An Odyssey Publication
© 1998 Pacific Century Publishers Ltd.
Text © 1998 Sources Far East Ltd.

Published by Pacific Century Publishers Ltd., Hong Kong

Editor: Nancy Johnston
Illustrator: Xie Qing
Designer: Aubrey Ise
Map: Tom Le Bas

Front cover photograph: Peter Danford
Back cover photograph: Mac McGowan of CHINAPIC at Grosvenor House, Shanghai
Inside photographs by Peter Danford;
except p.189 bottom © Hongkong and Shanghai Banking Corporation

Pacific Century Publishers Ltd., Hong Kong
Room 1003-5, Kowloon Centre,
29-43 Ashley Road, Tsimshatsui,
Kowloon, Hong Kong
Tel: (852) 2376-2085
Fax: (852) 2376-2137
E-mail: airman@gateway.net.hk

ISBN 962-217-531-7

Printed in Hong Kong

# LIVING IN
# SHANGHAI

*Photographed from the roof of the Portman Hotel, the Pudong television tower can be seen in the distance.*

# CONTENTS

# ABOUT THE AUTHORS

Americans Jennifer Jacoby Dawson and Douglas Dawson are business partners and the operators of Sources Far East Ltd., a relocation services company in Shanghai. They are also mother and son.

Jennifer Dawson arrived in Shanghai in 1988 from Algeria, one of many overseas postings. The knowledge and experience acquired from seventeen corporate moves led her to establish Sources in 1994. Douglas Dawson joined the company in 1995, and moved his family to Shanghai soon after.

Through their familiarity with Shanghai and a wealth of personal experience with numerous moves, Jennifer and Douglas are able to assist other expats as they cope with the transition to life in Shanghai.

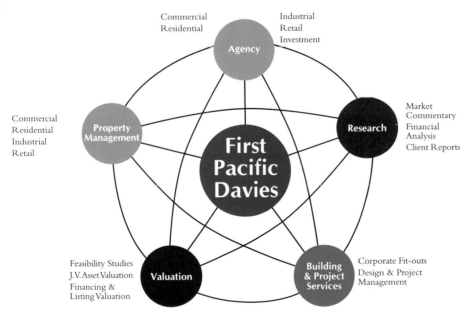

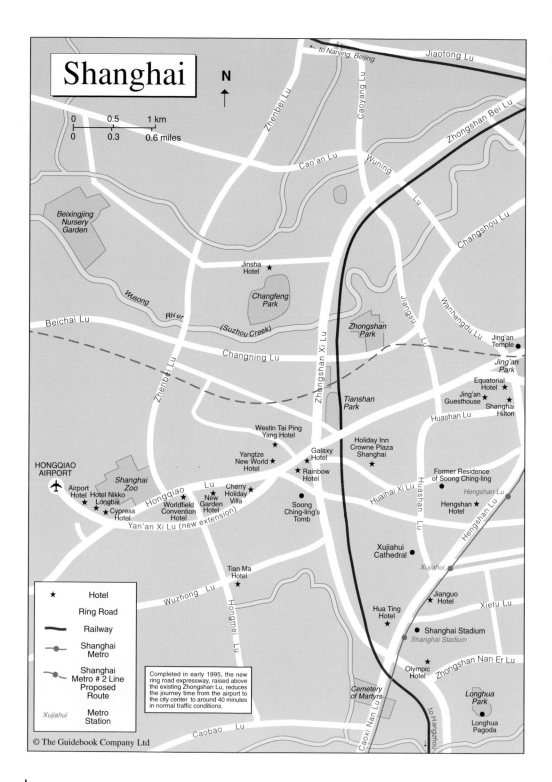

# Shanghai

N

0   0.5   1 km
0   0.3   0.6 miles

to Nanjing, Beijing

Jiaotong Lu

Zhenbei Lu

Caoyang Lu

Zhongshan Bei Lu

Cao'an Lu

Wuning Lu

Changshou Lu

Beixingjing Nursery Garden

Jinsha Hotel ★

Changfeng Park

Wusong River

(Suzhou Creek)

Zhongshan Park

Jing'an Temple ●

Beichai Lu

Changning Lu

Zhongshan Xi Lu

Jiangsu Lu

Wanhangdu Lu

Jing'an Park

Zhenbei Lu

Tianshan Park

Equatorial Hotel ★

Jing'an Guesthouse ★

Shanghai Hilton ★

Huashan Lu

Westin Tai Ping Yang Hotel ★

Yangtze New World Hotel ★

Galaxy Hotel ★

Holiday Inn Crowne Plaza Shanghai ★

HONGQIAO AIRPORT

Shanghai Zoo

Rainbow Hotel ★

Former Residence of Soong Ching-ling ●

Hengshan Lu

Airport Hotel ★

Hotel Nikko Longbai ★

Cherry Holiday Villa ★

New Garden Hotel ★

Hongqiao Lu

Huaihai Xi Lu

Hengshan Lu

Hengshan Hotel ★

Cypress Hotel ★

Worldfield Convention Hotel ★

Soong Ching-ling's Tomb ●

Huashan Lu

Yan'an Xi Lu (new extension)

Xujiahui Cathedral ●

Tian Ma Hotel ★

Xujiahui

Jianguo Hotel ★

Xietu Lu

Wuzhong Lu

Hongmei Lu

Hua Ting Hotel ★

Shanghai Stadium ●
Shanghai Stadium

Olympic Hotel ★

Zhongshan Nan Er Lu

Longhua Park

Cemetery of Martyrs

Caoxi Nan Lu

to Hangzhou

Longhua Pagoda

Caobao Lu

## Legend

★ Hotel

▬ Ring Road

▬ Railway

●━● Shanghai Metro

●━━● Shanghai Metro # 2 Line Proposed Route

*Xujiahui* Metro Station

© The Guidebook Company Ltd

Completed in early 1995, the new ring road expressway, raised above the existing Zhongshan Lu, reduces the journey time from the airport to the city center to around 40 minutes in normal traffic conditions.

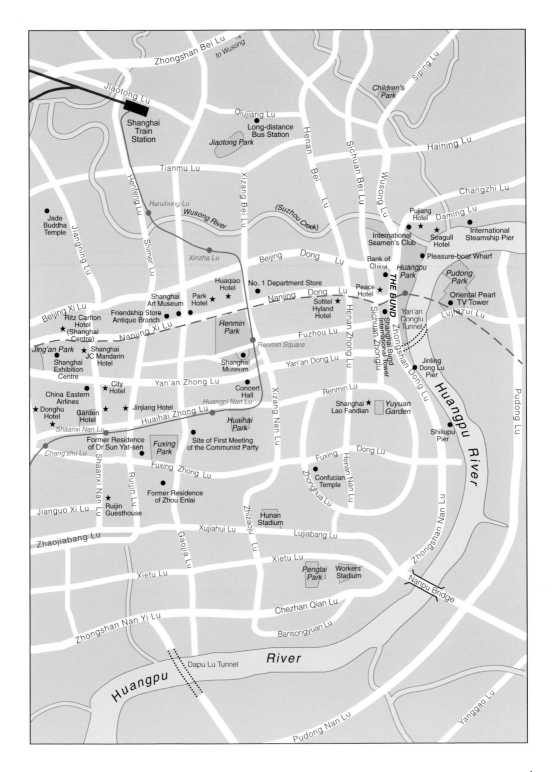

# ACKNOWLEDGEMENTS

*Living in Shanghai* sprang from rather inauspicious beginnings. Sources Far East Ltd provides relocation advice, orientation and assistance in the acquisition of housing and office space. Part of this service includes providing clients with printouts of information which is pertinent to relocating and living here. Over time, as new subjects were addressed, the handouts began to take on the characteristics of a book, and it became obvious that this information would be of great use to the general expatriate population of Shanghai. The fact that Shanghai's existing English-language telephone directories are not very comprehensive adds to the difficulty of going about life here in a "normal" way. What should take only a few minutes to accomplish in other countries can take half the day here, resulting in an overdependence on local support staff to accomplish even the most mundane tasks. It is hoped that this book will succeed in its objective of helping readers function more independently and self-sufficiently.

The material contained within this guide will be revised on a regular basis, in order to keep up with the constant changes this city is becoming so known for. Readers should feel free to offer suggestions for information and services they feel is of value to expats, to be included in subsequent editions. There is no such thing as too much information! Further, every attempt has been made to ensure that the information provided herein is current and accurate. However, there will be the inevitable error or omission, and again, readers are invited to point them out.

Certainly, a great deal of support was needed in acquiring and categorizing information, and the first person to lend a hand was Chuck Marzullo, a Hong Kong-based American expat. Chuck is at the top of the "thank you" list, as he assisted with securing a publisher, and then provided further encouragement in seeing the process to fruition.

Many thanks also go out to Kristi Hulett, Marguerite Shen and Zachary Zhang for providing the time and expertise in tracking down detailed research material.

Shanghainese artist Xie Qing made a vast contribution by providing the illustration for this book. A good friend, he also provided encouragement when most needed.

Heartfelt appreciation also goes out to Dr. Grace Hutcheson, Dr. Paul Chiang and Karin Schweitzer for the essays they provided in their respective fields of expertise, and to the many friends who were willing to scan text for mistakes and omissions.

Mac McGowan, a Shanghai-based American photographer with CHINAPIC, provided the authors' photo. He not only contributed his time, labor and expertise, but also made the authors look good! His efforts are most appreciated. CHINAPIC is listed in the "Services" section. The authors' photo was taken at Grosvenor House, which is part of the Jin Jiang Hotel complex. We thank them for the use of this lovely setting.

This book would not exist at all if not for all of Sources' clients, who inspired the compilation of this material. Sincere thanks to each and every one of you.

Jennifer J. Dawson
Douglas S. Dawson III

# SHANGHAI—A NEW CITY EMERGES

Not unlike the legendary phoenix arising from the ashes, Shanghai is undergoing tremendous, dynamic change that will likely make it one of the most vital cities in the world in the not-too-distant future. Change is everywhere from the skyline filled with construction cranes and the new buildings thrusting over the tops of billboards lining the road, to the enthusiasm of ever more well-dressed local business people who have discovered the thrill of relying upon their own abilities to succeed.

During the first half of this century, Shanghai was known as the "Paris of the East". Perhaps during the next century it will be dubbed the "New York of the East". It is said that one hundred skyscrapers are in the planning phase or are already under construction in Pudong. Of the one hundred buildings exceeding 104 meters already in China, Shanghai is home to twenty-six of them, whereas Beijing boasts only sixteen, Guangzhou nineteen and Shenzhen twelve. By the year 2001, Shanghai will be home to the tallest building in the world.

The population of Shanghai is officially estimated at 13.4 million with 7.5 million in the central urban area. This does not take into account, however, the transients from the countryside who are streaming into the city seeking a better life. In the past, movement was strictly regulated. Now, stringent regulation is proving to be impossible due to the vast numbers arriving in this city every day. This amazingly high number of people live in an area of 6,340 square kilometers. The urban area itself is comprised of 375 square kilometers, making it very densely populated. In 1987, Shanghai implemented numerous housing improvement projects. At that time, 47,000 households had less than 2.5 square meters of living space per person. In October 1996 there were 73,794 households with less than 4 square meters of living space per person. Today, 42% of Shanghai residents live in apartments with 6.1 square meters to 8 square meters per person. This is an improvement, but quarters are still cramped.

The indigent peasants arriving daily in Shanghai often find themselves in dire straits, which has led to an increase in the incidence of crime in Shanghai. However, the crime rate continues to be extremely low compared with the West. Earlier on, at least on the surface, there seemed to be no crime at all, and expatriates felt quite safe. Presently, one needs to bear in mind that crime exists, but that relatively speaking, it is probably much safer here than at home.

In the fall of 1988, the only way across the Huangpu River to Pudong was by ferry. Now tunnels and the fourth bridge spanning the river are in place. Hongqiao Lu, running from the Hongqiao Development Zone to the airport was only two lanes. Now Hongqiao Lu is four lanes wide and there is an elevated expressway running parallel to it. In the Hongqiao Development Zone, which now resembles a slice of Hong Kong, the first and only building (New Town Mansion) was still under construction. The Sheraton and Nikko hotels were open, and the Hilton had just opened. But the Garden Hotel, Shanghai Centre, Jinjiang Tower, Westin Hotel, Yangtze Hotel, and Galaxy Hotel didn't exist. Jessica, at the Jinjiang Hotel, and the small grocery store in the Hengshan Hotel were the only western grocery stores. No bagels there! In those days, expatriates carried heavy suitcases laden with food and toiletries back from R and Rs and home leaves. There were also few places for expatriates to live. The Hongqiao Villas and Longbai Apartments were brand new. Other options were Yandang Apartments, Huaihai Apartments, the

Hengshan Hotel, Shanghai Mansions, and the villas at the Cypress Hotel, since torn down and replaced with high-rise apartments and luxury villas. Housing options are still not optimum, but have vastly improved in both quality and selection. The authors had to bring in everything needed to set up house here, except for furniture. This required a large shipment from the one's home country and a stop in Hong Kong to buy appliances. Now one can arrive with two suitcases, make a local shop-ping trip, and have the basics accomplished almost overnight.

A heady experience, all of this change in such a short time, unparalleled in the history of the world. After living here for some time, this pace will seem to be the norm. On trips back home, the fact that nothing has changed since the last visit may seem a little strange and disconcerting.

# CLUBS AND ORGANIZATIONS

Shanghai's social life is very vibrant, offering everything from grand balls to tennis lessons. The organizations listed provide ideas about where to start when integrating oneself into the community. For further ideas, check out the "Leisure" section. For reference purposes, the listing below is in alphabetical order, NOT in order of membership! As you scan the information below, you'll find that there is more to do in Shanghai than meets the eye. It is typical for incoming expatriates to be at a loss as to how to spend free time. And it is even more typical that, after a being here for month or so, one HAS no free time!

## AL-ANON

Tel: 6270-5536

This group provides support to those who find that someone close is drinking too much. All calls, meetings, and members' names are confidential.

## ALCOHOLICS ANONYMOUS

Contact the American Consulate Health Unit's nurse at 6433-6880, x 244 for details. All calls, meetings, and members' names are confidential.

## ALLIANCE FRANCAISE DE SHANGHAI

297 Wusong Lu   吴淞路297号
Tel: 6357-5388
Fax: 6325-1183
Director: Olivier Salvan

This non-profit organization promotes French culture through cultural events and French language classes. Alliance Francaise was founded in Paris in 1883 by eminent figures in the arts, sciences and politics, as an international educational system to teach the French language. The organization was active in Shanghai between 1934 and 1951, and reopened in February, 1993. Although teaching French is the primary objective of this organization, cultural events are also held, including film nights, concerts, exhibitions, and stage shows.

## AMERICAN ALUMNI CLUB

Contact Thomas Tsui at 6351-1928 or Michele Lee at 6280-1288, x 420.

This group holds monthly meetings for graduates of American Universities who live in Shanghai. Each month, events are organized by a different university.

## THE AMERICAN CHAMBER OF COMMERCE (AMCHAM)

4th Fl, Ritz Carlton Hotel, Shanghai Centre
波特曼大酒店
1376 Nanjing Xi Lu 200040

南京西路1376号
Tel: 6279-7119
Fax: 6279-8802

Amcham is a non-profit organization of American business representatives in Shanghai. Their purpose is to promote American business by providing information to members, and meetings focus on topics of interest to the business community. Membership mixers are held on the fourth Wednesday of each month. For membership information and meeting venues, call the numbers above. An annual membership list is published. As an adjunct to Amcham meetings, there is also a U.S. Consulate briefing on the first Tuesday of each month at 5:30 pm, in room #631, East Tower, Shanghai Centre, at the US Consulate's Commercial Section. There is a social hour following the briefing. American passport holders and listed Amcham members who want to attend should advise Amcham of their intentions. Persons who do not hold American passports must let Amcham know that they wish to attend and state their name and nationality. No one will be admitted whose name does not appear on the Amcham RSVP list.

## AMERICAN WOMEN'S CLUB

President: Cathy Fletcher
Tel: 6279-8316

The inaugural meeting of the American Women's Club of Shanghai was held on September 25, 1996 and was attended by 117 women. As of March, 1998, membership had grown to approximately 250. The objectives of the club are to further the development of an American community in Shanghai through the sponsoring of events for its members in Shanghai as well as the rest of China, and to present the views of its membership on issues of concern to the American community. Tours and day trips are provided and many special interest groups have been formed. These include a book club, book and

magazine swap, bowling league, cooking classes, empty nesters group, golf league, mahjongg, pot luck dinner club, and tennis. A Big Sister - Little Sister group provides help to incoming members. Two types of memberships are available. Full memberships are available to any citizen of the United States and their expatriate spouses living in Shanghai. Associate membership is available to any expatriate who, in the opinion of the Board of Directors, has a close and abiding connection with the United States. Associate memberships cannot comprise more than 20% of the total membership. Annual dues for a full membership are RMB200. If interested in joining, please contact:
Sandra Beeman
Tel: 6262-4293
Fax: 6262-4296, or
Colleen Barnes
Tel: 6268-8598
Fax: 6268-9518

## AUSTRALIAN CHAMBER OF COMMERCE  东海商业中心
Suite 22C, East Ocean Center
588 Yan'an Dong Lu 200001
延安东路588号
Tel: 6352-3155,6,7
Fax: 6352-3116
For information as to schedule of activities and venues, contact the numbers above.

## AUSTRALIAN WOMEN IN SHANGHAI
Contact Sara Browne at 6268-9988 x 503
This organization offers support for Australian women. Monthly coffee meetings are held and evening social events include couples. Other events are planned for families. Helping Australian newcomers get settled is one of the group's primary objectives.

## THE BANANA AND EGG CLUB (BEC)
This group is interested in cross-cultural issues, especially relating to Asians born in other

countries, but not exclusive to them. The subject of monthly events varies. If you're interested in attending, contact either Patrick Snodgrass at 6279-1563, Jane Jiang at 6262-6477, or Justin Malley at 6278-7204.

## BEEFSTEAK AND BURGUNDY CLUB
Howard T. Bennett, Membership Secretary
Tel: 6875-2252
Fax: 6875-1605
E-mail: BandBClubShanghai@poboxes.com
The Beefsteak and Burgundy Club was founded in Adelaide, South Australia in April, 1954, and in 1996 186 clubs were active in eight countries. Membership totals about 4,800 who enjoy fellowship, good food and wine. The club meets on the first Friday of each month and the venues vary. If you want to expand and develop your knowledge of food and wine, contact Mr. Bennett for further information.

## BELGIUM BUSINESS ASSOCIATION
Please contact Gilbert Van Kerckhove at
Tel: 6472-2471 or
Fax: 6472-0640 for information concerning events and functions.

## BELGIUM NIGHTS
Badlands Cafe
897 Julu Lu  巨鹿路897号
Tel: 6279-4334
Belgians or friends of Belgians are welcome to attend this casual social evening held the second Friday of each month at Badlands at 8:00 pm.

## BRITISH CHAMBER OF COMMERCE
15C Jinming Building  锦明大厦
8 Zunyi Nan Lu  遵义南路8号
Contact Lisa De Abreu at
Tel: 6219-8185, 6278-5975 or
Fax: 6278-5975, 6219-7311.
The British Chamber of Commerce, Shanghai works closely with other organizations

promoting trade and investment with China and Shanghai. Key contacts are:

- British Consulate General, Shanghai
  Tel: 6279-7650
  Fax: 6279-7651
- China-Britain Trade Group, Shanghai
  Tel: 6219-8185
  Fax: 6219-7311
- British Council, Shanghai
  Tel: 6471-4849
  Fax: 6433-3115
- British Chamber of Commerce, China (in Beijing)
  Tel: (010) 6593-6611
  Fax: (010) 6593-6610
- Association of British Commerce in China (Guangzhou)
  Tel: (020) 8666-5756
  Fax: (020) 8666-5746
- British Chamber of Commerce in Hong Kong
  Tel: (852) 2824-2211
  Fax: (852) 2824-1333

    The British Chamber of Commerce, Shanghai is the independent voice of Britain's commercial and industrial presence here. It was founded in 1995 after nine years as the Association of British Commerce in China, Shanghai. The goals of the organization are to provide a forum at which members and guests can widen their contacts, provide regular and informative speaker meetings, create social and charitable fund raising events, develop more contacts with local government, offer access to other foreign Chamber of Commerce activities, provide a pool of experience for visiting UK companies to draw upon, and lobbying, when deemed appropriate. The organization also meets regularly with British government offices, the Chambers in Beijing and Hong Kong, the China-British Trade Group and other related bodies to coordinate events and disseminate information.

## BRITISH WIVES CLUB

For information on membership and a description of the group's activities, please contact Sue Kwan at 6219-1449.

## CANADIAN BUSINESS FORUM

Tel: 6279-8400
Contact Derek Read at the Canadian Consulate at 6279-8400 for information. Events are held monthly and new members are welcome.

## CERCLE FRANCOPHONE DE SHANGHAI

Welcomes French-speaking newcomers to Shanghai and organizes social events. Regular meetings are held on the first Monday of every month. Contact Annick de Benizamann at 6472-8762 or request information from the French Consulate, Twenty-First Floor, Qihua Tower, 1375 Huaihai Lu between 1:00 pm and 3:00 pm or telephone 6431-4301.

## CORNELL CLUB

Contact Thomas Tsui at 6351-1928 x 215 if you are an alumna or alumnus of Cornell and would like to trade war stories with fellow Cornellians.

## DANISH CLUB

Tel: 6212-0182
Fax: 6219-9735
Contact Anne Darsen for information. A variety of events are held every five or six weeks. There is some form of participation for singles, newcomers, and families. Luncheons and evening events are planned, and Danish holidays are celebrated.

## THE DUTCH BUSINESS ASSOCIATION (DBA)

Contact: Dutch Consulate General at 6209-9076 or Anne Darsen at 6212-0182
This association is open to anyone. Language spoken during meetings is English. Monthly

meetings usually feature a guest speaker. The Dutch Consulate can provide you with details of scheduled meetings and venues.

## THE DUTCH CLUB (NEDERLANDSE VERENIGING)

Contact: Dutch Consulate General
Tel: 6209-9076
Organized by Dutch women for the purpose of arranging get-togethers for the Dutch-speaking community. A newsletter (in Dutch) is distributed monthly. The Dutch Consulate General will provide a contact number for membership info.

## EXPATRIATE PROFESSIONAL WOMEN'S SOCIETY

For information about the time, venue, and subject of the monthly business/cultural/social meetings for expatriate women working and living in Shanghai, contact Melissa McFerrin at 6361-9485 or 6279-2559, or Grace Peppers at 6278-5900.

## FINNISH BUSINESS COUNCIL

Tel: 6474-0068
Fax: 6471-1338
Contact the Finnish Consulate General at the numbers above for schedules and information.

## FIRST AID AND PRENATAL CLASSES

Tel: 6466-1614
These classes are organized quarterly by World Link Medical Center.

## FRIENDS OF HOPE

Tel: 6384-0609, 6384-0369
Fax: 6385-0525
Founded in March, 1994, by a small group of expatriate women volunteers serving as language partners for students learning English through Project HOPE. (Project HOPE is discussed in the Medical Care chapter). The volunteer program, now known as "Friends of HOPE", has grown both in membership and

activities. Almost 100 volunteer expatriate men and women from all walks of life continue with their work at the Shanghai Normal University, sponsor an annual International HOPE Ball to raise funds, and support the pediatric patients at Xinhua Hospital through therapy and toy donations. Contact HOPE's office at the numbers above for participation information.

## GERMAN CENTRE

Haus der Deutschen Wirtschaft Shanghai
1233 Siping Lu　四平路1233号
Tel: 6501-5100
Fax: 6515-4648
Organization for promotion of German businesses.

## THE GREAT WORLD

Tel: 6471-1635 (Sandor Dani)
This association was formed by those who want to further their appreciation of Chinese culture through the study of it. The initial series of ten classes offered Chinese cooking, traditional Chinese massage, Taijiquan, calligraphy, and Qigong. This group takes its name from the famous Great World Entertainment Center, popular in the thirties.

## HONG KONG CHAMBER OF COMMERCE

Contact Michelle Lee at 6386-6688 x 420 or Wing Sham at 6352-8488 for information as to regular weekly and monthly events.

## HONG KONG CLUB

Social events, sports, and business oriented meetings are regularly held for expatriates from Hong Kong. Contact Michele Lee at 6280-1288, x 420 or Wing Sham at 6326-5935 for further details.

## IBEROAMERICAN SOCIETY

Contact: 6268-6022, Consuelo Cancellieri
There are currently about fifty members in this newly formed group which meets two to four

Thursdays a month. One Thursday is set aside for a rotating luncheon at a member's home. Another Thursday is dedicated to philanthropic work with nursing homes, day care centers, and individuals in need. Other Thursdays might involve visits to interesting sites in Shanghai. One goal of the group is to help members' children improve their Spanish language abilities. A newsletter is prepared monthly.

## INTERNET USERS GROUP
Tel: 6272-3205
Contact Breaux Walker for details. Basically, this group meets to discuss Internet related issues and accommodates all interested parties, from those not yet on the net but who want to be, to professionals. For further information concerning the Internet, see "Telecommunications".

## JEWISH COMMUNITY OF SHANGHAI
Contact Jay Goldberg at pager 128-287516 or Seth Kaplan at 6482-7230.

## MONTROSE WINE CLUB
Call 6468-3293 or 6468-6758 for information concerning meetings. These are usually casual wine tasting get-togethers.

## SCOUTS
The Shanghai American School (tel: 6221-1445) has groups for both Girl and Boy Scouts at the elementary level. Daisy Scouts, Brownies, and Junior Girl Scouts are options for girls in Kindergarten through 5th grade. Tiger scouts, Wolf, Bear, and Webelo Scouts are options for 1st grade through 5th grade. If your child wants to participate in scouting, but does not attend the American School, contact the school your child attends.

## SELF-SUPPORT GROUP
Tel: 6268-6005
Supported by the American Cancer Society and the Hong Kong Cancer Fund, this group meets regularly to provide support to cancer survivors and their families living in Shanghai. This group has recently broadened its scope to include group support for other personal concerns as well.

## SHANGHAI CIGAR SOCIETY
Cigar smokers are welcome at meetings at O'Malley's on the fourth Tuesday of each month. For further information please contact Rob Young at 6437-0667.

## SHANGHAI EXPATRIATE ASSOCIATION (SEA)
The most broad-based organization for foreigners in Shanghai provides a wonderful starting point for newcomers. Currently, there are over 1,650 members. Social events and local tours, as well as trips throughout China and other Asian countries are offered. In the spring of '95, the group organized a trip to Vietnam and in '96 to Burma. Destinations in '97 included Tibet, the Silk Road, Inner Mongolia, and the Yangtze River's Three Gorges. There are special interest groups as well, including arts and crafts, bible study, bridge, language study, quilting, mahjongg, mothers and toddlers, tennis, Tai Chi, band, choir, bowling, soccer for children, photography, and a book club. Two formal balls are organized each year, couples social functions are held on a regular basis, and family social activities are included on the agenda. Many activities are scheduled during the daytime for women. Membership base is multinational, with the largest percentage represented by Americans (about 25%). The group publishes a monthly newsletter and, more importantly, an annual membership list that includes telephone numbers, virtually the only expat telephone directory in town, aside from personal card files! Annual membership fees are RMB250 for individuals, and RMB400 for couples. For a membership form

and information, call 6268-8802 or 6268-6022. Membership applications are also accepted at a coffee morning held every second Wednesday, 10:00 am - noon at the Convention Hotel 上海世博会议大酒店 (Shanghai Sibuo Huiyi Dajiudian), 2106 Hongqiao Road 虹桥路2106号.

## SHANGHAI FOREIGN MEDICAL NETWORK
Tel/fax: 6488-3252 or 6433-4606
Shanghai's medical professionals gather regularly to discuss health issues in China.

## SHANGHAI SUNRISE
Tel: 6268-9411 (Bonnie Tucker)
 6433-0672 (Charlotte Ashby)
This expatriate organization sponsors underprivileged children in Shanghai, helping to provide them with an education.

## SHANGHAI TRAINERS NETWORK
Tel: 6451-5230 x 131 (Lawrence Chi), or
Tel: 5972-1434 x 4132 (Olive Lu)
This group is aimed at all training and development professionals and provides a forum to exchange information and discuss issues.

## SINGAPORE CLUB
For information, contact the Singapore Consulate General (新加坡领事馆),
400 Wulumuqi Lu 乌鲁木齐路400号
Tel: 6437-0776
Fax: 6433-4150

## SWEDISH BUSINESS LUNCHEON
Swedish Consulate, Tel: 6474-1311
Swedish Consulate Commercial Section,
Tel: 6474-3533
You may call the Swedish Consulate or its Commercial Section to obtain information on schedules and subjects of monthly luncheons. Speakers and presentations are usually on the agenda. Most programs are in English, but some are in Swedish only. Luncheons are attended by Swedish business leaders living in Shanghai, but others are also welcome.

## SWEDISH CLUB
Contact Lena Richardsson at 6258-9988 x 207 for details.

## SWISS CLUB
For information contact:
The Swiss Consulate General 瑞士领事馆 (Ruishi Lingshiguan)
Sun Plaza, 3rd Floor
仙霞路88号太阳广场3楼
88 Xianxia Lu, Hongqiao
Tel: 6270-0519
Fax: 6270-0522
This organization provides the Swiss community with a venue for social events.

## UNITED STATES - CHINA BUSINESS COUNCIL
Jinjiang Hotel 锦江饭店
Room 2331, West Building
59 Maoming Nan Lu 茂名南路59号
Tel: 6415-2579 or 6258-2582 x 2331
Fax: 6415-2584
E-mail: uschc@uninet.co.cn
Director, Shanghai Operations: Sheila Melvin
American Headquarters:
1818 N. Street, N.W. Suite 200,
Washington D.C. 20036 USA
Tel: (202) 429-0340
Fax: (202) 775-2476
This group is membership-based and acts as a liaison between the American government and American companies that have business interests in China.

## WHIRLIGIG
Tel: 6472-0517 (Lily)
This community theater group is open to Chinese and foreign actors, dancers, singers, and crew and production people.

# MEDICAL CARE

AMBULANCE   Tel: 120

Proper medical care is a major concern of every expatriate committed to living and working in Shanghai. Although conditions are improving rapidly with the addition of more foreign managed medical and dental clinics, the level of care we find at home still does not exist. The main area of difference lies with emergency medical care. If treated either in a foreign clinic or a hospital clinic catering to foreigners, no undue problems should arise. However, if emergency treatment is needed away from a treatment facility, the situation can become dire. Fancy ambulances or medi-vac helicopters are not generally available. On the bright side, you are much less likely to be mugged enroute!

# HOSPITALS and CLINICS

Presently, there are only about twelve hospitals in Shanghai that, officially, are "allowed" to see foreigners. These are classified as Grade III, Class I hospitals by the Chinese Ministry of Public Health.

## NEW PIONEER INTERNATIONAL MEDICAL CENTRES LIMITED
新峰医疗中心
(Xinfeng Yiliao Zhongxin)
2nd Fl, Geru Building　格如大楼2楼
910 Hengshan Lu　衡山路910号
24 hour emergency hotline: 6469-3090
Tel: 6469-3899, 6438-2283
Fax: 6469-3897
Medical Director: Dr. Paul Chiang
Medical Director Consultant: Dr. Eric Cheung
Information: Sabrina Lee
Hours: 24 hours a day, 365 days a year
The New Pioneer International Medical Centres Ltd. (NPIMC) was established in Shanghai in 1994. NPIMC is a comprehensive private medical network offering medical care to international standards to foreigners in Asia. NPIMC Shanghai specializes in primary care and offers outpatient and inpatient treatment. Dental service utilizing expatriate dentists are also available. NPIMC manages a network of 800 hospitals that provide cashless accidental medical services throughout Mainland China and has clinics staffed with expatriate doctors in Guangzhou, Singapore, Thailand, and affiliated hospitals in other parts of the world. NPIMC offers its patients direct billing with major insurance companies from the USA and Europe and assists patients with individual insurance claim procedures. Services include annual health checkups, pre/postnatal care, emergency ambulance service, house calls, and evacuation services.

## WORLD LINK MEDICAL CENTER §
瑞新国际医疗中心
(Ruixin Guoji Yiliao Zhongxin)
- Suite 203, Shanghai Centre
  上海商城203室
  1376 Nanjing Xi Lu　南京西路1376号
  Tel: 6279-7688
  Fax: 6279-7698
  Hours: Mon. and Thu. 8:00 am - 9:00 pm; Tue., Wed. and Fri. 8:00 am - 7:00 pm; Sat. and Sun. 10:00 am - 4:00 pm
- Room 30, Mandarine City　名都城30号房
  788 Hongxu Lu　虹许路788号
  Tel: 6405-5788
  Fax: 6405-3587
  Hours: Mon. - Fri. 9:00 am - 5:00 pm
Website: www.worldlink-shanghai.com
Medical Director: Dr. Joseph Kolars
The health care team has been recruited by Joseph C. Kolars, M. D. who serves as Medical Director of the Healthcare system. Dr. Kolars previously served as the Associate Chair of Medicine at the University of Michigan. Six expatriate physicians are fully trained and Board-certified in Western medicine and resumes are available upon request. This clinic is linked by fax modem to the University of Michigan in order to facilitate patient diagnoses. The clinic has a lab, x-ray facilities, and a pharmacy with imported medications. If hospitalization is required, the clinic uses the expatriate wing of Ruijin Hospital with care provided by the World Link medical staff. No membership to the clinic is required and walk-in patients are welcome. Corporate Plans are available as outlined:

## Corporate/Individual Plan 1

The cost of the plan is US$100/person/annum for group of 10 or less and US$80/person/annum for group of 11 or more. Large group rates are available. Benefits offered under this plan are:

- Cashless payment methods for members
- Access to After-Hours Medical Assistance Hotline by western-trained healthcare providers
- Guaranteed same-day appointment booking, if member calls for appointment before noon.
- Complimentary annual basic diagnostic investigation including total cholesterol, urinalysis (including sugar, protein, blood, etc. and microscopic exam)
- Special rates for medical and dental services including health maintenance services (during office hours)
- Newsletter

Corporate Memberships are transferable once per annum.

## Corporate/Individual Plan 2

This plan offers more extensive coverage for individual members. The plan covers all medical consultations for one year and an extensive annual medical investigation. The cost of the plan is US$500/year. The following benefits are included with this package:

- Access to After-Hours Medical Assistance Hotline by western-trained healthcare providers
- Guaranteed same-day appointment booking, if member calls for appointment before noon.
- Complimentary annual basic diagnostic investigation including total cholesterol, urinalysis (including sugar, protein, blood, etc. and microscopic exam), blood pressure monitoring, and an annual oral dental exam.

- Up to 10 medical consultations per year for routine illnesses.
- Newsletter

## Corporate/Individual Plan 3

This plan is mainly for companies who are insured but would like access to WorldLink's After-Hours Medical Assistance Hotline. This plan costs US$100/person/annum with group rates starting from 11 or more. Large group rates are also available. This plan offers the following benefits:

- Cashless payment methods for members
- Access to After-Hours Medical Assistance Hotline by western-trained healthcare providers
- Guaranteed same-day appointment booking, if member calls for appointment before noon.
- Special rates for medical and dental services (during office hours)
- Newsletter

### DRs. ANDERSON AND PARTNERS GENERAL MEDICAL CLINIC
上海晏打臣公济诊疗所
(Shanghai Yandachen Gongji Zhenliaosuo)
New Century Plaza　新世纪广场
Block D, 10th Fl, Room 1001
D座10楼1001室
48 Xingyi Lu　兴义路48号
Tel: 6270-3263

This clinic has operated in Hong Kong since 1870 and opened its first office in the PRC (in Shanghai) in May 1997. Drs. Anderson and Partners offers normal outpatient medical care and healthcare services in their clinic as well as inpatient services in cooperation with International Medical Care Center (IMCC), a branch of the Shanghai First People's Hospital. Healthcare services include medical consultations, X-ray, lab, vitalograph, audiogram, prescriptions, innoculations, annual and pre-employment medical check-ups, and 24 hour emergency services. Drs. Anderson and Partners provides a membership program, and walk-in patients are also welcome.

## HUASHAN HOSPITAL 华山医院

(Huashan Yiyuan)
19th Fl  19楼
12 Wulumuqi Zhong Lu  乌鲁木齐中路12号
Tel: 6248-3986, 6248-9999
Fax: 6249-8476
Director: Dr. May Yuan

Out-patient and in-patient services for foreigners on the 19th floor. Dr. Yuan is Chinese, but has lived and had training in the U.S. She has designed this clinic by American standards, and her staff speak English. In-patient rooms are private, clean and comfortable, with IDD telephones and televisions. (Chinese channels only). The clinic is open 24 hours. For an out-patient consultation, prescription medications are given on the spot. These are usually a combination of western and Chinese drugs. Prices for basic in-patient care range from RMB650 for a small room to RMB900 for a large room. Out-patient consultations are RMB60–90, plus medication. The basic charge for home visits is RMB120. Credit cards are accepted.

In the event of serious illness or trauma, Huashan can provide emergency evacuation through the SOS services.

## HUADONG HOSPITAL 华东医院

(Huadong Yiyuan)
221 Yan'an Xi Lu  延安西路221号
Tel: 6248-3180
Director: Dr. Liu Shao

Dr. Liu and staff speak English. In-patient rooms have telephones. In-patient services cost between RMB450 and RMB900. Out-patient consultations are RMB30–60, plus medication. 24-hour facilities. No credit cards accepted.

## IMCC (INTERNATIONAL MEDICAL CARE CENTER) OF SHANGHAI'S FIRST PEOPLE'S HOSPITAL

国际医疗保健中心(第一人民医院内)
(Diyi Renmin Yiyuan)
585 Jiulong Lu  九龙路585号
Tel: 6306-9480, 6306-9485

International Medical Care Center is an out-patient clinic for foreigners. Out-patient consultations cost from RMB80 to RMB120. In-patients will be charged RMB340–680. Credit cards are accepted. Facilities are open 24 hours. Contact Dr. Qin Xü at 6306-9478.

## RUIJIN HOSPITAL 瑞金医院

(Ruijin Yiyuan)
197 Ruijin Er Lu  瑞金二路197号
Tel: 6437-0045
Director: Dr. Li Hong Wei

This hospital has a clinic for foreigners (called the Guangxi Clinic). The staff speak English. Telephones in each of 12 rooms for foreigners. No credit cards. In-patient care RMB580–980. Out-patient basic fee is RMB75. Open 24 hours.

## SHANGHAI MEDICAL UNIVERSITY CHILDREN'S HOSPITAL 儿科医院

(Erke Yiyuan)
183 Fenglin Lu  枫林路183号
(3rd Fl for foreigners)
Tel: 6404-7129
Beeper: 127-203-7979 (wait for 2 beeps and hang up)
Director: Dr. Liu Mei Hua

Dr. Wu Jing Lei, a cardiologist, was trained in Hong Kong and speaks English. Dr. Liu speaks some English. Open 24 hours. In-patient basic treatment from RMB150 to RMB500. Out-patient care from RMB50 to RMB100, plus medication. Home visits are RMB150.

### RENJI HOSPITAL 仁济医院
(Renji Yiyuan)
145 Shandong Zhong Lu 山东中路145号
Tel: 6326-0930

### SHANGHAI #6 PEOPLE'S HOSPITAL
上海市第六人民医院
(Shanghai Diliu Renmin Yiyuan)
600 Yishan Lu 宜山路600号
Tel: 6436-9181

### SHANGHAI #9 PEOPLE'S HOSPITAL
上海市第九人民医院
(Shanghai Dijiu Renmin Yiyuan)
(dermatology specialists)
639 Zhizaoju Lu 制造局路639号
Tel: 6313-8341

### SHANGHAI RAILWAY CENTRAL HOSPITAL 上海铁路中心医院
(Shanghai Tielu Zhongxin Yiyuan)
301 Yanchang Lu 延长路301路
Tel: 5677-0588

### XINHUA HOSPITAL 新华医院
(Xinhua Yiyuan)
(pediatrics)
1665 Kongjiang Lu 控江路1665号
Tel: 6545-4630

### ZHONGSHAN HOSPITAL 中山医院
(Zhongshan Yiyuan)
180 Fenglin Lu 枫林路180号
Tel: 6404-1990

## TRADITIONAL CHINESE MEDICINE
Traditional Chinese medicine is practiced at the following two hospitals:

### LONGHUA HOSPITAL 龙华医院
(Longhua Yiyuan)
532 Lingling Lu 零陵路532号
Tel: 6438-5700
Also known as the Shanghai Traditional Chinese Medical Hospital, it is connected to Shanghai's Traditional Medical College.

### SHUGUANG HOSPITAL 曙光医院
(Shuguang Yiyuan)
185 Pu'an Lu 普安路185号
Tel: 6326-1650

## Massage and Acupuncture

### DR. WU WEN BING 吴文斌(医师)
Room 501, No. 8, Lane 2285
交通路2285弄8号501室
Jiaotong Lu
Home Tel: 5695-1718
Pager: 6275-7890 x 12060

Dr. Wu is a member of the Shanghai Municipal Association and the Chinese Medical Institute of Restoration of Health. He specializes in massage and acupuncture, and makes house calls for one hour massages. Fee: RMB150.

# MEDICAL CARE ISSUES
Karin Schweitzer
International SOS Assistance

Medical health care facilities in China are still not up to Westerners' expectations. In the larger cities, Western-owned clinics are coming on line, much to the relief of expatriates and travellers. However, these clinics are unfortunately still few in number and located only in large cities. While their facilities and equipment are usually excellent, their capabilities are limited with respect to in-patient treatment.

In major cities, foreigner wards can be found in Chinese hospitals. These wards are set up with Western standards in mind and the equipment is often the same found in Western hospitals. However, even though Western treatment can be received on a certain level, it's still very much influenced by the traditional Chinese way of practising medicine. Generally speaking, with the exception of a few hospitals with foreigner wards, standards at most of the hospitals within China fall far short of Western practices.

The best solution for handling a serious medical problem is to seek treatment in Hong Kong, which is the nearest city offering up-to-date Western medical facilities.

Prior to travel or relocation to China, it's important to secure comprehensive medical insurance as well as evacuation / repatriation coverage. This will provide peace of mind and a secure knowledge that, should you fall ill, you will be evacuated to a modern Western facility. When settling down into daily life in China, remember to familiarise yourself with local medical facilities so that you are prepared should a medical emergency occur.

*Author's note: Ms. Schweitzer resides in Shanghai and is the Shanghai Representative for SOS. She co-ordinates any medical evacuations from Shanghai authorised by SOS.*

# Other alternatives may be found through:

## AUSTRALIAN CONSULATE CLINIC
澳大利亚领事馆诊所
(Aodaliya Lingshiguan Zhensuo)
17 Fuxing Xi Lu  复兴西路17号
Open to Australian and New Zealand passport holders as well as expatriate personnel from other consulates in Shanghai. You will need to bring your passport with you.
Tel: 6433-4606

## UNITED STATES CONSULATE CLINIC
美国领事馆诊所
(Meiguo Lingshiguan Zhensuo)
1469 Huaihai Zhong Lu  淮海中路1467号
(need US passport)
Tel: 6433-6880

# JAPANESE ENCEPHALITIS
## DO I NEED THE VACCINE?

Grace A. Hutcheson, M.D.

World Link Medical Centre, Shanghai Centre

Many of us travelling or working in Asia have heard about Japanese Encephalitis (JE) and have probably been given all sorts of opinions and advice about whether or not to be vaccinated. While JE is a rare disease, it can cause severe or even fatal encephalitis, an inflammation and swelling of the brain. In an ideal world, the JE vaccine would provide us with 100% protection and would not have any side effects. Unfortunately, this is not the case. What do we know about the JE virus and the JE vaccine and who should be vaccinated?

## THE VIRUS

The JE virus is found throughout Asia and India; and is transmitted via the bite of the Culex mosquito. In temperate regions, including Shanghai and most of China, transmission from mosquitoes can occur from May through September. In tropical regions, mosquitoes can often survive year-round. The Culex mosquito, and thus the JE virus, is found mainly in rural and agricultural regions. The US Center for Disease Control estimates that the risk to travellers of contracting JE is less than one in a million in most usual tourist destinations in Asia and India.

Even when a human is infected with the JE virus, he or she very rarely develops symptoms. While this is somewhat reassuring, people unlucky enough to have symptoms often suffer severe encephalitis, which can result in brain damage or even death. Excellent supportive medical care is essential as currently there is no specific cure for JE.

When travelling to areas in which JE virus is found, we should take steps to decrease the chance of infection. The single most important thing is to prevent or decrease the number of mosquito bites. Wear mosquito repellent, preferably containing at least 30% DEET (use DEET sparingly on children), avoid outdoor activities from dusk to dawn if possible, wear protective clothing while outdoors including socks, pants and long sleeves, and try to sleep in a well-screened room or under mosquito netting. A vaccine against JE virus is also available.

## THE JE VACCINE

The vaccine against JE virus was developed in Japan and has been in use in Asia since 1954. The vaccination series consists of three shots given under the skin on days 0, 7, and 30. For proper protective immunity, you should begin the series at least 40 days prior to travelling to a high risk area. The exact length of protections is unknown; a booster shot may be given at 2 years.

Some people will have a reaction to the vaccine. About 1 in 5 people have some pain, swelling and redness at the injection site. As many as 1 in 10 people may develop fever, chills, nausea, abdominal pain or headache. Rare cases (<0.01%) of itchy rash, hives, throat or tongue swelling, or very low blood pressure have occurred; if you experience any of these more unusual reactions you should obtain medical care immediately as they can, in extreme cases, result in death. After you receive the JE vaccine you should be observed in the office for 30 minutes following each injection and should stay in an area with readily available medical care for 10 days in case delayed reactions occur. Your chance of a reaction increases with each injection; having no problem with the first or second injection is no guarantee that you will not have a reaction to the third.

If you are travelling or working in an urban area or spend less than 30 days in a rural area, you probably do not need the JE vaccine, according to the US Center for Disease Control and the American College of Physicians. Children under one year of age, pregnant women, persons who have had a reaction to the JE vaccine, and persons with a history of hives or allergy to bee stings should not receive the JE vaccine. As with other vaccines and medications, the decision to receive the JE vaccine should be based on the risks and benefits to you individually. This is best discussed with your healthcare provider.

*Author's note: Dr. Hutcheson most graciously gave her permission for this essay to be reprinted from the March 1997 issue of the "Courier". JE is an issue that we are frequently asked about during our orientations for incoming expatriates.*

# VACCINATIONS RECOMMENDED FOR CHINA

Dr. Paul Chiang

Director, New Pioneer Medical Centre

Living and working in China can be a worthwhile and enjoyable experience, however there are some precautions you should take to ensure that you do not put yourself or your family at a health risk.

## IS A VACCINATION RECORD AN ENTRY REQUIREMENT FOR CHINA?

A primary concern for many people entering China is immunisation against various diseases. There are no compulsory vaccinations required for entry to China, however there are several vaccines recommended before coming to China or at least commenced before departure from your home country.

## HEPATITIS A

Three injections (shots) are required. The first and second injection are given one month apart. The third injection is given 6 - 12 months after the first injection. There is a new product, called HAVRIX, available in some countries that requires only two injections followed by a booster shot 8 - 10 years after the primary course.

## HEPATITIS B

Three injections are required over a period of 6 months. The first and second injections are given one month apart. The third injection is given 6 months after the first one. A booster shot is necessary 3 - 4 years after the primary course.

## JAPANESE ENCEPHALITIS

Three injections are given over a one month period. The first and second injections are given 7 - 14 days apart and the third injection is given 28 days after the first injection. A booster shot is necessary every two years. While the risk of contraction in urban areas is low, many people prefer not to take the risk and have the vaccine.

## TYPHOID

This vaccine is available in oral (capsule) form as well as injectable form. The oral vaccine is the most popular for obvious reasons. Your doctor will advise you on how and when to take the capsules.

## TETANUS

You probably had a tetanus vaccination as a child or teenager. If you did, then it is necessary to have a booster every 5 - 10 years. If you are not certain whether or not you had a primary course, discuss with your doctor the best course of action. It is most important that you have this protection.

## DIPHTHERIA

A booster every 10 years is all you need, assuming that you had your childhood immunisations. Adults can have a combined Tetanus and Dipthena booster known as A.D.T. (Adult Dipthena and Tetanus).

## POLIO

You should have a booster dose every 10 years, but if you are uncertain about the last time you had the vaccine, check with your doctor.

Additional vaccines you may wish to consider are:

## CHOLERA, RABIES, FLU, AND MERUVAX

If children are accompanying you, it is necessary to bring their vaccination records along with you. If possible have their vaccine schedule completed before departure. Remember to bring your vaccination record as well. Sometimes it's hard to remember what vaccines you had five years ago.

**YOU MUST REMEMBER, TO RECEIVE MAXIMUM PROTECTION, YOU AND YOUR FAMILY MUST COMPLETE EVERY COURSE OF VACCINATION YOU COMMENCE AND KEEP YOUR BOOSTER SHOTS UP TO DATE.**

*Author's note: Dr Chiang is a highly respected member of Shanghai's medical community and we thank him for taking the time to outline his recommendations, as health issues are a primary concern for all expatriates in China.*

# DENTAL CARE

In order to address a major expat concern, American Healthcare plans to open a clinic in Shanghai, with a dentist on staff. Current options include the following:

## KOSEI DENTAL CLINIC 厚诚医院

(Houchen Yiyuan)
666 Changle Lu 长乐路666号
Tel: 6247-6748, 6247-7386
Managing Director: Mr. Zhu (Tel: 247-7386)
Medical Director: Dr. Lou Yun Fei
Hours: 8:00 am - 12:00 noon,
      1:00 pm - 6:00 pm
Originally a Sino/Japanese joint venture, now solely Chinese. Credit cards are accepted.

## NEW PIONEER (INTERNATIONAL) MEDICAL CENTRES 新峰医疗中心

2nd Fl, Geru Building 格如大楼2楼
910 Hengshan Lu 衡山路910号
Tel: 6469-7259
Fax: 6469-3897

## SHANGHAI DENTAL MEDICAL CENTRE COOPERATIVE, LTD.
上海口腔医疗中心

(Shanghai Kouqiang Yiliao Zhongxin)
Ninth Peoples' Hospital 第九人民医院
7th Fl, Out-patient Service Building
639 Zhizaoju Lu 200011 制造局路639号
Tel: 6313-3174
Fax: 6313-9156
8:00 am - 5:00 pm Mon. - Sat.
This is a Sino/Canadian joint venture clinic which specializes in preventive and general dentistry. Chinese dentists and visiting foreign consultants staff this modern facility. Services include:
- Basic family dentistry
- Esthetic restoration
- Endodontic and periodontal treatment
- Orthodontic treatment
- Crowns and bridges
- Dentures

- Dental surgery and implants

## SHANGHAI SHEN DA DENTAL CLINIC
上海申大齿科医院

(Shenda Chike Yiyuan)
83/1 Taiyuan Lu 太原路83弄1号
Tel: 6437-7987, 6415-2697
Fax: 6415-2697
Director: Mr. Gao
Hours: 8:30 am - 8:30 pm Mon. - Sat.
      8:30 am - 5:00 pm Sun.
Complete dental care services and cosmetic dentistry. Most of the doctors and nurses can speak some English. Consultations are by appointment. Credit cards are accepted. Fees are similar to those of most Western-trained dentists in Hong Kong.

## WORLDLINK MEDICAL CENTER
瑞新国际医疗中心

Room 30, Mandarine City 名都城30号房
788 Hongxu Lu 虹许路788号
Tel: 6405-5788
Fax: 6405-3587
Hours: 9:00 am - 5:00 pm Mon. - Fri.
Led by Dr. William Xu, Chief Dentist, the dental team has advanced training in Canada and Japan and is experienced with providing care to the expatriate community. Local and foreign specialists serve as consultants for services such as orthodontics and surgery. Dental services cover a comprehensive range of general and cosmetic dentistry including teeth cleaning, X-rays, fillings, crowns dentures, root canal therapy and restorative dentistry.

As the choices above may not appeal, it is best to take care of dental needs while on home leave. If emergency treatment is needed, one option is to visit the following Western expat dentists in Hong Kong.

## DR. DAVID ROLAND

Room 703A, Manning House
48 Queen's Road, Central
Tel: (852) 2622-8151 or (852) 2625-0966

## THE DENTAL CLINIC

Adventist Hospital
40 Stubbs Road
Tel: (852) 2574 6211
Fax: (852) 2572-9813

## DR. SHEILA HURST-GREEN

Matilda Hospital
41 Mount Kellett Road
The Peak
Tel: (852) 2849-6467

# Emergencies

In the event of a serious emergency, there are medical evacuation companies in Shanghai, and it pays to consider joining one.

## INTERNATIONAL SOS ASSISTANCE

国际SOS援助公司上海代表处
Kunlun Hotel, Suite 447　昆仑饭店447房间
2 Xinyuan Nan Lu　新源南路2号
Chaoyang District　朝阳区
Beijing 100004
Beijing 24-hour Alarm Center:
(010) 6590-3419
Hong Kong 24-hour Alarm Center:
(852) 2545-0868
24-hour alarm centers in Beijing and Hong Kong arrange full emergency medical evacuations by helicopter, private jet, and commercial flights. Even if you are traveling in remote parts of China, SOS can perform services to take members home.

## AEA INTERNATIONAL (ASIA EMERGENCY ASSISTANCE)

亚洲国际紧急救援中心
Suite 2606, Shartex Plaza　协泰中心2606室
88 Zunyi Nan Lu　遵义南路88号
Shanghai Alarm Centre: 6295-0099
Office tel: 6295-9951
Office fax: 6295-8277
Contact: Corinna Tan Reisia

Beijing Office:
Ta Yuan Diplomatic Office Building 2-1-1
塔园外交人员办公楼2-1-1
Ground Fl, 14 Liangmahe Nan Lu
亮马河南路14号
Chaoyang District
Beijing 100600
Administration: (010) 6462-9199
24-hour Alarm: (010) 6462-9100
Clinic: (010) 6462-9112
Fax: (010) 6462-9111
AEA's office in the Hongqiao area of Shanghai opened in the last quarter of 1997 as an alarm center. Services do not include a clinic at this time. AEA, of course, provides services to its members, but will also accommodate non-members, such as tourists, should dire need exist. In addition to medical evacuation services, AEA provides 16 hour Red Cross Courses that include CPR training and certification. They also have existing working relationships with the Shanghai hospitals that provide service for expatriates and with tourist medical clinics.

# FOUNDATIONS

## PROJECT HOPE

(Health Opportunities for People Everywhere) is a non-profit organization, committed to helping children through health education. It was founded in 1958 and has had a presence in China since 1983.

Currently, the main focus of Project HOPE in China is a collaboration with the Shanghai Second Medical University for the development of the Shanghai Children's Medical Center (SCMC). This 250 bed state-of-the-art hospital will become a national model for clinical care and serve as a primary pediatric referral center for children from the Chinese and expatriate communities. However, one of its most important roles is health education for Chinese healthcare personnel. Under HOPE's colla-borative educational programs, selected physicians, nurses, biomedical engineers, health care administrators, and allied health sciences personnel are being prepared to assume leadership positions in SCMC. This preparation includes three months overseas Fellowships to the United States and mentoring and collaboration with the HOPE foreign faculty of educators that come to work in China. HOPE's faculty, who are health care professionals from major medical centers in Canada and the United States, serve in one of two capacities: either as volunteer short-term consultants or as paid long-term educators. Currently, four long-term educators work on a day-to-day basis with their Chinese counterparts at Xinhua Hospital, HOPE's training site for SCMC.

This "volunteer spirit" is not limited to the healthcare educators, but extends to the Shanghai expatriate community. In the fall of 1993, Project HOPE offered its first intensive English language course at Shanghai Normal University for SCMC designated staff. In order for HOPE's international partnerships to work, the partners need to be able to communicate with each other. This is particularly important for the Chinese Fellowship candidates selected for specialized training in the U.S. In March 1994, a small volunteer group consisting of six Shanghai expatriate women volunteered to serve as language partners for the students learning English in HOPE's program. Today the volunteer program, now known as "Friends of HOPE", has grown both in membership and activities. Almost 100 volunteer expatriate men and women from all walks of life, continue with their work at the Shanghai Normal University, sponsor an annual International HOPE Ball to raise funds, and support the pediatric patients at Xinhua Hospital through therapy and toy donations.

If you are interested in their work or would like more information about Shanghai's health facilities and nutrition standards, you may contact Project HOPE in Shanghai at:
280 Chongqing Nan Lu, 200023
Tel: 6384-0609, 6384-0369
Fax: 6385-0525
Inquiries about the "Friends of HOPE" volunteer program should be directed to the Project HOPE numbers listed above.

## SCMC

Shanghai Children's Medical Center
1678 Dongfang Road
Pudong
Tel: 5881-5377
Fax: 5839-3915

# EDUCATION

Sources, a company that aids newcomers with their relocation to Shanghai, has found that most people with children that are considering moving here are very pleased with the available educational resources. Class sizes are small in Shanghai's expatriate schools, allowing for a typical student to teacher ratio of about 15:1. Additionally, expat schools here have virtually no discipline problems compared with schools in other countries. The expatriate student population in Shanghai is growing at a frantic pace, making social interaction among young people consistently easier. Facilities may not yet be up to standards of schools "back home", but are improving at a steady pace. Intramural sports programs are not equal to those at home, but "where there's a will there's a way". Most parents feel the things their children must give up at home are more than offset by the cultural learning experience their children will be exposed to. Tuition prices quoted below are quite high, unfortunately, but most companies cover tuition costs for transferring employees, as it is regarded as a cost of doing business in China.

# For expatriate children, from pre-kindergarten through high school

## CONCORDIA INTERNATIONAL SCHOOL SHANGHAI

Huangyang Lu　黄杨路
Jinqiao, Pudong　金桥浦东
Administrative Office: 11th Fl, East Ocean Center, 618 Yan'an Dong Lu 200001
延安东路618号
Tel: 5306-5192
Fax: 5306-5190
E-mail: aschmidt@uninet.co.cn
Director: Allan H. Schmidt
Admissions: Sandra Schmidt
CISS is a sister school to Hong Kong International School and is a co-educational private day school with an American style curriculum. The program is offered in a Christian setting. English is the language of instruction. High school grades will be added in the fall of 1999. The Pinghe School is the temporary site of CISS, while the permanent campus is being constructed nearby.

## SHANGHAI AMERICAN SCHOOL
美国学校

(Meiguo Xucxiao)
If mailed in the USA:
c/o American Consul General Shanghai
PSC 461, Box 200
FPO A.P. 96521-0002
Administrator: Ronald Montgomery
Assistant Superintendent for Instruction:
Dr. Robin R. Leveillee
High School Principal: Larry Cummins
Middle School Principal: Dr. Bill Parker
Elementary School Principals:
Victoria Montgomery, Deborah Karmozyn
Business Manager: Ruby Laney

SAS is an independent coeducational school incorporating grades pre-K through 12. It offers an educational program based on standard curriculums found in the best schools in the United States. Accreditation was granted to SAS in 1988 by the Western Association of Schools and Colleges. Emphasis is on reading, math, science, language arts, music, drama, Chinese language and culture, and physical education. English as a Second Language is offered to students requiring additional assistance with English. SAS is able to incorporate non-English speaking students into their program while they are learning the language. Over 35 countries are represented within the student body, creating a diverse and multinational campus environment. Boarding facilities are available.

Due to the exponential growth of the foreign community in Shanghai, in 1996 the school moved to two new campuses - one in western Shanghai near the airport, and the other in Pudong.

## WESTERN CAMPUS
美国学校[西部校区] (Xibu Xiaoqu)
50 Jidi Lu　纪翟路50号
Zhudi Township　诸翟镇
Minhang District　闵行区
High School Principal: Larry Cummins
Middle School Principal: Dr. Bill Parker
Elementary School Principal:
Victoria Montgomery
Tel: 6221-1445
Fax: 6221-1269
SAS West is located in Zhudi Township immediately west of Hongqiao Airport, an approximate twenty minute ride. The full pre-K through grade 12 (ages 4-18) program began for students on September 9, 1996 in a new building with expanded facilities. The site accommodates up to 800 students and will serve while a new permanent campus is being built near the present facility. The first building on the permanent site which will house the high school will be in use by fall of 1998.

## EASTERN CAMPUS
美国学校[东部校区] (Dongbu Xiaoqu)
2700 Huaxia Dong Lu, Pudong
华夏东路2700号, 浦东新区
Tel: 5892-5334
Principal: Deborah Karmozyn
Within the confines of the Shanghai Links Executive Community, the first permanent building on this site will be ready for use in 1998, offering a comprehensive program for students in Pre-K through Grade 12. This program will parallel what is offered on the western campus and will include the core curriculum as well as Chinese language, English as a Second or Other Language (ESOL), physical education, art, and music.

SAS is governed by a seven member Board of Directors, six of whom are elected from the members of the SAS Parents' Association. Membership in the group is open to all parents with children enrolled at SAS, however one non-parent may be elected to the board. One member is appointed by the American Consul General.

For the 1997-98 year, SAS features:
- Certified experienced teaching staff from eight countries
- Ongoing staff in-service program
- Chinese language for all students in Kindergarten through Grade 5
- Foreign language choices of Chinese, Spanish, and French for secondary students
- Elective hot lunch program
- Elementary enrichment and remedial resource teacher
- Immersion ESOL for beginners
- Full accreditation by the Western Association of Schools and Colleges
- Member of the East Asian Regional Council of Overseas Schools (EARCOS)
- Member of the European Council of International Schools
- Member of the Asian Pacific Activities Conference (a regional league for high school athletics and activities)
- Advanced Placement courses offered in seven subjects at the high school level
- Frequent instructional field trips
- Regular program of after school activities
- Model United Nations program
- Associated Student Body (student government) at all levels
- Instrumental and vocal music programs
- Eclectic teacher-determined instrumental methodology
- Small class sizes (student-teacher ratios average less than 15:1)
- Comprehensive curriculum
- Chicago Mathematics (hands on manipulative) at the elementary level

Approximately 96% of the school's income is derived from tuition. An annual fundraising campaign in the corporate communities provides additional contributions. A debenture program has been in place for two years to help fund the building of the two permanent campuses. Purchasing a debenture for US$30,000, one is given priority for a place in the school for one student for ten years. A US$35,000 permanent debenture is also available. A capital fee will be added to the tuition of any student who is not covered by a debenture.

*Tuition (1997-1998 school year)*
Pre-K: (1/2 day) US$11,500 per annum
K- grade 5: US$12,500 per annum
Grades 6-8: US$13,000 per annum
Grades 9-12: US$14,000 per annum
A capital fee of US$3,000 per semester is levied in addition to tuition if a student's seat is not offset by the purchase of a debenture.

## YEW CHUNG SHANGHAI INTERNATIONAL SCHOOL  耀中国际学校
(Yaozhong Guoji Xuexiao)
11 Shuicheng Lu  水城路11 号
Tel: 6242-3242

18 Ronghua Xi Lu, Gubei 荣华西路18号古北
Tel: 6242-3243

SIS operates nine schools - seven in Hong Kong, one in the USA, and one in Shanghai. Curriculum is based upon the UK National Curriculum with special emphasis on information technology and multiculturalism. Subjects include Chinese and English languages and cultures (with the option of a third language), mathematics, science and technology, history and geography, art and craft, drama, music and movement, physical education, social studies, computer studies, environmental studies, and life management skills. Form 5 students will take the General Certificate of Secondary Education (International) GCSE (1). Students may continue for the International Baccalaureate. This school goes through grade 10 and is comprised of two campuses in the western area of the city.

*Tuition:*
Reception to Primary 6   US$17,325/annum
Secondary School         US$17,655/annum
*Fees:*
Registration fee         US$200
Miscellaneous charges, Reception to Primary
                         US$630/annum
Miscellaneous charges, Secondary
                         US$840/annum
*School lunch:*
Reception to Primary 4   US$1,155/annum
Primary 5 and 6          US$1,265/annum
Secondary                US$1,265/annum
Transportation (depending on location)
                         US$1,210–1,672/
                         annum

## SHANGHAI CHANGNING INTERNATIONAL SCHOOL
上海长宁国际学校
(Shanghai Changning Guoji Xuexiao)
155 Jiangsu Lu   江苏路155号长宁区
Changning District
Tel: 6212-2328
Fax: 6212-2330

E-mail: jmichael@uninet.com.cn
Principal: Michael Jones

This school offers a pre-school through 8th grade US-based, international school curriculum for expatriate children. Materials are primarily from the United States, with teaching strategies and curricular enhancements designed to prepare children for transition to other academically challenging schools. Presently, the faculty is from the United States, Australia, and New Zealand. Changning International in Shanghai is applying for accreditation from the Western Association of Schools and Colleges in California, the European Council of International Schools, and the East Asia Regional Council of Overseas Schools. Students follow a text-based program in English, mathematics, social studies, science, Mandarin, computing, English as a Second Language, physical education, music, and arts. Facilities include computer and science labs, a 4,000+ volume library, music and art rooms, theater/gymnasium, nurse's station, and twenty climate-controlled classrooms. School uniforms are mandatory. Lunches are RMB30 per day. In addition to tuition fees, a Capital Levy Certificate (CLC) must be purchased for each student attending SCIS. This certificate is a bond which depreciates 35%, 35%, and 30% over a three year period, and is refundable until its validity expires. Through this bond, the parent community subsidizes building facilities costs and other capital expenditures. The principal may approve the payment of an annual capital fee in lieu of CLC purchase. No CLC is required for pre-school.

*Fees:*
Application fee          US$100
                         (non-refundable)

Pre-Kindergarten 1       US$4,500
Pre-Kindergarten 2       US$6,500
Pre-Kindergarten 3       US$8,000
Kindergarten tuition     US$8,500
Grade 1-5 tuition        US$12,000

Grade 6-8 tuition US$13,000
Bus fee US$100/month
Lunch fee RMB30/daily
Capital fee US$4,000/year
Capital Levy Certificate (valid for 3 years)
US$12,000

*Note: SCIS is offering "Summer Camp" programs for students aged 8 to12. In 1997, the camp ran from June 30th until July 25th, Monday - Friday from 8:00 am to noon. The "Fun Camp" offers activities such as arts and crafts, English, creative writing, games, playground activities, computer study, swimming, field trips, painting, and use of the library. The cost is US$500. The "ESL/Academic Camp" provides students with a chance to achieve higher competency in the English language and also includes academic programs in math, science, and computer enrichment. This camp costs US$800. The Camps are organized and run by qualified teachers. Enrollment will be on a first come, first served basis. To register, please call Ms. Hu at the school office.*

## SHANGHAI GERMAN/FRENCH SCHOOL 上海德国，法国学校

Shanghai Deguo Faguo Xuexiao
437 Jinhui Lu   金江路437号
German School tel: 6405-9220
German School fax: 6405-9235
French School tel: 6405-1123
French School fax: 6405-9227

This school provides classes for German-speaking and French-speaking children. Only children whose parents are members of the German School Association are accepted by the German school. Membership in the French School Association is now also prerequisite for enrollment in this school. Membership forms are available at the school. The school offers Kindergarten and regular school curriculum through Grade 4. A school bus service is available for which the annual fee is US$1,000. Lunches are available for RMB25.

Tuition is as follows:
German School annual tuition
US$12,000
German Kindergarten (Full day)
US$10,000
German Kindergarten (Half day)
US$8,000
French School Maternelle
US$10,000
French School Primaire
US$12,000
French School Secondaire
US$13,000

## SHANGHAI JAPANESE SCHOOL
上海日本人学校

(Shanghai Ribenren Xuexiao)
3085 Hongmei Lu
虹梅路3085号
Tel: 6406-8027
Fax: 6401-2747

This school accepts children from six to fifteen years of age. Monthly tuition is RMB1,200. Bus fee is RMB660. Parent meeting fee is RMB25. Japanese passport is required for attendance.

## SHANGHAI HIGH SCHOOL (INTERNATIONAL DIVISION)
上海中学国际部

(Shanghai Zhongxue Guoji Bu)
400 Shangzhong Lu
上中路400号
Tel: 6476-5516
Fax: 6453-5008

The International Division was established on June 1, 1993 by Shanghai High School in conjunction with the Shanghai Municipal Education Bureau. The International Division selectively admits qualified international

*Gubei Xinqu is a residential area close to the airport in which many expatriates live.*

students for Grades 5 through 12, including, but not limited to, overseas Chinese, students from Taiwan, Hong Kong, Macau, and other countries. The curriculum includes English, Chinese, mathematics, physics, chemistry, computer science, natural science, history, geography, physical education, arts, music, and others. The school provides facilities for both day and boarding students, and provides private buses for day students on five routes. Dormitories for boarding students have air-conditioning, hot water, and other necessities.

Full-time specialists are available to serve students' everyday needs. Faculty of the International Division is Chinese and multi-national. A bilingual teaching approach is utilized and both Chinese and English text-books are available for mathematics, English, computers, and other major subjects. Facilities include a science laboratory, library, computer rooms, audio-visual lab, cinema, language lab, gymnasium, basketball, volleyball and tennis courts, table tennis, swimming pool, soccer field, and skating rink. The school is located in southwestern Shanghai and covers over 300 mu (20 hectares) of park-like area. Current tuition is US$4,000 per semester.

## INTERNATIONAL PLAY POINT (IPP)

Ground Fl, Block 2, Longbai Service Apart-ments 龙柏高级公寓2号楼底楼
Longbei Gaoji Gongyu 2 Haolou Dilou
2461 Hongqiao Lu 虹桥路2461号
Tel: 6268-8462, 6270-9250
A non-profit "play group" for pre-school children in which parents of children attending are participants. The aim of IPP is to provide expat pre-school children with an opportunity to develop appropriate social and early academic skills under the guidance of a qualified counselor/early childhood educator. IPP is open to all pre-school age children who are at least two years and nine months old. Acceptance and placement (morning or afternoon session) of children is subject to the evaluation of a professionally qualified teacher. Children must be toilet trained. The half-day sessions are 9:00 am - noon and 1:00 pm - 4:00 pm Monday through Friday. Days of operation will follow those of Shanghai American School. The language of instruction is English. Maximum enrollment of IPP is twenty-six children (thirteen per session). Parents must provide transportation for their child. Each school year is comprised of two semesters and tuition is US$750/semester,

of which US$50 is used to purchase materials and supplies.

## RAINBOW BRIDGE INTERNATIONAL SCHOOL 虹桥国际幼儿园

2381 Hongqiao Lu 虹桥路2381号
Tel: 6268-9773
Fax: 6269-1294
International preschool for children two years old to six years old. English and Chinese instruction. Located on the grounds of Shanghai Zoo.

## SOONG CHING LING KINDERGARTEN 宋庆龄幼儿园

(Songqingling You'er Yuan)
3908 Hongmei Lu 虹梅路3908号
Tel: 6242-9851
Fax: 6242-2881
Soong Ching Ling International Education Center (SCLIEC) is jointly established by Soong Ching Ling Kindergarten (SCLK) in Shanghai and Soong Ching Ling Children's Foundation of Canada, and admits children aged 3-6 from Taiwan, Hong Kong, Macau, and foreign countries. It strives to create an environment of multiculturalism. English and Chinese bilingual instruction is provided. The International Class at the kindergarten is conducted in English. The school also offers a Montessori Program. Fees for the Inter-national Division are:
Registration fee (non-refundable)   US$150
Tuition fee     Autumn term (Sept. - Dec.)
US$800 x 4 months = 3,200 (Full time)
US$500 x 4 months = 2,000 (Part time)
          Spring term (Jan. - April)
US$800 x 4 months = 3,200 (Full time)
US$500 x 4 months = 2,000 (Part time)
          Summer term (May - July)
US$800 x 3 months = 2,400 (Full time)
US$500 x 3 months = 1,500 (Part time)
Miscellaneous fees    US$100 per term
School lunch and snack
     Autumn Term     US$175 (Full time)

|  |  |
|---|---|
|  | US$53 (Part time) |
| Spring term | US$150 (Full time) |
|  | US$45 (Part time) |
| Summer term | US$125 (Full time) |
|  | US$ 37 (Part time) |
| Transportation fee |  |
| Autumn term | US$400 |
| Spring term | US$350 |
| Summer term | US$250 |

## ZONG GONG HUI KINDERGARTEN
上海市总工会幼儿园

Shanghai Shi Zonggonghui Youeryuan

Yangguang Hotel　阳光大酒店

2264 Hongqiao Lu　虹桥路2264号

Tel: 6242-7932

Fax: 6242-9080

This kindergarten accommodates children aged 3-1/2 to 6-1/2 years old. All classes are conducted in Chinese and foreign students are accepted only if they speak Chinese. Most students are local Chinese. Tuition is approximately RMB1,300 per month.

# ADULT EDUCATION

## ALLIANCE FRANCAISE DE SHANGHAI
法语培训中心

(Fayu Peixun Zhongxin)

297 Wusong Lu　吴淞路297号

Tel: 6357-5388

Fax: 6325-1183

Director: Olivier Salvan

This non-profit organization promotes French culture through cultural events and French language classes. Alliance Francaise was founded in Paris is 1883 as an international French Language educational system. Active in Shanghai from 1934 to 1951, it reopened in 1993 as a venture with the Shanghai Hangkou Spare Time College (HKU). General French courses are offered at all levels. Specialized courses such as Secretarial French, French for the Hotel Industry, and Business French are also available. Although teaching the French language is the primary objective of this organization, cultural events are also held, including film nights, exhibitions, and stage shows.

## CHINA EUROPE INTERNATIONAL BUSINESS SCHOOL (CEIBS)
中文国际工商学院

(Zhongwen Guoji Gongshang Xueyuan)

Jiaotong University, Minhang

交通大学闵行分校

800 Dongchuan Lu　东川路800号

Tel: 6463-0200

Fax: 6463-1265

E-mail: ceibspr@fudan.ihep.ac.cn

CEIBS is a joint-venture operation between Shanghai Jiaotong University and the European Foundation for Management Development. Its primary goal is to train Chinese managers in the ways of the global economy. However, as classes are conducted in English by visiting foreign professors, expatriates can also join the programs. Two programs are offered by CEIBS: a full-time MBA program and a part-time Executive MBA program taught over long weekend sessions once per month. The 18-month MBA program is targeted at bright, young Chinese applicants and a small number of foreign students, usually between the ages of 24 and 35, with a maximum age of 40. All candidates should have a minimum of 2 years work experience, excellent academic credentials, and a good knowledge of English. The Executive MBA program is aimed at managers already working in the Chinese business environment. The EMBA program has two parallel classes - one in English and one with Chinese translation. The EMBA program runs over a two-year period with classes held on four consecutive days over one weekend a month. Targeted to entrepreneurs in the 30 - 45 old year age group, who have at least eight years work experience, including five years in a managerial position. Fees for the EMBA program are US$20,000 plus extra for food and accommodation.

## DA SHI JIE 大世界
(The Big World)
Tel: 6471-1635
This expatriate group offers courses related to Chinese culture. Initial classes have dealt with Chinese cooking and Chinese massage. Each session runs for ten weeks with meetings once a week. Classes are taught in English. Fees differ for each type of class but are usually around RMB1,500.

## FUDAN UNIVERSITY'S MANDARIN CENTER 复旦大学
(Fudan Daxue)
College of Humanities 人文学院汉语中心
Study and Research Center of Chinese and Foreign Cultures
10 Songyuan Lu 宋园路10号
Tel: 6270-7668
Fax: 6270-7661
E-mail: mandarin@online.sh.cn
Contacts: Director Mr. Zhou Cheng Yu and his assistant Sam.
This extension of Fudan University offers interactive lectures on Chinese culture, training classes, tours, and art appreciation. They also offer Chinese language classes, Chinese painting classes, Martial Arts classes, and classes in antique porcelain. The Chinese language classes are offered at four levels (basic, elementary, intermediate, and advanced) and can be taken during the daytime (8:45-noon) Monday to Thursday or the evening (6:30-9:00) on Mondays and Wednesdays. Terms begin in January, July, and September. Fees for daytime classes for the Spring Term (5 months) run US$1,100, Autumn Term (3 months) US$660, and the Summer Term (2 months) US$440. Evening classes for the Spring Term are US$550, Autumn Term US$330. and Summer Term US$220. One may join classes during the middle of the term and the fee will be prorated accordingly. Classes are also available for teenagers 14-18 years of age for eight weeks during the summer. The intensive Chinese Program that runs 120 hours over four weeks runs US$500. Classes can also be custom-tailored for groups and private tutoring can be arranged. Instruction is also provided in Shanghainese.

## MACH MANDARIN
Morningside China
380 Wuyuan Lu 五原路380号
Wuyuan Lu 380 Hao
Tel: 6437-3174
Mobile: 9106-5770
Fax: 6431-0999
Contact: Michelle Keyte, Senior Marketing Manager
MACH Mandarin was established in Hong Kong in 1993 and began pilot Putonghua (Mandarin) courses in Shanghai in 1996. Emphasis is placed on communication skills, along with reading and writing of Chinese characters using computer software. Classes average four or five students, and can be held at Morningside China or in your office. Beginner, intermediate, and advanced courses are offered, each course running for eight weeks with two hour classes twice a week. Courses are RMB8,000 per person. An intensive ten day course is available as an alternative at RMB10,000 per person.

# HOUSING

Housing is the most urgent matter for the majority of incoming expatriates. Newcomers naturally focus first on their housing needs upon arrival in Shanghai.

Most foreigners who arrive in Shanghai on "look-see" visits arranged by their employers find overall living conditions here to be much better than they had expected. After about a half-day of looking at housing, some degree of relaxation takes place. Often, preconceived notions originate when outdated guidebooks have been consulted for information. The housing situation in Shanghai has improved significantly in recent years, and is not as grim as most available (outdated) information sources would lead one to believe.

Expats can rest assured that homes here are more than adequate for a comfortable existence, even if they are not completely up to Western standards. Although price is a key factor in what can be had here, the norm usually includes air conditioning, dishwashers, smoke detectors and adequate living space.

Housing costs are indeed a major issue here, with prices being among the highest in the world, anywhere from US$1,000 to US$15,000 for monthly rents. Most of Sources' clients who are with major multi-national firms pay an average of US$8,000 per month for housing. Accommodation in the lower price range often lacks such things as an adequate kitchen, quality furnishings, healthclub and restaurant facilities and English-speaking property management. Mid-range prices offer on-site facilities, more nicely finished living space and English-speaking management. The high-end, upscale properties provide excellent service and management, high-quality living quarters, excellent facilities and well-manicured surroundings.

Most first-time visitors experience "sticker-shock" when initially viewing housing options, though within a day or two, the realization that a good place in the US$7,000 range is a good value begins to settle in. Often, those who arrive alone on fact-finding missions for their firms have a very hard time convincing the managers back home that adequate

housing truly "costs" in Shanghai.

When selecting a residential area, the expatriate community gravitates primarily to the western and central areas of Shanghai, though Pudong (East Shanghai) is becoming an increasingly attractive option for housing. However, significant movement "across the river" has only just begun.

Central Shanghai has numerous high-rise apartment complexes which vary widely in quality and price, from very high-end to very low. There are some free-standing houses in this area as well, but not many. The main advantage to being in central Shanghai is convenience and proximity to shopping, services, restaurants and meeting venues. The drawbacks are noise, pollution and lack of green space. In the better neighborhoods of the central area, much less space for the dollar can be had than in the less "in-demand" parts of the city.

Many expats reside in the area which spreads from the western edge of the city to Hongqiao Airport, with the primary concentration being in the Hongqiao and Gubei areas. There is a much higher number of free-standing houses here than in central Shanghai, along with a tremendous number of newer apartment buildings. Advantages to living here include cleaner air, better green space, and more actual living space. The main drawback is the longer commuting times to central Shanghai, Pudong and other areas. At least half an hour is required for the frequent drive into the city's center. The western area attracts many families with school-age children, as most of Shanghai's international schools are located here, with the exception of Shanghai American School's Pudong campus. Another "family" factor which makes this area attractive is abundance of single-family houses with yards and gardens.

The best way to locate suitable housing in Shanghai is through a real estate or relocation company. Sources has established relationships with many of the real estate companies in Shanghai, similar to the American style multiple-listing system. Sources also keeps in close touch with developers of new housing projects, which enables newcomers to be exposed to a very wide selection of properties. Real estate companies show only their own listings, making it necessary for customers to visit many companies in order to see all that is available for their needs.

It is standard practice in Shanghai for the potential tenant or buyer to pay a commission to the real estate company. Standard fees are half a month's rent for leases less than one year, and one month's rent for leases from one to three years. Three year (or longer) contracts usually require a commission fee of two months' rent. When purchasing housing, a percentage (usually about 3%) of the total sales price of the home is paid as commission.

Most expats in Shanghai lease their homes and offices. However there is a growing interest in purchasing, due to high rental rates. Hesitation still exists among expat buyers due to China's legal system (or lack thereof), fears of political instability and poor construction quality in many projects, though the situation on these fronts is improving.

When choosing a home in Shanghai, property management is one of the most important considerations. Non-Chinese speaking tenants naturally need to have access to on-site English-speaking management personnel for obvious reasons, such as ordering repairs, calling for taxis and possible emergencies. It is the responsibility of the professional who is assisting with home-search to be aware of the quality and reputation of each property's management team.

During the search for living quarters, it becomes apparent that certain trade-offs must be made. Through extensive experience with home-search, Sources has found that it is virtually impossible for a prospective tenant to be 100% satisfied. For example, the apartment or house itself may be ideal, but there may be a trade-off with respect to location convenience, facilities or price level, and vice-versa. It is reasonable to expect that about 75% of one's needs will be met by any particular place.

With the rapid growth and development of Shanghai, security is naturally becoming another important consideration. Relative to the rest of the world, Shanghai's crime rate remains low. However, compared to just a few years ago, the incidence of crime has increased here. All housing for foreigners has security, but the degree varies widely. Again, the housing agent is responsible for assessing the security situation for each development tenants are interested in.

Many housing communities provide a wide range of facilities, such as swimming pools, gyms, tennis courts and restaurants, etc. Surprisingly, price is not necessarily a guarantee, as there are many high-priced places that lack such facilities, and vice versa.

Housing complexes seem to have their own "personality", and draw tenants accordingly. Obviously, a successful housing search culminates in finding a social setting one is comfortable with. For the most part, expatriates in Shanghai are warm and welcoming, with frequent get-togethers among neighbors being common. Some complexes hold organized activities like bridge, mahjongg, and aerobics on a regular basis, and this can be a particularly important source of support and stimulation for the non-working spouse. One's instincts should be heeded when visiting various residential buildings and complexes, as your choice will either allow you to enjoy your stay in Shanghai or make you want to catch the next plane home.

# SHOPPING

The most popular leisure-time activity in Shanghai, for locals and expats alike.

# IMPORTED FOODS

A great variety of imported food items and familiar Western brand names can now be found in Shanghai's grocery stores, particularly those that cater to the expat market, and even in many of the smaller local stores. The problem lies in not being able to do a Western-style "one-stop" shopping trip once a week. Grocery stores are scattered throughout the city, and no single place ever carries everything on one's list. It is usual for shoppers to have to make rotation trips to various stores that carry particular items. For example, it's Glenmore Deli for fresh meats and cheese, Park 'n Shop for Bisquick pancake mix and City Shopping for Hormel's canned meat products, as none of these places carries all three things. This of course requires much extra time and planning. It helps to have a separate storage freezer at home for stocking up and cutting down on numerous trips. And, if there are certain items that are needed on a regular basis and can't be done without, keep an ample supply in a kitchen pantry. Adding to shopping frustration is the fact that an item may appear on the store shelves one day and be gone the next, with no future delivery date known by store staff. Overall, bear in mind that many products and brands from home are not yet available here. However, the supply of Western-style goods is more adequate than one would expect, and an increasing number of products are becoming available.

## BAUERNSTUBE

2nd Fl, Westin Tai Ping Yang
太平洋大酒店
(Taipingyang Dajiudian)
5 Zunyi Nan Lu, 200335    遵义南路5号
Tel: 6275-8888
Fax: 6205-5420, 6275-0750
Hours: 10:00 am - 8:30 pm
A wide selection of Swiss cheeses, baked goods, imported wines, and homemade chocolates can be found at Bauernstube, which means "farmer's living room". This expanded store has replaced the original Westin Deli. The lounge area outside the shop has been converted into a coffee bar serving drinks and snacks.

## CARREFOUR   家乐福超市

(Jialefu Chaoshi)
- 560 Quyang Lu    曲阳路560号
  Tel: 6555-8078
  Fax: 6552-3550
- 20 Wuning Lu    武宁路20号
  Tel: 6227-7788
  Fax: 6227-5848
- 268 Shuicheng Nan Lu    水城南路268号
Hours: 8:30 am - 10:00 pm
This large store carries just about everything. The 2nd floor offers office supplies, VCD's, clothing, bedding, appliances, toys, and more. To enter the grocery store on the ground floor, proceed down a ramp from the second floor. The grocery section is very large and well-stocked, with low prices. However, there

is not a heavy concentration of imported goods. Selection seems to be aimed at the local market and the store is consistently crowded.

## CITY SUPERMARKET 上海城市超市
(Shanghai Chengshi Chaoshi)
3822 Hongmei Lu, Hongqiao
虹梅路3822号
Tel: 6262-3345
1233 Zhangyang Lu, Pudong
浦东张扬路1233号
Tel: 6875-2312
Hours: 8:00 am - 10:00 pm
This is the supermarket run by the City Shopping Delivery Service, mentioned below in "Food Delivery Services". It is just south of the Worldfield Convention Hotel in Hongqiao, and is located near Next Age Department store in Pudong in the Krest Garden housing complex. City Supermarket carries products from all over the world and receives a shipment from the US every two months. Carries over fifty varieties of cheese, twenty kinds of cereals, fresh breads, wines, quality meats and sausages, and cake mixes. See "Food Shopping Services" below for home delivery.

## FABERMART 华英白选商城
(Huaying Zixuan Shangcheng)
Hongqiao Location:
3901 Hongmei Lu   虹梅路3901路
Tel: 6262-6605
Hours: 9:00 am - 9:30 pm
A small store with a treasure-trove of European and American items. Things here are not found elsewhere, including a wide selection of cake mixes, canned frosting, canned walnuts, French-cut green beans, Pillsbury flour, brown sugar, and minced dried onions.

## FRIENDSHIP SHOPPING CENTER
虹桥友谊商城
(Hongqiao Youyi Shangcheng)
6 Zunyi Nan Lu   遵义南路6号

Tel: 6270-0000
Hours: 10:00 am - 10:00 pm
Located on the first floor of the shopping center, this store carries a combination of imported and local items. There is also an Italian deli stocked by Pasta Fresca just outside the entrance.

## GLENMORE DELI 悉谊食品商行
(Xiyi Shiping Shanghang)
501 Wuzhong Dong Lu (near Guyi Lu)
吴中东路501号
Tel: 6464-8665
Fax: 6464-3043
Pager: 127-2094058
Hours: Mon. - Fri. 10:00 am - 6:30 pm,
       Sat. 10:00 am - 4:00 pm,
       Sun. noon - 4:00 pm
Imported meats, seafood, wines, and grocery items from Australia (including Vegemite) at wholesale prices. This place is a treasure, albeit "hidden" on a side street in a part of town that is off the beaten path. It's well worth the trip, however. From the intersection of Wuzhong Dong Lu and Guyi Lu, look south for a relatively small green "G" jutting from the side of a building on the left side of Guyi Lu about 200 yards down. Call for a catalogueue.

## GREEN VALLEY VILLAS 绿谷别墅
(Lügu Bieshu)
1500 Hami Lu   哈密路1500号
Tel: 6268-9988
This housing complex has a large grocery store that is open to the entire community. Carries many hard-to-find items. Let the formidable security guards at the gate know that you want to shop in the store.

## IMM (INTERNATIONAL MERCHANDISE MART) 南方商场
(Nanfang Shangcheng)
7388 Humin Lu   沪闵路7388号
Tel: 6412-3888

Hours: 9:00 am - 9:00 pm
Operated like a Price Club in the US, one may buy items in bulk after paying a membership fee of RMB20. Information on other articles carried by IMM is under the heading "Mega-Marts".

## JESSICA GROCERY   老锦江饭店
59 Maoming Nan Lu   茂名南路59号
Tel: 6258-2582
Hours: 9:00 am - 10:00 pm
Located on the "Food Street" adjacent to the Old Jinjiang Hotel, this was one of the first stores to carry imported food in Shanghai. To find it, enter the front gate of the hotel, immediately turn right, and go halfway down the walkway.

## LONGBAI APARTMENTS GROCERY
龙柏高级公寓
(Longbai Gaoji Gongyu)
2461 Hongqiao Lu   虹桥路2461号
Tel: 6268-8320
Hours: 9:00 am - 9:00 pm
Located at the front of the first block of apartments, this is a very small grocery store with a limited selection. OK in a pinch. Baked goods from Pucci bakery are sold in the Longbai coffee shop next door.

## LOTUS SUPERCENTER   莲花超市
(Lianhua Chaoshi)
1126-1128 Yanggao Nan Lu, Pudong
200127   浦东 扬高南路1126-1128号
Tel: 6312-0922
Hours: 9:00 am - 10:00 pm
"Everyday Low Prices!" is this store's credo. A vast grocery store is on the first floor, aimed at the local market, but also carries many items of use to expats.

## PARK 'N SHOP   百佳超市
(Baijia Chaoshi)
- 1190 Quxi Lu, Luwan District
  瞿溪路1190 号，卢湾区

- 242 Julu Lu, Luwan District
  巨鹿路242号，卢湾区
- 200 Shunchang Lu, Luwan District
  顺昌路200号，卢湾区
- 14 Xietu Lu, Luwan District
  斜土路14号，卢湾区
- 362-370 Dezhou Lu, Pudong
  德州路362-370号，浦东
- 700 Laoshandong Lu, Pudong
  崂山东路700号，浦东
- Gubei Store: Ronghua Xi Dao, #8 Lane 28, Changning District
  荣华西路，28弄 8号，长宁区
- 1-8 Renmin Dadao, Huangpu District
  人民大道1-8号，黄浦
- 889 Liyuan Lu, Luwan District
  丽园路889号，卢湾区
- 401 Zhiyuan Lu, Zhabei District
  芷园路401号，闸北区
- Minhang Store: 131 Humin Lu, Minhang District
  沪闵路131号，闵行区
- Qibao Store: Qixing Lu, Qibao Department Store, 1st Floor, Qibao District
  七辛路，七宝商场1楼，七宝区
- 218 Wusheng Lu, Huangpu District
  武胜路218号，黄浦
- 16 Lishan Lu, Putuo District
  骊山路16号，普陀区

This Hong Kong chain is expanding rapidly in Shanghai. Stores are well stocked with foreign products and housewares.

## SHANGHAI ORIENT SHOPPING CENTER
上海东方商厦
(Dongfang Shangxia)
8 Caoxi Bei Lu   漕溪北路8号
Tel: 6487-0000
On the basement level of this store, you will find a large grocery store offering a combination of imported and local goods, bakery counter, candy shop, and housewares.

*Shoppers walking the streets of Huaihai Lu, a busy Shanghai street which is popular with window shoppers. Many western shops sell their goods along it. The streets are lined with advertisements for goods from the west and east.*

## UNCLE SAM'S STORE 赛姆便利店

(Saimu Bianli Dian)
Basement Shop 4-5　地下商场4-5
Kerry Everbright City　嘉里不夜城
218 Tianmu Xi Lu　天目西路218号
Zhabei District　闸北区
Tel: 6354-1068, 6354-1069
Fax: 6354-0180
Hours: 10:00 am - 10:00 pm daily
More than 90% of the goods in this store are manufactured in the USA and the rest are from Canada, France, the United Kingdom, Italy, Brazil, Malaysia, Indonesia, Thailand, and China. You'll find name brands of household cleaners, detergents, air fresheners, personal health items, glassware, plastic household items, microwave cookware, hair accessories, toys, infant and children's items, as well as food and beverages. All products are sold for RMB15 or a multiple of RMB15.

## WELLCOME SUPERMARKET
惠康超级市场

(Huikang Chaoji Shichang)
Level 1 West, Shanghai Centre
上海商城底楼
1376 Nanjing Xi Lu, 200040
南京西路1376号
Tel: 6279-8018
Delivery service tel: 6279-7077
Offers the best selection of imported foods, albeit at some of the higher prices in town. Carries many Western-style, South Asian and Japanese grocery items. Also find a freezer section, extensive dairy case and the high-quality Portman Deli (and bakeshop).

# FOOD SHOPPING SERVICES

## A LA CARTE
隆事达中国上海贸易有限公司

(Rongshida Zhongguo Shanghai Maoyi Youxian Gongsi)
8 Gao'an Lu　高安路8号
Tel: 6474-2163, 6474-2162
Fax: 6474-2221
Delivers French wine and cheese to your door. Wine prices range from RMB95 to 275 per 750 ml bottle. Cheeses are sold by weight. Allow 24 hours for delivery.

## AMERICAN GARDEN
原创美西园艺有限公司

(Yuanchuang Meixi Yuanyi Youxian Gongsi)
Sales Contact: Tang Bi Yun
Tel: 6459-3694
Fax: 6459-3695
Pager: 126-633715
Organize some friends and place a weekly group order for vegetables grown using American techniques.

## CITY SHOPPING SERVICE COMPANY
城市购物服务公司

(Chengshi Gouwu Fuwu Gongsi)
3822 Hongmei Lu　虹梅路3822号
Tel: 6215-0418, 6267-4248
Fax: 6215-0418, 6267-4248
Hours: 9:00 am - 8:00 pm
Order before 3:30 pm, and receive goods the same evening. Goods ordered after 3:30 pm will be delivered the next day. Instant delivery can be arranged as well. Delivery in Shanghai is always free of charge, regardless of the amount ordered. This is a very popular service and has a good reputation. City Shopping Service also delivers food to Suzhou, Wuxi, and Hangzhou with no charge for delivery.

Expatriates in Ningbo, Nanjing, Jinan, Qingdao, Yantai, Xuzhou, and Xiamen are also served, with a modest delivery charge. Delivery to other cities can be arranged. Call for a catalog.

## JING CHENG FOODSTUFF CENTER
金城食品总汇

(Jincheng Shiping Zonghui)
172 Nanjing Dong Lu　南京东路172号
Visit this store for a large variety of German wines. If you prefer delivery, have a Chinese speaker call or fax 6321-7918 and ask for Jiang Zhu Wei or Ying Xiao Mei.

## MONTROSE HOME DELIVERY
杰信国际贸易有限公司

(Jiexin Guoji Maoyi Youxian Gongsi)
Shimen Er Lu, #4, Lane 179, Room 404
石门二路179弄1号404室
Tel: 6468-3293 or 6468-6758
American beer from Saranac Beers - Matt Brewery. Wines from Wente Brothers in California, Concannon Vineyards in California, Banfi Vintners in Italy, Miguel Torres in Spain, and Bochot in France. Everything is sold by the case. Per bottle, wine runs from RMB102 to 552. Three day delivery time.

## SHANGHAI BAGEL FACTORY
上海贝谷食品有限公司

(Shanghai Beigu Shipin Youxian Gongsi)
2024 Zhongshan Xi Lu　中山西路2024号
Tel: 6427-7788
Mobile: 1391845969
Fax: 6468-6352
E-mail: bagelman@prodigychina.com
With a minimum order of RMB200 delivery is free within Shanghai west of the Huangpu River. There is a service charge of RMB30 for orders under RMB200. You may chose from twelve flavors of bagels in either sandwich size (RMB6.50 each) or cocktail size (RMB4.50 each). Bagel chips, muffins, donuts, and cream cheese are also available from this outlet. For a full description of their product line, we suggest you contact them and ask for their list of products and prices.

## SHANGHAI HOME SHOPPING SERVICE
上海家园电话购物有限公司

(Shanghai Jiayun Dianhua Gouwu Youxian Gongsi)
Room 301, 804 Huaihai Zhong Lu
淮海中路804号301室
Tel/fax: 6242-3134
Hours: 9:00 am - 8:00 pm, 7 days. Call for catalogueue. This grocery shopping service will deliver items before 7:00 pm if ordered by 3:00 pm.

## THE FRENCH WINE CLUB
法国葡萄酒俱乐部

(Faguo Putaojiu Julebu)
Tel/fax: 6282-1572
Open: 9.00 am - 6:00 pm
French wines delivered to your door! Call for a list of available wines. Current lists offer about 50 selections, ranging from Cote du Rhone at RMB80 per bottle to Champagne Michel Gonet at RMB340 per bottle. Chardonnay is about RMB65 and Riesling is about RMB95. Order between 9:00 am and 6:00 pm for delivery within 24 hours. Orders placed before 3:00 pm will be delivered before 7:00 pm. In an emergency, immediate delivery can be arranged. Cash is due upon delivery. Service personnel are available to help you with choices. If you live outside Shanghai within 300 kilometers, the transportation fee is RMB70 per kilometer (doubled, since a round-trip is involved) or free if your order exceeds RMB5,000. Delivery exceeding 300 kilometers can be arranged. Prepayment is required for the wine and transportation.

# WATER DELIVERY

## DRINS PURE DISTILLED WATER
俊仕纯蒸馏水
(Junshi Chunzheng Liushui)
299 Fule Lu (Pudong)  浦东福乐路299号
Tel: 5854-9988
Fax: 5854-1188

## GRAND CANYON PURE DISTILLED WATER  大峡谷蒸馏水
(Daxiagu Zhengliushui)
49 Haiying Lu  海盈路49号
Tel: 5920-4761

## HIGH PURITY WATER  大雅矿泉水
(Daya Kuangquan Shui)
Tel: 6234-5678 or 6219-1486

## PURE WATER  碧纯饮用水
(Bichunshui)
396 Changping Lu  昌平路396号
Tel: 6256-8400

## SPARKLING PURE DISTILLED WATER
斯柏克林蒸馏水
(Sibaikelin Zhengliushui)
488 Hunan Lu  沪南路488号
Tel: 5891-4195

# BAKED GOODS

## CROISSANTS DE FRANCE
可颂坊面包房
(Kesongfang Mianbaofang)
- 144 Wulumuqi Lu  乌鲁木齐路144号
  Tel: 6431-9718
- 1109 Xiangying Lu  翔鹰路1109号
  Tel: 6511-3172
- 92 Tianlin Lu  田林路92号
  Tel: 6436-6546
- 399 Lingling Lu  零陵路399号
  Tel: 6417-5590 x 573
- 366 Chifeng Lu  赤峰路366号
  Tel: 6553-1674
- 80 Nandan Lu  南丹路80号
  Tel: 6438-1100
- 509 Damuqiao Lu  大木桥路509号
  Tel: 6417-5887
- 785–789 Baotou Lu  包头路785-789号
  Tel: 6524-1980 x 3036
- 818 Linfen Lu  临汾路818号
  Tel: 5688-0450
- 144 Ruijin Er Lu  瑞金二路144号
  Tel: 6433-3851
- Minhangxinan Shangcheng 闵行西南商城
- 244 Dongxin Lu  东新路244号
  Tel: 5290-3741
- 47 Lanxi Lu  兰溪路47号
  Tel: 6297-1743
- 550 Dalian Xi Lu  大连西路550号
  Tel: 6351-1900 x 2258

Wellcome Grocery Store at Shanghai Centre also carries this brand.

## PUCCI  葡吉面包
(Puji Mianbao)
Tel: 5306-1111 x 120
Ground Floor, Isetan Department Store 伊势丹 (Huating Yisidan),
527 Huaihai Zhong Lu  淮海中路527号
3rd Fl, Westgate Mall  梅龙镇广场
(Meilongzhen Guangchang)
1038 Nanjing Xi Lu  南京西路1038号
Tel: 62187477
(There is also a counter at Longbai Apartments clubhouse.)

# ICE CREAM

## HAAGEN-DAZS ICE CREAM
哈根达斯冰淇淋
(Hagendasi Binqiling)
1038 Nanjing Xi Lu　南京西路1038号
Tel: 6218-2248
2077 Yan'an Xi Lu　延安西路2077号
Tel: 6219-2941
A very stylish ice cream store. Buy in bulk downstairs, or go upstairs to their spacious café area and order from the menu.

## SWENSON'S　双圣
(Shuang Sheng)
139 Ruijin Yi Lu　瑞金一路139号
Tel: 5306-5009
Hours: 11:00 am - 3:00 am
The San Francisco ice cream chain has arrived in Shanghai. Along with their famous sundaes, steaks and sandwiches, salads, and other light fare is available. Live music in the evenings.

# CANDY

## CANDIANA　全国土产食品公司
(Quanguo Tuchan Shipin Gongsi)
491 Huaihai Zhong Lu　淮海中路491号
Jelly beans in a vast array of choices! Pay by weight at RMB15.50 for 100 grams.

Imported fruits and vegetables can be found at the adjoining food store. Located a couple of store fronts east of Isetan Department Store.

Luxury chocolates can be found at hotel delis such as the Hilton, Westin, or Sofitel.

# TEA

## TEN FU'S TEA SHOP　天福名茶
(Tianfu Mingcha)
116 Changshu Lu　常熟路116号
918 Huaihai Zhong Lu　淮海中路918号
Office: 6303-5838
Aside from the two addresses above, these high-quality teas are sold in the Super Emporium at the Oriental Pearl Television Tower (东方明珠), #2 Lane 504, Lujiazui Lu, Pudong (陆家嘴路504弄2号，浦东), in the food section at the Taipingyang Pacific Department Store (上海太平洋百货 Tel: 6487-8888 x 801), and at the Hong Kong Underground Shopping Center (人民广场地下商场) in People's Square (人民广场内).

# DEPARTMENT STORES

## CHINESE TOURIST SOUVENIR CORPORATION
中华旅游纪念品总公司
(Zhonghua Lüyou Jinianpin Zonggongsi)
1000 Yan'an Zhong Lu　延安中路1000号
Tel: 6279-0279 x 62224, 6247-2180
Hours: 8:45 am - 6:30 pm
Antique reproductions, hand-crafted items, and merchandise from all over China. Located in the Exhibition Center.

## FRIENDSHIP STORE　友谊商店
(Youyi Shangdian)
40 Beijing Dong Lu, near the Bund
北京东路40号
Tel: 6329-4600
This government-run store carries goods from all over China such as Chinese carpets, arts and crafts, antiques, furniture, dishes, leather goods, Chinese medicines, liquors, small

appliances, cashmere sweaters, and more. They also carry imported merchandise.

## GOLDEN EAGLE ARCADE
金龙丝绸呢绒公司
(Jinlong Sichou Nirong Gongsi)
858-864 Huaihai Zhong Lu
淮海中路858-864号
Huaihai Lu at Maoming Lu    淮海路 茂名路
Tel: 6473-6691
Hours: 10:00 am - 10:00 pm

## HONG KONG UNDERGROUND SHOPPING CENTER AND D MALL
人民广场地下商场
(Renmin Guangchang Dixia Shangcheng)
People's Square    人民广场内
Tel: 6359-6946
Located under People's Square, this newly-developed Japanese style mall offers marble flooring and contemporary fashions. Boutiques and shoe stores, sportswear shop (including Columbia and Puma), Park-N-Shop Express, Kodak Express, and much more! D Mall is adjacent, and features even more stores including a 2-floor Watson's.

## HUALIAN DEPARTMENT STORE
华联商厦
(Hualian Shangsha)
635 Nanjing Dong Lu    南京东路635号
Tel: 6422-4466
This store is well known and popular in Shanghai. It carries everything from cosmetics, clothing, and household goods to large appliances and television sets.

## ISETAN DEPARTMENT STORE    伊势丹
(Huating Yisidan)
527 Huaihai Zhong Lu    淮海中路 527号
Tel: 5306-1111
Opened in 1993, you'll find many casual wear boutiques, a Pucci bakery, international brand cosmetics, a large children's department, a video arcade, and more. A good place to look if you need to replace an important item of clothing, from San-ai, D'Urban, Zero, Studio Ray, and Episode lines.

## JIN JIANG DICKSON SHOPPING CENTER    锦江迪生
(Jinjiang Disheng)
400 Changle Lu    长乐路 400号
Tel: 6472-6888
A posh high-end mall located across from the Garden Hotel and the Old Jin Jiang Hotel. Boutiques include  Polo, Charles Jourdan, Nina Ricci, Guy Laroche, Jack Nicklaus, Kuppenheimer, Jean Estelle, and Borghese among others.

## JUSCO    佳世客购物中心
(Jiashike Gowu Zhongxin)
218 Tianmu Xi Lu    天目西路218号
Tel: 6354-1110
Located just across from the train station at Kerry Everbright City (嘉里不夜城), this is a new mega commercial and residential complex. Jusco Department Store is in this five-story mall of stores such as Watson's, Laura Ashley, Theme, and Esprit. More stores of this caliber will open as the remaining top floors arc completed. A large Japanese-style grocery store is in place as well as McDonalds, a cafe, and a diner.

## THE LANDMARK    上海置地广场
(Shanghai Zhidi Guangchang)
409 Nanjing Dong Lu    南京东路409号
Tel: 6360-8205
Hours: 10:00 am - 10:00 pm
Head east from the Sofitel toward the river past Sincere Dept. Store and Manhattan Plaza. The first floor of the Landmark offers cosmetics, scarves, hair accessories, etc. The second and third floors are dedicated to women's clothing and men's clothing is on the fourth. Other floors carry appliances, children's clothing, toys, shoes and bags.

## MAISON MODE DEPARTMENT STORE
美美百货商店

(Meimei Baihuo)

1312 Huaihai Zhong Lu (at Changshu Lu)
淮海中路1312号

Tel: 6431-0100

Top-end clothing with a high price tag such as Yves St. Laurent, Ferregamo, Chanel, Christian Dior, Prada, BOSS, and Escada. International brand cosmetics and western furniture (in the basement level) are also fixtures of the store.

## MANHATTAN PLAZA    曼哈顿广场

(Mahhadun Guangchang)

463 - 477 Nanjing Dong Lu, near the Sofitel Hotel   南京东路463-477号 近海仑宾馆

Tel: 6322-2239

Closes at 10:00 pm

Features casual international boutiques with some of the most up-market shops for funky and casual wear. Hong Kong designer fashions, cosmetics, children's clothing and jewelry along with a children's play area, coffee shop, and Chinese restaurants.

## MEILIHUA DEPARTMENT STORE
美丽华商厦

(Meilihua Shangsha)

180 Xizang Zhong Lu   西藏中路180号

Tel: 6322-1660

## MOSTA COMMERCIAL BUILDING
摩士达商厦

(Moshida Shangsha)

889 Nanjing Xi Lu   南京西路889号

Tel: 6217-5076, 6256-6992

Hours: 10:00 am - 10:00 pm

Department store containing a wide variety of daily use articles and clothing.

## NEW WORLD WOMEN'S AND CHILDREN'S DEPARTMENT STORE
新世界妇女儿童用品商店

(Xin Shijie Funu Ertong Yongpin Shangdian)

558 Nanjing Dong Lu   南京东路558号

Tel: 6322-6226

## NEW WORLD DEPARTMENT STORE
新世界商厦

(Xinshijie Shangsha)

2 Nanjing Xi Lu   南京西路2号

Tel: 6358-8888

Just about anything is available in this new department store with an extensive toy department. Carries a wide variety of household items and clothing for the whole family.

## PARKSON SHOPPING CENTER
百盛购物中心

(Baishen Gouwu Zhongxin)

918 Huaihai Zhong Lu   淮海中路918号

Tel: 6415-8818

Hours: 10:00 am - 10:00 pm

## PRINTEMPS DEPARTMENT STORE
上海巴黎春天百货

(Shanghai Bali Chuntian Baihuo)

939 Huaihai Zhong Lu at Shaanxi Nan Lu
淮海中路939号

Tel: 6431-0118

Popular in France, the one in Shanghai is a joint-venture between Hong Kong Top Form International and Shanghai Yimin and is housed in a newly constructed Art Nouveau building. Six floors offer international boutiques.

## SHANGHAI ARTS AND CRAFTS TRADING CO.   上海工艺品商店

(Shanghai Gongyipin Shangdian)

1000 Yan'an Zhong Lu (in the Exhibition Center)   上海展览中心 延安中路1000号

Tel: 6279-0279 x 2111, 6247-2180

This store displays hand-crafted articles from all over China as well as carpets, antique reproductions, medicine, and more.

## SHANGHAI HONGQIAO FRIENDSHIP SHOPPING CENTER
上海虹桥友谊商城

(Hongqiao Youyi Shangcheng)
6 Zunyi Nan Lu    遵义南路6号
Tel: 6270-0000
Designed as an indoor mall, this store offers a grocery store on the first level, housewares, a bakery, designer makeup, toiletries, health care products, CDs, TVs, large and small household appliances, clothing, shoes, jewelry, luggage, sports equipment, toys, bedding, oriental carpets, trinkets, Chinese handicrafts, jewelry, and more.

## SHANGHAI NO. 9 DEPARTMENT STORE
上海第九百货商店

(Shanghai Dijiu Baihuo Shangdian)
50 Wanhangdu Lu    万航渡路50号
Tel: 6253-6350

## SHANGHAI NUMBER ONE DEPART-MENT STORE   上海第一百货商店

(Diyi Baihuo)
830 Nanjing Dong Lu    南京东路830号
Tel: 6322-3344
This store is an older state-owned venture, but offers a wide selection of merchandise. Pricing is aimed at the local market, allowing for some good bargains. Be forewarned that it is always crowded.

## SHANGHAI ORIENT SHOPPING CENTER
上海东方商厦

(Dongfang Shangsha)
8 Caoxi Bei Lu    漕溪北路8号
Tel: 6487-0000
A good place to look when furnishing a home. Large and small appliances, furniture, TV's, stereo systems, drapes, carpeting, linens, and more. The basement level is a large grocery store that carries many housewares. In the sub-basement there is access to the subway. The second and third floors are dedicated to clothing with the majority of large appliances

and televisions on the fourth floor and small appliances on the first floor. The fifth floor has Chinese and Western restaurants. If you'd prefer Kentucky Fried Chicken, just exit the shopping center front door and turn left.

## SHANGHAI PACIFIC DEPARTMENT STORE   上海太平洋百货

(Taipingyang Baihuo)
932 Hengshan Lu    衡山路932号
Tel: 6487-8888
An excellent range of clothing for men, women, and children including a large selection of shoes, purses, accessories, cosmetics and perfumes.
Note: You can travel from the Orient to the Pacific without even stepping outside. A subway tunnel at the entrance of either store will take you directly to the other. Along the way you can shop in the stores (mainly grocery) located in the tunnel itself.

## SHANGHAI SUNRISE DEPARTMENT STORE   中兴百货

(Zhongxing Baihuo)
718 Caoxi Bei Lu    漕溪北路718号
Tel: 6438-7420
This store features clothing and household goods, including a large drapery and uphol-stery department and grocery.

## SINCERE DEPARTMENT STORE
西施公司

(Xisi Gongsi)
479 Nanjing Dong Lu    南京东路479号
Tel: 6322-1953
Closes at 10:00 pm
Six stories, featuring a large variety of trendy, up-market goods. Adjacent to the Sofitel Hotel on the east side.

## SOUTH DEPARTMENT STORE
八百伴南方商城

(Babaiban Nanfang Shangcheng)
7388 Humin Lu    沪闵路7388号
Tel: 6412-0800

## TIANSHAN SHOPPING CENTER
天山商厦
(Tianshan Shangsha)
789 Tianshan Lu　天山路789号
Tel: 6229-5010
Hours: 9:30 am - 9:30 pm

## TIME INTERNATIONAL　时代广场
(Shidai Guangchang)
550 Huaihai Zhong Lu, across from Isetan
淮海中路550号
Tel: 6327-5566
This store is managed by Lane Crawford and provides leading international men's boutiques (such as Hugo Boss). If hungry, try the large Western restaurant or dance the night away later at THE TIME. The large clock with swinging pendulum on the storefront makes for easy locating.

## TIMES SQUARE　上海时代广场
(Shanghai Shidai Guangchang)
500 Zhangyang Lu, Pudong 200122
浦东张杨路500号
Tel: 5836-8888
Fax: 5836-7777
This huge department store and office complex is located in the heart of Lujiazui in Pudong. The store has several levels of merchandise and food outlets and a car park is provided under the building.

## VOGUE DEPARTMENT STORE
万象帝王百货
(Wanxiang Diwang Baihuo)
258 Nanjing Xi Lu　南京西路258号
Tel: 6358 -7978

## YAOHAN DEPARTMENT STORE
上海第一八佰伴新世纪商厦
(Babaiban)
501 Zhangyang Lu, Lujiazui, Pudong
上海浦东新区张扬路501号
Intersection of Pudong Lu and Zhangyang Lu

(close to the new tunnel from West Shanghai)
Tel: 5830-1111
Hours: 9:00 am - 9:00 pm, 7 days.
Also called "Next Age", this store goes by the Chinese name of "Ba Bai Ban". Whatever name you use, this store is spectacularly large and impressive. This huge shopping complex opened in December, 1995 and was the first significant store to open in Pudong. It is a joint-venture between Japanese Yaohan and the Shanghai Number One Department Store. Next Age is designed to provide one-stop shopping, with goods from Hong Kong, Japan, the US, South Korea, China and elsewhere. It aims to be "The Great Mall of China", with an extraordinary range of selections and facilities. Taxis are available from the underground parking area. There are several appealing restaurants and cafes scattered throughout the store. The first floor is a car showroom and also offers cosmetics, paintings, exercise equipment, and various other goods, while the second and third floors offer women's clothing. The fourth floor is dedicated to men's fashions and sporting goods, and a children's department and Chinese crafts are on the fifth floor. All manner of household items can be found on the sixth and seventh floors. The eighth and ninth floors offer restaurants and a supermarket. The tenth floor is relegated to entertainment and games of chance. There's a merry-go-round for the kids, a video game arcade, and bowling. If you're moving to Shanghai or are looking to update your home here you can find everything that you need in this one place. However, prices are rather high.

## YU YUAN DEPARTMENT STORE
豫园商厦
(Yuyuan Shangsha)
84 Yuyuan Lu　豫园路84号
Tel: 6328-9850

## WESTGATE MALL　梅龙镇广场

(Meilongzhen Guangchang)
1038 Nanjing Xi Lu　南京西路1038号
Tel: 6218-7878
This large mall contains an Isetan Department Store and many other stores of every description. You'll find Burberrys, Gore Weather Zone, Ermenegildo Zegna, Watson's and Park 'n Shop, to name a few. You won't go hungry while you're shopping as there is a Haagen-Dazs store, Cafe de Tulip, Kentucky Fried Chicken, The Gap Cafe, a Chinese restaurant, and a food court. For entertainment, there's a video game center, a night club, and a cinema.

## WINGS DEPARTMENT STORE
鸿翔百货

(Hongxiang Baihuo)
869 Nanjing Xi Lu　南京西路869号
Tel: 6258-2688
Closes at 10:00 pm
This store offers clothing of international origin such as Burberry, Valentino, Viva, Dunhill, Bally and Jessica. International credit cards are accepted. Good selection of quality, stylish clothing.

## XINXIN DEPARTMENT STORE
新新商厦

(Xinxin Shangsha)
567 Gonghexin Lu　共和新路567号
Tel: 5697-4600

# MEGA-MARTS

## INTERNATIONAL MEGA MART (IMM)
南方商城

(Nanfang Shangcheng)
7388 Humin Lu near the corner of Caoxi Lu and Humin Lu, about one block from Jinjiang Amusement Park 上海市闵行区沪闵路7388号
Tel: 6412-0800
Similar to Western-style bulk membership supermarkets. Purchase of a RMB20 membership card, which admits three persons and is valid for two years, is required for admittance. (Card applications can be made any day at the service center.) A range of imported and Chinese goods are available in single-item or bulk quantities, including produce, meats and dairy items. Upper floors offer furniture, bathroom and lighting fixtures, and interior building accessories. Also plentiful are men's, women's and children's fashions at low prices, hence the department's expat moniker of "Bargain Basement". This place is worth the trip to the southwestern fringe of the city, especially for purposes of stocking up.

## LOTUS SUPERCENTER　莲花超市

(Lianhua Chaoshi)
1126 - 1128 Yanggao Nan Lu, Pudong 200127　浦东 扬高南路1126-1128号
Tel: 6312-0922
This is another place for one-stop shopping and reasonable prices. The first floor of this vast two-story building houses a grocery store, with household goods and large and small appliances. The second floor offers bicycles, an optical shop, clothing, sporting goods, shoes, jewelry, clocks, office supplies, a flower shop, cosmetics, handbags, bedding, toys, hardware and plumbing supplies, cleaning products, toiletries, televisions, audio equipment, computers, printers, CDs and more.

## METRO　麦德龙

(Maidelong)
1425 Zhenbei Lu, Putuo District
普陀区 真北路1425 号
Tel: 6265-8888
Fax: 6265-4521
Hours: 3:00 am - 10:00 pm
Membership card is required. To qualify for

membership, one must provide a passport and residency card or business card. Check all bags at the front desk, including small purses, upon entering. Children under 12 are not allowed in the store, and no delivery is provided. Parking is available for 600 cars.

# MAIL ORDER

## THE CATALOG STORE

P.O. Box 700
Greenhurst, New York  14742-0700
Tel:  519-442-1646  (24 hours)
Fax: 519-442-6897

Shop at Bloomingdale's and Neiman Marcus right here in Shanghai. This company features some of the finest and most well known catalogues from the US. The catalogues listed below are all available. You may pay for the catalogues in US funds by check, money order, VISA, Mastercard, or American Express. You may fax or phone your order for catalogs or write your name, address, and telephone number along with your selection of catalogues and mail to the address above. Allow 8-10 weeks for delivery.

### Barnes and Noble

America's largest bookseller. Each issue of their bargain book catalog features a collection of exclusive editions, plus publishers' closeouts, overstocks, remainders, and other hard-to-find titles, all offered at discounts of up to 80%. US$5.

### Barrie Pace

A collection of clothing for professional women from such designers as Austin Reed, Jones New York, Burberry's of London, and Freedberg of Boston. 68 pages, full color. US$5.

### Bloomingdale's By Mail

Bloomingdale's By Mail brings you American fashion and innovative home design. US$6.00.

### Brooks Brothers

Founded in 1818, Brooks Brothers is known for tailored classic clothing with an American attitude. Offers a selection of business clothing, Fridaywear, sportswear, outerwear, formal-wear, and furnishings for both men and women. US$5.

### Clifford and Wills

Clifford and Wills offers a collection of versatile clothing sized to fit everyone including petites. US$5.

### The Disney Catalog

Apparel, collectibles, art, accessories and more for both young and old, decked out with Mickey Mouse, Donald Duck, The Lion King, and Winnie the Pooh. US$5.

### Henry F. DuPont Winterthur Collection

An eclectic collection of unique gifts from the world's premier American decorative arts museum. Select from home accessories, jewelry, garden statuary and many other fine gifts, many of which are adaptations or reproductions from the Winterthur collection. US$6.

### Horchow Fine Linen Collection

Fine linens for bed and bath, decorative accessories, toiletries, special gifts and more. Catalog price of US$10 is applicable toward first purchase.

### Land's End

Known for traditionally styled casual clothing for men, women, and children as well as fashion accessories, luggage, bed linens, bath products, and more. Everything is unconditionally guaranteed. Free catalog.

## The Lew Magram Catalog
This catalog offers a collection of women's apparel for office and casual wear as well as elegant evening wear... at value prices. This catalog features the latest suits, dresses, outerwear, and sportswear. US$6.

## Lilliput Motor Company
Tin toys for the collector and fancier of mechanical wind-up toys. Comprehensive collection of cars, ships, carousels, figures, animals and other whimsies. US$6.

## The Metropolitan Museum of Art
Select from a collection of holiday cards and ornaments, unique jewelry and scarves, sculpture, distinctive tabletop items, posters, prints, books and more. US$5.

## National Wildlife Federation
America's largest conservation organization offers a 52-page catalog of unique cards, stationery, nature-themed apparel, gifts, decorative items, outdoor accessories, fashion accessories, educational and fun children's items. Purchases support the educational and conservation activities of the Federation. US$6.

## Neiman Marcus
From designer fashions and fine jewelry to imaginative gifts and home furnishings. Receive a selection of catalogues including the famous Neiman Marcus Christmas book. US$15, applicable toward first purchase.

## 1-800-Pro-Team
Authentic American sportswear–caps, jackets, jerseys, T-shirts, sweatshirts, and more that the superstars of baseball, football, basketball, and hockey work and play

in. US$6.

## Signals
Gifts that inform, enlighten, and entertain such as hard to find videos, distinctive clothing and jewelry, collectibles, toys, great books and music, and more. US$6.

## The Smithsonian Institute Catalog
Reflecting the diversity of its collections, the Smithsonian Catalog offers fine gifts, decorative home accessories, jewelry, scarves, ties, books, educational toys, and more. US$6.

## Victoria's Secret
Here is another way to get the Victoria's Secret Catalog. Inside you'll find their renowned collection of lingerie and the latest fashions. US$5.

## Wireless
Wireless is packed with unique and upbeat gifts of all kinds including high spirited sweatshirts and T-shirts, classic American memorabilia, vintage and contemporary radio shows, great music, books, games, jewelry, and plenty of "just plain fun stuff"! US$5, refundable on first purchase.

## VICTORIA'S SECRET
You may request a mail order catalog by writing to:
Victoria's Secret Catalog
North American Office
3425 Stelzer Road
Columbus, OH 43299
If you prefer to fax or phone:
Tel: 614-337-5122
Fax: 614-337-5555
Air mail or orders are an additional US$30 to the shipping charge listed in the catalog. You may order by phone, fax, or mail. Renowned collection of luxury lingerie and clothing.

# UPMARKET BOUTIQUES

## BALLY
- Jinjiang Tower, 2nd Fl (Xin Jinjiang)
  新锦江2楼
- 161 Changle Road  长乐路161号
- Wings Department Store (Hongxiang Baihuo Shangdian)  鸿翔百货
- 869 Nanjing Xi Lu, 1st Fl.
  南京西路869号1楼
- Maison Mode Department Store (Meimei Baihuo)  美美百货商店
- 1312 Huaihai Zhong Lu  淮海中路1312号

## BURBERRY
Shanghai Hilton (Jing'an Xierdun)
静安希尔顿
250 Huashan Lu  华山路 250号
Burberry can also be found in certain department stores, including Wings.

## CALVIN KLEIN
Shanghai Orient Shopping Center
上海东方商厦
(Dongfang Shangxia)
8 Caoxi Bei Lu  漕溪北路8号
Tel: 6487-0000
A small collection for men can be found in the men's department.

## CARTIER  卡地亚
(Kadiya)
1376 Nanjing Xi Lu  南京西路1376号
Tel: 6279-8038
Hours: 10:00 am - 9:00 pm
Located on the east street side of the Shanghai Centre complex. Watches and leather goods, but no jewelry per se.

## CERRUTI
1376 Nanjing Xi Lu  南京西路1376号
This men's clothing store is next to Ferregamo in the Nanjing Road facade of Shanghai Centre.

## CHRIS AND CHRIS  格诗
- 1160 - 1164 Huaihai Zhong Lu
  淮海中路1160-1164号
  Tel: 6431-9587, 6431-4569
  Hours: 10:00 am - 10:00 pm
- 3rd Fl, Sunrise Shopping Center
  中兴百货3楼

The new store on Huaihai Lu near Consulate Row offers stunning Euro-style furniture, a huge floral center and cafe. Along with clothing, you'll also find decorative items for the household.

## CHRISTIAN DIOR (SHANGHAI) PERFUME AND COSMETICS
克丽斯汀迪奥(上海)香水化妆品有限公司
(Kelisiting Diao Shanghai Xiangshui Huazhuangpin Youxian Gongsi)
91 Xingguo Lu  兴国路91号
Tel:  6474-5325
Fax: 6437-6680
Hours: 9:00 am - 5:30 pm
All the large department stores and Watson's carry Christian Dior cosmetics.

## CREACHINE  礼物商店
(Liwu Shangdian)
- Gift Shop, Portman Ritz-Carlton, Shanghai Centre, 2nd Fl  上海商城
  1376 Nanjing Xi Lu
  南京西路1376 号
  Tel: 6279-8888, x gift shop
- Discoveries, Westin Tai Ping Yang, 2nd Fl  太平洋大酒店
  5 Zunyi Nan Lu  200335  遵义南路5 号
  Tel: 6275-8888, x Discoveries
- Company store, Shanghai Sunrise Department Store, 3rd Fl  中兴百货
  718 Caoxi Bei Lu  漕溪北路718 号
  Tel: 6438-7420 x 3311

This company has talented craftspeople

fashioning natural Chinese materials into useful items for home and personal use. Items include scarves made of wild silk from Manchuria, silk and brocade cushions, silk pouches, beaded clothing, and silk ties.

## ERMENEGILDO ZEGNA  杰尼亚
(Jieniya)
- Jinjiang Tower, 2nd Fl  新锦江2楼
  161 Changle Road  长乐路161号
- Hilton Hotel  静安希尔顿
  250 Huashan Lu  静安希尔顿华山路250号

## FENDI
Shanghai Hilton  静安希尔顿
250 Huashan Lu  华山路250号
Located in the lobby.

## FERREGAMO  费力加姆
(Feili Jiamu)
1376 Nanjing Xi Lu  南京西路1376号
Tel: 6279-8838
This store for men's and women's clothing can be found in the Nanjing Road facade of the Shanghai Centre east of the entrance. Women's shoe sizes stop at size 38, which is equivalent to an American size 8.

## GIANNI VERSACE  范思哲
(Fansizhe)
Jinjiang Dickson Shopping Center  锦江迪生
400 Changle Lu  长乐路400号
Tel: 6472-6888

## GIVENCHY  纪梵喜
(Jifanxi)
Jinjiang Tower, 2nd Fl  新锦江2楼
161 Changle Lu  长乐路161号
Tel: 6415-1188 x 80212
Hours: 10:00 am - 10:00 pm

## GUESS
Shanghai Orient Shopping Center
上海东方商厦
(Dongfang Shangsha)

8 Caoxi Bei Lu  漕溪北路8号
Tel: 6487-0000
One can find a small selection of Guess for men and women in the men's department.

## ISETAN DEPARTMENT STORE  伊势丹
(Yi Shi Dan)
527 Huaihai Zhong Lu
淮海中路527号
Tel: 5306-1111

## JEANSWEST  真维斯
(Zhenweisi)
114 Nanjing Dong Lu  南京东路114号
Tel: 6321-3730
Hours: 9:00 am - 10:00 pm

## LOUIS VUITTON  路易威登
(Luyi Weideng)
1376 Nanjing Xi Lu  南京西路1376号
Tel: 6279-8093
Hours: 10:00 am - 8:00 pm
On Nanjing Lu, to the right of the entrance to Shanghai Centre.

## NAUTICA/CHRISTINA
Manhattan Plaza  曼克顿广场
463 - 477 Nanjing Dong Lu
南京东路463-477号
920 Nanjing Xi Lu  南京西路 920号
939 Huaihai Zhong Lu  淮海中路 939号

## PASSAPORTO  万象
(Wanxiang)
134 Nanjing Dong Lu  南京东路134号
Tel: 6321-3145
Hours: 10:00 am - 10:00 pm
Young, trendy fashions.

## STEFANO RICCI
Portman Ritz-Carlton  上海商城
1376 Nanjing Xi Lu  南京西路 1376号
This store is in the lobby near the reception desk.

**Hats** can be found at Mon Chapeau, 366 Changle Lu (长乐路366号)

**Larger sizes** for men can be found at Men's 12 at 256 Shimen Yi Lu (石门一路256号) and Benetton sells clothing in their original Western sizes. Marlboro Classics is a good bet. They can be found at Wings (鸿翔百货), 869 Nanjing Xi Lu (南京西路869号) and at the Shops at the Huating Hotel and Towers (华亭宾馆). One can also find real Levis at Wings (鸿翔百货). Women can find larger sizes at 456 Nanjing Xi Lu (南京西路456号) between 10:00 am and 8:00 pm. Another shop at 1527 Nanjing Xi Lu (南京西路1527号) is also a good bet.

## HUATING CLOTHING MARKET (华亭路服装市场) is an alley market for bargain clothing off Changle Lu (长乐路), not far from the Hilton Hotel. Numerous individual booths offering everything from sportswear to luxurious silks, and some famous label export items as well. Prices are marked, but bargaining is expected.

Many shoe stores in Shanghai don't carry women's shoes in sizes larger than 38 (American size 8). However, you can usually find larger size shoes at:

## 4/F EVERBRIGHT CITY SHOPPING CENTER  不夜城商厦4楼

(Buyecheng Shangsha)

188-198 Tianmu Xi Lu  天目西路188-198号

Tel: 6354-7367

This is a very large shoe store with a vast selection.

## SHANGHAI FAMOUS BRAND SHOE STORE  上海名款鞋城有限公司

(Shanghai Mingkuan Xiecheng Youxian Gongsi)

1220 Nanjing Xi Lu  南京西路1220号

Tel: 6253-0212

Western-style quality costume **jewelry** can be found at Seed Company and Ogle on the ground floor of Isetan Department Store, 527 Huaihai Zhong Lu (淮海中路527号) and at World of Silver, on Changshu Lu (常熟路), just north of Changle Lu (长乐路).

# WATCHES

## HENG DA LI CLOCK AND WATCH SHOP
亨达利钟表商店
(Hengdali Zhongbiao Shangdian)
262 Nanjing Dong Lu　南京东路262号
Tel: 6329-1514

## HENG DE LI CLOCK AND WATCH SHOP
亨得利钟表商店
(Hengdeli Zhongbiao Shangdian)
417 Jinling Dong Lu　金陵东路417号
Tel: 6328-0691
456 Nanjing Dong Lu　南京东路456号
Tel: 6352-2498

## SHANGHAI CLOCK AND WATCH SHOP
上海钟表商店
(Shanghai Zhongbiao Shangdian)
478-492 Huaihai Zhong Lu
淮海中路478-492号

Tel: 6327-8921, 6327-3268
This store carries many brands including Rolex and Movado and also has straps and watch repair.

## SWATCH SHOP　斯沃奇专卖店
(Siaoqi Zhuanmaidian)
217 Changle Lu　长乐路217号
Tel: 6473-2303
Hours: 10:00 am - 9:00 pm
Swatch watches can also be found on the first floor of the Hongqiao Friendship Shopping Center, the first floor of the Friendship Store on Beijing Lu, the fourth floor of Isetan, the second floor of Next Age, the second floor of the Landmark, the second floor of the Pacific Department Store, the first floor of Printemps, and the first floor of the Emperor Department Store.

# ESPECIALLY FOR CHILDREN

## C & B　大集成
(Da Jicheng)
441 Nanjing Xi Lu　南京西路441 号
Tel: 6359-0742
Hours: 9:30 am - 10:00 pm
Children's clothing and toys

## ISETAN DEPARTMENT STORE　伊势丹
527 Huaihai Zhong Lu　淮海中路527号
Their children's department is well stocked with quality items.

## LOONEY TUNES
Printemps Department Store
上海巴黎春天百货
Huaihai Lu at Shaanxi Lu　淮海路近陕西路
Cartoon-theme novelty items such as stuffed animals, mugs, and paper items.

## MICKEY'S CORNER
马兰花儿童服装商店
(Mulahua)
819 Huaihai Zhong Lu　淮海中路819号
Tel: 6431-3432

## YI FENG MODEL STORE
翼风模型商店
Yifeng Moxing Shangdian
437 Nanjing Xi Lu　南京西路437号
Tel: 6327-6897
Plane, car, and boat models.

# TAILORS

If the desired item can't be found in the shops listed above, another option is to have special items custom-made by one of Shanghai's many tailors.

## ASCOT CHANG  诗格服装专卖店

(Shige Fuzhuang Zhuanmaidian)
Jinjiang Dickson Shopping Center  迪生商厦
400 Changle Lu, Room 211
长乐路 400号 211室
Tel: 6472-6888
Manager: Mr. Ha (speaks English)
Specializes in men's suits, overcoats, and pants. Measurements are faxed to shops in the Prince's Building or the Peninsula Hotel in Hong Kong. Items take about two weeks. If fittings are needed, it will take about one month. Prices and quality are high.

## BAROMAN WESTERN STYLE CLOTHING CO.  培罗蒙西服商店

(Peiluomeng Xifu Shangdian)
- Shop 1: 580 Nanjing Dong Lu
  南京东路580号
  Tel: 6322-6611
  Hours: 10:00 am - 10:00 pm
- Shop 2: 403 Jinling Dong Lu
  金陵东路403号
  Tel: 6326-8001
  Hours: 9:00 am - 8:00 pm

## BLUE G  蓝旗

(Lanqi)
4th Fl, 177 Pu'an Lu  普安路177号4楼
Tel: 6384-6000, 6468-8292
Fax: 6384-6333
If you're too busy to shop for shirts or can't find the right style or size, call 6474-3779. Within three hours a representative can provide ready-made shirts for instant delivery, or tailor-made shirts that will be ready within 10 days.

## LEO MEN'S WEAR  里奥

(Liao)
- Shop 1: 3rd Fl, 527 Huaihai Zhong Lu
  淮海中路 527号 3楼
  Tel: 5306-1111 x 325
  Hours: 10:00 am - 9:00 pm
- Shop 2: 4th Fl, 869 Nanjing Xi Lu
  南京西路 869号4楼
  Tel: 6258-2688 x 245
  Hours: 10:30 am - 10:00 pm

## QIFA FOREIGN DRESS COMPANY

启发西服公司
(Qifa Xifu Gongsi)
835 - 841 Huaihai Zhong Lu
淮海中路835-841号
Tel: 6437-5123
Hours: 9:00 am - 10:00 pm

## SAKURAI YOFUKU  樱井

(Yingjing)
2nd Fl, Friendship Shopping Center
友谊商城2楼
6 Zunyi Lu  遵义路 6号
Tel: 6270-0000 x 2031
Hours: 10:00 am - 10:00 pm
Men's clothing only. Suits start at RMB900.

## SANG JING QUAN  桑景全

128 Wulumuqi Nan Lu
乌鲁木齐南路128号
Tel/fax: 6437-8824
Mr. Sang speaks English and is accustomed to working with foreigners. He will come to your home if necessary.

## WING'S  鸿翔服装

(Hongyang Fuzhuang)
2nd Fl, Friendship Shopping Center

友谊商城2楼
6 Zunyi Lu　遵义路6号
Tel: 6270-0000 x 2031
Hours: 1:00 pm - 8:00 pm
Women's clothing only. There can be a one month wait for fittings unless an additional 100% surcharge is paid for express service. Suits will run about RMB600, blouses about RMB200, and dresses about RMB400.

## TAILOR LANE

This is the least expensive place in Shanghai to have something made, but there are no fitting rooms and little English is spoken. However, it's not too difficult to have clothing copied from an original. The tailors work at tables in the lane from 3:30 pm until dark. Located on Wuyuan Lu (五原路) (near Maison Mode) between houses #52 and #72.

One can have a **qipao** (Chinese-style dress) custom made at Long Feng, 942 Nanjing Xi Lu (南京西路942号). Choose from an extensive selection of silk, brocade, velvet or lame, or bring your own fabric. On the initial visit, fabric is selected, design details specified and measurements taken. After two weeks and one or two fittings, your qipao will be ready.

## FABRICS

| Cashmere | Shanyang rong | 山羊绒 |
|---|---|---|
| Cotton | Mian | 棉 |
| Silk | Si | 丝 |
| Wool | Yangmao | 羊毛 |

A large selection of silk can be found at the silk store on the corner of Sichuan Lu (四川路) and Jinling Lu (金陵路).

## GOLDEN DRAGON SILK AND WOOL COMPANY　上海金龙丝绸呢绒公司
(Shanghai Jinlong Sichou Nirong Gongsi)
816 Huaihai Zhong Lu　淮海中路816号
Tel: 6473-6691, 6473-0290

Hours: 10:00 am - 10:00 pm
Many types of fabrics can be found here.

## JINLING SILK COMPANY
老介福金陵商厦
(Laojiefu Jinling Shangsha)
363 Jinling Dong Lu　金陵东路363号
Tel: 6320-1449
Hours: 9:00 am - 8:00 pm
This store offers a wide variety of silk.

## JINGUANG SILK AND WOOL STORE
金光丝绸呢绒商店
(Jinguang Chouduan Nirong Shangdian)
373 Nanjing Dong Lu　南京东路373号
Tel: 6351-4240
Hours: 9:00 am - 10:00 pm
Silk, cotton, and wool.

## LAOJIEFU STORE　老介福商厦
(Laojiefu Shangsha)
257 Nanjing Dong Lu　南京东路257号
Tel: 6321-8481
Hours: 9:00 am - 10:00 pm
Silk, cotton, and wool.

## LUWAN AIJIAN TEXTILE STORE
卢湾爱建纺织品百货经营部
(Shanghai Aijian Fangzhipin Baihuo Jingyingbu)
98 Maoming Nan Lu　茂名南路98号
Tel: 6437-9206
Hours: 9:30 am - 5:30 pm
Cotton.

## LUWAN FABRIC STORE
卢湾工商联纺织品服装经营部
(Luwan Gongshanglian Fangzhipin Fuzhuang Jingyingbu)
132 Maoming Nan Lu　茂名南路132号
Tel: 6471-7023
Hours: 8:30 am - 5:30 pm
This store carries a variety of fabrics.

**SHANGHAI SILK COMMERCIAL COMPANY** 上海真丝商厦有限公司
(Shanghai Zhensi Shangsha Youxian Gongsi)
139 Tianping Lu, Xujiahui
天平路139号近徐家汇
Tel: 6282-5021 6282-5013
Fax: 6282-5017
Hours: 9:00 am - 6:00 pm
Three floors of silk.

**SICHOU ZHUAN MAI SILK**
上海徐汇纺织品公司
(Shanghai Xuhui Fangzhipin Gongsi)
1226 Huaihai Zhong Lu  淮海中路1226号
Tel: 6437-3370
Fax: 6282-5017
Hours: 9:00 am - 6:00 pm
Silk.

# COSTUMES

**BEIJING OPERA STORE**
上海戏剧服装用品厂商场部
(Shanghai Xiju Fuzhuang Yongpinchang Shangchangbu)
181 Hennan Zhong Lu  河南中路181号

Tel: 6323-8344
Corner of Nanjing Lu and Henan Lu
This store, near the Bund, carries operatic costumes and accessories.

# FURNITURE

**BAKER FURNISHINGS**
2nd Fl, Consulate Square  领馆广场2楼
4 Hengshan Lu  衡山路4号
Tel: 6473-3686
Hours: 10:00 am - 7:00 pm daily
This store features Baker brand furniture, known for quality and elegance.

**BO CONCEPT**  丹麦家俱
(Danmai Jiaju)
4th Fl, Hongqiao Friendship Shopping Center
虹桥友谊商城4楼
6 Zunyi Nan Lu, Hongqiao
遵义南路6号 (虹桥开发区)
Tel: 6270-0000 x 4091/4092

**CHRIS AND CHRIS**  格诗
(Ge Shi)
1160-1164 Huaihai Zhong Lu
淮海中路1160-1164号
Tel: 6431-9587, 6431-4569
Hours: 10:00 am - 10:00 pm
If you're looking for very stylish, high-end furnishings, you definitely need to check out this store. The pieces are very distinctive, albeit expensive. This store offers tasteful accessories and a wide selection of fresh and dried flowers as well. A visit here makes one wants to redecorate.

**FURNITURE WAREHOUSE**
十六铺家俱商厦
(Shiliupu Jiaju Shangsha)
2nd Fl, 111 Zhongshan Dong Er Lu
中山东二路111号 客运站2楼
Tel: 6374-6467
This warehouse on Shilupu Dock near the river has a  sampling of many different kinds of furniture. A little bargaining is sometimes acceptable.

**GALLERIA LAMEX**  美时家具
(Meishi Jiaju)
27-33 Shuicheng Nan Lu
水城南路27-33号
New Gubei Area/Changning
古北新区/长宁区
Tel: 6219-7576

Stylish European-designed classic furniture and lighting, fabric and accessories. The furniture at Lamex Galleria is imported from Italy, Spain, France, Australia and many other Western countries.

## GALLERY M　家乐丽家俱

(Jialeli Jiaju)
Shanghai Gallery Furniture
Decoration Co. Ltd.
上海家乐丽家俱装璜有限公司
37 Chengjiaqiao Lu, Hongqiao
程家桥路37号
Tel: 6406-5260, 6406-5246, 6406-5249

## IKEA　宜家家俱

(Yijia Jiaju)
Shanghai Swede Furnishing Co., Ltd.
中海申瑞家俱有限公司
Harvest Building　华富大厦
585 Long Hua Xi Lu　龙华西路585号
Tel: 6487-7030
Fax: 6469-5978
Aside from affordable, modern furniture, you'll find this store to be a treasure trove of items you can use in setting up house here.

## INTERIORS　北欧风情

Block F, Victoria Towers　维多利亚大厦F座
126 Ronghua Dong Lu, Gubei
荣华东路126号(古北新区)
Tel: 6278-0886, 6278-0887
Hours: 9:30 am - 10:00 pm
Modern European furniture and accessories.

## MASTER FURNITURE

万事德实业有限公司
(Wanshide Shiye Youxian Gongsi)
1150 Jinshajiang Lu　金沙江路1150号
Tel: 6406-6671 Ask for Thomas Mao
Run by brothers who have spent time in the West and speak English, this store will custom design upholstered furniture and draperies.

## MINGYI CLASSIC FURNITURE MANU-FACTURING CO. LTD.

明艺红木家具有限公司
(Mingyi Hongmu Jiaju Youxian Gongsi)
555 Zhumei Lu　朱梅路555号
Tel: 6476-1582
Fax: 6476-7116
Mahogany and rosewood furniture is recognized for its unique style, combining old Chinese traditional elegance with the flow of contemporary design. Custom-made furniture or carved works of art can be designed according to spec.

## MONTEREY FURNITURE　蒙特利家俬

(Mengteli Jiasi)
17 Shuicheng Nan Lu, Gubei
水城南路17号古北新区
Tel: 6270-2306, 6270-2307
Fax: 6270-2354
Furniture and lamps. Much is available through catalog-order within a few days.

## SLUMBERLAND SOFT FURNITURE

上海斯林百来有限公司
(Shanghai Silingbailai Youxian Gongsi)
227 Luchen Lu　绿春路227号
Minhang District　200240
Tel: 6430-9977, 6430-6800
Fax: 6430-3355
This Sino/British joint venture manufactures mattresses, sofas, and easy chairs. One can custom order sizes and fabrics. The address above is their factory site where one can go to place orders.

## THOMASVILLE

1131 Huaihai Zhong Lu　淮海中路1131号
Tel: 6431-7783
Hours: 10:00 am - 9:30 pm
Thomasville is an American furniture company. The store carries furnishings for every room.

## UNIVERSAL 环美家具

(Huanmei Jiaju)
1547 Huashan Lu 华山路1547号
Tel/fax: 6283-0117
Western-style furniture that will make you feel right at home. The Huashan Lu store has two floors. You'll also find another smaller outlet in the basement at Maison Mode and at Yaohan Department Store in Pudong.

# CARPETS

## THE CARPET SHOP 地毯之家

(Ditan Zhijia)
783 Honggu Lu 200335 虹古路783号
Tel: 1391603148
This shop carries handmade silk and woolen carpets from the Jiangsu Animal By-Product Import and Export Group.

## CHINA NATIONAL ARTS AND CRAFTS
建材商城

(Jiancai Shangcheng)
Shanghai showroom: Shanghai Construction Materials Building
407 Yishan Lu 宜山路407号
Tel: 6438-8812, 6438-2873 or
      6468-4468

## FRIENDSHIP STORE 友谊商店

(Youyi Shangdian)
40 Beijing Dong Lu 北京东路40号
Tel: 6329-4600
Hours: 9:30 am - 10:00 pm

## GERDA SCHOLLAERT

7886 Humin Lu 沪闵路7886号
Tel: 6412-4605
Ms. Schollaert sells excellent quality Chinese carpets from her home.

## SHANGHAI ARTS AND CRAFTS TRADING CO. 上海工艺品商店

(Shanghai Gongyipin Shangdian)
Shanghai Exhibition Center 上海展览中心
1000 Yan'an Xi Lu 延安西路1000号

Tel: 6279-0279 x 62222
Hours: 8:30 am - 6:30 pm
Worth checking out. Small discounts can be negotiated.

## T & D ARTS PLAZA CO. LTD.
上海天地工艺美术城公司

(Shanghai Tiandi Gongyi Meishicheng Gongsi)
25 Zhaobao Lu 漕宝路25号
Tel: 6218-8460
Hours: 9:00 am - 5:30 pm
Deputy Gen. Manager: Wu Zhong Zi
Large silk rugs

## WYNE'S CARPETS

673 Xianxia Lu 仙霞路673号
Tel: 6273-7745
Hours: 10:30 am - 6:30 pm

## ZHAO HU CARPET FACTORY
召沪地毯联营总厂

(Zhaohu Ditan Lianying Zongchang)
98 Gubei Nan Lu 古北南路98号
Mobile: 1391711047
Fax:     6209-9058
Pager: 6438-9300 x 67876
Manager: Tom (Dai Jian Guo) (戴建国)
"Running Horse" brand silk carpets from Henan at discount prices. Tom, the manager, speaks excellent English and is extremely easy to work with. This store claims to sell at about 50% of the price of other large dealers.

# ELECTRONICS

Audio visual equipment such as TVs and VCRs can be purchased at the following stores as well as at major department stores listed in the shopping section. It's always best to shop around and compare prices as the difference in pricing may be significant.

**CHEN JIANQIAO**  剑桥实业有限公司
(Jianqiao Shiye Youxian Gongsi)
235 Tangzijing Lu Near Kaixuan Lu
塘子泾路235号近凯旋路
Tel: 6403-1180
Hours: 9:00 am - 5:00 pm
Beeper: 126 x 672176

**HITACHI**
上海日立家电专营公司
(Shanghai Rili Jiadian Zhuanying Gongsi)
268 Jinling Dong Lu   金陵东路268号
Tel: 6326-0902
Hours: 9:00 am - 5:00 pm

**INCHCAPE GILMAN OFFICE MACHINES**
新亚—英之杰信息工程有限公司
(Xinya Yingzhijie Xinxi Gongcheng Youxian Gongsi)
7th Fl, 1303 Yan'an Xi Lu
延安西路1303号7楼
Rooms A and B
Tel: 6212-6765
Fax: 6257-8757
Hours: 9:00 am - 5:30 pm

**INTERNATIONAL AUDIO AND VIDEO**
国际音视电器公司
(Guoji Yinshi Dianqi Gongsi)
Electrical Appliance Co.
739 Nanjing Dong Lu   南京东路739号
Tel: 6322-3118
Hours: 9:30 am - 10:00 pm

**MODERN AUDIO AND VIDEO APPLI-
ANCES**  现代音像电器有限公司
(Xiandai Yinxiang Dianqi Youxian Gongsi)
1008 Huaihai Zhong Lu   淮海中路1008号

Tel: 6467-3606, 6473-0958
Hours: 9:00 am - 9:00 pm

**QUN YIN AUDIO AND VIDEO EQUIP-
MENT CO.**  群英视听设备商店
(Qunying Shiting Shebei Shangdian)
518 Nanjing Dong Lu   南京东路518号
Tel: 6351-1147
Hours: 9:30 am - 10: 00 pm

**SHANGHAI INDEX COMPUTER COM-
PANY LTD.**  上海索因电脑有限公司
(Shanghai Suoying Diannao Youxian Gongsi)
423 Wuning Lu   武宁路423号
Tel: 6257-9218
Fax: 6257-8757
Hours: 8:30 am - 5:00 pm

**SHANGHAI INTERNATIONAL
ACOUSTIC EQUIPMENT MALL**
上海国际音响广场
(Shanghai Guoji Yinxiang Guangchang)
111 Qufu Lu   曲阜路111号
Tel: 6306-0264
Hours: 9:30 am - 5:30 pm
This huge electronics mall is aimed at the local market making it a lower priced alternative to department stores. You'll find computers, software, printers, sound systems, VCD players, televisions, and more here.

**SHANGHAI SEA & SKY ELECTRONICS
CO.**  上海西斯凯电子公司
(Shanghai Xisikai Dianzi Gongsi)
207 Xiangyang Nan Lu 200031
向阳南路207号
Tel: 6433-5042
Fax: 6431-7960
Hours: 8:30 am - 5:00 pm

## SHANGHAI SEIYU TRADE CO., LTD.
上海西友贸易有限公司
(Shanghai Xiyou Maoyi Youxian Gongsi)
779 Beijing Xi Lu　北京西路779号
Tel: 6267-4207
Fax: 6215-0232

## SISO　上海思索科技实业公司
(Shanghai Sisuo Keji Shiye Gongsi)
232 Fanyu Lu  200050　番禺路232号
Tel: 6283-5643, 6282-2127,
　　　6282-2128, 6282-2122
Fax.: 6282-2119, 6282-2124
This store carries a full range of Hewlett
Packard products.

## TRAYTON SYSTEMS
上海特雷通系统公司
(Shanghai Teleitong Xitong Gongsi)
Suite 5-E2, Chengzhou World Trade Building
增泽世贸大厦5楼E2室
1590 Yan'an Xi Lu　延安西路1590号
Tel: 6280-6598 x 2528
Hours: 9:00 am - 5:30 pm
Computer software.

## ZHONG WAI COMPUTER STORE
中外电脑商都
(Zhongwai Diannao Shangdu)
5th Fl, 233 Nanjing Dong Lu
南京东路233号5楼
Tel: 6329-1180
The fifth floor in this building houses several
small companies.

# BEDDING

Listed below are a few specialty stores. Bedding is also sold at most
department stores.

## SHANGHAI BEDDING CO.
上海床上用品商店
(Shanghai Chuangshang Yongpin Shangdian)
806-812 Huaihai Zhong Lu
淮海中路806-812号
Tel. 6473-9149, 6473-8458, 6473-0550

Hours: 10:00 am - 10:00 pm
Excellent selection at good prices. Mr. Yuen
speaks English

## SHANGHAI BEDROOM ARTICLES CO.
740 Nanjing Dong Lu　南京东路740号

# ANTIQUES

*Please note that only items dated after 1797 can be exported.
The following are wood types commonly used in Chinese antique furniture. It's nice to know what
you're buying!

| Pinyin | Hanzi or Chinese Characters | English | Pinyin | Hanzi or Chinese Characters | English |
|---|---|---|---|---|---|
| Xiang | 橡木 | Camphor | Limu | 梨木 | Pear |
| Zimu | 紫木 | Catalpa | Yangmu | 扬木 | Poplar |
| Nanmu | 楠木 | Cedar | | | (Aspen) |
| Baimu | 柏木 | Cypress | Youmu | 油木 | Teak |
| Wumu | 乌木 | Ebony | Hualimu | 花梨木 | Rosewood |
| Jumu | 榉木 | Elm | Huang | 黄花梨木 | Yellow |
| Huaimu | 槐木 | Locust | hualimu | | Rosewood |
| Songmu | 松木 | Pine | Hongmu | 红木 | Black wood |
| Hongsong | 红松 | Red pine | Yingmu | 影木 | Burl |
| Zitanmu | 紫檀木 | Red sandal-wood | Zhangmu | 樟木 | Camphor |

# ANTIQUE STREET MARKETS

## "CRICKET STREET" 古商品市场

(Dongtai Lu Gudong Shichang)

Dongtai Lu off Xizang Lu 东台路近西藏路

Also called the "Dongtai Lu Market", here one may bargain for antiques and curios every day. This street market is becoming more sophisticated with time. The market received its name from expatriates in the late '80s, when there were crickets, cricket cages, and cricket paraphernalia sold in the market. The stalls were decrepit and the prices once very low, but as time went on and more foreigners came to Shanghai, the stalls were renovated. The government forbade the sale of crickets due to the fact that they are used for gambling. The street is becoming more and more sophisticated, but one can still enjoy an afternoon of browsing and bargaining. It is a good idea to offer about 1/3 to 1/2 of the price requested for an item. You will usually end up by paying about 2/3 of what was asked originally. Dealers use calculators and body language to communicate, and you respond in the same manner. One buys "antiques" at one's own risk, but some get lucky. It is best to just buy things that appeal, and don't pay more for them then you feel comfortable with for their visual appeal alone. Of course, there is Chinese porcelain and some furniture, but also Mao buttons and "Little Red Books" from the cultural revolution, brass candlesticks, jewelry, swords, old clothing, and boxes and baskets galore. An interesting afternoon can be had mingling with the locals and picking up local color. The market opens in the early morning and tends to close, one booth at a time, around dinnertime. On rainy days, some stalls aren't open, and pickings may be slim.

## LIUHE LU ANTIQUE MARKET

浏河路古玩市场

(Liuhe Lu Guwan Shichang)

Tel: 6326-5254

Hours: 10:00 am - 5:00 pm

Located near the Dongtai Lu (东台路) market (Cricket Street). Over 150 stalls offering baskets, embroideries, ivory, porcelain, jade, artifacts from the cultural revolution and more.

## SUNDAY MARKET 星期天旧货市场

(Xingqitian Jiuhuo Shichang)

457 Fangbang Lu, near Henan Lu

方滨中路457号近河南路

This market operates on Saturday and Sunday. It used to be a street market on Fuyou Lu, but has moved into a building not far from its former location. As before, the early bird gets the best antique, as the best finds are snapped up very early in the morning. Sellers (about 800 of them) are sometimes there are early as 4:00 am or 5:00 am. This place is a definite "must" if you're into collecting. You'll find trash and treasures of many kinds, including antiques. Don't forget to bargain.

## ZHAOJIABANG OLD COINS AND STAMP COLLECTING MARKET

上海太原路云州集邮市场

(Shanghai Taiyuan Lu Yunzhou Jiyou Shichang)

Taiyuan Lu at Zhaojiabang Lu

上海太原路近肇家滨路

Tel: 6417-2268 x 302, 6417-2268 x 3022

This market specializes in old coins, stamps, and model cars. You may buy, sell, or trade. It is rumored that this market may move to 88 Damuqiao Lu (大木桥路88号).

## ZHONGHUA XIN LU MARKET

中华新路旧货市场

(Zhonghuaxin Lu Jiuhuo Shichang)

100 Hengfeng Lu near Zhonghua Xin Lu

恒丰路100号 近中华新路
Tel: 5672-9892, 5630-1058
This is the largest street market in Shanghai

and is open to private traders. Some antiques, but for the most part this market sells everything from soup to nuts.

# ANTIQUE STORES

## ANNLY'S ANTIQUE WAREHOUSE
安丽家具有限公司
(Anli Jiaju Youxian Gongsi)
1255 Wuzhong Lu   吴中路1255号
Tel: 6406-0242
Fax: 6419-6070
Annly carries antique furniture and reproductions, but is unique in that she can also provide custom made upholstered sofas and chairs, draperies and cushions. Services also include picture framing, for a one-stop home decor shop.

## CHINE ANTIQUES
刘海粟美术馆家具经营部
(Liuhaisu Meishuguan Jiaju Jingyingbu)
1660 Hongqiao Lu   虹桥路1660号
38 Liuhe Lu at the corner of Dongtai Lu
浏河路38号
Store tel: 6270-1023
Warehouse tel: 5914-4424
Mobile: 9109-1441
Fax: 5914-6985
Hours: 9:00 am - 5:00 pm
The Liuhe Lu store is very small and is located in the Cricket Street market. The showroom on Hongqiao Lu is much larger. The warehouse is located west of the airport. Furniture is very nicely finished.

## CHUANGXIN ANTIQUE STORE
创新旧工艺品商店
(Changxinjiu Gongyipin Shangdian)
1297 - 1305 Huaihai Zhong Lu
淮海中路1297-1305号
Tel: 6437-2559   6437-0138
Hours: 10:00 am - 6:00 pm
Corner of Huaihai Lu and Changshu Lu

Clocks and watches, jewelry, and leather goods.

## DRAGON ERA   龙韵实业有限公司
(Longyun Shiye Youxian Gongsi)
377 Huqingping Cong Lu (National Route #318)   沪青平公路377号
Minhang District
Tel: 6421-9106
Fax: 6421-0208
Hours: 9:00 am - 5.00 pm
This great warehouse has a wide selection of antique furniture, with refinishing services.

## G. E. TANG ANTIQUE AND CURIO SHOP   古玩商店
(Guwan Shangdian)
- Head Office: 85 Dongtai Lu, located adjacent to the elementary school in the antique street market   东台路85号
  Tel: 6326-3355
  Fax: 6384-7288
- North Branch: 50 Liuhe Kou Lu
  浏河口路50号
  Tel: 6326-3355
You may also call the Sales Director, Mr. Sulan Su's pager at 128 x 225177.
A relatively new addition to the "Cricket Street" market. It is operated along the outside wall of the school in the market and is affiliated with the school. Teachers man the shop and claim that proceeds go towards the teachers' salaries. Articles are somewhat different from most antique furniture in that the finish is of medium darkness. New pieces are made from undamaged parts of old pieces. Although this probably affects the value, the result is quite modern and the prices are reasonable.

## GUO HUA CHINAWARE STORE
国华瓷器商店
(Guohua Ciqi Shangdian)
550 Nanjing Dong Lu　南京东路550号
Tel: 6322-4537
Hours: 10:00 am - 10:00 pm

## HUA BAO LOU　华宝楼
(Huabaolou)
265 Fangbang Lu　方滨中路265号
Tel: 6355-9999
Hours: 8:30 am - 9:00 pm
Located in the basement of the Huabao Building in the Old City near Yuyuan Garden. Nearly 250 stalls filling 1,500 square meters of space, offering porcelain, embroideries, calligraphy, jade, rubbings, carvings, and more. This is one-stop antique shopping! Since this area is aimed at the tourist trade, asking prices are fairly high. Try to cut asking prices considerably.

## SHANGHAI ANTIQUE AND CURIO STORE　上海文物商店
(Shanghai Wenwu Shangdian)
218 - 226 Guangdong Lu　广东路218-226号
Hours: 10:00 am - 5:00 pm
Tel: 6321-4697, 6321-6529
This is a municipal government antique store, so bargaining is not usually an option. However, what you buy will be authentic and easily exportable. Proper customs receipts are issued.

## SHANGHAI FRIENDSHIP STORE
北京东路友谊商店
Main Store, 40 Beijing Dong Lu
北京东路40号
Antiques and Curios Branch,
694 Nanjing Xi Lu　南京西路694号

## SHANGHAI HONG MEI ANTIQUE FURNITURE SHOP
上海虹梅古典家俱
(Shanghai Hongmei Gudian Jiaju)
1268 Wuzhong Lu　吴中路1268号
Tel: 6406-1275
Ask for Li Xin Shen

## SHANGHAI YINGUI ANTIQUE FURNITURE SHOP　上海银桂古典家俱
(Shanghai Yingui Gudian Jiaju)
1232 Hongmei Lu　虹梅路1232 号
Tel: 6484-1125
Mobile: 9182-4495
Hours: 9:00 am - 5:00 pm
This warehouse is run by the Li brothers. Aside from selling antique furniture, they repair, refinish, custom-make and copy furniture, and ship overseas.

## SHANGHAI LYCEUM JEWELRY AND ANTIQUES　兰馨珠宝文物商行
(Lanxin Zhubao Wenwu Shanghang)
398 Changle Lu　长乐路398号
Tel: 6255-1667, 6253-8459
Hours: 10:00 am - 9:00 pm
Jewelry, porcelain, ivory, antiques, seals, and paintings.

## SHAANXI ARTS AND CRAFTS
陕西工艺品商店
(Shaanxi Gongyipin Shangdian)
557 Yan'an Zhong Lu　延安中路557号
Tel: 6256-5489
Hours: 9:00 am - 6:30 pm
Porcelain, antique clocks and watches, etc.

## WAN BO ARTS AND CRAFTS
1430 Hongqiao Lu　虹桥路1430号
Beautiful pieces, but limited selection with rather high prices.

## WANG'S ANTIQUE FURNITURE SHOP
卢湾红木家具店
(Luwan Hongmu Jiajudian)
307 Shunchang Lu　顺昌路307号
Tel: 6328-3813
Proprietor: Wang Junli
High-end antique furniture, including some Ming pieces, can be found here. This store

# ANTIQUITIES TABLE

When shopping for antiques, it is helpful to know just how old something from the Ming or Qing Dynasty is supposed to be.

| DYNASTY | EMPEROR | DATES |
|---|---|---|
| HSIA | | BC 2205-1766 |
| SHANG | | BC 1766-1122 |
| CHOU | | BC 1122-770 |
| SPRING and AUTUMN ANNALS | | BC 770-476 |
| WARRING STATES | | BC 476-221 |
| CHIN | | BC 221-206 |
| HAN | | BC 206 - AD 220 |
| THREE KINGDOMS | | AD 220 - 263 |
| TSIN | | AD 265- 420 |
| SOUTHERN and NORTHERN | | AD 420- 589 |
| SUI | | AD 589-618 |
| TANG | | AD 618-907 |
| FIVE DYNASTIES | | AD 907-960 |
| SONG | | AD 960-1280 |
| YUEN | | AD 1280-1368 |
| MING | | AD 1368-1644 |
| | Hung Wu | AD 1368-1399 |
| | Chien Wen | AD 1399-1403 |
| | Yung Lo | AD 1403-1425 |
| | Hung Hsi | AD 1425-1426 |
| | Hsuan Toh | AD 1426-1436 |
| | Cheng Tung | AD 1436-1450 |
| | Ching Tai | AD 1450-1457 |
| | Tien Shun | AD 1457-1465 |
| | Cheng Hwa | AD 1465-1488 |
| | Hung Chih | AD 1488-1506 |
| | Cheng Toh | AD 1506-1522 |
| | Chia Ching | AD 1522-1567 |
| | Lung Ching | AD 1567-1573 |
| | Wan Lee | AD 1573--1620 |
| | Tai Chang | AD 1620-1621 |
| | Tien Chi | AD 1621-1628 |
| | Chung Cheng | AD 1628-1644 |
| QING | | AD 1644-1911 |
| | Shun Chih | AD 1644-1662 |
| | Kang Hsi | AD 1662-1723 |
| | Yung Cheng | AD 1723-1736 |
| | Chien Lung | AD 1736-1796 |
| | Chia Ching | AD 1796-1821 |
| | Tao Kuang | AD 1821-1851 |
| | Hsien Fong | AD 1851-1862 |
| | Tung Chih | AD 1862-1875 |
| | Kuang Hsu | AD 1875-1908 |
| | Hsuan Tung | AD 1908-1911 |

has a reputation for high quality and prices.

## XINGUANG OPTICAL INSTRUMENT STORE　新光光学仪器商店
(Xinguang Guangxue Yiqi Shangdian)
538 Huaihai Zhong Lu　淮海中路538号
Tel: 6327-5111
Hours: 9:00 am - 10:00 pm
At the corner of Huaihai Zhong Lu and Yandang Lu, this store deals in old and new optical instruments. The staff repairs old cameras as well.

## YU GARDEN ANTIQUE MARKET　豫园
(Yu Yuan)
老城隍庙九曲桥旁边
There is a charming antique store within the garden itself, close to the exit, to the right, through a gate. The store sells many porcelains, jewelry, jade ornaments, baskets, etc, with a separate room where a calligrapher is at work.

# CHINESE ARTS AND CRAFTS

## CHONG SHIN OLD ARTS AND CRAFTS STORE　创新旧工艺品商店
(Chuangxinjiu Gongyipin Shangdian)
1297-1305 Huahai Zhong Lu
淮海中路1297-1305号
Tel: 6437-2559, 6437-0138
Hours: 10:00 am - 6:00 pm
Cloisonné clocks, watches, porcelain, pottery ware, and furniture.

## DUO YUN XUAN ART STUDIO　朵云轩
(Duo Yun Xuan)
422 Nanjing Dong Lu　南京东路422号
Tel: 6322-3410, 6322-3939
Hours: 9:30 am - 6:30 pm
Seals and seal cutting, calligraphy, paintings, rubbings, and stationery.

## RAINBOW PAVILION
上海小雨亭刻字工艺品商店
(Shanghai Xiaoyuting Kezi Gongyipin Shangdian)
609 Changle Lu　长乐路609号
Tel: 6473-7042
Hours: 9:00 am - 6:00 pm
Chops and seals.

## RUI HUA ARTS AND CRAFTS
瑞华工艺品商店
(Ruihua Gongyipin Shangdian)
1207 Nanjing Xi Lu　南京西路1207号
Tel: 6247-2350
Hours: 10:00 am - 10:00 pm

## SECOND MARKET　赛肯德商行
(Saikende Shanghang)
3824 Hongmei Lu　虹梅路3824号
(next to City Shopping)
Tel: 6262-3094
Fax: 6242-9178
Hours: 9:00 am - 9:00 pm
Rosewood furniture, antiques, porcelain, pearl jewelry, gifts, oil paintings, vases, baskets, and teapots. They will also make lamps from your favorite vase and/or lamp shades from your fabric.

## SHANGHAI ARTS AND CRAFTS IMPORT/EXPORT
上海工艺品进出口公司
(Shanghai Gongyipin Jinchukou Gongsi)
89 Siping Lu　四平路89号
Tel: 6522-2888
Hours: 9:00 am - 7:00 pm

## SHANGHAI ARTS AND CRAFTS INSTITUTE 上海工艺美术研究所旧工艺品复修部

(Shanghai Gongyi Meishu Yanjiusuo Jiugongyipin Xiufubu)
79 Fenyang Lu　汾阳路79号
Tel: 6437-0509
Hours: 8:30 am - 4:30 pm

## SHANGHAI ARTS AND CRAFTS SALES SERVICE CENTER 上海工艺美术商厦

(Shanghai Gongyi Meishu Shangsha)
190 Nanjing Xi Lu　南京西路190号
Tel: 6327-5299, 6327-6530
Hours: 9:30 am - 9:00 pm
Jade, ivory, gold and silver jewelry, carpets, leather goods, screens, and embroideries.

## SHANGHAI ARTS AND CRAFTS TRADING CO. 上海工艺品展销公司

(Shanghai Gongyipin Zhanxiao Gongsi)
1000 Yan'an Zhong Lu　延安中路1000号
Tel: 6247-4781
Hours: 9:00 am - 6:00 pm

## NO. 52, SHANGHAI BUILDING MATERIALS COMMERCIAL CENTER 上海建材商城

(Shanghai Jiancai Shangcheng)
407 Yishan Lu　宜山路407号
Tel: 6438-8812 x 3352
Hours: 9:00 am - 5:30 pm
Blue and white batik.

## SHANGHAI FOREIGN TRADE EMPORIUM 上海外贸商厦

(Shanghai Waimao Shangsha)
24 Nanjing Dong Lu　南京东路24号
Tel: 6323-0148, 6323-0174
Hours: 10:00 am - 9:00 pm
Handicraft articles, medicine, and daily necessities.

## THE SHANGHAI HUANGSHAN TEA CO. 黄山茶叶商店

(Huangshan Chaye Shangdian)
853 Huaihai Zhong Lu　淮海中路853号
Tel: 6437-7627
Hours: 9:00 am - 10:00 pm
This store offers a wide selection of tea and Yixing teapots.

## SHANGHAI GOLD STONE CO. 上海金石企业有限公司

(Shanghai Jinshi Qiye Youxian Gongsi)
Room103, 1376 Nanjing Xi Lu
南京西路1376号103室
Tel: 6279-8335
Hours: 7:30 am - 10:00 pm

## SHANGHAI JINGDEZHEN PORCELAIN ART WARE SERVICE DEPT. 上海景德镇艺术瓷器服务部

(Shanghai Jingdezhen Yishu Ciqi Fuwubu)
1175 Nanjing Xi Lu　南京西路1175号
Tel: 6253-0885, 6253-3178
Hours: 10:00 am - 9:00 pm
Porcelain and handicrafts.

## SHANGHAI OLD TOWN GOD'S TEMPLE ARTS AND CRAFTS STORE 上海老城皇隍庙小商品市场

(Shanghai Laochenghuangmiao Xiaoshangpin Shichang)
1 Anren Lu　安仁路1号
Tel: 6326-0858
Hours: 9:00 am - 6:00 pm

## SHANGHAI SUPERB ARTS AND CRAFTS CO 上海华丽工艺品商店

(Shanghai Huali Gongyipin Shangdian)
Hotel Equatorial Shanghai　国际贵都大饭店
65 Yan'an Xi Lu　延安西路65号

## YU HUA ARTS AND CRAFTS STORE
玉华工艺品商店
(Yuhua Gongyipin Shangdian)

Huaihai Zhong Lu at the corner of Chongqing Lu. Opening in September 1998
淮海中路重庆路附近(九八年九月开张)

# PHARMACIES (WESTERN-STYLE)

## WATSON'S 屈臣氏
(Quchensi)

This store is opening new shops at a steady pace.

- Level 1 West, Shanghai Centre
  上海商城底楼西
  1376 Nanjing Xi Lu　南京西路1376号
  Tel: 6279-8381
- 789 Huaihai Zhong Lu　淮海中路789号
- Westgate Mall, 2nd Fl,　梅龙镇广场2楼
  (Meilongzhen Guangchang)
- 1038 Nanjing Xi Lu　南京西路1038号
  Tel: 6218-0598

- Kerry Everbright City　嘉里不夜城
  (Jiali Buyecheng)
- 218 Tianmu Xi Lu　天目西路218号
  Tel: 6354-5825
- Ya Xin Shopping Mall　亚新生活广场
  401 Changshou Lu　长寿路401号
  Tel: 6276-7649
- Di Mei Shopping Center　迪美购物中心
  (Dimei Gouwu Zhongxin)
- Underground Shopping Mall, People's Square　人民广场地下商场
  (Renmin Guangchang Dixia Shangchang)
  Tel: 6358-2319

# CHINESE MEDICINE

## CAI TONG DE DRUGSTORE
蔡同德堂
(Caitongde Tang)
320 Nanjing Dong Lu　南京东路320号
Tel: 6322-3991
Rare medicinal herbs.

## HU QING YU TANG CHINESE MEDICINE STORE 胡庆余堂国药店
(Huqingyu Tang Guoyao Dian)
620 Xizang Zhong Lu　西藏中路620号
Tel: 6352-9260

## JIN SONG GINSENG AND DRUGSTORE
劲松参药店
(Shenyaodian)
823 Huaihai Zhong Lu　淮海中路823号
Tel: 6437-6700

## JIU HE TANG DRUGSTORE　九和堂
(Jiuhetang)
964 Nanjing Xi Lu　南京西路964号

Tel: 6218-5753

## LEI YUN SHANG CHINESE MEDICINE
雷允上中药店
(Leiyunshang Zhongyaodian)
719 Nanjing Xi Lu　南京西路719号
Tel: 6255-2708

## THE ORIENTAL DISPENSARY 华美药房
(Huamei Yaofang)
356 Fuzhou Lu　福州路356号
Tel: 6322-4179
Hours: 8:30 am - 5:00 pm

## SHANGHAI #1 DISPENSARY
第一医药商店
(Diyi Yiyao Shangdian)
616 Nanjing Dong Lu
南京东路616号
Tel: 6322-4567
Shanghai's largest and primary "drug" store for Chinese and Western medicine. Many

Western items, such as antibiotics and Prozac sold over the counter here. The best bet for a "hard to find" item.

## SHANGHAI CHINESE MEDICINE TRADE CENTER 上海中药贸易中心
(Shanghai Zhongyao Maoyi Zhongxin)
506 Henan Zhong Lu 河南中路506号
Tel: 6325-1990, 6321-4174
Hours: 9:00 am - 7:00 pm
Rare medicinal herbs.

## TONG HAN CHUN TANG TRADITIONAL CHINESE MEDICINE STORE
老城隍庙童函春国药公司
(Laochenghuangmiao Tonghanchun Guoyao Gongsi)
20 Xinyuyuan Lu 豫园新路20号
Tel: 6373-1232, 6328-5230
Hours: 8:30 am - 9:00 pm
Western medical instruments, Chinese herbal medicine, western medicine.

# PICTURE FRAMING

## HUAGUANG PICTURE FRAMING
华光画框
30 Gao'an Lu (entrance on Hengshan Lu)
高安路30号 近衡山路
Tel: 6466-0644
Hours: 9:00 am - 6:00 pm

## VANTALY GALLERIE AND FRAMES
凡达利画廊
(Fandali Hualang)
• 458 Fuzhou Lu 福州路458号

Tel: 6322-5453
Fax: 6352-0456
• 1 Changshu Lu, Lane 108
常熟路108弄1号
Tel: 6248-7911
• 137 Xianxia Lu 仙霞路137 号
Tel: 6259-7953, dial 0, then x 7640
Vantaly also has a store in Suzhou at:
9 Renmin Lu Jiayufangbei
人民路嘉余坊北9 号
Tel: 0512-523-7652

# SPORTING GOODS

Many of the department stores have special sections dedicated to sporting equipment and clothing. A few other stores around the city may be worth checking out.

## COLUMBIA SPORTSWEAR
Located in the Hong Kong Underground Shopping Mall 人民广场地下商场
(Renmin Guangchang Dixia Shangchang)
People's Square 人民广场内

## EAST SPORTS GOODS STORE
东方体育用品公司
(Dongfang Tiyuyongpin Gongsi)
322 Shaanxi Nan Lu 陕西南路322号
Tel: 6473-6052
Hours: 9:00 am - 9:00 pm

## NIKE 耐克
(Naike)
400 Huaihai Zhong Lu 淮海中路400号
A wide range of Nike products at this store, but another source is the Shanghai Centre Health Club, where purchases can be made with either cash or credit card.

## PUMA 飘马
(Piaoma)
1000 Huaihai Zhong Lu 淮海中路1000号
Hong Kong Underground Shopping Mall
人民广场地下商场

(Renmin Guangchang Dixia Shangchang)
People's Square　人民广场内

Tel: 6325-0727
Hours: 9:30 am - 8:30 pm

## SAN YUAN SPORTING GOODS
三元健美用品商店
(Sanyuan Jianmei Yingpin Shangdian)
604 Nanjing Xi Lu　南京西路604号
Tel: 6253-0232
740 Fengyang Lu　凤阳路740号
Tel: 6256-3816

## SHANGHAI GENERAL SPORTING GOODS　上海运动鞋总厂商店
(Shanghai Yundongxie Zongchang Shangdian)
1400 Sichuan Bei Lu　四川北路1400号

## SHANGHAI SPORTING GOODS
上海体育用品总店
(Shanghai Tiyu Yongpin Shangdian)
160 Nanjing Dong Lu　南京东路160号
Tel: 6329-1343, 6323-2773

## SHANGHAI SPORTS EQUIPMENT SHOP
上海体育用品公司
(Shanghai Tiyuyongpin Gongsi)
160-166 Nanjing Dong Lu
南京东路160-166号
Tel: 6321-4789

# OPTICAL SHOPS

## AMERICAN EYES　美式眼镜城
(Meishi Yanjing Cheng)
- 481 Jinling Dong Lu　金陵东路481号
  Tel: 6326-3030
  Hours: 9:00 am - 9:00 pm
- 1st Fl, 2118 Sichuan Bei Lu
  四川北路2118号1楼
  Tel: 5671-1202
  Hours: 9:30 am - 10:00 pm
- 35 Huashan Lu　华山路35号
  Tel: 6248-2207
  Hour: 9:30 am - 9:30 pm
- 789 Tianshan Lu　天山路789号
  Tel: 6259-8764
  Hours: 9:00 am - 9:00 pm
- 21-23 Hongkong Underground Mall
  People's Square
  人民广场香港名品街21-23号柜台
  Tel: 6358-0000
  Hours: 10:00 am - 9:00 pm
- 1669 Kongjiang Lu　控江路1669号
  Tel: 6501-5879
  Hours: 9:30 am - 9:30 pm
- 1038 Nanjing Xi Lu　南京西路1038号
  Tel: 6218-0414

  Hours: 10:00 am - 10:00 pm
- 1004 Huaihai Zhong Lu　淮海中路1004号
  Tel: 6466-5838
  Hours: 9:15 am - 9:15 pm
- 505 Nanjing Dong Lu　南京东路481号
  Tel: 6351-7576
  Hours: 9:30 am - 10:00 pm
- 1149 Nanjing Xi Lu　南京西路1149号
  Tel: 6253-6720
  Hours: 9:30 am - 9:00 pm

## PARIS MIKI (SHANGHAI)　巴黎三城
(Bali Sancheng)
- 280 Jinling Dong Lu　金陵东路280号
  Tel: 6373-9634
  Hours: 9:30 am - 8:30 pm
- 838 Nanjing Dong Lu　南京东路838号
  Tel: 6267-3907
  Hours: 10:00 am - 9:30 pm
- 1st Fl, The Landmark　置地广场底楼
  409 Nanjing Dong Lu　南京东路409号
  Tel: 6360-8205
  Hours: 10:00 am - 10:00 pm
- 83 Zunyi Lu　遵义路83号
  Tel: 6209-4807
  Hours: 10:00 am - 9:00 pm

- 2nd Fl, Kerry Everbright City
  嘉里不夜城2楼
  218 Tianmu Xi Lu　天目西路218号
  Tel: 6354-2383
  Hours: 9:30 am - 9:30 pm
- 1351 Sichuan Bei Lu　四川北路1351号
  Tel: 6324-6167
  Hours: 10:00 am - 9:00 pm
- 63 Tianyaoqiao Lu　天铜桥路63号
  Tel: 6469-9920
  Hours: 10:00 am - 10:00 pm
- Billion Auspice Shopping Center
  九州名品城
  1328 Dingxi Lu　定西路1328号
  Tel: 6211-9626
  Hours: 9:30 am - 8:30 pm
- 1088 Yiangying Lu　翔鹰路1088号
  Tel: 6511-2071
  Hours: 9:00 am - 9:00 pm
- 1667 Kongjiang Lu　控江路1667号
  Tel: 6501-9238
  Hours: Mon. - Thur. 9:00 am - 8:00 pm,
  　　　　Fri. - Sun. 9:00 am - 8:30 pm

## SWANK OPTICAL　斯维卡眼镜店
(Siweika Yanjingdian)
- 1350 Sichuan Bei Lu　四川北路1350号
  Tel: 6324-8047
  Hours: 9:00 am - 9:30 pm
- 22 Hong Kong Underground People's Mall Square
  人民广场香港名品街22号柜台
  Tel: 6358-2560
  Hours: 10:00 am - 10:00 pm
- 1126 Yiangying Lu　翔鹰路1126号
  Tel: 6511-9446
  Hours: 9:30 am - 9:30 pm
- 3rd Fl, Westgate Mall　梅龙镇广场3楼
  1038 Nanjing Xi Lu　南京西路1038号
  Tel: 6218-3668
  Hours: 10:00 am - 10:00 pm
- 305 Changshou Lu　长寿路305号
  Tel: 6227-6946
  Hours: 8:30 am - 8:30 pm
- 185 Zhidan Lu　志丹路185号
  Tel: 5694-0564
  Hours: 9:00 am - 9:00 pm
- 218 Tianmu Xi Lu　天目西路218号
  Tel: 6354-7748
  Hours: 10:00 am - 10:00 pm

# HOLIDAY FARE

### THE CHRISTMAS SHOP　长乐百货商店
(Changle Baihuo Shangdian)
384 Changle Lu　长乐路384号
Tel: 6256-3686
Hours: 9:00 am - 10:00 pm
Artificial trees and a wide assortment of decorations are sold here year 'round. They also stock a good supply of candles for use anytime.

### GOLDEN EAGLE SHOPPING CENTER
金龙丝绸呢绒公司
(Jinlong Sichou Nirong Gongsi)
858-864 Huaihai Zhong Lu
淮海中路858-864号
Huaihai Lu at Maoming Lu

淮海路 茂名路
Tel: 6473-6691
Hours: 10:00 am - 10:00 pm
Christmas decorations.

### ISETAN DEPARTMENT STORE
华亭伊势丹
(Huating Yishidan)
527 Huaihai Zhong Lu　淮海中路527号
Tel: 5375-1111
Christmas cards, trees, and decorations.

### PET MARKET
104 Jiangning Lu　江宁路104号
Christmas trees and a wide selection of ornaments.

# FLOWERS

## SHANGHAI JINGWEN FLOWER MARKET 金门精文花市交易市场

(Shanghai Jingwen Huahui Jiaoyi Shichang)
225 Shaanxi Nan Lu (between Fuxing Zhong Lu and Yongjia Lu)  陕西南路225号
Hours: 5:00 am - 10:00 pm
This covered market is found through a gate on the east side of the address listed. Prices are reputed to be less in the evening when additional street vendors open their stands.

Along with cut flowers and potted plants at great prices, you'll find ribbons and bows, wrapping paper, vases, baskets, and flower pots. Outdoor furniture is also available. If you're looking for a landscape architect to plan your garden, go to stall #41-44 and talk to Sang Ye (桑叶). He can also design flower arrangements for large parties or make customized dry flower arrangements. His telephone number is 6467-6500 x 3066.

# BOOKS AND PUBLICATIONS

English-language materials can be found at the **Foreign Languages Bookstore** at 390 Fuzhou Lu (福州路390号). Also browse at a nearby small bookstore on the corner that has a large selection. Old China Hand Press (tel: 6471-2637) carries many books that capture China's past through photographs. Most hotels also have bookstores catering to foreigners.

## CHINESE ANCIENT BOOKSTORE 上海古籍书店

(Shanghai Guji Shudian)
424 Fuzhou Lu  福州路424号
Tel: 6322-4984 x 20, 6320-7745
Hours: 9:00 am - 6:00 pm
Aside from antique books, you'll find stationery, calligraphy and paintings, and hand-crafted items.

The **Book of the Month Club** now has an international service through which you can order books in English. You may contact them by mail at BOOK-OF-THE MONTH, INC., Camp Hill, Pa., 17012-8804, USA, by telephone at 1-717-697-1209, or by fax at 1-717-795-1670.

## SHANGHAI POT LUCK

This collection of recipes was put together by the Shanghai Expatriates Association and includes dishes containing ingredients easily found in Shanghai. All proceeds go to charity. To order a copy, call: 6279-8624, 6270-9231, 6270-9346, 6268-7718, or 6268-9761.

Stephanie Dawson provides **laminated Chinese/English address cards** which can be shown to taxi drivers. Included are the most popular destinations among the expat crowd here. Addresses are shown in English, Pinyin, and Chinese characters. They sell for RMB200. Stephanie can be reached at tel 6268-6947 or 6268-9541, fax: 6268-8004, e-mail: sources@public.sta.net.cn.

## SHANGHAI TALK 上海趣谈

(Shanghai Qu Tan)
Room 201, 939 Yan'an Xi Lu
延安西路939号201室
Tel/fax: 6252-3914
E-mail: 75223.1646@compuserve.com
This is a monthly newspaper with current information for the expatriate community. Current events are listed and informative

articles keep one up-to-date. Subscribe by contacting them directly or look for complimentary issues in hotel lobbies and reception areas of businesses that cater to foreigners.

## SHANGHAI STAR  上海英文星报

(Shanghai Yingwen Xingbao)
Room 3021, Hengshan Hotel
衡山宾馆3021房间
534 Hengshan Lu  200030  衡山路534号
Tel: 6437-7050, 6437-3021
Fax: 6433-6515
This is a state-owned English language newspaper. You'll find articles on current events in Shanghai and also a directory of upcoming events. Available in hotel lobbies or subscribe to it at any post office. *Shanghai Star* was the first local English language newspaper in China. It was founded in 1992 and is published bi-weekly, on Tuesday and Friday. With a focus on Shanghai and the Yangtze River region, *Shanghai Star* provides a wide coverage of the region's economic and social development.

## THE SHANGHAI TICKET

Tel:  6437-1768 (English and Chinese),
      6233-2250 (Chinese language only)
Coupon Shopper's Club has come out with a new book of coupons that can be redeemed at over 150 locations in Shanghai. The price is RMB100.

## THE WESTERN FOOD LOVER'S GUIDE TO SHANGHAI

Nancy Johnston
Tel/fax: 64312055
Written by a resident expat and available directly from the author, in hotel bookstores or at Glenmore Deli, City Shopping and 1221 The Dining Room. The only complete listing of Shanghai's Western and Southeast Asian restaurants, bakeries, ice cream and grocery stores, and nightclubs, plus a section listing Chinese restaurants that have English-language menus. Portable and informative, with listings given in English, Pinyin and Chinese characters, a definite "must-have". RMB125.

# COUNTRY CLUBS AND
# CITY CLUBS

# CITY CLUBS

## EXECUTIVE CLUB　精英会所

(Jingying Huisuo)

8th Fl, Golden Gate Square　金门广场8楼

1188 Xin Jinqiao Lu near Yu'an Lu

新金桥路1188号近裕安路

Tel: 5899-0011

Fax: 5899-5859

Hours: 9:00 am - 5:00 pm

Tennis, golf driving range, and gym are included in this business club's facilities. Individual memberships are RMB399 annually and corporate memberships are RMB699 annually. The purpose of the club is to facilitate business networking and information exchange.

## G'S CLUB SHANGHAI　知名俱乐部

(Zhiming Julebu)

Club: 41 Hengshan Lu, Xuhui area

衡山路41号(徐家汇)

Sales office: Lane 506/1, Jianguo Xi Lu

建国西路506弄1号

Tel: 6431-1035

Fax: 6471-5519

Hours: 9:00 am - noon,
　　　　2:00 pm - 5:00 pm

This 5-story, members-only club is located in the old French quarter of Shanghai. On the ground floor is the main lobby, the Members' Lounge, the Reading Room, and a restaurant called "The Verandah" which is adjacent to G's private garden and lawn. The lower ground floor houses a health center with a Roman-style indoor swimming pool. One can workout in the gym and use the sauna, steam bath, and hot spa or just relax with a drink at the Health Bar. The first floor serves as a function venue for private banquets, seminars, and conferences while the second floor offers Cantonese, Sichuan, Chaozhou, and Shanghainese cuisine in the Dining Room. The Continental Seafood Restaurant can be found on the third floor along with the cocktail bar, billiard room, movie theater, and private karaoke rooms. The Peninsula Group has been appointed as the club's manager. Memberships are available at US$20,000.

## SHANGHAI AMERICAN CLUB

上海美国俱乐部

(Shanghai Meiguo Julebu)

3rd, 28th, and 29th Fl, Shanghai Bund International Tower　上海滩国际大厦3,28,29楼

99 Huangpu Lu　黄浦路99号

Tel: 6393-2880

Fax: 6393-6766

Hours: 8:30 am - 5:00 pm

Shanghai American Club offers an atmosphere of sophisticated elegance encompassing 4,500 square meters of dining and recreation. Facilities include the American Grill Room for fine dining, a casual cafe and lounge, and a Chinese restaurant. There's also a fitness center, business center, pro shop, library and reading room, and a deli along with a formal lounge that provides entertainment. Membership is by invitation and inquiries concerning membership should be directed to the telephone number above. Members may take advantage of a reciprocal network with more than 100 other clubs run by American Clubs International.

# COUNTRY CLUBS

## AMERICAN CLUB AT SHANGHAI LINKS
(see Shanghai Links Golf and Country Club listed below)

## GRAND SHANGHAI INTERNATIONAL GOLF AND COUNTRY CLUB
大上海国际高尔夫乡村俱乐部
(Dashanghai Guoji Guoerfu Xiangcun Jùlebu)
Shanghai office: Room 306-308, Yixiang Building, 1599 Yan'an Xi Lu  200050
延安西路1599号 怡翔大厦306-308室
Tel: 6210-3350
Fax: 6213-0406
Hours: 8:00 am - 5:00 pm
Country Club: P.O. Box 18, Zhengyi Township, Kunshan City, Jiangsu Province 215347
Tel: (0520)-789-2111
Fax: (0520)-789-2305
Hours: 8:00 am - 5:00 pm
This club is located in Kunshan (昆山), 60 kilometers west of Shanghai and 30 kilometers northeast of Suzhou between Yangcheng Lake and Yangcheng East Lake (home of hairy crabs). It is halfway between Shanghai and Wuxi along the Shanghai - Nanjing Expressway. The Singapore Industrial Township near Suzhou is eight kilometers away. The championship eighteen hole course is a par 72 with a length of 6,420 meters and was designed by the Ronald Fream Golf Plan Design Group. The three-story clubhouse, which is located on the lake, provides such amenities as locker rooms, spa, pool bar, pro shop, restaurants, coffee shop, function rooms, pro shop, swimming pool, tennis courts and driving range. Plans for future development include a five-star hotel, theme park, marina, and residential villas. The driving range is open to the public by appointment for RMB80 per hour, but use of the golf club is restricted to members and their guests. Individual Memberships are being sold for US$39,999

and Corporate Memberships cost US$80,000. Guests must be accompanied by a member and need pay a green fee of RMB410 on weekdays and RMB600 on weekends.

## GRAND YACHT CLUB
淀山湖格兰特国际游艇俱乐部
(Dianshanhu Guoji Youting Jùlebu)
Shanghai office: 1860 Hongqiao Lu
虹桥路1860号
Tel: 6242-3632, 6242-4794
Fax: 6242-4047
Club: Dianshan Lake Tourism Development Area, Dianshan Lake, Kunshan, Jiangsu
Office hours: 8:30 am - 5:30 pm Mon. - Fri., 8:30 am - 11:30 am Sat.
This members-only club has facilities that consist of a clubhouse, swimming pool, restaurants, and bars. Sea Ray motor boats, Hunter, Catalina, and Hobie Cat sailboats, jet skis, water skis, kayaks, surfboards, and parasailing are available for water sports on Dianshan Lake. Marina berths are provided with security and utility lines. Lakefront cabins are provided for overnight stays. A Corporate Membership is US$12,000 with an annual fee of US$600; Individual Transferable Membership is US$8,000 with an annual fee of US$400; Individual Non-transferable Memberships are US$3,000 with an annual fee of US$150.
Hours: 9:00 am - 5:30 pm

## HANGZHOU WEST LAKE INTERNATIONAL GOLF AND COUNTRY CLUB
杭州西湖国际高尔夫乡村俱乐部
(Hangzhou Xihu Guoji Gaoerfu Xiangcun Jùlebu)
200 Zhijiang Dadao   之江大道200号
Tel: (0571) 797-0060
Fax: (0571) 796-1005

Hours: 8:30 am - 5:30 pm

Situated near Hangzhou. The driving range opened in April '97 and nine holes opened in July, '97. A temporary clubhouse is in place. The permanent clubhouse facility will open in approximately two years and will include a swimming pool, tennis, and bowling. Individual memberships are being sold for US$35,000 and corporate memberships for US$70,000.

## JINGLI GOLF ENTERTAINMENT CLUB
上海景丽高尔夫游乐村有限公司

(Shanghai Jingli Gaoerfu Youlecun Youxian Gongsi)

888 Kanglu Gong Lu　康乐公路888号

Jinqiao Development Zone, Pudong 201206

Tel: 5854-0777 x 2107

Fax: 5834-3317

Open 24 hours

This par 3 course with 18 holes that range in length from 80 to 120 yards opened in June, 1996. There is also a 36-bay driving range. The clubhouse is outfitted with an outdoor pool, sauna, gym, billiards, a laser disc projection room, restaurant, beauty salon, and mahjongg room. In addition, there is a fishing pond. Six holiday villas and nineteen guest rooms are also provided. Memberships are sold out, but guests accompanied by members are welcome for RMB200.

## SHANGHAI CHANG YING XINFA GOLF AND BUSINESS CLUB　上海长盈
欣发高尔夫练习场商务俱乐部

(Shanghai Changying Xinfa Gaoerfu Lianxichang Shangwu Jülebu)

Club: 551 Yanggao Lu (Pudong)

浦东扬高路551号

Facilities include dining hall, cafe, bar, bathing room, sauna, massage, shops, golf practice fields, business center, game room, table tennis, tea room, and night-club which are open every day.

## SHANGHAI COUNTRY CLUB
上海国际高尔夫乡村俱乐部

(Shanghai Guoji Gaoerfu Xiangcun Jülebu)

Qinpu Zhujiajiao　青浦 朱家角

Qingpu County 201713　青浦镇

Tel: 5972-8111, 5972-9229

Fax: 5972-8520

Hours: 7:00 am - 5:00 pm

Course Architect: Robert Trent Jones Jr.

This par 72, 18-hole golf course opened in 1991. Included is a 3-hole practice course, a driving range, and three tennis courts. The main clubhouse has a restaurant, bar, billiards room, library, and pro shop. Another building houses ten guest rooms, another restaurant, a swimming pool, and mahjongg rooms. The last memberships were sold for US$150,000 (cor-porate). One must now buy from established members seeking to sell. Green fees for a guest accompanied by a resident member are RMB450 on weekdays and RMB700 on weekends and holidays. If a guest is accom-panied by a non-resident member, the green fee is RMB700 on weekdays and RMB900 on weekends and holidays. Introduced guests pay RMB950 on weekdays and RMB1,150 on weekends and holidays. Each person, including members, pays an additional RMB200 general fee. Reservations for play must be made by a member, either by phone or fax.

## SHANGHAI EAST ASIA GOLF CLUB
上海东亚高尔夫球俱乐部有限公司

(Shanghai Dongya Gaoerfuqiu Jülebu Youxian Gongsi)

135 Jianguo Xi Lu　建国西路135号

Tel: 6433-1351, 6433-1198

Fax: 6433-1296

Hours: 6:00 pm - 11:00 pm Mon - Sat
　　　 1:00 pm - 11:00 pm Sun

This 2-story public driving range at Luwan Stadium has 46 bays, open from 6:00 pm to 11:00 pm. Also included are tennis courts, a pro shop, sauna, bar, and restaurant. Non-members may use the facilitites by paying an entrance fee of RMB100, but memberships are available for RMB6,800 per year, for three years at RMB12,800, or for five years at RMB16,800. Transferable life memberships run RMB46,800 for individuals and RMB98,300 for a corporate membership with two nominees. Members pay RMB20 for a bucket of 50 balls, while non-members must pay RMB30. Half hour golf lessons run RMB50 for members and RMB60 for non-members. Golf clubs rental runs RMB8 for members and RMB10 for non-members. Carpark, sauna, shower, and locker facilities are free to members.

## SHANGHAI GOLF CLUB
上海高尔夫俱乐部
(Shanghai Gaoerfu Jülebu)
12 Jiadingqu Tanghangzhen Shuangtangcun
嘉定区唐行镇双塘村12号
Tel: 5995-0111
Fax: 5995 0222
Hours: 7:30 am - 5:00 pm Tue - Fri
        7:00 am - 6:00 pm Sat - Sun
This 18-hole, par 72 golf club is located in Jiading, 40 minutes north of Shanghai's city center. Facilities include a restaurant, Japanese baths, gym, tennis, swimming pool, massage, and guest rooms. Individual memberships sell for US$53,000 and corporate memberships sell for US$106,000.

## SHANGHAI GRAND CITY GOLF CLUB
上海大都会国际高尔夫俱乐部
(Shanghai Daduhui Guoji Gaoerfu Jülebu)
Club: Qibao 5188 Huaxing Road, 201101
七宝 华星路5188号
Office: 11D, 686 Gubei Road 200335
古北路686号11D
Tel: 6478-9251
Fax: 6419-3892
Hours: 6:00 am - 10:00 pm
Located on Huaxing Road in Qibao, 4 km from the Hongqiao International Airport, this golf course offers nine holes and a driving range. There are also a wide variety of other activities including an indoor/outdoor pool, gym, tennis courts, library, game rooms, and billiards.

## SHANGHAI GRASSLANDS GOLF CLUB
上海草原高尔夫俱乐部有限公司
(Shanghai Caoyuan Gaoerfu Jülebu Youxian Gongsi)
1366 Huqingping Gong Lu Highway
青浦县徐泾318国道1366号
Xujing, Qingpu County 201702
Tel: 5976-6666 x 3304
Fax: 5976-7676
Hours: 10:00 am - 10:00 pm
Located at the beginning of highway #318, 5 km from the Hongqiao International Airport, this facility includes a 90-bay golf driving range, a 9-hole putting green, pro shop, coffee shop, and a play center with a video arcade for children. Plans for the future include an Olympic-size swimming pool, and 18-lane bowling alley, tennis and badminton courts, billiard room, sauna, massage, steam rooms, beauty salon, cinema, restaurants, pubs, business center, and holiday villas. Memberships continue to be available and individual memberships begin at US$16,000. However, the driving range is open to the public for a RMB100 user fee and RMB50 for 50 balls.

## SHANGHAI HONGQIAO GOLF COURSE 上海虹桥高尔夫球场
(Shanghai Hongqiao Gaoerfu Qiuchang)
Office: Shanghai International Trade Center, Room 1906 上海国贸中心1906室
2200 Yan'an Xi Lu 延安西路2200号
Fax: 6275-2789
Club: 567 Hongxu Lu
虹许路567号 近吴中路
Tel: 6406-5606, 6401-6666
This 9-hole course is located in the western area of the city and will have a clubhouse

## Tianma Country Club
### 天馬鄉村俱樂部

---

# International Golf Community

---

---

## Tianma Country Club

Tianma Country Club will incorporate a championship 27-hole golf course, country clubhouse, athletic clubhouse and lodging. Professional management by the world's leading sports management firm, International Management Group (IMG), ensures a world-class golfing experience and an international atmoshpere the entire family can enjoy.

---

## Tianma Villas

Tianma Villas offers a residential lifestyle that is unique in Asia. Designed by Klages Carter Vail of California, each home is a perfect blend of Chinese Courtyard style with western lifestyle and interior design.With an American Elementary School on-site and just 35 minutes from the Hong Qiao International Airport, Tianma is sure to become Shanghai's benchmark in suburban living.

IMG
*Golf Management*

For more information, please contact:
Tianma Country Club and Villas
Tel: (8621)6268-5500   Fax: (8621)6268-2525

with tennis, swimming pool, and a restaurant. The price of membership is yet to be determined as the club will not open until 1999.

## SHANGHAI LINKS GOLF AND COUNTRY CLUB
## 上海林克司高尔夫乡村俱乐部

(Shanghai Linkesi Gaoerfu Xiangcun Jülebu)
Tianxu Township, Sanjia Bay, East China Sea, Pudong
浦东三甲港近东海
Tel: 5882-2700
Fax: 5882-9018
This club is now selling memberships. The course consists of a 165-acre, 18-hole championship Jack Nicklaus Signature Design Course approximately 7,100 yards (6,490 meters) long with ocean views and breezes, a driving range, and multiple tees. The property will be professionally landscaped with a state-of-the-art irrigation and drainage system. Over 4,000 mature trees and 6,000 other trees will be transported to the site. There will be two separate clubhouses, a 20,000 square foot clubhouse for the exclusive use of Golf Course members as well as an 80,000 square foot American Club at Shanghai Links that will offer squash, bowling, tennis, indoor and outdoor swimming pools, and a host of other fitness facilities with professional expatriate instructors and trainers. A Western-style housing community will also be built on the site. The current selling price of golf memberships is US$70,000 for individual memberships and US$120,000 for a corporate membership with two nominees. Spouses and children under 21 are also allowed privileges. Membership inquiries for the American Club at Shanghai Links and for golf membership should be directed to the numbers above.

## SHANGHAI RIVIERA GOLF RESORT
## 上海富升体育有限公司

(Shanghai Fusheng Tiyu Youxian Gongsi)
Jiading, Nanxiang, Xiang Er Village
嘉定 南翔 翔利路
Lots 8, 17, and 18
Shanghai 201802
Tel: 5912-6888 x 129
Fax: 5912-9712
Hours: 8:00 am - 6:00 pm Tue - Fri
7:00 am - 6:00 pm Sat - Sun
Shanghai office: 128 Tongren Lu 200040
铜仁路128号
Tel: 6247-5470
Fax: 6247-9573
Hong Kong office: DC Club International Limited, 7th Fl, Southwest Tower, Convention Plaza, 1 Harbour Road, Wanchai, Hong Kong
Tel: (852) 2829-7968
Fax: (852) 2829-7905
This club is located northwest of Shanghai In Jiading. Currently offers a 48-bay driving range, clubhouse, and an 18-hole, 3,788-yard floodlit course. Facilities also include tennis and swimming. Shuttle buses are available to and from Shanghai Centre daily, and to and from the Yangtze Hotel on weekends.

## SHANGHAI SILPORT GOLF AND COUNTRY CLUB
## 淀山湖(旭宝)国际高尔夫俱乐部

(Dianshanhu Guoji Gaoerfu Jülebu)
Dianshan Lake Township, Kunshan District
昆山，淀山湖镇
(Kunshan, Dianshan Huzhen)
Club tel: (0520) 748-111
Club fax: (0520) 748-2544, 748-1970
Hours: 6:30 am - dusk
Located on Dianshan Lake west of Qingpu, this 27-hole golf course designed by Bobby J. Martin is newly completed. There is a driving range and the clubhouse has Chinese and Western restaurants, locker rooms, sauna,

coffee shop, pro shop, swimming pool, media center, and suites. Individual memberships with two nominated members go for US$56,000 and corporate memberships with two nominated members go for US$120,000.

## SHANGHAI SUN ISLAND INTERNATIONAL CLUB
上海太阳岛国际高尔夫俱乐部
(Shanghai Taiyangdao Guojl Gaoerfu Jülebu)
Sun Island, Shenxiang, Qingpu County
201714 青浦县 沈巷镇
Tel: 5983-0888
Fax: 5983-1625
Open 24 hours
Located on an island at the junction of the Mao, Taipu and Huangpu Rivers, about 35 minutes southwest of Hongqiao Airport. The 18-hole course was designed by Nelson Wright Haworth Golf Architects. The 30-bay driving range is unique in that the greens are on a separate island. The clubhouse contains restaurants, a pub, individual private karaoke rooms, pro shop, business center, sauna, beauty salon, shops, horseback riding, swimming pool (contained within a large water amusement park), and tennis courts. Villas are available. Memberships are currently available for US$54,000 (Individual). Guests may be introduced by members via fax. Guest green fees are RMB400 on weekdays and RMB800 on weekends.

## SHANGHAI TIANMA COUNTRY CLUB
上海天马乡村俱乐部
(Shanghai Tianma Xiangcun Jülebu)
#1 Tianma Shan Precinct, Shanghai
Songjiang Xian 201603
Tianma Country Club is located at the foot of Sheshan (She Mountain) in Songjiang County approximately 30 minutes southwest of Shanghai. This 27-hole course will have a minimum of nine holes open for play in October, 1998 along with the golf and athletic clubhouse. An additional country club

facility will be added along with villas and, possibly a satellite campus of the Shanghai American School for grades Pre-K through 5. The golf community will also have a medical clinic on site. Club facilities will be managed by International Management Group (IMG). As of now memberships are available at the founding level. For additional information concerning membership, please contact 6268-5500 (telephone) or 6268-2525 (fax).

## SHANGHAI TOMSON GOLF COURSE
汤臣高尔夫上海有限公司
(Tangchen Gaoerfu Shanghai Youxian Gongsi)
1 Longdong Lu, Pudong 浦东龙东大道1号
Tel: 5833-8888
Fax: 5833-9698
Hours: 7:00 am - 10:00 pm
This is a new club that held its soft opening in October 1996 and its official opening in May 1997. This 18-hole course, designed by Shunsuke Kato, has a clubhouse that includes restaurants, gym and sauna, bowling, billiards, function rooms, business center, tennis courts, and indoor/outdoor swimming pools. The course includes a driving range. Residential villas are also available on-site. Membership is required for the golf course, but the driving range is open to the public for RMB200. Memberships presently are US$100,000. Guests of members pay RMB830 as a green fee on weekdays and RMB1,130 on weekends.

## SHANGHAI WESTERN GOLF COUNTRY CLUB 西上海高尔夫乡村俱乐部
(Xi Shanghai Gaoerfu Xiangcun Jülubu)
Office: 5th Fl, 89 Taixing Lu
泰兴路89号5楼
Tel: 6318-4642
Club: Songjiang County, Che Dun Zhen city, near highway #320
松江县车墩镇近320国道

Tel:  5760-1494

Hours: closed Tue - Wed

   8:00 am - 6:00 pm Mon, Thu, Fri

   6:30 am - 7:30 pm Sat - Sun

This 18-hole course has a clubhouse which contains a gym, tennis courts, a bowling alley, business center, swimming pool, and barbecue facilities. A fishing lake is also available with its own marina. Individual memberships are sold for RMB100,000 annually and corporate memberships are available for RMB120,000 annually. The site also has condominiums and villas.

Following page:
*Nanjing Lu, Shanghai's main street, where neon signs advertising Chinese-made goods compete for space alongside those from Hong Kong and the West.*

# SIGHTSEEING AND LEISURE ACTIVITIES

Expatriates in Shanghai seem to spend most of their time working, either in the office or at home.

This is most likely due to a combination of business demands and the lack of tempting distractions. Available entertainment for newcomers includes sightseeing and exploration for purposes of satisfying the initial curiosity about a new place. Long-timers need to be a bit more resourceful, and have been by creating their own group activities and events.

Perhaps it is possible after all, to discover an activity or two that encourages one to turn off the computer and have some well-deserved fun.

# MOVIES, MUSIC, AND STAGE PRESENTATIONS

## Movies

English-language films are screened only at one or two places in Shanghai. However, several foreign-backed multiplex cinemas are in the planning stages, so hopefully the selection and screening frequency of Western films will continue to improve.

### FRENCH CINEMA 法国电影

(Faguo Dianying)
Alliance Francaise de Shanghai
法语培训中心
297 Wusong Lu 吴淞路297号
Tel: 6357-5388
Fax: 6325-1183
Films in French with English and/or Chinese subtitles are shown on Fridays at 6:30 pm.

### GERMAN FILM NIGHT 德国电影

(Deguo Dianying)
German Consulate General 德国领事馆
181 Yongfu Lu 永福路181号
Tel: 6433-6953
Call the Consulate at 6433-6951 for details concerning their weekly Wednesday evening German-language movie presentation. Films begins at 7:00 pm in the German Consulate auditorium. Programs can also be picked up at the cultural section and can be seen posted on the bulletin board in front of the consulate.

### HOLLYWOOD WONDERS
平安动感电影

(Ping'an Donggan Dianying)
1193 Nanjing Xi Lu 南京西路1193号
Tel: 6279-0827
Hours: noon - midnight
Admission price: RMB15–25
Experience thrill rides here through simulation. There are 17 films in stock that run about 10 minutes each. Upon entering the theater, one must watch an introductory film warning that children under 122 cm, pregnant women, and those suffering from heart disease or high blood pressure should not partake. Seats consist of six convertible cars that hold four persons, and move and rock. Films shown include "Dracula's Haunted House", "Cosmic Pinball", "Space Race", car racing, motor-biking, and high-speed trains.

### JUDY'S MOVIES 杰迪录像馆

(Jiedi Luxiangguan)
176 Maoming Nan Lu 茂名南路176号
Tel: 6473-1417
Judy's Too shows two films every Sunday at 7:30 pm and at 9:30 pm on its large-screen projector.

### MARINE MOVIE NIGHT
玛林家庭电影院

(Malin Jiating Dianyingyuan)
Marine House
17th Fl, Shanghai Centre West Tower
上海商城西峰17楼
For movie schedule, call 6279-8036
The U.S. Marines show recently released films every Friday night at 7:00 pm. Doors open at 6:00 pm and seats are limited. Passport is required for admission.

### PARADISE CINEMA 永乐宫

(Yongle Gong)
308 Anfu Lu 安福路308号
Tel: 6431-2961
Hours: 8:00 am - midnight
Call the theater for a schedule of films. Foreign films are shown here in their original languages with Chinese subtitles, much to the delight of expats.

*The following theatres screen Chinese-language films only:*

## CATHAY CINEMA 国泰电影院
(Guotai Dianyingyuan)
870 Huaihai Zhong Lu 淮海中路870号
Tel: 6473-0415

## CHINA THEATER 中国大戏院
(Zhongguo Daxiyuan)
704 Niuzhuang Lu 牛庄路704号
Tel: 6351-7839

## DAWUTAI THEATER 人民大舞台
(Renmin Dawutai)
663 Jiujiang Lu 九江路663号
Tel: 6322-6068

## GRAND CINEMA 大光明电影院
(Daguangming Dianyingyuan)
216 Nanjing Xi Lu 南京西路216号
Tel: 6327-3399

## LANXIN THEATER 兰心大戏院
(Lanxin Daxiyuan)
57 Maoming Nan Lu 茂名南路57号
Tel: 6253-0788

## SHANGHAI PEOPLE'S ART THEATER 上海人民艺术剧院
(Shanghai Renmin Yishu Juyuan)
284 Anfu Lu 安福路284号
Tel: 6433-0069

## YIFU CINEMA 逸夫舞台
(Yifu Wutai)
701 Fuzhou Lu 福州路701号
Tel: 6322-6270, 6322-5487, 6351-4668

# Music

## CHAMBER MUSIC 静安室内音乐会
(Jing'an Shinei Yinyuehui)
San Diego Hall, Jing'an Hotel 静安宾馆
(Jing'an Bin Guan)
370 Huashan Lu, 200040 华山路370号
Tel: 6248-1888 x 617
Fax: 6248-2657
This weekly chamber concert is held on Friday evenings at 8:00 pm. Admission is RMB20.

## HUJU, BEIJING, AND SHAOXING OPERA 逸夫舞台
Yifu Theater (Yifu Wutai)
701 Fuzhou Lu 福州路701号
Tel: 6322-6270, 6322-5487, 6351-4668
Opera is performed at this theater on a regular basis. Call for upcoming schedules.

## JINJIANG CHAMBER MUSIC SERIES 缪斯音乐行
(Miaosi Yinyuehang)
8 Fenyang Lu 汾阳路8号
Tel: 6433-7336
A different collection of classical music is presented each Friday at 8:00 pm.

## OLD JAZZ BAND 老年爵士乐团
(Laonian Jueshi Yuetuan)
Peace Hotel 和平饭店
(Heping Fandian)
20 Nanjing Dong Lu 200002
南京东路20号
Tel: 6321-6888 x 6210
Fax: 6329-0300
Hours: 8:00 pm - 11:00 pm, nightly

# Stage presentations

## BALLROOM DANCE LESSONS
Ballroom Dance School
Jingan Cultural Palace　静安区文化馆
(Jinganqu Wenhuaguan)
459 Wulumuqi Bei Lu　乌鲁木齐北路459号
Tel: 6248-4420 (Cao Hong)
You can take lessons from beginning to advanced here, and even enter competitions. Classes in the Waltz, Tango, Quick Step, Fox Trot, Cha Cha, Rumba, Paso Doble, Samba, and Jive are available.

## CHINESE OPERA　逸夫舞台
(Yifu Wutai)
701 Fuzhou Lu　福州路701号
Tel: 6351-4668
Performance: Every Sunday, 1:30 pm
Ticket price: RMB5 - 20
Students from the Shanghai School of Music and Opera perform various operatic selections. The same location also hosts professional performances of Beijing Huju and Shaoxing Opera. Contact the box office for scheduled performances.

## SHANGHAI ACROBATIC CIRCUS
上海杂技团表演
(Shanghai Zajituan Biaoyan)
Shanghai Centre Theater　上海商城
1376 Nanjing Xi Lu　南京西路1376号
Tel: 6279-8600 x 6744
Show from 7:30 pm - 9:00 pm
Price: RMB 60, 45, or 30 depending on location of seating. Check which evening the circus is scheduled either by telephone or by stopping at the Shanghai Centre Box Office box office on the street in front of Shanghai Centre. Schedule changes monthly due to other events at the theater. On average, there are about twenty performances a month. The show is worth seeing and includes acrobats, jugglers, contortionists, and more.

## SHANGHAI CENTRE THEATER
上海商城剧场
(Shanghai Shangcheng Juchang)
1376 Nanjing Xi Lu　南京西路1376号
Tel: 6279-8663
The Shanghai Centre Theater Management Office can be reached at 6279-8614. Presentations scheduled at this venue range from "Broadway" type shows, concerts, and dramas, more frequently in Chinese, but sometimes in English. Upcoming events are usually listed in *Shanghai Talk*, *Shanghai Star*, *Culture and Recreation*, and Shanghai Centre's newsletter. Tickets may be purchased at the Box Office in front of Shanghai Centre on Nanjing Lu. In the spring of 1997, season subscriptions became available and the line-up of shows was greatly enhanced. Stars signed up for the '97-'98 season included Joni Mitchell, Luther Johnson, Coco Montoya, The Nylons, and Todd Rundgren to name a few. One cannot attend any of these shows without a season subscription. Prices for individuals run RMB800 - 5,000.

## SHANGHAI GRAND THEATRE ARTS CENTER　上海大剧院艺术中心
(Shanghai Dajuyuan Yishu Zhongxin)
190 Huangpi Bei Lu　黄陂北路190号
Tel: 6387-5480
Tel/fax: 6372-8141
Don't head here yet! This magnificent theater is still under construction. It was designed by French architect Jean-Marie Charpentier and is located just north of People's Square. With a seating capacity of more than 1800, it is designed to meet demands for performances of world class ballet, opera, and orchestra. There is also a smaller theater that seats 300 that will function as a venue for chamber concerts and dramatic presentations.

## BOWLING 保龄球

(Baolingqiu)

Bowling leagues are gradually being formed through some of the clubs and organizations in town, but if you're not involved with organized bowling there are still plenty of bowling alleys where you can have a good time with friends. One, with automatic score keeping is at the Exhibition Center (on the Nanjing Lu side) and others are at the Cypress Hotel, Galaxy Hotel, Huating Hotel, Equatorial Hotel, and New Town Mansion. More seem to be opening every week as this sport becomes increasingly popular. Following are a few more bowling centers:

### BEI GONG BOWLING CO.
北宫保龄球馆有限公司
818 Linten Lu 临汾路818号
Tel: 5681-3823

### BUCKINGHAM BOWLING CENTER
白金汉保龄球馆有限公司
825 Dingxi Lu 定西路825号
Tel: 6281-9988

### GUO XIN BOWLING CO.
国信保龄球馆有限公司
849 Zhongshan Xi Lu 中山西路 849号
Tel: 6270-1210

### JIN GANG BOWLING CLUB
金港保龄球俱乐部有限公司
860 Caoyang Lu 曹杨路860号
Tel: 6243-8818 x 3043

### LAI LAI BOWLING CENTER
来来保龄球健身中心有限公司
765 Wuyi Lu 武夷路 765号
Tel: 6234-5657

### LUCKY BOWLING 鸿运保龄球馆
1127 Kongjiang Lu 控江路1127号
Tel: 6570-3328,29,30

### NAN YANG BOWLING CLUB
南洋保龄娱乐有限公司
295 Zhongshan Nan Er Lu
中山南二路295号
Tel: 6416-4755

### QI QI QI BOWLING CLUB
七七七保龄球馆
777 Dongchang Zhi Lu 东长治路777号
Tel: 6535-8866

### SHANGHAI BAO MA CLUB
宝马保龄球娱乐有限公司
688 Pudong Chuanbei Gong Lu
浦东川北公路688号
Tel: 5892-6275

### SHANGHAI HEAVENLY DRAGON BOWLING RECREATIONAL CO.
天上神龙保龄球娱乐有限公司
271 Weifang Lu 维坊路271号
Tel: 5820-6736, 5820-5843

### SHANGHAI LI ZHONG BOWLING CO.
利众保龄球有限公司
Room 201, 425 Yanping Lu
延平路 425号201室
Tel: 6267-3320

### SHANGHAI HIGH POINT SPORTS
高点保龄球馆
456 Dongjiangwan Lu 东江湾路456号
Tel: 5671-1111

### SHANGHAI NEW PALACE ALLEY BOWLING 新皇宫保龄球馆
1333 Nanjing Xi Lu 南京西路1333号
Tel: 6247-4723 , 6247-7530

## SILVER STAR BOWLING CLUB
新银城保龄球馆

299 Fahuazhen Lu　法华镇路299号
Tel: 6280-8001

## XUJIAHUI BOWLING CENTER
徐家汇保龄球馆有限公司

5th Fl, 205 Yude Lu　裕德路205号5楼
Tel: 6468-1771

## ZHENG DA BOWLING CO.
正大保龄球运动馆有限公司

5th Fl, 183 Jiadingqu, Meiyuan Lu
嘉定梅园路183号5楼
Tel: 55991-1166

## CRICKET　板球
(Banqiu)

Tel/fax: 6212-7477 (Joan Taylor, Secretary)
Tel: 6279-7161　Fax: 6279-7160
(Richard Graham, Captain)

Cricket was revived in Shanghai in 1994 by Richard Graham and a group of multinational enthusiasts. The first match in almost fifty years was held in November 1994 against a team from Hong Kong (Craigengower Cricket Club). The Shanghai Cricket Club (SCC) visited Hong Kong in 1995 and held its first game against Beijing in 1996. SCC reached the final of the Beijing International 6's in October 1996. SCC holds regular sets at the Xingguo Guest House (Xingguo Binguan) 兴国宾馆, 72 Xingguo Lu　200052　兴国路72号 and games from time to time (including winter indoor games) at the Meilong Ground, (750 Lao Humin Lu　老沪闵路750号, 10 minutes south of the Huating Hotel) of the Shanghai Sports Institute, tel: 6477-0058 (上海体育运动技术学院). The main season is late August - early November. Enthusiasm, not skill or experience, is the qualification of most, and all ages are welcome.

## DARTS LEAGUE　标枪
(Biaoqiang)

Held once a week on Tuesdays at 8:30 pm at rotating locations - Ch Euro's, Churchill's, Green Valley Villas, Jurassic Pub, Huating Hotel, Tequila Mama, Judy's, Malone's, Shanghai Sally's, the Dragon Pub, the Sofitel Hotel, and the Novotel. Each of these sponsors has ten members on a team. To join, contact one of the locations above for more details or Wolfgang Simdon at 5662-5804, x 228.

## EAST DISCO ICE SKATING CLUB
东方迪斯科溜冰俱乐部

(Dongfang Disike Liubing Jülebu)
777 Dongfang Lu　东方路777号
Tel: 5888-1732
Hours: 11.00 am - 10:00 pm
RMB9 per hour, RMB11 per hour after 6:00 pm.

## HASH HOUSE HARRIERS　健身俱乐部
(Jianshen Jülebu )

This group meets every Sunday at 3:00 pm in winter and 4:00 pm in summer to run a course that's laid out in different areas of the city each week by a rotating group volunteer, called a "hare". Anyone who would like to run or walk the course with the group is welcome. There are presently about fifty participants each week. The idea originated with British soldiers in Malaysia, circa the 1930s, who, for something to do, ran through the jungle to another British camp known as "The Hash House". Many cities in the world now have a group of Harriers. After the run, there is socializing over well-earned drinks and dinner. For information, you may contact Brad by telephone at 6219-2906.

## THE HONG KONG ASSOCIATION

Weekly tennis, golf, badminton, and soccer games. To participate, call Lucy Wang at 6352-3453.

## KICK BOXING

D.D.'s Personal Club
387 Panyu Lu　番禺路387号
8:00 pm - 9:30 pm, Monday and Thursday
Tel: 6281-5639 (Freddy) or
　　　6406-8674 (Mark)
Classes for beginners.

## LASER TAG

People's Park　人民公园
Daily until 10:00 pm
Huxi Gongren Wenhua Gong
沪西工人文化宫
71 Wuning Lu　武宁路71号
Tel: 6244-0046
Daily until 10:00 pm
Teams battle each other with laser guns in indoor arenas.

## NETBALL

Games are played every Saturday morning. Call Alison Rigby at 6433-2546.

## PAINTBALL

Zhongshan Park　中山公园
780 Changning Lu　长宁路780号
Tel: 6210-5805
Hours: 8:30 am - 11:00 pm
Price: RMB20 adults, RMB10 student ID holders.
Weicheng Paintball Shooting Center provides camouflage outfits for team or one-on-one battle.

## POOL　台球

(Taiqiu)
Shanghai Sally's　故乡餐厅
(Guxiang Canting)
4 Xiangshan Lu　香山路4号
Tel: 6327-1859 or 6375-3348 (Monica Zhou)
Tournaments are held twice a week on Sundays at 3:00 pm and Mondays at 8:30 pm. Also see the public billiard halls listed below.

## SOCCER (FOOTBALL)　足球

(Zuqiu)
The Jing'an Ball Games Hall at 681 Weihai Lu is the indoor venue for the Wednesday evening matches from 6:30 pm til 8:00 pm. If that's not enough, play again on Saturday from noon - 3:00 pm, outdoors, at the Shanghai East Asia Golf Club, 139 Jianguo Lu. Contact Tom Bus at 6469-7993 or Jan Berges at 1391916504.

## SOFTBALL　垒球

(Leiqiu)
Just show up or call China Jim at 6279-4336 for current information. Participants meet at Shanghai Centre, 1376 Nanjing Lu at 10:30 am Sunday mornings to catch a bus to the field. Extra gloves and equipment are available. The spring schedule runs from March until June and play resumes in the fall. The games end at about 2:00 pm and then everyone is invited to go to a sponsoring bar for free hors d'oeurves and a drink.

## SQUASH

Telephone Mark Thomas at 6415-5588 to obtain schedule details.

## TENNIS 网球

(Wangqiu)

Public courts are not yet plentiful in Shanghai, though there are a few. Some of the major hotels have courts, such as the Portman Ritz-Carlton, JC Mandarin, Garden Hotel, Huating Hotel, Hilton, Novotel, Evergreen, et al. The new Regal International East Asia Hotel has the best international-calibre tennis complex in the city, but it is members-only. Many of the newer housing developments such as Windsor Park, Green Valley Villas, Sassoon Park, Rose Garden, and Vanke City Garden, have courts as well, but you must be accompanied by a resident to play there. Still, there are other options.

### CHANGNING COURTS 长宁网球场

Huashan Lu, 1038 Lane, No. 173
华山路1038弄173号
Tel: 6252-4436
Three older, slightly worn red clay courts. Call for reservations, especially on weekends. RMB40 per hour.

### CHANGNING XIANXIA TENNIS CLUB
长宁仙霞网球中心

1885 Hongqiao Lu (near Xijiao Sports Center)
虹桥路1885号
Tel: 6262-8327
A new group of lighted outdoor public courts. Eight courts, including one stadium court. Hourly rates: RMB50 weekday days, RMB80 weekday nights; weekend rate are RMB80 and RMB100 respectively.

### FUXING LU COURTS 复兴路体育场
1380 Fuxing Zhong Lu 复兴中路1380号
Tel: none (reserve courts in person)
Four hard courts. The Shanghai professional teams work out here on weekdays from 9am to 3pm, but courts are available between noon and 1pm. RMB50 per hour.

### SHANGHAI INTERNATIONAL TENNIS CENTER 上海国际网球中心
Regal International East Asia Hotel
516 Hengshan Lu 衡山路516号
Tel: 6415-5588
Eight outdoor lighted courts (including one stadium court) and two indoor courts, clubhouse, VIP spectator tower. Memberships are US$24,000.

### WAIGAOQIAO XUHUI CLUB
外高桥徐汇俱乐部

85 Hengshan Lu 衡山路85号
Tel: 6437-2847
A new complex located at a metro stop with six outdoor lighted courts and two indoor courts and clubhouse. Open to the public. RMB50 per hour.

### XIJIAO SPORTS CENTER 西郊体育中心
1921 Hongqiao Lu 虹桥路1921号
Tel: 62198800 x 575
State-owned club with two indoor and four outdoor courts, clubhouse, fitness center, restaurants and bowling. Hourly rates: RMB50 weekday days, RMB80 weekday nights; weekend rates are RMB80 and RMB100 respectively.

## TOUCH RUGBY  橄榄球

(Ganlanqiu)
Jincai Middle School
2788 Yanggao Lu at Yuanshen Lu, Pudong
杨高路2788号 近源深路(浦东)
Games are held every Saturday at 3:30 pm.
Telephone Andrew Cox at 6219-1219 or
Mark Thomas at 6415-5588 for additional
information.

## VOLLEYBALL  排球

(Paiqiu)
You can find a game every Tuesday at 6:30
pm at the Jingan Ball Games Hall at 681
Weihai Lu. Telephone Kevin Cookman for
details at 6257-9218.

# Shooting Clubs

## PUDONG SHOOTING CLUB
浦东射击场

(Pudong Shejichang)
Hunan Highway End
沪南公路到底南汇县滨海旅游渡假区
Tel: 5805-8262
Hours: 8:00 am - 5:00 pm

## SHANGHAI SAN HE SHOOTING CLUB
上海三和射击场

(Shanghai Sanhe Shejichang)
1330 Hami Lu  哈密路1330号
Tel: 6259-3562
Hours: 8:00 am - 4:00 pm

# Public Billiard Halls

## FORUM SNOOKER CLUB
富临桌球俱乐部

(Fulin Zhuoqiu Jülebu)
Floors 2 - 6, Jinjia Business Building
776 Huaihai Zhong Lu   200020
淮海中路776号
Tel: 6431-6667
Hours: 10:00 am - 6:00 am
This club is on five carpeted floors and has a
tournament stage. This is so far the newest
and nicest club in town. There is a Japanese
restaurant, Kanetanaka. Prices start at RMB48
per hour. White Gold Card membership is
also available for Chinese citizens or
foreigners who are 18 or older for a fee of
RMB3,800 per year. White Gold Membership entitles one to a pool cue and case, a
bottle of Famous Grouse Gold Reserve, a
watch, RMB1,000 credit, and a 10% discount on food.

## QIANG SHENG BILLIARDS CENTER
强生经济发展公司

(Qiangsheng Jingji Fazhan Gongsi)
920 Nanjing Xi Lu  南京西路920号
Tel: 6258-0000
Open 24 hours
This club is a little older and consists of two
floors. Six private rooms are available.
Noodles are available. No smoking allowed.

## SHIYUN BILLIARDS ENTERTAINMENT CENTER  时运购物城

(Shiyun Gouwucheng)
988 Suzhou Bei Lu (北苏州路988号) just north
of Suzhou Creek
Tel: 6306-0264
Hours: 8:30 am - 6:00 pm
There are more American pool tables here
than at the other locations, along with table
tennis facilities and an Asian Food Court
located beneath the club. RMB18 per hour.

# Theme Parks

## AMERICAN DREAM PARK
美国梦幻乐园

(Meiguo Menghuan Leyuan)
4498 Cao'an Lu 漕安路4498号
Tel: 6279-8928
Hours: 9:00 am - Closing time varies with the season.
Admission: Adults: RMB100, children and senior citizens: RMB80. Group and student rates are available.

This new theme park is located about 30 minutes northwest of the city off the Jiading Highway. The park contains five theme areas: Main Street USA, USA Today, Children's Treasure Island, American Heritage Area, and The Wild West. Rides include a log flume (expect to get wet), a roller coaster called the Hurricane, a parachute ride, a swinging pirate ship, a ferris wheel, and a tilt -a- whirl. There are also many games of skill, a haunted house, and a 360-seat theater showing Chinese history films. There are several shows such as medieval jousting, cowboys on horses, magic, and water-skiing. There is also a children's play area and several restaurants.

## EUROPEAN THEME PARK
欧罗巴世界乐园

(Ouluoba Shijie Leyuan)
Sheshan, Songjiang 佘山镇
Tel: 5765-1582
Admission: RMB30, children under 1.2 meters tall: RMB20
Hours: 8:00 am - 4:00 pm
A Magic Castle is one of the attractions in this park where the Tenglong Magic Troupe provides a variety of illusions and tricks. You can also use row boats, play laser tag, and visit a house run totally via robotics. A Chinese restaurant and hotel are available. Double rooms at the hotel run RMB130.

## FUNDAZZLE 翻斗乐

(Fandoule)
780 Changning Lu in Zhongshan Park
长宁路780号中山公园内
Tel: 6210-7388, 6210-7288
Hours: 9:00 am - 5:00 pm
Tickets: RMB25
This building in Zhongshan Park has ball pens, giant tubes for children to crawl around in, and jungle gyms. Supervision is provided and fast-food is available.

## GLOBAL PARADISE 古琦园

(Guqiyuan)
Located in Nanxiang County (南翔镇), off the Hujia Highway, this 1,200 hectare site has recreations of Mount Rushmore, Niagara Falls, an Egyptian pyramid, a Thai Buddha, a Russian church, and a replica of the Grand Canyon with man-made, temperature-controlled lake for swimming, water-skiing, and parasailing. Thirty-six famous sites are planned in all. The park cost RMB500,000,000 to build and can accommodate up to 30,000 visitors daily. It was developed by a joint-venture comprised of ten mainland Chinese companies.

## HUAHUA LONG WATER AMUSEMENT PARK 长风公园花花龙水上乐园

(Changfeng Gongyuan Huahualong Shuishang Leyuan)
Changfeng Park 长风公园
189 Daduhe Lu 大渡河路189号
Tel: 6260-4905
Hours: 9:00 am - 4:30 pm

## JINJIANG JOYLAND 锦江乐园

(Jinjiang Leyuan)
201 Hongmei Lu 虹梅路201号
Tel: 6436-4956
Hours: 8:30 am - 4:00 pm

## JINJIANG WATERWORLD
### 锦江水上世界
(Jinjiang Shuishang Shijie)
Sheshan National Holiday Resort
Songjiang County
This park features a long, man-made stream which winds through scenic areas, a musical fountain lighted with lasers, a water screen that can be used to show films, and other recreational activities.

## JIANGWAN WAVE SWIMMING POOL
### 江湾造波游泳池
(Jiangwan Zaobo Youyongzhi)
346 Guohe Lu  国和路346号
Tel: 6548-1789
Hours: 9:00 am - 7:00 pm

## SHANGHAI HENGSHA HAWAII WATER PARK  上海横沙夏威夷水上乐园
(Shanghai Hengsha Xiaweiyi Shuishang Leyuan)
Hengsha Island   横沙东滨村
Tel: 5689-0256
Located in the east part of the island, the Water Amusement Park is equipped with motor boats, surf boards, parasailing and more.

## SHANGHAI WILD ANIMAL PARK
### 上海野生动物园
(Shanghai Yesheng Dongwuyuan)
Nanhui County, Pudong, 40 kilometers from People's Square.
Tel: 5803-6000
Admission: RMB50 weekdays, RMB60 weekends
Enclosed buses drive visitors through 337 hectares of park. Five thousand wild animals of 130 species roam freely, including elephants, bears, tigers, giant pandas, lions, takins (Tibetan goats), Asiatic asses, wild horses, and Bactrian camels. This year an additional 40 species will be added to the park, with the goal of having 13,000 wild animals of 230 species in the park within three years. After the first year of operation the facility has already seen the birth of fourteen lion cubs, four tigers, and two lesser pandas. The zoo is also trying to breed flamingos and golden monkeys. Currently there are zones for Manchurian and Bengal tigers, lions, bears, monkeys, and one cheetah, plus a 17-hectare herbivore habitat where horses, deer, elephants, Asiatic asses, and giraffes live together. This year, a new water amusement center will be built to house sea lions and seals. A lake in the southwest corner of the zoo is home to forty species of water fowl. There is a teahouse on the lake where visitors can rest and watch the birds and animals. The Children's Garden has baby animals for children to pet and feed. The zoo has four stalls where visitors can buy fruit and vegetables to feed the animals. Visitors may feed themselves at several places throughout the park. The largest restaurant near the main gate serves Chinese food. Animal shows are held daily.

## DANCING DOLPHINS   海豚表演
(Haitun Biaoyan)
Peace Park   和平公园
891 Tianbao Lu   天宝路891号
Tel: 6503-9073
Hours: 10:30 am, 1:30 pm, 3:00 pm
Price: RMB20 for adults, RMB10 for children
You can watch dolphins leap from the water, play ball, dance to music, kiss people, and calculate math by splashing their tails. Seals and sea lions also perform.

# Exploring Shanghai

In addition to visiting the well-known attractions listed here, another way to explore Shanghai is to take a taxi to various spots around town on different days and casually wander adjacent streets, poking in and out of shops. Something new and interesting is always discovered, and this is also a good way to learn one's way around the city.

## THE BUND  外滩
(Wai Tan)

Called *Waitan* by the Chinese, this is the most famous landmark in Shanghai. A photo of this water-front promenade appears almost without exception in any publication about the city. The name "Bund" is derived from an Anglo-Indian word meaning "embankment". The architectural style of the buildings is turn-of-the-century European. Due to lack of progress during the reign of Chairman Mao, and municipal guidelines protecting the buildings from being altered, the street appears to have been preserved in a time capsule from the late 1930s. A pleasant day can be had by starting at the Friendship Store on Beijing Dong Lu, just west of the Bund. The Friendship Store has seven floors of products, from all corners of China. From here, return to the Bund and, using one of the underground tunnels, cross the street to the river front. Once across, take the short stairway to the wide esplanade along the river and observe activity both on the water and of the many visitors from all over China and the world. Returning to the west side of the street, find the historic Peace Hotel on the corner of the Bund and Nanjing Dong Lu. Make use of either the bar off the lobby for a drink or try the Dragon and Phoenix restaurant on the eighth floor, offering ambiance straight out of 1930s Shanghai. Try for one of the window tables and observe the river and the Bund from a different, and more comfortable angle. This popular restaurant serves Chinese food (the menu is in English and Chinese). After lunch, take a right out of the hotel, and stroll along Nanjing Lu, China's Fifth Avenue, until the crowds of shoppers become too much to bear.

The outline on the next page provides an overview of the original and present-day uses of the buildings along the Bund, which stretch from Suzhou Creek on the north to Yan'an Lu on the south. At present, some buildings are undergoing transition of ownership, and are empty.

*Note: It's quite apparent that Suzhou Creek is very polluted, dirty, and odorous. Fortunately a massive clean-up project is underway to end the discharge of sewage, clear up poisonous and radioactive silt from the riverbed, channel clean water into the river, and dredge its associated waterways. Currently, four programs are underway in Huangpu, Zhabei, Hongkou, and Jing'an districts to beautify the embankment along the creek. Each of these districts has agreed to beautify its section of the embankment by planting trees and flowers. Houses and factories along the creek will be cleared to create a 15 meter strip of open space along each bank. The area near the Waibaidu Bridge on the Bund is targeted for earliest completion.*

## GREAT WORLD ENTERTAINMENT CENTER  大世界
(Dashijie)
1 Xizang Nan Lu   西藏南路1号
Tel: 6326-3760
Hours: 9:00 am - 9:00 pm

| Guide to Structures on the Bund | | | |
|---|---|---|---|
| Original use | Present use | Address | Constructed |
| British Consulate | Second General Office of the Shanghai Municipal People's Government | 33 Zhongshan Dong Yi Lu 中山东一路33号 | 1873 |
| China Merchants Bank | Bangkok Bank | 6 Zhongshan Dong Yi Lu 中山东一路6号 | 1897 |
| Russo-Chinese Bank | In transition | 14 Zhongshan Dong Yi Lu 中山东一路14号 | 1901 |
| Palace Hotel | Peace Hotel, south wing | 19 Zhongshan Dong Yi Lu 中山东一路19号 | 1906 |
| China Merchants Bank | In transition | 7 Zhongshan Dong Yi Lu 中山东一路7号 | 1907 |
| Waibaidu Bridge | Same | Spans Suzhou Creek as an extension of Zhongshan Lu | 1907 |
| Shanghai Club | Dongfeng Hotel | 2 Zhongshan Dong Yi Lu 中山东一路2号 | 1910 |
| Astor House | Pujiang Hotel, home of the Shanghai Stock Exchange | 15 Huangpu Lu 黄浦路15号 | 1910 |
| Banque de Indo-Chine | In transition | 29 Zhongshan Dong Yi Lu 中山东一路29号 | 1914 |
| Yangtze Building | In transition | 26 Zhongshan Dong Yi Lu 中山东一路26号 | 1916 |
| Asiatic Petroleum Building | In transition | 1 Zhongshan Dong Yi Lu 中山东一路1号 | 1916 |
| Russian Consulate | Same | 20 Huangpu Lu 黄浦路20号 | 1917 |
| Jardine Matheson and Co. | Shanghai Foreign Trade Bureau | 27 Zhongshan Dong Yi Lu 中山东一路27号 | 1920 |

| Original use | Present use | Address | Year Built |
|---|---|---|---|
| North China Daily News | Guilin Building | 17 Zhongshan Lu<br>中山路17号 | 1921 |
| Union Insurance Company | In transition | 4 Zhongshan Dong Yi Lu<br>中山东一路4号 | 1922 |
| Glen Line Building | In transition | 28 Zhongshan Dong Yi Lu<br>中山东一路28号 | 1922 |
| Chartered Bank | Shanghai Textiles Import and Export Corporation | 18 Zhongshang Dong Yi Lu<br>中山东一路18号 | 1923 |
| Hongkong and Shanghai Bank | Pudong Development Bank | 12 Zhongshan Dong Yi Lu<br>中山东一路12号 | 1923 |
| Yokohama Species Bank | The Industrial and Commercial Bank of China | 24 Zhongshan Dong Yi Lu<br>中山东一路24号 | 1924 |
| Creek Nishan Navigation Company | Huaxia Bank | 5 Zhongshan Dong Yi Lu<br>中山东一路5号 | 1925 |
| Taiwan Bank | In transition | 16 Zhongshan Dong Yi Lu<br>中山东一路16号 | 1926 |
| Jiang Hai Customs House | In transition | 13 Zhongshan Dong Yi Lu<br>中山东一路13号 | 1927 |
| Sassoon House (Cathay Hotel) | Peace Hotel, north wing | 20 Zhongshan Dong Yi Lu<br>中山东一路20号 | 1929 |
| Broadway Mansion | Shanghai Mansions, (three-star hotel) | 2 Suzhou Bei Lu<br>北苏州路2号 | 1930-1934 |
| Bank of China | Bank of China | 23 Zhongshan Lu<br>中山路23号 | 1937 |
| Bank of Communications | Shanghai Federation of Trade Unions | 14 Zhongshan Dong Yi Lu<br>中山东一路14号 | 1940 |

Corner of Yan'an Lu and Xizang Lu
This huge entertainment center dates from the 1930s. Inside are acrobats, a hall of mirrors, a Guinness Book of Records display, a ghost ride, and computerized fortune telling. The first floor features variety shows while the second floor is home to various opera, comedy and magic shows, and acrobatics. Games and bowling are on the third floor and a dance hall, tea room, and coffee shop are on the fourth floor.

## HUANGPU RIVER CRUISE　浦江游览

(Pujiang Youlan)
239 Zhongshan Dong 2 Lu
中山东二路239号
Tel: 6374-4461
Hours: 8:00 am - 6:30 pm
Day cruises to Wusong, at the mouth of the Yangtze River, run Monday through Friday leaving at 2:00 pm, returning at 5:30 pm. Price per person is RMB100, 70, 55, or 45 depending upon accommodation. Saturday and Sunday the ship leaves at 3:30 pm and returns at 7:00 pm. Price per person is RMB118,98, or 88. A buffet is provided for these cruises. Scenery along the way is mainly industrial. Other cruises go between the Yangpu Bridge and the Nanpu Bridge at 10:45 am and 3:15 pm daily for RMB30.

## PEARL TELEVISION TOWER　东方明珠

(Dongfang Mingzhu)
#2 Lane 504, Lujiazui Lu, Pudong
陆家嘴路504弄2号, 浦东
Tel: 5879-1888
Hours: 8:00 am - 9:30 pm
Price:  RMB50,
　　　　children under 1.3M, RMB30
This new super-structure on the Pudong side of the Huangpu River is one of those things one either loves or hates. Resembling a space ship, it is definitely a modern counterpoint to the historic structures on the Bund. Some are very proud of the structure and equate it with the Eiffel Tower; others find it to be an eyesore. Regardless, it does provide an unmatched view of Shanghai from the top. There is also a revolving restaurant (tel: 5878-8888) that serves a buffet lunch from 11:30 am to 2:00 pm for RMB161. Tea is served from 2:30 pm to 5:00 pm for RMB88 and a buffet dinner is served from 5:30 pm to 9:00 pm for RMB253. Cuisine is a combination of Western and Chinese. Children are charged half price for all meals.

## REGAL CHINA CRUISES
中国皇家公主号

(Zhongguo Huangjia Gongzhuhao)
108 Huangpu Lu　黄埔路108号
Tel/fax: 6356-3269
Pager:　128 x 215221
Regal provides an overnight cruise, called "The Spirit of Shanghai", to Wusong at the mouth of the Yangtze River and back daily. One boards the ship at 5:30 pm for a Western and Chinese buffet dinner served at 6:00 pm. The ship departs at 8:30 pm and a one-hour show begins at 9:00 pm. Movies are also shown. Additionally there is a live band, a piano bar, and a fitness room. A Western and Chinese buffet breakfast is served at 7:30 am and docking is at 8.00 am. Rates: standard twin room: US$70, superior twin room: US$75, deluxe twin room: US$80, deluxe single room: US$120, and deluxe double suite: US$150. Reservations are required.

Regal also provides a daily evening cruise, called "Shanghai Best", that boards at 5:30 pm, provides a Western and Chinese buffet dinner at 6:00 pm, departs at 7:30 pm, has a show at 8:30 pm, and docks at 9:30 pm. Disembarkment must take place by 10:00 pm. One may dance to a live band, enjoy the piano bar, watch movies, or use the fitness room. The ship sails between the Nanpu and Yangpu bridges. Price is US$45 per person. Reservations are required.

This company also provides cruises on the Yangtze River from Chongqing to Wuhan or from Wuhan to Chonqing that include the Three Gorges in the itinerary. The cruise from Chongqing to Wuhan requires four days while the Wuhan to Chongqing cruise has more stops requiring six days. The Three Gorges area will soon be merged by the Gezhouba Dam project, so see it now.

## YU GARDEN AND OLD TOWN
## 豫园及老城隍庙

(Yuyuan Jilao Chenghuangmiao)
Open daily 9:00 am - 4:30 pm, 6:00 pm - 9:30 pm
An entrance fee of RMB15 during the day, and RMB20 in the evening is payable at the gate.

Built between 1559 and 1577 by mandarin Pan Yunduan, this is a typical Chinese garden surrounding classical Chinese architecture. Located in the northern part of the Old Town, the 20,000 square meter garden contains forty Ming dynasty buildings and is surrounded by a long wall topped by an elaborately carved dragon. When the garden was originally built, it was adjacent to the Temple of the City God. In the 1700's, the garden was sold to the Temple and the area became a market and entertainment center. It remained as such until British troops occupied Shanghai during the Opium War and used the complex as its headquarters.

The area surrounding Yu Garden is fun to explore before or after you visit the garden itself. Outside the main gate is a carp pond and famous "willow pattern" Huxingting Tea House accessed by a "bridge of nine turnings", designed to ward off evil spirits. Immediately in front of the tea house watch steamed pork dumplings being made from scratch. There is always a long line of locals waiting to be served these delicious "xiao long bao". Small specialty shops line the adjacent narrow streets. In particular, look for the Chopsticks Store and the Walking Stick Store. An appealing Chinese meal and pleasant ambience can be had at the Green Wave Restaurant near the entrance to the garden, and TCBY yogurt also has a store in the area. This part of town is being ambitiously restored by the city of Shanghai. New buildings of traditional style house a seemingly endless variety of shops. There are also very tiny lanes adjacent to the central area offering a broad selection of notions (buttons, thread, ribbons, elastic tape) and various knickknacks and small toys. These small lanes are very crowded and difficult to find. The best way is to start from the parking lot in front of the Shanghai Restaurant. Walk toward the entrance to Old Town on the left side of the restaurant, but don't enter there. Continue straight down the road a short way and you'll soon find the entrance to the narrow lanes on your left. If at all possible, plan your excursion to Yu Garden and Old Town for a weekday as weekends are very busy.

## Historic Sites

## FORMER RESIDENCE OF DR. SUN YAT-SEN   孙中山故居纪念馆
(Sun Zhong Shan Guju Jinianguan)
7 Xiangshan Lu   香山路7号
Tel: 6437-2954
Hours: 1:00 pm - 4:00 pm
Dr. Sun and his wife, Madame Soong Ching Ling, lived here from 1919 to 1924.

## LU XUN MEMORIAL HALL AND TOMB
## 鲁迅纪念馆
(Lu Xun Jinianguan)
Lu Xun Park   鲁迅公园
146 Jiangwan Dong Lu   东江湾路146号
Tel: 5696-2093
Park hours: 5:00 am - 10:00 pm
Memorial Hall hours: 8:30 am - 11:30 am,

1:30 pm - 4:00 pm
On display here are the renowned writer's statue, manuscripts, literature, and photos.

## FORMER RESIDENCE OF MADAME SOONG CHING LING  宋庆龄故居

(Song Qing Ling Guju)
1843 Huaihai Zhong Lu  淮海中路1843号
Tel: 6433-5033
Hours: 9:00 am - 11:00 pm,
        1:00 pm - 4:30 pm
Madame Soong resided and worked at this address from 1948 until 1963.

## SITE OF THE FIRST NATIONAL CONGRESS OF THE CHINESE COMMUNIST PARTY
中国共产党成立第一次代表大会会址
(Zhongguo Gongchandang Chengli Diyici Daibiao Dahui Huizhi)
76 Xingye Lu  兴业路76号
Tel: 6328-1177
Hours: 8:00 am - 11:00 am,
        1:00 pm - 4:00 pm
A secret meeting was held here in July 1921, resulting in the formation of the Communist Party of China. The first Party constitution was written and the Party's founding central committee was elected here. The building has been restored to its 1921 condition.

# Shanghai's Parks and Zoos

## CHANGFENG PARK  长风公园

(Changfeng Gongyuan)
189 Daduhe Lu  大渡河路189号
Tel: 6245-3270
Hours: 8:00 am - 6:00 pm
This large park features army training ground equipment for children, who must make their way down Yonggan Zhedao Lu (Road for the Brave) within the park, displaying courage and ability to navigate. Kids who want to pretend they're at boot camp should enjoy this park. Changfeng Park is also home to 350,000 tulip bulbs imported from the Netherlands. It is located in Putuo district, northwest of the city.

## FUXING PARK  复兴公园

(Fuxing Gongyuan)
2 Gaolan Lu  皋兰路2号甲
Tel: 6372-0662
Hours: 6:00 am - 6:00 pm
This park is of classic European design. It was opened as "The French Park" in 1909. One may fish or dine at the posh new Park 97 restaurant.

## GONGQING WOODS  共青森林公园

(Gongqing Senlin Gongyuan)
2000 Jungong Lu  军工路2000号
Tel: 6548-0528
Hours: 6:00 am - 4:00 pm
This park is densely wooded and is located in the northeast Yangpu area.

## GUILIN PARK  桂林公园

(Guilin Gongyuan)
1 Guilin Lu  桂林路1号
Tel: 6436-0042
Hours: 7:00 am - 5:00 pm
This park, in the Xuhui district, is famous for sweet smelling osmanthus, which blooms from October to November.

## HONGKOU PARK  虹口公园

(Hongkou Gongyuan)
2288 Sichuan Bei Lu  四川北路2288号
Tel: 5696-2894, 5666-0311
Hours: 6:00 am - 6:00 pm
Located in the northeastern part of the city, this park was opened in 1905. Row boats for hire and the Lu Xun Memorial are in this park.

## HUANGPU PARK   黄埔公园

(Huangpu Gongyuan)
28 Zhongshan Dong Yi Lu
中山东一路28号
Tel: 6329-2636
Hours: 6:00 am - 10:00 pm
This park, previously called "Public Gardens", is reputed to have had an infamous sign that read "No Dogs and Chinese Allowed". In actuality, the park's regulations included a clause that stipulated that the only Chinese allowed in the park were nannies. Another sign said "No Dogs Allowed". Although the notorious sign never existed, the intent, in essence, did. This park is located at the northern tip of the Bund along the river, adjacent to the Suzhou Creek Bridge.

## JING'AN PARK   静安公园

(Jing'an Gongyuan)
1649 Nanjing Xi Lu  (at Huashan Lu)
南京西路1649号 华山路口
Tel: 6256-5640
Hours: 6:00 am - 6:00 pm

## RENMIN PARK   人民公园

(Renmin Gongyuan)
231 Nanjing Xi Lu   南京西路231号
Tel: 6327-1333
Fax: 6327-1071
Hours: 6:00 am - 6:00 pm
This park, also known as "People's Park", is located in the center of the city and occupies 30 acres of land encompassing flower beds, trees, ponds (one for fishing), a fairground, seating areas, and a large open square. The land it occupies now was once the race track. Shanghai's new museum and city hall are on the peripheries of the park. The new Grand Theater is also now under construction in the park. People's Park is famous for its "English Corner" where Chinese meet to practice their English with each other and tourists alike.

## SHANGHAI BOTANICAL GARDEN

上海植物园
(Shanghai Zhiwuyuan)
1111 Longwu Lu   龙吴路1111号
Tel: 6451-3369
Hours: 8:00 am - 5:00 pm
Admission: RMB 6 (For bonsai exhibition only, RMB 5)
This large garden offers a wide variety of flowers, plants, trees, and bonsai for display or sale. Many people are attracted to the annual spring fair sponsored by the park.

## SHANGHAI ZOO   上海动物园

(Shanghai Dongwuyuan)
2381 Hongqiao Lu   虹桥路2381号
Tel: 6268-7775
Hours: 6:00 am - 6:00 pm
Admission: RMB15
The area that now is home to the zoo, established in 1954, is now a major part of the city proper. However, before 1949, the area was countryside and was a large golf course. The zoo's primary attraction is, of course, its pandas. There are currently 580 animal species on display. To raise funds, the zoo has established a program called "Friends of the Shanghai Zoo" wherein companies and individuals pay a fee to adopt an animal. Each spring, the zoo stages an Animal Art Festival, showcasing such things as baby elephants wandering the park, monkeys motorcycling on high-wires, snakes and dancing girls, and a housecat beauty contest.

## SQUARE PAGODA PARK   方塔公园

(Fangta Gongyuan)
Songjiang Country   松江镇
Tel: 5783-3310
This park in Songjiang County features an ancient square pagoda.

## TIANSHAN CHILDREN'S TRAFFIC PARK
## 天山儿童交通公园

(Tianshan Ertong Jiaotong Gongyuan)
101 Zunyi Lu　遵义路101号
Tel: 6259-9446
Hours: 8:00 am - 5:00 pm
Children learn traffic rules in this park by following traffic lights and signs through miniature streets. This facility has been open for about five years, and hopefully, in another ten, results will be evident.

## TIAN SHAN PARK　天山公园

(Tianshan Gongyuan)
1743 Yan'an Xi Lu　延安西路1743号
Tel: 6259-4887
Hours: 6:00 am - 6:00 pm
In the Changning area.

## XIANGYANG PARK　向阳公园

(Xiangyang Gongyuan)
1008 Huaihai Zhong Lu　淮海中路1008号
Tel: 6473-2208
Hours: 6:00 am - 6:00 pm
This small, centrally located park in one of Shanghai's better neighborhoods attracts many citizens for morning exercise and camaraderie.

## ZHONGSHAN PARK　中山公园

(Zhongshan Gongyuan)
780 Changning Lu　长宁路780号
Tel: 6252-1478
Hours: 6:00 am - 6:30 pm
This park is home to Fundazzle, an amusement park for children.

# Temples

## CONFUCIUS TEMPLE　孔夫子庙

(Kong Fu Zi Miao)
183 Nanda Lu, Jiading District
Tel: 5953-0379
Hours: 8:00 - 11:00 am,
　　　　1:30 pm - 5:00 pm
An Imperial Examination Hall is adjacent to this temple built in 1219 and is open to visitors.

## JADE BUDDHA TEMPLE　玉佛寺

(Yufusi)
170 Anyuan Lu　安远路170号
Tel: 6266-3668
Open daily from 8:00 am to 11:00 am, and 1:00 pm to 5:00 pm. Small admission fee. Originally built in Jiangwan in 1882, the temple was moved to Anyuan Lu in the Putuo District in 1918. The Jade Buddha in residence was brought to China from Myanmar in 1882. Made of white jade, it measures 6'2" (1.9 meters) high and weighs 2,200 pounds (1,000 kilos). The Buddha is in a seated position and wears a jewel encrusted robe. Other Buddhas in the temple date back as far

as 386 AD. The temple also houses a collection of Buddhist scriptures and paintings from the Tang, Song, and Ming dynasties. Seventy monks are active here, sometimes chanting and ringing bells. Supposedly, an abbot protected the temple from harm during the Cultural Revolution by posting pictures of Chairman Mao all over the gates, making them inviolable to the Red Guards.

## JING'AN TEMPLE　静安古寺

(Jing'an Gusi)
1700 Nanjing Xi Lu
南京西路1700号
Tel: 6248-6366
This temple is believed to be the oldest in Shanghai and is reputed to have been built between 220 - 280 AD. Today, it is still a busy temple. Its most important artifact is a bell that was cast in 1183. A fair is held here each year on the eighth day of the fourth lunar month.

## LONGHUA TEMPLE AND PAGODA
龙华古寺
(Longhua Gusi)
2853 Longhua Lu     龙华路2853号
Tel: 6456-6085
Hours: 7:00 am - 4:00 pm
This traditional temple and pagoda in the southwestern area of the city contains ancient Buddhist scriptures. In the third month of the lunar calendar a temple fair is held. The octagonal pagoda, constructed of brick and wood, is seven stories (40 meters) high. One may climb to the top for views of the city to the north and open countryside to the south.

Longhua Temple is more than 1,750 years old and houses an ancient bell that is rung every Chinese New Year's Eve by monks and tourists alike. Visitors may ring the bell for RMB10, but photos are not allowed.

## ZEN TEMPLE 真如寺
(Zhenrusi)
5 Hou Shan Men     后山门5号
Tel: 6254-6340
Hours: 8:00 am - 4:00 pm
This small temple is located in the center of the downtown area and contains two jade Buddhas from Myanmar.

# Art Galleries and Exhibitions

## Galleries

## SHANGHAI ART MUSEUM 上海美术馆
(Shanghai Meishuguan)
456 Nanjing Xi Lu   南京西路456号
Tel: 6327-0976
Hours: 9:00 am - 11:00 am
           1:00 pm - 4:00 pm
The Art Museum is a state-run entity that holds constantly changing art exhibitions.

## SHANGART
2nd Fl, Portman Ritz-Carlton Hotel
波特曼大酒店2楼
1376 Nanjing Xi Lu
南京西路1376号
Tel: 6279-7135
Fax: 6289-1602
E-mail: shangart@uninet.co.cn
Web page: www.shangart.com
Hours: 9:00 am - 9:00 pm
Director: Mr. Lorenz Helbling
Each month this casual gallery features the work of different contemporary artists. ShangArt's web page provides firsthand information about comtemporary art in China.

## SOURCES FAR EAST LTD.
渊源远东有限公司
(Yuanyuan Yuandong Youxian Gongsi)
Longbai Apartments, 1-11B
龙柏公寓1号楼11层B座
2461 Hongqiao Lu, 200335
虹桥路2461号
Tel:  6268-9850, 6268-9541
Fax: 6268-8004
E-mail: sources@public.sta.net.cn
Web page: www.shanghaisources.com
Contact: Jennifer Dawson
Sources is a "home" gallery where one can see, by appointment, the works of Xie Qing. Mr Xie's oil paintings are realistic, detailed, and tend to be large in size. Some of his paintings are still-lifes and landscapes, and he is highly skilled in painting figures and portraits.

# Auction Houses

## CHRISTIE'S 佳士得
(Jiashide)
Suite 404, American International Center
Shanghai Centre
1376 Nanjing Xi Lu  南京西路1376号
Tel: 6279-8773
Fax: 6279-8771
Representative: Lillian Chu

## SHANGHAI DEKANG ART AUCTION HOUSE 上海德康艺术品拍卖公司
(Shanghai Dekang Yishupin Paimai Gongsi)
Shanghai Art Museum (Shanghai Meishuguan)
上海美术馆后楼
456 Nanjing Xi Lu  南京西路456号
Tel: 6318-1666
Fax: 6372-5748

# Museums and Libraries

## SHANGHAI LIBRARY 上海图书馆
(Shanghai Tushuguan)
1555 Huaihai ZhongLu  淮海中路1555号
Tel: 6445-5555
Hours: 8:30 am - 8:30 pm
This new library is the second largest of its kind in China, after the National Library in Beijing, and one of the ten largest in the world. The library's collection contains 13 million books and manuscripts, 1.7 million of which are antiquarian, with some 1,400 years old. Twenty reading rooms house Chinese, foreign, electronic and audio-visual publications, as well as access to the Internet and books in Braille.  There are also eleven exhibition halls with 4,000 items on display. The fourth floor is an English and other languages floor, with a comprehensive collection of international newspapers, periodicals and books. A reading card must be obtained (bring RMB25, a passport and one photo) in order to access this floor.

## SHANGHAI HISTORY MUSEUM 上海历史博物馆
(Shanghai Lishi Bowuguan)
1286 Hongqiao Lu  虹桥路1286号
Tel: 6275-5595
Hours: 9:00 am - 3:30 pm

## SHANGHAI MUSEUM 上海博物馆
(Shanghai Bowuguan)
People's Square, 201 Renmin Dadao
人民大道201号
Tel: 6372-3500
Hours: 9:00 am - 5:00 pm Sun. - Fri.,
         9:00 am - 8:00 pm Sat.
This magnificent new museum has eleven galleries that showcase paintings, bronzes, sculpture, ceramics, calligraphy, jade, furniture, coins, seals, and Chinese minority art. The facility is modern, quiet, and the displays are expertly exhibited. The large, sky-lighted atrium provides benches. Admission is RMB20. Acoustic guides available in several languages for an admission price of RMB60. Leave your passport or a security deposit at the acoustic guide desk.

## SHANGHAI NATURAL HISTORY MUSEUM 上海自然博物馆
(Shanghai Ziran Bowuguan)
260 Yan'an Dong Lu  延安东路260号
Tel: 6321-3548
Hours: 9:00 am - 3:30 pm
Admission: RMB10

## BAO CHANGSHAN'S COLLECTION OF MATCHBOOKS AND KEYRINGS
包昌善火柴梗，钥匙圈收藏
(Bao Changshan Huochaigeng, Yaoshiquan Shoucang)
#6, Lane 406, Yan'an Xi Lu
延安西路406弄6号

## BAO WANRONG'S THEATRICAL COSTUMES EXHIBITION
戏剧服装展览
(Xiju Fuzhuang Zhanlan)
#11, Lane 138, Rushan Lu, Pudong
浦东 乳山路138弄11号

## CAO HUIZHONG'S COLLECTION OF MINI-SCULPTURES
曹惠忠微艺术陈列室
(Cao Huizhong Weidiao Yishi Chenlie Shi)
57 Yangyue Lu, Wusong District
吴淞区 杨月路 曹家宅57号

## CHEN BAOCAI'S BUTTERFLY COLLECTION 蝴蝶收藏品
(Hudie Shouzangpin)
#2, Lane 77, Zichang Lu, Pudong
浦东 子长路77弄2号

## CHEN BAODING CALCULATION INSTRUMENTS EXHIBITION
算具陈列室
(Suanju Chenlie Shi)
#8, Lane 379, Jianguo Xi Lu
建国西路379弄8号
Abacuses are Mr. Chen's passion - they even comprise the door of his store.

## CHEN YUTANG'S COLLECTION OF ANCIENT JARS 古容器收藏
(Gu Rongqi Shoucang)
326 Xizang Nan Lu 西藏南路326号
Chen Yutang keeps a collection of about 500 jars dating back to the early Qing Dynasty.

These jars are of many materials including porcelain, pottery, bronze, jade, mahogany, lacquerware, crystal, glass, and marble.

## DU BAOJUN'S COLLECTION OF RAIN FLOWER STONES 雨花石收藏
(Yuhuashi Shoucang)
Room 501, 268 Meiling Nan Lu
梅岭南路268号501室

## HUANG GUODONG'S COLLECTION OF PAPER FAN COVERINGS 纸扇收藏
(Zhishan Shoucang)
#1, Lane 47, Ninghe Lu, Nanshi District
南市区凝和路47弄1号

## HU RENFU'S COLLECTION OF ROOT SCULPTURES 根雕艺术收藏
(Gendiao Yizhu Shoucang)
#13, Lane 470, Loushanguan Lu
娄山关路470弄13号

## LAN XIANG'S COLLECTION OF CHOPSTICKS 蓝翔筷子陈列室
(Lanxiang Kuaizi Chenlie Shi)
3rd Fl, back door, 170 Yongshou Lu
永寿路170号后门3楼

## PENG TIANMIN'S COLLECTION OF NATURAL MODELS 自然标本
(Ziran Biaoben)
#23, Lane 60, Linyin Lu 林荫路60弄23号

## SHANGHAI FOLK COLLECTION EXHIBITION HOUSE
上海民间房屋展览
(Shanghai Minjian Fangwu Zhanlan)
1551 Zhongshan Nan Lu 中山南路1551号

## SHEN WEI'S COLLECTION OF BEIJING OPERA MASKS 沈伟京剧脸谱陈列室
(Shen Wei Jingju Lianpu Chenlie Shi)
Room 103, #6 Lane 221, Taopu Lu
桃浦公路221弄6号103室

## WANG ANJIAN'S COLLECTION OF CLOCKS AND WATCHES
王安坚家庭钟表博物馆

(Wang Anjian Jiating Zhongbiao Bowuguan)
Tel: 5663-8110

## WANG XIANBAO'S COLLECTION OF NINE DRAGON FANS　九龙扇收藏

(Jiulongshan Shoucang)
#1125, Waiyumatou Lu　外鱼码头路1125号

## WEI ZHI'AN'S MUSEUM OF AGATES
玛瑙博物馆

(Manao Bowuguan)
#6, Lane 21, Balin Lu　巴林路21弄6号

## XU BINJIE'S COLLECTION OF BOAT MODELS　航模收藏

(Hangmo Shoucang)
#131, Lane 1143, Yuhang Dong Lu
东余航路1143弄131号

## XU SIHAI'S HOUSE OF TEA ART
茶道艺术

(Chadao Yishu)
332 Xingguo Lu　兴国路332号

## YAN HANXIANG'S COLLECTION OF MATCHBOX LABELS
严汉祥火花陈列室

(Yan Hanxiang Huohua Chenlie Shi)
320 Qingyun Lu　青云路320号

## YU LIULIANG'S NUMISMATIC COLLECTION　古币收藏

(Gubi Shoucang)
267 Hongzhen Laojie　虹镇老街267号

## ZHAO JINZHI'S MUSEUM OF GOLDEN KEYS　锁匙收藏

(Yaoshi Shoucang)
11 Xueye Lu, Pudong　浦东 学业路11号

## ZHAO ZHENGXIN'S COLLECTION OF CLASSICAL CAMERAS
赵振新古典相机博物馆

(Zhao Zhenxin Gudian Xiangji Buwuguan)
25 Linshan Lu　临山路25号

## ZHENG GENHAI'S COLLECTION OF RARE SHELLS　珍烯贝壳类收藏

(Zhenxi Beikelei Shoucang)
#42, Laoshan Village 2, Pudong
浦东 崂山二村42号

## ZHOU CHANGXING'S COLLECTION OF MINI-SCULPTURES
周长兴微雕工艺摆件陈列室

(Zhou Changxing Weidiao Gongyi Baijian Chenlie Shi)
Room 103, #45 Lane 749, Tianmu Zhong Lu　天目中路749弄45号103室

## ZHU GUOQUAN'S COLLECTION OF CIGARETTE LABELS
朱关权烟标陈列室

(Zhu Guoquan Yanbiao Chenlie Shi)
#5 Lane 174, Jiangning Lu
江宁路174弄5号

## ZHU XIAOHUA'S COLLECTION OF CELEBRITIES' HANDWRITING
朱晓华名人封陈列室

(Zhu Xiaohua Mingrenfeng Chenlie Shi)
Room 602, 223 Tongzhou Lu
通州路223号602室

# Day Tours

## GRAND VIEW GARDEN  青浦大观园

(Qingpu Daguanyuan)

Situated beside Dianshan Lake 淀山湖 in Qingpu County 青浦镇 65 kilometers southwest of central Shanghai, this park's design was based on the book "Dream of the Red Mansion" written by Cao Xueqin 曹雪芹. The story concerns the gradual downfall of an aristocratic family and is a classic of Chinese literature. A white stone tablet stands at the entrance to the park, depicting the "Twelve Beauties of Jinling" who are major characters in the story. The buildings represent the fictional family's compound and are new reproductions. Among them you'll find the home of the book's hero, Jia Baoyu, and the nunnery where Miaoyu, one of the twelve beauties, cloistered herself. This large park covers 106.7 hectares and is crisscrossed with ponds and streams. One can hire small boats and leisurely explore the waterways amidst greenery and fresh air.

## SHESHAN HILL  佘山

(Sheshan)

This area 36 kilometers southwest of Shanghai is designated by the government as one of China's seven important resorts. Sheshan is unique in that it is the only "mountain" (though only 100 meters high) anywhere near Shanghai, and also boasts an active Catholic Church, "Our Lady of China" at its peak. Rock climbing aficionados also come here to perfect their techniques. Sheshan was a sacred Buddhist enclave until the mid-1800s when the buildings were destroyed. A new Catholic church was built in 1873 and many Catholics make an annual pilgrimage to Sheshan in May. One may drive a car to the top of the hill or walk along winding paths where the stations of the cross may be performed. There is also a cable car to the top of the mountain. The European Amusement Park and Sea

Wonderland are recent additions to the area.

## SUZHOU  苏州

(Suzhou)

Marco Polo visited this picturesque city and dubbed it the "Venice of the East". Suzhou still retains some of its Song and Ming dynasty charm, but is also becoming a center for industry due to a US$20 billion Sino/Singaporean investment. Access from Shanghai has also recently been improved via the construction of a superhighway. The trip takes 90 minutes either via this highway or by double-decker express train. Modernization of Suzhou is being balanced by efforts to preserve cultural heritage. The city has begun to clean the waterways of the Old City which is crisscrossed by a network of in-use canals connected to the Grand Canal. The famous American architect, I. M. Pei, whose family is originally from Suzhou, has been retained to help restore the old buildings of the city. Suzhou is most famous for its gardens, the oldest being the Pavilion of Waves, which dates from the 11th century. The Garden of the Master of Fishing Nets built in the 12th century is the smallest, but is considered the most beautiful. The New York Metropolitan Museum has duplicated this garden's Hall for Staying Spring as an example of the classical Chinese garden. The most popular and representative garden is probably the Humble Administrator's Garden which has ornamental pools and elegant pavilions linked by winding corridors of carved, red lacquered wood.

## ZHOUZHUANG VILLAGE  周庄

(Zhouzhuang)

Located near the west side of Dingshan Lake 60 kilometers west of Shanghai, is this quaint village of canals and picturesque bridges. Expect the trip to take about one hour and fifteen minutes from Hongqiao Airport. The prominent Chinese artist, Chen Yi Fei, helped bring Zhouzhuang to world attention with a painting which depicts the famous Bridge of Peace and the Bridge of Virtue. The village's narrow streets are lined with traditional Chinese buildings, some of which date back to the Ming Dynasty. Upon arrival in present-day Zhouzhuang, visit the Zhouzhuang Travel Agency to buy a ticket and then walk two blocks to the entrance of the old city. This ticket will allow entry into the several buildings cum museums within the old city.

# EATING OUT IN SHANGHAI

Due to busy schedules and frequent business dining obligations, the expatriate community in Shanghai tends to dine out a lot. In the past, safe choices were limited to the known and trusted hotel restaurants, but fortunately that is changing due to the rapidly expanding roster of new, clean and well-managed establishments. Some of the more obvious choices are listed, with a star indicating those that are particularly good.

# WESTERN RESTAURANTS

## Upscale

### SHANGHAI AD RESTAURANT
上海安多那罗亚意式餐厅
3896 Hongmei Lu    虹梅路3896号
Tel/fax: 6262-5620
This great new addition to Shanghai's restaurant scene offers an extensive and delicious menu. The ambience, with its huge fireplace, leaves little to be desired.

### CONTINENTAL ROOM    欧陆餐厅
33rd Fl, Garden Hotel (Huayuan Fandian)
花园饭店33楼
58 Maoming Nan Lu    茂名南路58号
Tel: 6415-1111
Hours: 7:00 am - 9:30 am, 11:30 am - 2:30 pm, and 5:30 pm - 10:00 pm
The beautiful view and fine French menu make for an elegant dining experience in Shanghai for lunch and dinner. Excellent venue for business-related dining, with a quiet and unobtrusive atmosphere.

### DAVINCI'S ☆ 达芬奇西餐厅
Shanghai Hilton Hotel, Ground Fl
静安希尔顿底楼 (Xiardun Fandian)
250 Huashan Lu    华山路250号
Tel: 6248-0000
Hours: 6:00 pm - 10:30 pm
A refined, elegant ambience and fine Italian food and wines. At the back of the restaurant, is a Japanese Teppan section where a Japanese-trained chef prepares dishes in front of your eyes.

### GIOVANNI'S ☆ 意大利餐厅
Westin Taipingyang Hotel
(Taipingyang Fandian)    太平洋大酒店
5 Zunyi Nan Lu    遵义南路5号
Tel:  6275-8888 x 4276
Fax: 6275-5420
Open daily for lunch: noon - 2:00 pm, dinner:

6:00 pm - 10:30 pm
Reservations required.
This Italian restaurant is located at the top of the hotel and offers great views. Small and quiet with a pleasant ambience.

### PARK '97
Fuxing Park    复兴公园
2 Gaolan Lu    皋兰路2号
Tel: 6318-0785
Fax: 6287-4716
Restaurant hours: noon - 3:00 pm and
                6:00 pm - 11:00 pm, daily
Cafe hours: 10:00 am - 2:00 am from
                Monday to Thursday and 24
                hours on Fridays and Saturdays
                11:00 am - 4:00 pm Brunch
                menu only on Sundays
Ultra Late Lounge hours: 11:00 pm - 2:00 am Thursdays and 11:00 pm - 4:00 am on Fridays and Saturdays.
This new restaurant is unique in several ways. Its location in Fuxing Park affords it a truly sumptuous front yard. During daytime hours when the park is open, one may approach the restaurant from any park entrance. Once the park has closed for the evening, one must use the Gaolan Lu entrance. The 6,000 square foot interior has been decorated in rich shades of saffron, gold, plum, and red accented with emerald green. One wall is painted with a six meter long mural of a reclining female nude. There are two restaurants with two separate menus. The "restaurant" is decorated with table linens and has an elegant ambience while the "cafe" is far more casual and contains the bar. The restaurant's menu is upscale in price and selection while the cafe offers more affordable casual dining selections. The atmosphere and the food is distinctly Western. You needn't hesitate to dine alone as there is

a wide selection of current foreign magazines on a rack by the door. Reservations are recommended for the more formal restaurant section.

## SHANGHAI JAX ☆ 佳客餐厅

Level 1, East Wing 东峰底楼
Shanghai Centre 上海商城
(Shanghai Shangcheng)
Tel: 6279-8847
Hours: 11:30 am - 2:30 pm,
        5:30 pm - 10:30 pm
Open for lunch and dinner with a relaxing bar and live entertainment. A good quiet venue for business lunches. Dinnertime is a bit noisier because of the live vocalist. On Sundays, from 11:30 am - 2:30 pm, a brunch offers a buffet including foie gras and caviar preceding a choice of main course and dessert.

## TICINO 意大利餐厅

(Yidali Canting)
Shanghai New Asia Tomson Hotel
新亚汤臣大酒店
(Xinya Tangcheng Dajiudian)
777 Zhangyang Lu 张扬路777号
Pudong 2000120
Tel: 5831-8888 x 3323
Hours: 5:30 pm - 10:00 pm
Overlooking the Atrium, this cozy, Art Deco restaurant offers Northern Italian dishes with a Swiss touch.

## More Casual

## 50 HANKOU ROAD 汉口路50号

Located at the same address near the Bund.
汉口路50 号
Tel: 6329-8999, 6323-8383
Hours: 11:00 am - midnight
Fine continental food with everything from sandwiches to more elegant fare. The decor is unique and attractive with a rustic Balinese flair. This private restaurant offers an alternative to hotel dining when you are in the mood for good Western food.

## ATRIUM CAFE 连天阁

(Liantiange)
Lobby level, Shanghai Hilton Hotel
静安希尔顿
(Jing'an Xierdun)
250 Huashan Lu 华山路250号
Tel: 6248-0000
Hours: 6:00 pm - 10:00 pm
        12:00 pm - 2:00 pm
A huge skylight in the atrium ceiling provides welcome light. Breakfast, lunch, and dinner buffets are offered along with an a la carte menu. The cuisine is a blend of Western and Asian dishes.

## BACANA BRASIL 巴西烤肉

1st Fl, Lion Garden East, Gubei
里昂花园E座1楼 (古北新区)
Tel: 6209-7670
Hours: 11:00 am - 11:00 pm
Brazilian food has come to Shanghai, encompassing a wide variety of meats grilled over an open flame. If you chose the set menu, at lunch, RMB68 and at dinner, RMB98, you will be served a variety of grilled meats and have full access to the buffet of vegetables, soups, rice and pasta dishes, fresh fruits, and desserts.

## BAVARIAN STEAK HOUSE 百威灵牛排屋

(Baiweiling Niupaiwu)
Equatorial Hotel 上海国际贵都大饭店
(Shanghai Guoji Guidu Dafandian)
65 Yan'an Xi Lu 延安西路65号
Tel: 6248-1688 x 2383
Hours: 6:00 pm - 10:00 pm

## BRASSERIE ORIENTALE 香榭郦舍

(Xingxielishe)
4th Fl, Hyland Sofitel Hotel 海仑宾馆4楼
(Hailen Binguan)

505 Nanjing Dong Lu    南京东路505号
Tel: 6351-5888
Hours: 6:00 am - midnight
The window tables are especially pleasant, affording a bird's eye view of activities in the heart of the shopping district along Nanjing Lu.

## BRASSERIE TATLER   达乐餐厅
(Dale Canting)
Shanghai J C Mandarin    锦沧文华大酒店
(Jincang Wenhua Jiudian)
1225 Nanjing Xi Lu    南京西路1225号
Tel: 6279-1888
Open 24 hours

## CAFE BISTRO    咖啡厅
(Kafeiting)
Lobby level, The Westin Tai Ping Yang Hotel
太平洋大酒店
(Taipingyang Dajiudian)
5 Zunyi Nan Lu    遵义路5号
Tel: 6275-8888
Hours: 6:00 am - 1:00 am
The glass walls of this round restaurant afford a view of a Chinese garden. There is a breakfast buffet as well as menu items. Lunch and dinner provide a choice of Western or Asian food. This is a popular place with the business lunch crowd.

## CAFE VIENNA    城市咖啡
(Chengshi Kafei)
City Hotel    城市酒家
(Chengshi Jiujia)
5-7 Shaanxi Nan Lu    陕西南路5-7号
Tel: 6255-1133
Hours: 6:00 am - 1:00 am

## CHEERS    西餐厅
(Xicanting)
Holiday Inn Crowne Plaza    银星假日酒家
388 Panyu Lu    番禺路388号
Tel: 6280-8888
Hours: 5:00 pm - 9:30 pm
This small restaurant has a bar and a lot of charm.

## COMPASS ROSE BUFFET RESTAURANT
玫瑰罗盘餐厅
(Meigui Luopan Canting)
Westin Tai Ping Yang    太平洋大酒店
(Taipingyang Dajiudian)
5 Zunyi Nan Lu    遵义南路5号
Tel: 6275-8888
Hours: 6:00 pm - 10:00 pm
A Mediterranean buffet offers salads, appetizers, entrees, and desserts. Australian oysters and prawns abound.

## FLAMINGO RESTAURANT    柏丽中餐厅
(Baili Zhongcanting)
Radisson SAS Lansheng Hotel    兰生大酒店
1000 Quyang Lu    曲阳路1000号
Tel: 6542-8000
Hours: 6:00 am - 11:00 am,
       5:30 pm - 11:00 pm

## FOUNTAIN RESTAURANT    喷泉西餐厅
(Penquan Xicanting)
Hotel Nikko Longbai    日航龙柏饭店
(Rihang Longbai Fandian)
2451 Hongqiao Lu    虹桥路2451号
Tel: 6268-9111
Hours: 6:30 am - 11:30 pm
Large white wicker dining chairs lend a colonial flavor to the decor of this establishment.

## GIURLANI RISTORANTE ITALIANO
(班地) 意卢意大利餐厅
(Yilu Yidali Canting)
3rd Fl, Jinjiang Tower    新锦江3楼
(Xin Jinjiang)
161 Changle Lu    长乐路161号
Tel: 6415-1188 x 80303
Fax: 6415-0048
Hours: 10:00 am - 11:30 pm
The semi-buffet dinner is RMB220 and includes antipasti and salad, choice of soup, choice of four main courses, and dessert bar.

## HARD ROCK CAFE  硬石咖啡

(Yingshi Kafei)
Shanghai Centre Retail Plaza  上海商城底层
Suites A05 and 110
1376 Nanjing Xi Lu  南京西路1376号
Tel: 6279-8133
Fax: 6279-8399
Hours: 11:30 am - 2:00 am (Sunday - Thursday), 11:30 am - 3:00 am (Friday-Saturday and Eve of Public Holidays)
Offering some of the best hamburgers in Shanghai. The menu is authentically American - even the blue cheese salad dressing tastes right!

## KAFEI TING RESTAURANT  咖啡厅

(Kafeiting)
Lobby level, Huating Hotel and Towers
华亭宾馆 (Huating Binguan)
1200 Caoxi Bei Lu  漕溪北路1200号
Tel: 6439-1000 or 6439-6000 x 2610
Hours: 6:00 am - 11:00 pm
Coffee shop fare, from sandwiches and soup to hot dishes and a buffet. Their "hard to find in Shanghai" crab meat cocktail is a feature.

## LATINA  拉丁餐厅

(Lading Canting)
South Building, Jinjiang Hotel
59 Maoming Nan Lu  茂名南路59号
Tel: 6472-2718
Fax: 6472-1269
Hours: noon - 12:00 am
Brazilian music accompanies dishes from France, Italy, Spain, Portugal and Brazil. From 10:00 pm until midnight their live band performs Bossa Nova music. One can order from the menu or partake of the "All You Can Eat Buffet" for RMB150. Once you've had your fill of the buffet, you place a "Stop" flag on your table to signal for coffee and dessert.

## LUIGI'S  意大利餐厅

Huating Hotel and Towers  华亭宾馆
(Huating Binguan)
1200 Caoxi Bei Lu  漕溪北路1200号
Tel: 6439-1000, 6439-6000 x 2616
Hours: 5:30 pm - 10:30 pm
Shanghai's oldest Italian restaurant offers a menu of perennial favorites and regional specials.

## THE METROPOLE  名都餐厅

(Mingdu Canting)
Yangtze New World Hotel  扬子江大酒店
(Yangzijiang Dajiudian)
2099 Yan'an Xi Lu  延安西路2099号
Tel: 6275-0000
Open 24 hours

## PAULANER BRAUHAUS  宝莱纳啤酒城

(Baolaina Pijiucheng)
150 Fengyang Lu  汾阳路150号
Tel: 6474-5700
Fax: 6474-5814
Hours: 5:30 pm - 2:00 am
This slick three story restaurant, part of a worldwide chain, has a seating capacity of 400 and encompasses a restaurant, microbrewery, bakery, and butchery. The food is authentic German and the decor is high-end with imported oak furniture and stained glass.

## RESTAURANT EL GALLO  卡罗坊

(Kaluofang)
1704 Huaihai Zhong Lu  淮海中路1704号
Tel: 6433-9427
Hours: 10:00 am - midnight
The cuisine in this restaurant is a blend of Chinese and Spanish cooking. The owner is a Chinese gentleman who has spent considerable time in Spain.

## ROSE GARDEN  玫瑰咖啡厅

(Meigui Kafeiting)
Garden Hotel  花园饭店
332 Maoming Nan Lu  茂名南路332号
Tel: 6253-6958
Hours: 6:00 am - 2:00 am
Casual, Italian-influenced cafe fare.

## SAVINI'S  意大利餐厅

(Yidali Canting)
823 Huangjin Cengdao, Lyon Garden, Gubei
古北新区黄金城道823号(里昂花园)
Tel: 6278-9878
Fax: 6278-9878
Hours: 8.00 am - 10:00 pm
This Italian restaurant also has a deli full of
products from Italy, France, and Japan.

## THE TEA GARDEN  茶园

Level 1, East Wing  东峰底楼
(Dongfend Dilou)
Shanghai Centre  上海商城
Tel: 6279-8888 x 5986
Open 24 hours
Generous buffets are served for breakfast,
lunch, and dinner. Selections from the menu
are also available.

## TERRACE CAFE  绿茵咖啡馆

(Luyin Kafeiting)
Shanghai New Asia Tomson Hotel
新亚汤臣大酒店
(Xinya Tangcheng Dajiudian)
777 Zhangyang Lu, Pudong  张扬路777号
Tel: 5831-8888 x 3302
Hours: 6:30 am - 11:00 pm
A buffet with tiger prawns, beef tenderloin,
salmon, Australian rock oysters, deli meats and
cheeses, 17 hot dishes, Asian regional
specialties, and a wide selection of desserts.
No charge for children under eight who are
with two paying adults.

# Very Casual

## BADLANDS  心缘餐厅

(Xinyuan Canting)
897 Julu Lu  巨鹿路897号
Tel: 6466-7788 x 8003
Hours: noon - 2:00 am (Sun. - Thurs.),
noon - 5:00 am (Fri. - Sat.)
This restaurant features Mexican food such as
tacos, chimichangas, burritos, and Mexican-
style hamburgers.

## BLUE HEAVEN REVOLVING
## RESTAURANT  蓝天旋转餐厅

(Lantian Xuanzhuan Canting)
Jinjiang Tower, 161 Changle Lu
新锦江长乐路161号
Tel: 6415-1188

Hours: 6:00 am - 10:00 am,
11:30 am - 2:00 pm,
and 6:00 pm -10:00 pm
Great views of Shanghai, ultra-modern decor
and a Western buffet.

## CAPPUCCINO (ITALIAN SNACK HOUSE)
卡比基诺

(Kabijinuo)
4th Fl, Equatorial Hotel
上海国际贵都大酒店
(Shanghai Guoji Guidu Dafandian)
65 Yan'an Xi Lu, 200040  延安西路65号
Tel: 6248-1688 x 2384
Hours: noon - 2:00 pm,
6:30 pm - 10:00 pm
Pizzas, pasta and other Italian dishes. Select
pasta types from a wall chart.

## CHALON　沙龙餐厅

(Shalong Canting)
3rd Fl, Jusco Shopping Mall
佳世客购物中心3楼
(Jiashike Gewu Zhongxin)
218 Tianmu Xi Lu　天目西路218号
Tel: 6354-3060
Hours: 10:00 am - 9:30 pm
This attractive, fast-food restaurant is Japanese run and offers Western and Asian dishes and a wide range of set menus ranging from RMB30 to RMB55.

## THE CHINNERY　淮香楼海鲜酒家

(Huixianlou Haixian Jiujia)
Xiangdao Food Plaza
7th Fl, Shanghai International Shopping Center　上海国际购物中心7楼
527 Huaihai Zhong Lu　淮海中路527号
Tel: 5306-1616
Hours: 11:30 am - 4:00 pm,
　　　　5:30 pm - 10:30 pm

## CHURCHILL'S PUB AND DELI
丘吉尔酒吧

(Qiujier Jiuba)
Old Wing, Donghu Hotel　东湖宾馆
167 Xinle Lu　新乐路167号
Tel: 6415-8158, x 12131
Hours: Pub 11:00 am - 2:00 am
　　　　Deli 11: 00 am - 2:00 am
Traditional English pub grub and atmosphere.

## DANNY'S PUB　丹尼思酒吧

(Dannisi Jiuba)
141 Maoming Nan Lu　茂名南路141号
Tel: 6473-2849
Hours: 11:30 am - 3:00 am
Lunch, dinner, and cocktails are served. Western and Asian dishes in a bistro-type atmosphere.

## ESPRESSO AMERICANO　意美咖啡厅

(Yimei Kafeiting)
Level 1, West Tower, Shanghai Centre

上海商城西峰底楼
Tel: 6247-9750
Hours: 7:00 am - 10:00 pm, Mon. - Fri.
　　　　8:00 am - 9:00 pm, Sat. and Sun.
A small coffee bar offering latte, cappuccino, and many other varieties of coffee and beans. Coffee makers, coffee grinders, and other coffee related paraphernalia are also available for purchase, as are a limited variety of sandwiches and cookies.

## FEST BREW HOUSE　菲斯特啤酒坊

(Feisite Pijiufang)
11 Hankou Lu　汉口路11号
Tel: 6323-0965
Hours: 11:00 am - 1:00 am
Micro-brewery and German restaurant near the Bund.

## FLAMINGO RESTAURANT　柏丽西餐厅

(Bailixi Canting)
2nd Fl, Lansheng Hotel　兰生大酒店2楼
1000 Quyang Lu　曲阳路1000号
Tel: 6542-8000 x 8555
Hours: 6:00 am - 11:00 am and
　　　　6:00 pm - 11:00 pm
Western food in a subdued atmosphere of mahogany and beveled mirrors.

## THE GAP　锦明酒店

(Jinming Jiudian)
Ground Fl, Jingming Bldg.　锦明大厦底楼
8 Zunyi Nan Lu, Hongqiao
遵义南路8号虹桥新区
Tel: 6278-2900, 6278-0248, 6278-0249
Hours: 11:00 am - 1:00 am
Western and Chinese food. Western decor and entertainment.

## GOLDEN WORLD BEVERLY
## RESTAURANT　比伏利中西餐厅

(Bifoli Zhongxi Canting)
139 Yan'an Xi Lu　延安西路139号
Tel: 6248-2755
Hours: 11:00 am - midnight

Splashy cabaret-style floor shows and Western food on three over-the-top floors.

## JUDY'S TOO　杰迪酒吧

(Jiedi Jiuba)
176 Maoming Nan Lu　茂名南路176号
Tel: 6473-1417
Fax: 6275-0076
Hours: 11:30 am - 1:00 am, weekdays
　　　11:30 am - 2:00 am, weekends
Popular nightspot and pizzeria with largely expat clientele.

## LE JARDIN　百花厅

(Baihuating)
Novotel Yuanlin Hotel　园林宾馆
(Yuanlin Binguan)
201 Baise Lu　200231　百色路201号
Tel: 6470-1688
Hours: 6:00 am - 1:00 am
The hotel's coffee shop with a fairly extensive menu of Western and SE Asian items.

## MALONE'S AMERICAN CAFE
马龙美式酒楼

(Malong Meishi Jiulou)
255 Tongren Lu (just west of the Portman)
铜仁路255号
Tel: 6247-2400
Hours: 11:00 am - 1:00 am
This "American" cafe is actually Canadian. A good place to have a drink or play pool and darts among expats.

## BISTRO METROPOLE
名都西餐厅

(Mingdu Xicanting)
Yangtze New World Hotel　扬子江大酒店
2099 Yan'an Xi Lu　延安西路2099号
Tel: 6275-0000
Open 24 hours and serves mostly Western food.

## PASTA FRESCA　沙华多利意式面食

(Shahuadaoli Yishi Mianshi)
Hongqiao Friendship Shopping Center
虹桥友谊商城内
6 Zunyi Nan Lu　遵义南路6号
Tel: 6270-4693
Also at:
115 Changshu Lu and 4 Hengshan Lu
常熟路115号及衡山路4号
Tel: 6248-1705
Hours: 11:00 am - 3:00 pm,
　　　5:00 pm - 10:30 pm
Popular pizza and pasta bistro-type restaurant Italian owned and managed.

## PINES BISTRO BAR AND GRILL
松坊西餐厅

(Songfang Xican Ting)
3901 Hongmei Lu　虹梅路3901号
Tel: 6262-6447
Western grilled meats are available along with a salad bar at reasonable prices. Wines are available by glass, carafe, or bottle. Located on the second floor over Faber Supermarket, you'll find the décor to be very western and clean.

## SHANGHAI BARBYLON FRESH BEER CITY　上海巴比龙鲜啤城

(Shanghai Babilong Xianpicheng)
4th Fl, Universal Mansion Shopping
168-172 Yuyuan Lu　200040
愚园路168-172号环球商厦4楼
Tel: 6249-6511
Fax: 6271-1006
Hours: 1:00 pm - 1:00 am
Several dining areas in a wide-open "Western saloon" type place with steakhouse.

## SHANGHAI EXPRESS　沪江特快

(Hujian Tekuan)
Hilton Hotel, lower level
250 Huashan Lu
静安希尔顿地下室
Tel: 6248-0000 x 8607

Open 24 hours. Offers a variety of dim sum, noodles, and other Chinese dishes supplemented by several Western dishes.

## SHANGHAI SALLY'S 故乡餐厅
(Guxiang Canting)
4 Xiangshan Lu (opposite Sun Yat Sen's former residence) 香山路4号
Hours: 11:00 am - 2:00 am
Tel: 6358-1859 or 6375-3348
Hours: 5:00 pm - 2:00 am Mon. - Sat.,
        Sun. open at 11:00 am
A traditional English pub where you can relax and feel at home. Sally's offers a variety of games including pool, chess, dice games, and darts. Darts buffs can inquire about Sally's darts team. American inspired menu items such as BBQ sandwiches, chili fries, and apple pie.

## SUNSHINE CAFE
(Shenshen Canting)
8 Fuxing Xi Lu, at Huaihai Zhong Lu
复兴西路8号淮海路复兴路口
Tel: 6473-3182 x 126
10 Hengshan Lu 衡山路10号
Tel: 6474-6545
Hours: 11:00 am - 4:30 am
This restaurant serves Chinese and Western food in a lively pubby environment.

## SUPPER BOWL DELI 大堂美食店
(Datang Maishidian)
Huating Hotel and Towers 华亭宾馆
1200 Caoxi Bei Lu 漕溪北路1200号
Tel: 6439-1000, 6439-6000
Open 24 hours, light Western fare and deli.

## TEQUILA MAMA 巴哈玛
(Bahama)
24A Ruijin Er Lu (between Huaihai Lu and Nanchang Lu) Basement Level
瑞金二路24号
Tel: 6433-5086
Hours: 11:30 am - 4:00 am
Drinks are half-price between 5:00 pm and

8:00 pm. This establishment serves Mexican and Western dishes as well as some Asian items. The decor is best described as Mexican/Caribbean. Dance, play darts or pool, or use a KTV room.

## TERRACE CAFE 兰香阁
(Lanxiangge)
2nd Fl, Lansheng Hotel 兰生大酒店2楼
1000 Quyang Lu 曲阳路1000号
Tel: 6542-8000 x 2255
Hours: 11:00 am - 11:00 pm
Pleasant and quiet, offering Euro-style dishes.

## TIME CAFE 时代咖啡厅
(Shidai Kafeiting)
550 Huaihai Zhong Lu 淮海中路550号
Tel: 6327-5566
Hours: 9:30 am - 2:00 am
Live bands, singers, Western food and exotic drinks.

## TONY ROMA'S ☆ 多利萝玛餐厅
(Duoliluoma Canting)
#109 Retail Plaza, Shanghai Centre
上海商城西峰109室
1376 Nanjing Xi Lu, 200040
南京西路1376号
Tel: 6279-7129
Hours: 11:00 am - 11:00 pm, daily
Famous for American-style ribs and also salads, hamburgers, and chicken dishes. Their good blue cheese dressing is a welcome surprise.

## VIVA EL POPO ☆ 墨西哥餐厅
(Moxige Canting)
Bldg. 12, Lane 19, 12 Ronghua Xi Dao
荣华西道19弄12号
Golden Lion Garden 金狮公寓
Gubei New Area 古北新区
Tel: 6219-9279
Fax: 6275-0076
Hours: 11:00 am - late
Shanghai's first authentic Mexican restaurant

and bar. Noteworthy T-bone steaks and margaritas. Named for a volcano in southern Mexico. The fare is close to what's found in California.

# Fast Food

## KENTUCKY FRIED CHICKEN 肯德基
(Kendeji)

- 3 Zhongshan Dong Yi Lu,
  Dongfeng Fandian, Tel: 6321-5004
  中山东一路3号 东风饭店内
  Hours: 9:30 am - 10:00 pm
- 69 Wuning Lu, Tel: 6244-1013
  武宁路69 号
  Hours: 9:30 am - 10:00 pm
- 800 Changning Lu, Tel: 6212-1528
  长宁路800 号
  Hours: 8:00 am - 11:00 pm
- 50 Xuzhen Lu, Tel: 6438-7286
  徐镇路50 号
  Hours: 9:00 am - 10:00 pm
- 2150 Sichuan Bei Lu, Tel: 6540-3563
  四川北路2150 号
  Hours: 9:30 am - 10:30 pm
- 1117 Xiangyin Lu, Tel: 6511-1795
  翔鹰路1117 号
  Hours: 9:00 am - 11:00 pm
- 800 Pudong Nan Lu, Tel: 5882-0731
  浦东南路800 号
  Hours: 10:00 am - 10:00 pm
- 700-724 Xizang Zhong Lu,
  Tel: 6352-1353
  西藏中路700-724 号
  Hours: 10:00 am - 10:30 pm
- 66-68 Xizang Zhong Lu,
  Tel: 6322-5001 西藏中路66-68 号
  Hours: 9:30 am - 10:30 pm
- 888 Tianshan Lu, Tel: 5253-0354
  天山路888 号
  Hours: 8:00 am - 11:00 pm
- 15 Wujiang Lu, Tel: 6267-2571
  吴江路15 号
  Hours: 10:00 am - 10:30 pm
- 955 Huaihai Dong Lu, Tel: 6467-4974
  淮海东路955 号
  Hours: 9:00 am - 11:00 pm

- 627-641 Huaihai Zhong Lu,
  Tel: 6358-8564 淮海中路627-641号
  Hours: 9:00 am - 11:00 pm
- 1298 Huaihai Zhong Lu,
  Tel: 6474-7044 淮海中路1298 号
  Hours: 9:30 am - 10:30 pm
- 585 Hengfeng Lu, Tel: 6353-4517
  恒丰路585 号
  Hours: 9:00 am - 11:00 pm
- 1500 Pingliang Lu, Tel: 6520-2199
  平凉路1500 号
  Hours: 10:00 am - 10:00 pm
- 1165 Kongjiang Lu, Tel: 6501-7466
  控江路1165 号
  Hours: 9:00 am - 11:00 pm
- 1829 Beijing Xi Lu, Tel: 6240-8505
  北京西路1829 号
  Hours: 9:00 am - 11:00 pm
- Songjiang County, 99 Zhongshan Zhong
  Lu, Tel: 5772-0124
  松江县中山中路99 号
  Hours: 10:00 am - 9:30 pm
- 234 Fuyou Lu, Tel: 6326-4913
  福佑路234 号
  Hours: 9:30 am - 11:00 pm
- 1818 Sichuan Bei Lu, Tel: 6540-1058
  四川北路1818 号
  Hours: 9:30 am - 10:30 pm
- 880 Huaihai Zhong Lu, Tel: 6467-6766
  淮海中路880 号
  Hours: 8:30 am - 10:00 pm
- 333 Changle Lu, Tel: 5874-3962
  昌里路333 号
  Hours: 10:00 am - 9:00 pm
- 558 Nanjing Dong Lu, Tel: 5353-0144
  南京东路558 号
  Hours: 9:00 am - 10:30 pm
- 888 Wanhangdu Lu, Tel: 6212-9214
  万航渡路888号
  Hours: 9:30 am - 10:00 pm

- 1359 Zhonghua Lu  Tel: 6368-4318
  中华路1359号
  Hours: 9:00 am - 11:00 pm
- 231 Nanjing Xi Lu  Tel: 6372-3982
  南京西路231号
  Hours: 8:00 am - 11:00 pm
- 1318 Sichuan Bei Lu  Tel: 5354-1165
  四川北路1318号
  Hours: 9:30 am - 10:30 pm
- 976 Lujiabang Lu  Tel: 5357-0150
  陆家浜路976号
  Hours: 9:30 am - 10:00 pm
- 43 Tianmu Dong Lu  Tel: 6393-1182
  天目东路43号
  Hours: 9:30 am - 10:30 pm
- 137 Lanxi Lu  Tel: 6260-4031
  兰溪路137号
  Hours: 9:00 am - 10:00 pm
- 235 Tianmu Xi Lu  Tel: 6353-3312
  天目西路235号
  Hours: 9:00 am - 10:00 pm
- 1550 Gonghexin Lu  Tel: 5603-9814
  共和新路1550号
  Hours: 8:00 am - 11:00 pm

## MCDONALD'S  麦当劳
(Maidanglao)
Hours: 8:00 am - 11:00 pm
- 588 Huaihai Zhong Lu, Luwan District
  Tel: 5306-9608  卢湾区淮海中路588号
- 12-24 Wanhangdu Lu, Jing'an District
  Tel: 6256-3970  静安区万航渡路12-24号
- 588 Nanjing Dong Lu, Huangpu District
  Tel: 6352-1746  黄浦区南京东路588号
- 2052 Huangxing Lu, Yangpu District
  Tel: 6549-6817  扬浦区黄兴路2052号
- 500 Luochuan Dong Lu, Zhabei District
  Tel: 5670-3175  闸北区洛川东路500号
- 1380 Zhonghua Lu, Nanshi District
  Tel: 6377-6805  南市区中华路1380号

- 770 Changning Lu, Changning District
  Tel: 6252-4672  长宁区长宁路770号
- 22-50 Tianaizhi Lu, Hongkou District
  Tel: 5666-6742  虹口区甜爱支路22-50号
- 577 Fuzhou Lu, Huangpu District
  Tel: 6322-5807  黄浦区福州路577号
- 1963-1967 Sichuan Bei Lu, Hongkou
  District Tel: 5666-7643
  虹口区四川北路1963-1967号
- 88 Nanjing Xi Lu, Huangpu District
  Tel: 6358-9690  黄浦区南京西路88号
- 181 Lanxi Lu, Putuo District
  Tel: 6297-0081  普陀区兰溪路181号
- Lane 1088 Liyang Lu, Hongkou District
  Tel: 5666-7570  虹口区溧阳路1088弄
- 218 Tianmu Xi Lu, Zhabei District
  Tel: 6317-3753  闸北区天目路218号
- 898 Xiexu Lu, Luwan District
  Tel: 6418-9465  卢湾区斜徐路898号
- 1500 Sichuan Bei Lu, Hongkou District
  Tel: 6357-1035  虹口区四川北路1500号

## PIZZA HUT  必胜客
(Bishengke)
Hours: 11:00 am - 10:30 pm
- 700  Xizang Zhong Lu,
  Tel: 6352-3026 for take-out
  西藏店西藏中路700 号
- 770 Changning Lu, Tel: 6212-7788
  中山公园店长宁路770 号
- 88 Nanjing Xi Lu, Tel: 6358-8831, x 201
  and x 208  88总汇店南京西路88 号
- 887 Huaihai Zhong Lu, Tel: 6467-6764
  二百永新店淮海中路887 号

Pan pizza or thin and crispy, Shanghai Pizza Hut has it all, along with pasta, garlic bread, onions rings, soup, and salad bar. No delivery, however.

# Delivery / Take-out

## PIZZA KING 匹萨王

(Pisa Wang)
38 Shuicheng Lu, Changning district
水城路38号长宁区
Tel: 6242-4126
Hours: 9:00 am - midnight

Homemade tomato sauce and mozzarella cheese make up the basic pizza for RMB30. Each vegetarian topping runs an additional RMB5 (mushroom, onion, green pepper, chili, garlic, black olives, pineapple, corn, tomato, capers) and each meat topping adds an additional RMB10 (sausage, salami, bacon, sardines, ham, shrimp, pepperoni, chopped beef). Or order from their standard pizza menu. All come with tomato sauce and mozzarella plus:

| Regina | Mushroom and basil | RMB35 |
|---|---|---|
| Margarita | Basil | RMB35 |
| Veneziana | Shrimp and garlic | RMB40 |
| Shanghai Special | Sausage, onion, and chili | RMB40 |
| Re | Ham | RMB40 |
| Southern | Salami and chili | RMB40 |
| Vegetariana | Mushroom, green pepper, and onion | RMB40 |
| Taco Pizza | Chopped beef and chili | RMB40 |
| Hawaii | Ham and pineapple | RMB40 |
| Bolognese | Chopped beef | RMB40 |
| Shrimp Pizza | Shrimp and capers | RMB45 |
| Napoli | Sardines and black olives | RMB45 |

## YELLOW SUBMARINE 三友餐厅

(Sanyou Canting)
122 Fumin Lu 富民路122号
Tel/fax: 6279-4336
61 Yili Lu, Huangqiao 伊犁路61号虹桥
Tel: 6275-3630 x 2427

Primarily a take-out sandwich and pizza place.

Their "niche" is delivering hero sandwiches to your home or office if you aren't too far away. About 10 or 15 minutes from either the Portman or the Hilton. Expat manager "China Jim" Nicholson plans to open a similar restaurant in Gubei in the near future.

# CHINESE RESTAURANTS

China's EIGHT GREAT CUISINES are classified by regional culinary traditions. The eight are Beijing, Sichuan, Guangzhou (Cantonese), Fujian (Ming), Zhejiang (Zhe), Suzhou-Wuxi (SuXi), Anhui (Hui), and Muslim (Qingzheng). The three that are considered the best by gourmet standards are the cuisines of Guangzhou, Sichuan, and Beijing. Shanghai food is criticized by experts for its complicated preparation and its oiliness. However, Shanghai cuisine is notable for its hairy crab and its delicious pastries. Vegetarian restaurants are easy to find as it is a Buddhist tradition to eat vegetarian food.

Those unfamiliar with Chinese food can initiate themselves gradually by sampling "foreigner-friendly" dishes such as sweet and sour pork, lemon chicken, wonton soup, steamed dumplings and spring rolls. The chance to try more exotic dishes will come soon enough at the many dinners and business banquets one is constantly invited to in China. Special dishes are invariably ordered to impress foreign guests, allowing for the opportunity to increase one's repertoire of newly discovered dishes, and enhancing one's future ordering ability. One ordering guideline to adhere to is ordering a minimum of seven different types of dishes when dining with guests. These would include fish, fowl, meat, soup, and vegetable dishes for sure. The others could be dessert, rice or noodles, or dim sum. You may want to add an assortment of appetizers to the menu as well. One eventually learns through trial and error to put together a decent meal in a restaurant.

Listed below is a sampling of Shanghai's more popular Chinese restaurants. There are two major "food streets" in Shanghai, one on Zhapu Lu (in the Hongkou district) and one on Huanghe Lu (between Nanjing Lu and Beijing Lu near the Park Hotel.) These restaurant rows are especially appealing at night when awash in neon and tiny lights.

## AH YAT ABALONE FORUM SEAFOOD RESTAURANT ☆
阿一鲍鱼富临海鲜酒家
(A Yi Baoyu Fulin Haixian Jiujia)
2nd Fl, Shartex Plaza
88 Zunyi Nan Lu    遵义南路88号
Tel: 6219-2777, 8219-2666
Fax: 6219-7177
Hours: 11:00 am - 2:00 pm,
        4:00 pm - 11:00 pm
This restaurant is pricey, but good, specializing in delicacies such as salmon sashimi, shark's fin, bird's nest soup, and of course, abalone. The original restaurant is still operating in Hong Kong. On special holiday occasions, there are interesting set menus. Menus are printed in English and Chinese.

## BAI YU LAN  白玉兰中餐厅
(Baiyulan Zhongcanting)
Garden Hotel    花园饭店
(Huayuan Fandian)
58 Maoming Nan Lu    茂名南路58号
Tel: 6415-1111
Hours: 7:00 am - 9:30 am,
        11:30 am - 2:30 pm,
        5:30 pm - 10:00 pm
Cantonese cuisine.

## BAMBOO GARDEN ☆  竹园
(Zhu Yuan)
Jinjiang Tower    新锦江
161 Changle Lu    长乐路161号
Tel: 6415-1188
Hours: 7:00 am - 10:00 am, 11:30 am -
        2:00 pm, and 5:30 pm - 10:00 pm.
Sichuan-style restaurant that is quiet and refined. The ambiance is enhanced by soft Erhu

music, and Peking duck doesn't require the usual one-hour wait.

## CASH BOX 钱柜
(Qian Gui)
- 200 Yandang Lu 雁荡路200号
  Tel: 6358-3888
  Open 24 hours
- 457 Wulumuqi Bei Lu 乌鲁木齐北路457号
  Tel: 6248-6888
  Open 24 hours
- 200 Ninghai Dong Lu 宁海东路200号
  Tel: 6374-9909
  Open 24 hours. KTV palace and restaurant.

## CHAOZHOU GARDEN 潮州园
(Chaozhou Yuan)
Yangtze New World Hotel 扬子江大酒店
(Yangzijiang Dajiudian)
2099 Yan'an Xi Lu 延安西路2099号
Tel: 6275-0000
Hours: 11:00 am - 2:15 pm,
　　　　6:00 pm - 10:15 pm

## CHAOZHOU CUISINE 如意厅
(Ruyi Ting)
Dahua Guesthouse 达华宾馆
914 Yan'an Xi Lu 延安西路914号
Tel: 6251-2512
Hours: 5:00 pm - 11:00 pm
Fangshan-style Chaozhou cuisine of the Imperial Qing Dynasty.

## DONGFENG RESTAURANT 东风饭店
(Dongfeng Fandian)
3 Zhongshan Dong Yi Lu 中山东一路3号
Tel: 6321-8060
Hours: 11:00 am - 8:30 pm
Jiangsu style, favoring the methods of braising, stewing and simmering. Specialties include chicken leg Dongfen style and roast crisp duck.

## DRAGON AND PHOENIX RESTAURANT
☆ 龙风厅
(Longfengting)
Peace Hotel 和平饭店
(Heping Fandian)
20 Nanjing Dong Lu 南京东路20号
Tel: 6321-6888 x 6202
Hours: 11:30 am - 2:30 pm,
　　　　5:30 pm - 11:00 pm
This restaurant on the eighth floor has window tables offering a wonderful view of the Huangpu River and the Bund. Several types of Chinese cuisine are offered. A trip to Shanghai would be incomplete without a visit to this historic landmark.

## DYNASTY RESTAURANT 满福楼
(Manfulou)
Yangtze New World Hotel 扬子江大酒店
(Yangzijiang Dajiudian)
2099 Yan'an Xi Lu
延安西路2099号
Tel: 6275-0000
Hours: 11:00 am - 2:30 pm,
　　　　6:00 pm - 10:30 pm
Cantonese food.

## DYNASTY RESTAURANT 京华楼
(Jinghualou)
Ocean Hotel 远洋宾馆
1171 Dongdaming Lu 东大名路1171号
Tel: 6545-8888
Hours: 7:00 am - 10:30 am, 11:00 am -
　　　　2:30 pm, 5:00 pm - 10:00 pm
Chaozhou cuisine.

## EMERALD GARDEN 翡翠园
(Feicuiyuan)
Westin Tai Ping Yang 太平洋大酒店
(Taipingyang Dajiudian)
5 Zunyi Nan Lu, 200335 遵义路5号
Tel: 6275-8888
Hours: 11:30 am - 2:30 pm,
　　　　5:00 pm - 10:00 pm
Cantonese cuisine.

## FIVE GRAND WONDERS RESTAURANT
五岳厅
(Wu Yueying)
Jianguo Fandian　建国饭店
(Jianguo Binguan)
439 Caoxi Bei Lu　漕溪北路439号
Tel: 6439-9299 x 3320
Hours: 10:30 am - 2:00 pm,
　　　5:00 pm - 9:00 pm
Chaozhou cuisine.

## FOLK RESTAURANT　鲜墙房川菜
(Xianqiangfang Chuancai)
57 Nanchang Lu　南昌路57号
Tel: 6372-9893
Hours: 11:00 am - midnight
Unusual selection of rare treats, and unusual
Shanghainese dishes.

## FOOD PLAZA　美食广场
(Meishi Guangchang)
Radisson Lansheng Hotel　兰生大酒店
(Lansheng Dajiudian)
1000 Quyang Lu　曲阳路1000号
Tel: 6542-8000
Hours: 6:30 am - 1:00 am
Chaozhou cuisine.

## FORTUNE PALACE RESTAURANT
天府楼
(Tianfu Lou)
3rd Fl, East China Hotel　华东大酒店3楼
(Huadong Dajiudian)
111 Tianmu Xi Lu　天目西路111号
Tel: 6317-8000
Hours: 10:30 am 11:00 pm Mon. - Fri.,
　　　9:30 am - 11:00 pm Sat. and Sun.
Sichuan cuisine.

## FORUM PALACE CHIUCHOW RESTAURANT　富临皇宫
(Fulin Huanggong)
3rd Fl, 965 Huaihai Zhong Lu
淮海中路965号
Tel :6415-7301

Hours: 11:00 am - 10:30 pm Mon. - Fri.,
　　　9:30 am - 10:30 pm Sat. and Sun.
Nice atmosphere, reasonable prices, excellent
seafood.

## FORUM PALACE NO. 1 YAOHAN RESTAURANT
富临皇宫第一八佰伴酒楼
(Fulin Huanggong Diyi Babaiban Jiulou)
8th Fl, Yaohan Next Age Department Store
上海第一八佰伴新世纪商廈
(Babaiban)
501 Zhangyang Lu, Lujiazui, Pudong
上海浦东新区张扬路501号
Intersection of Pudong Lu and Zhangyang Lu
(close to the new tunnel from West Shanghai)
Tel: 5830-2855
Hours: 11:00 am - 10:00 pm

## FRIENDSHIP RESTAURANT　如意酒家
(Ruyi Jiujia)
58 Yuanmingyuan Lu　园明园路58 号
Tel: 6321-2434
Hours: 11:00 am - 2:30 pm,
　　　5:00 pm - 10:30 pm,
　　　8:00 am - midnight (Sun. only)
Expatriates seem to like this Cantonese restau-
rant located at the top of the Exhibition Center.
Prices are moderate and the food is good.

## FRIENDSHIP RESTAURANT　友谊餐厅
(Youyi Canting)
Jinjiang Hotel, Jinjiang Food Street
锦江美食街
59 Maoming Nan Lu　茂名南路59号
Tel: 6258-2582
Open 24 hours.
Cantonese cuisine.

## FULIN XUAN　富临轩鱼翅海鲜酒家
(Fulinxuan Yuchi Haixian Jiujia)
37 Sinan Lu　思南路37号
Tel:6358-3699, 6372-1777
Fax:6372-5151
Hours: 11:00 am - 11:00 pm

On Sinan Lu near Xiangshan Lu. Pricey, but good. Nice decor.

## FU RONG ZHEN　芙蓉镇
Shanghai Crowne Plaza
银星假日酒家
(Yinxing Jiare Jiujia)
388 Panyu Lu, 200052　番禺路388号
Tel: 6280-8888
Hours: 11:00 am - 2:00 pm,
　　　 5:00 pm - 10:00 pm
Sichuan cuisine.

## THE GAP　电影文艺沙龙锦亭
(Dianying Wenyi Shalong Jinting)
127 Maoming Nan Lu, near the entrance to the old Jin Jiang Hotel: 茂名南路127号
Tel: 6433-9028
Hours: 11.00 am - 2:00 am
The food is Chinese, but the ambience is Western, with checkered tablecloths, stone floors and a spacious interior. The main dining room's ceiling is two stories high with a mezzanine for a additional tables. The second floor also has several well-appointed private dining rooms.

## GOLDEN PHOENIX　金凤楼
(Jinfeng Lou)
2nd Fl, Equatorial Hotel
上海国际贵都大饭店二楼
(Shanghai Guoji Guidu Dafandian)
65 Yan'an Xi Lu　延安西路65号
Tel: 6248-1688
Hours: 11:30 am - 2:00 pm,
　　　 5:30 pm - 10:00 pm
Cantonese cuisine.

## GONGDELIN VEGETARIAN RESTAURANT　功德林素餐馆
(Gongdelin Sucanguan)
445 Nanjing Xi Lu　南京西路445号
Tel: 6327-1532
Hours: 7:30 am - 5:30 pm
Open for over 50 years, this restaurant borrows from Beijing, Sichuan, Yangzhou and Guangdong cuisines to create its own famous vegetarian dishes.

## GRAPE RESTAURANT
上海格瑞普酒家
(Shanghai Geruipu Jiujia)
55 Xinle Lu　新乐路55号
Tel: 6472-0486
Hours: 11:00 am - 12:30 am
Great prices, good food. Sister establishment to the New Grape.

## THE NEW GRAPE　新葡萄园酒家
(Xin Putaoyuan Jiujia)
142 Xinle Lu　新乐路142号
Tel: 6472-0499
Hours: 11:00 am - 11:00 pm
A small establishment frequented by the expat community. Food is good, prices are low, and the menu is in English.

## GREEN WAVE RESTAURANT ☆
绿波廊酒楼
(Lu Bolang Jiujia)
115 Yuyuan Lu　豫园路115号
Tel: 6373-7020
Hours: 11:00 am - 2:00 pm,
　　　 5:00 pm  8:30 pm
Shanghainese cuisine in an unusually nice ambience. Located in the old city, adjacent to Yu Garden.

## GREEN WILLOW VILLAGE RESTAURANT
绿扬村酒家
(Luyangcun Jiujia)
763 Nanjing Xi Lu　南京西路763号
Tel: 6255-0359
Hours: 7:00 am - 10:00 pm

## GUAN YUE TAI　观月台
(Guanyuetai)
Huating Hotel and Towers　华亭宾馆
(Huating Binguan)
1200 Caoxi Bei Lu　漕溪北路1200号

Tel: 6439-1000, 6439-6000 x 2611
Hours: 11:30 am - 2:00 pm,
        5:30 pm - 10:00 pm
Cantonese cuisine.

## HAI YU LAN GE SHANGHAINESE RESTAURANT 海粤厅

(Haiyueting)
Hyland Sofitel Hotel 海仑宾馆
(Hailun Binguan)
505 Nanjing Dong Lu 南京东路505号
Tel: 6351-5888
Hours: 11:30 am - 2:30 pm,
        5:30 pm - 10:30 pm
Shanghainese cuisine.

## HAI TIAN RESTAURANT 海天餐厅

(Haitian Canting)
516 Jungong Lu, Yangpu District (on the campus of the Shanghai Fisheries University)
军工路516号
Tel: 6571-0253
Hours: 11:00 am - 2:00 pm,
        5:00 pm - 8:00 pm
Open seven days a week.
Haitian means Sea Sky, but the accent here is clearly on the sea. This is the school's showcase for SFU's mission to promote fresh and saltwater fish and shellfish of every description. The extensive menu is in Chinese, Pinyin, and English. Enter the main gate, head toward the statue of Chairman Mao, turn left at the second road, and continue about 1,000 meters. The university manufactures its own tofu, and it's also on the menu. Beef, pork, and chicken dishes are also available and prices are very reasonable.

## HAI YUE TING CANTONESE RESTAURANT 海粤厅

(Haiyueting)
5th Fl, Hotel Sofitel 海仑宾馆5楼
505 Nanjing Dong Lu 南京东路505号
Tel: 6351-5888

Fax: 6351-4088
Hours: 7:00 am - 2:00 pm,
        5:30 pm - 10:30 pm
Noted for authentic Cantonese dim sum prepared by a master chef from Hong Kong and served daily for lunch and for breakfast buffet every Saturday and Sunday.

## HANSE RESTAURANT AND BAR

121 Zunyi Lu 遵义路121号
Hours: 11:00 am - 2:00 am
Despite its German name, this restaurant, located about two blocks north of the Westin Hotel in Hongqiao, serves Shanghainese and Fujian cuisine. The three-story venue has a Mexican design theme with Chinese art thrown into the mix. The atmosphere is casual and service is fast.

## HAO CHENG RESTAURANT 豪城餐厅

(Haocheng Canting)
235 Fahuazhen Lu 法华镇路235号
Tel: 6281-8308, 6281-7303
Hours: 10:30 am - 4:00 am
Haocheng is located directly across the street from the Crowne Plaza (银星假日酒家对面). Patrons rave about the low prices and good food.

## JIA QING TANG 佳庆堂餐厅

(Jiaqingtang Canting)
Rainbow Hotel 虹桥宾馆
(Hongqiao Binguan)
2000 Yan'an Xi Lu 延安西路2000号
Tel: 6275-3388
Hours: 6:00 am - 9:00 am,
        11:30 am - 1:00 pm,
        5:30 pm - 9:30 pm
Cantonese cuisine.

## JIE ER JING SICHUAN RESTAURANT 洁而精川菜馆

(Jie Er Jing Chuancaiguan)
82 Yandang Lu 雁荡路82号

Tel: 6372-8574

Hours: 10:00 am - 2:00 pm,
        5:00 pm - 8:30 pm

## JIN JIANG FOOD STREET RESTAURANT
锦园

(Jinyuan)

Shanghai Worldfield Convention Hotel
上海世博会议大酒店
(Shanghai Sibuo Huiyi Dajiudian)
2106 Hongqiao Road    虹桥路2106号
Changning District, Shanghai
Tel: 6270-3388
Hours: 11:00 am - 2:30 pm,
        5:00 pm - 10:30 pm

Cantonese cuisine

## JUE LIN VEGETARIAN RESTAURANT
觉林蔬食馆

(Juejin Shushi Guan)
250 Jinling Dong Lu    金陵东路250号
Tel: 6326-0115
Hours: 6:00 am - 10:00 am,
        11:00 am - 1:30 pm,
        5:00 pm - 7:30 pm

## JUXING (SUPERSTAR) RESTAURANT
巨星餐厅

(Juxing Canting)

Building #1, 155 Xinhua Lu    新华路155号
This 3-story restaurant is located near the
Holiday Inn Crowne Plaza and the Shanghai
Film Center. An extensive menu offers
Japanese, Taiwanese, Shanghainese,
Cantonese, and Sichuanese food.

## LONG CHENG RESTAURANT    蓉城餐厅

(Rongcheng Canting)
City Hotel    城市酒家
(Chengshi Jiujia)
5-7 Shaanxi Nan Lu    陕西南路5-7号
Tel: 6255-1133
Hours: 11:30 am - 2:30 pm,
        5:30 pm - 9:30 pm
Sichuanese cuisine.

## LOTUS (HE HUA TING)    荷花厅

(Hehuating)
Novotel Yuanlin Hotel    园林宾馆
(Yuanlin Binguan)
201 Baise Lu    百色路201号
Tel: 6470-1688
Hours: 11:00 am - 2:00 pm,
        6:00 pm - 1:00 am
Cantonese cuisine.

## LULU RESTAURANT    鹭鹭酒家

(Lulu Jiujia)
69 Shimen Yi Lu    石门一路69号
Tel: 6258-5645
Hours: 11:00 am - 1:30 pm,
        5:00 pm - 9:00 pm
It's sometimes hard to get a table here, but
the food is good. Seafood is the specialty.

## LUYANGCUN RESTAURANT    绿扬村

(Luyangcun Jiujia)
763 Nanjing Xi Lu    南京西路763号
Tel: 6253-7221
Hours: 7:00 am - midnight
Specialties include crisp chicken Luyang style
and bean curd Luyang style. Dishes offered in
both Sichuan and Yangzhou style.

## MEILONGZHEN RESTAURANT
梅龙镇酒家

(Meilongzheng Jiujia)
1081 Nanjing Xi Lu at Jiangning Lu
南京西路1081号
Tel: 6256-6688, 6256-2718
Hours: 11:00 am - 1:30 pm,
        5:00 pm - 9:00 pm
This renowned restaurant has been open since
1938. Its dishes, served in classical Sichuan
style influenced by Shanghai cuisine, include
snake, duck, stir-fried chicken legs in soup,
and pork. Seating capacity is 600 throughout
seven diversely styled dining halls.

## MOON-NIGHT RESTAURANT
月杨城餐厅
(Yueyangcheng Canting)
105 Yandang Lu 雁荡路105号
Tel: 6372-3649
Hours: 6:00 am - 11:00 pm
Shanghainese cuisine.

## MOON SHANGHAI XIJIAO
## RESTAURANT 夜上海西郊园酒家
(Ye Shanghai Xijiaoyuan Jiujia)
1119 Hongqiao Lu 虹桥路1119号
Tel: 6270-9777, 6270-3468
Fax: 6270-3475
Hours: 11:00 am - 1:00 am
The ambience is upscale and nicely done. A jazz combo plays during the peak dinner hours but is unobtrusive and pleasant. This is considered a Shanghainese restaurant and the food is nicely presented and good. Pricing is moderate to high.

## MUSLIM HUIFEN RESTAURANT
回风楼菜馆
(Huifenglou Caiguan)
89 Henan Lu at Remnin Lu
河南路89号人民路口
Tel: 6328-1795
Hours: 6:30 am - 9:30 pm

## NAN XING YA RESTAURANT
新雅粤餐馆
(Xinyayue Canguan)
457 Nanjing Dong Lu 南京东路457号
Tel: 6351-4718
Hours: 10:30 am - 9:00 pm
Pork, duck, fish and chicken served in traditional spicy Sichuan style.

## NEW SEAFOOD CITY RESTAURANT
新海鲜城大酒店
(Xin Haixiancheng Dajiudian)
122 Shaanxi Nan Lu 陕西南路122号
Tel: 6279-2111 x111

Hours: 10:30 am - 2:00 am
Shanghainese cuisine.

## PEACH GARDEN ☆ 鸿桃轩
(Hongtao Xuan)
JC Mandarin Hotel 锦伧文华大酒店
1225 Nanjing Xi Lu 南京西路1225号
Tel: 6279-1888
Hours: 11:30 am - 2:30 pm,
        5:30 pm - 10:30 pm
Beautiful setting in which to enjoy good Cantonese cuisine.

## PLUM BLOSSOM ROOM 梅花厅
(Meihua Ting )
Jinjiang Tower 新锦江
(Xin Jinjiang)
161 Changle Lu 长乐路161号
Tel: 6415-1188
Hours: 11:30 am - 2:00 pm,
        5:30 pm - 10:00 pm
Chaozhou cuisine.

## RAINBOW FOOD PALACE 虹桥食馆
(Hongqiao Shifu)
Rainbow Hotel 虹桥宾馆
(Hongqiao Binguan)
2000 Yan'an Xi Lu 延安西路2000号
Tel: 6275-3388, 6275-3399
Hours: 7:00 am - 10:00 am,
        11:30 am - 2:00 pm,
        5:30 pm - 9:30 pm
Beijing cuisine.

## RESTAURANT SHANGHAI NIGHT CLUB
上海滩酒家夜总会
(Shanghaitan Jiujia Yezonghui)
Shartex Plaza 协泰中心
88 Zunyi Nan Lu 遵义南路88号
Tel: 6275-9678
Hours: 11:00 am - 2:00 pm,
        5:30 pm - 11:00 pm
Authentic Shanghainese cuisine.

## REVOLVING 28  怡珀旋宫餐厅

(Yipo Xuangong Canting)
28th Fl, Ocean Hotel  远洋宾馆28楼
1171 Dongdaming Lu  东大名路1171号
Lunch: 11:15am -2:30 pm
Tea:    3:00 pm - 5:00 pm
Dinner:5:15 pm - 10:30 pm
Tel: 6545-8888
Stunning ever-changing views of the city near
the Bund. Just north of Suzhou Creek near the
river, offering Cantonese-Sichuan cuisine.

## SEA PALACE  海龙海鲜舫

(Hailong Haixianfang)
东昌路1号 浦东新区
Tel: 5887-7111, 5887-5123, 5840-6858
Fax: 5887-2277
Hours: 11:00 am - 2:00 pm,
       5:00 pm - 10:30 pm
Situated at Youlong Wharf in Pudong, not far
south of the Oriental Pearl television tower.
Seafood is the specialty of this large floating
restaurant affiliated with the Jumbo Seafood
floating restaurant in Hong Kong.

## SEA PALACE CHAO ZHOU
## RESTAURANT  上海海上皇宫潮州酒家

(Shanghai Haishang Huanggong Chaozhou
Jiulou)
Shanghai Hotel   上海宾馆
(Shanghai Binguan)
505 Wulumuqi Bei Lu   乌鲁木齐路505号
Tel:  6248-0088 x 6388 or for reservations
call 6248-1388
Hours: 11:00 am - 10:00 pm
Chaozhou cuisuine.

## SHANGHAI EXPRESS  沪江特快

(Hejiang Tekuan)
Hilton Hotel, basement level  静安希尔顿
(Jing'an Xi'erdun)
250 Huashan Lu   华山路250号
Tel: 6248-0000
Open 24 hours
Chinese food and an assortment of Western
items.

## SHANGHAI LAO FANDIAN
上海老饭店

(Shanghai Lao Fandian)
242 Fuyou Lu    福佑路242号
Tel: 6328-2782
Hours: 11:00 am - 2:00 pm,
       5:30 pm - 10:00 pm
Noted for its exceptional Shanghai cuisine,
including stewed turtle. The ambience leaves
something to be desired and it's quite cold in
the wintertime, but this restaurant is a famous
Shanghai institution.

## SHANGHAI MEI GIAO  美侨娱乐总汇

(Meiqiao Yule Zonghui)
120 Jinxian Lu   进贤路120号
Tel: 6256-4168
Hours: 11:30 am - 10:30 pm
Upscale Chinese restaurant with excellent
service and food.

## SHANGHAI RESTAURANT  沪江轩

(Hujiangxuan)
City Hotel   城市酒家
(Chengshi Jiujia)
5th Fl, 5-7 Shaanxi Nan Lu
陕西南路5-7号5楼
Tel: 6255-1133 x 1351
Hours: 11:30 am - 2:30 pm,
       5:30 pm - 11:00 pm
Shanghainese cuisine.

## SHANG PALACE  ☆ 香宫餐厅

(Xianggong Canting)
Portman Ritz-Carlton   波特曼大酒店
(Shanghai Shangcheng)
1376 Nanjing Xi Lu   南京西路1376号
Tel: 6279-8888 x 4770
Hours: 11:30 am - 2:30 pm,
       5:30 pm - 10:30 pm,
       Sundays from 10:30 am
Level 2, Shanghai Centre, over the Tea
Garden Coffee Shop (上海商城2楼).
One of the most elegant Chinese restaurants
in Shanghai. Order exclusively from a vast

dim sum menu at lunch. Prices reflect the superior food quality.

## SHAO TANG JIU JIA　少棠酒家
488 Xianxia Lu　仙霞路488号
Tel: 6219-1415
Mobile: 139-177-5776
Hours: 11:00 am - 10:00 pm
Good food, good service and clean (with some of the tidiest restrooms in town). The only catch is the Chinese/Spanish menu.

## SICHUAN COURT　四川天府楼
(Tianfu Lou)
Hilton Hotel　上海希尔顿
250 Huashan Lu　华山路250 号
Hours: 6:00 pm - 10:30 pm daily
Reservations tel: 6248-0000 x 8686
Serves Sichuan cuisine such as Chengdu tea and wok charred beef fillet with Sichuan vegetables. Classical Chinese music is offered along with spectacular views of the city.

## SICHUAN COURT　四川天府楼
175 Zhapu Lu　乍浦路175号
Tel: 6306-9898
Hours: 11:00 am - 2:00 pm,
　　　　5:00 pm - 2:00 am
448 Zunyi Lu　遵义路448号
2nd Fl, Yueping Hotel　玉屏宾馆
Tel: 6233-1147
Hours: 11:00 am - 2:00 pm,
　　　　5:00 pm - midnight
Both locations of this restaurant serve authentic Sichuanese dishes and hotpot.

## SICHUAN RESTAURANT　四川餐厅
(Sichuan Canting)
Jinjiang Hotel, Jinjiang Food Street
锦江饭店美食街
59 Maoming Nan Lu　茂名南路59号
6258-2582 x 9121
Hours: 11:30 am - 2:00 pm,
　　　　5:30 pm - 10:00 pm

## SOUTH BUILDING RESTAURANT
汇中厅
(Huizhong Ting)
Peace Hotel　和平饭店
(Heping Fandian)
20 Nanjing Dong Lu　南京东路20号
Tel: 6321-6888
Hours: 11:15 am - 2:00 pm,
　　　　5:15 pm - 10:30 pm
A new concept in Shanghai cuisine. Dishes that are already prepared are displayed with their price for "fast food" Shanghai-style.

## SUIYUAN ☆ 随园
(Suiyuan)
2nd Fl, Hilton Hotel
上海希尔顿饭店2楼
250 Huashan Lu　华山路250 号
Tel: 6248-0000
Hours: 11:30 am - 2:00 pm,
　　　　6:00 pm - 10:30 pm
Cantonese cuisine in a pleasant setting.

## TIANLUN　天伦酒楼
(Tianlun Jiulou)
117 Shaanxi Nan Lu　陕西南路117号
Tel: 6437-5109
Hours: 11:30 am - 2:00 am

## TIAN YUAN　恬园
(Tian Yuan)
Shanghai Crowne Plaza　银星假日酒家
(Yinxing Jiare Jiujia)
388 Panyu Lu　番禺路388号
Tel: 6280-8888
Hours: 11:30 am - 2:30 pm,
　　　　5:30 pm - 10:30 pm
Cantonese cuisine.

## TAI SHENG YUAN RESTAURANT
苔圣园餐厅
(Taishenyuan Canting)
50 Huanghe Lu　黄河路50号
Tel: 6375-0022
Open 24 hours.

Very popular and crowded, so arrive early. This restaurant serves a wide variety of dishes and prides itself on unique flavors.

## TAOLI RESTAURANT  桃李
(Taoli)
Nikko Hotel  日航龙柏饭店
(Rihang Longbai Fandian)
2451 Hongqiao Lu  虹桥路2451号
Tel: 6268-9111
Hours: 7:00 am - 9:30 am,
          11:30 am - 2:00 pm,
          6:30 pm - 9:30 pm
Cantonese cuisine.

## THANKSGIVING GARDEN  感恩苑
(Gan'en Yuan)
62 Fuxing Xi Lu  复兴西路62号
Tel: 64/4-2002  9108-4555
Fuxing Lu at Yongfu Lu  复兴路近永福路
Hours: 9:00 am - 2:00 am
Good food, low prices, and it's open 24 hours a day, every day.

## 1221 THE DINING ROOM  1221 餐厅
(1221 Canting)
1221 Yan'an Xi Lu  延安西路1221号
Tel: 6213-6585, 6213-2441
Manager: Michelle Liu
This is a step above other local eateries that provide good food at moderate prices. The ambience is modern and spare and the Chinese dishes are nicely presented. A group of ten can easily feast well and drink seemingly endless pitchers of beer for RMB800. Located on the west side of the Pan Pacific Building at the end of the alcove running alongside, with a "speakeasy" type entrance.

## TUNG AH CHAOZHOU RESTAURANT
东亚潮州酒家
(Dongya Chaozhou Jiulou)
3rd and 4th Floor, Hongqiao Freindship Shopping Center  虹桥友谊商城3-4楼
6 Zunyi Nan Lu  遵义南路6号

Tel: 6270-4690, 6270-3668
Hours: 10:00 am - 3:00 pm,
          5:00 pm - 10:00 pm
          (last order taken at 9:45 pm)
Cobra and "Five Step" pit viper are on the menu, as well as hare and pheasant.

## VILLAGE RESTAURANT  家乡饭店
(Jiaxiang Fandian)
137 Tianping Lu  天平路137号
Tel: 6282-4273
Hours: 11:30 am - 2:00 pm,
          5:30 pm - 10:00 pm
Comfortable atmosphere, good food. This restaurant is run by a mother and daughter team from Hong Kong.

## WANG BAO HE RESTAURANT
王宝和酒楼
(Wangbaohe Jiulou)
603 Fuzhou Lu  福州路603号
Tel: 6322-3673
Hours: 11:00 am - 1:30 pm,
          5:00 pm - 8:00 pm
Sichuan Food.

## WHITE CLOUD  白云厅
(Baiyun Ting)
Jianguo Hotel Shanghai  建国饭店
(Jianguo Binguan)
439 Caoxi Bei Lu  漕溪北路439号
Tel: 6439-9299 x 6
Hours: 6:00 am - 10:00 am,
          11:00 am - 4:00 pm,
          5:00 pm - 10:00 pm
Cantonese cuisine.

## XINGHUALOU RESTAURANT
杏花楼酒家
(Xinghualou Jiujia)
343 Fu Zhou Lu  福州路343 号
Tel: 6355-3777
Hours: 6:30 am - 2:00 am
Known for its cured meats, this century-old restaurant specializes in dishes such as cat,

chicken and masked civet cat.

## XIN YA RESTAURANT　新雅粤厅馆

(Xinyayue Canguan)
556 Fuzhou Lu　福州路556 号
Tel: 6322-3176
Hours: 11:00 am - 2:00 pm,
　　　5:00 pm - 9:00 pm
Appreciated by many, this restaurant specializes in Guangdong style dishes.

## YANYUNLOU RESTAURANT
燕云楼饭店

(Yanyunlou Fandian)
755 Nanjing Dong Lu　南京东路755号
Tel: 6322-1563

Hours: 10:45 am - 1:45 pm,
　　　5:00 pm - 10:30 pm
Known for its authentic Beijing style cuisine. A trip to this restaurant would not be complete without an order of Beijing roast duck.

## YOUYI JIU JIA　友谊酒家

(Youyi Jiujia)
1000 Yan'an Zhong Lu　延安中路1000号
Tel: 6279-0279 x 63505
Hours: 11:00 am - 2:00 pm,
　　　5:00 pm - 10:00 pm
Located at the Shanghai Exhibition Center, this large restaurant is one of the best places in town for authentic Cantonese cuisine.

# INDIAN RESTAURANTS

## JIN JIANG BOMBAY TANDOOR
## RESTAURANT　印度餐厅

(Yindu Canting)
Jinjiang Hotel, New South Building
锦江饭店南楼
59 Maoming Nan Lu　茂名南路59 号
Tel: 6258-2582 x 9301 or 6472-5494

Fax: 6252-2335
Hours: 11:00 am - 2:30 pm,
　　　5:30 pm - 10:30 pm
This establishment has become very popular with the expatriate community of Shanghai. The decor is stunning and the food is unique to Shanghai.

# JAPANESE RESTAURANTS

## BENKAY RESTAURANT　卉庆日餐厅

(Huiqingri Canting)
Hotel Nikko Longbai　日航龙柏饭店
(Rihang Longbai Fandian)
2451 Hongqiao Lu　虹桥路2451号
Tel: 6268-9111 x 1625
Hours: 11:30 am - 2:00 pm,
　　　6:00 pm - 9:30 pm

## EVERGREEN (TAIWAN AND JAPAN)
## RESTAURANT　四季餐厅

(Siji Canting)
Shanghai Centre　上海商城
1376 Nanjing Xi Lu　南京西路1376号

Tel: 6279-8888 x 5898
Hours: 11:00 am - 3:00 am

## GINZA JAPANESE RESTAURANT AND
## KARAOKE BAR　银座

(Yinzuo)
Shanghai Worldfield Convention Hotel
上海世博会议大酒店
(Shanghai Sibuo Huiyi Dajiudian)
2106 Hongqiao Lu　虹桥路2106号
Tel: 6270-3388
Hours: 11:00 am - 2:30 pm,
　　　5:00 pm - 10:30 pm

## HANAZEN　花膳

(Huashan)
574 Yongjia Lu at Wulumuqi Lu
永嘉路574号近乌鲁木齐路
Tel: 6474-6427
Hours: 11:30 am - 2:00 pm,
　　　　5:30 pm - 10:30 pm
Located in the Consulate area, this restaurant is beautifully decorated down to the last detail.

## INAGIKU RESTAURANT　日本餐厅

(Riben Canting)
Westin Taipingyang Hotel
太平洋大酒店
(Taipingyang Dajiudian)
5 Zunyi Nan Lu　遵义南路5号
Tel: 6275-8888
Hours: 7:00 am - 9:00 am,
　　　　11:30 am - 2:00 pm,
　　　　5:30 pm - 10:00 pm

## ITOYA　伊藤家

(Yi Teng Jia)
- 24 Ruijin Er Lu　瑞金二路24号
  Tel: 6473-0758
- Longhua Xidao, #6 Lane 19, Gubei
  荣华西道19弄6号(古北新区)
  Tel: 6219-2286
- 2nd Fl, 400 Changle Lu
  长乐路400号2楼
  Tel: 6466-2929
- 111 Ruijin Yi Lu　瑞金一路111号
  Tel: 6318-4722

Hours: 11:30 am - 11:30 pm
Those who can't read the menu can satisfy themselves at the sushi bar which is one of the best in town. Fresh fish is flown in daily.

## KAMPUCHI JAPANESE RESTAURANT
勘八日本料理

(Kanba Riben Liaoli)
4th Fl, Equatorial Hotel
上海国际贵都大饭店
(Shanghai Guoji Guidu Dafandian)

65 Yan'an Xi Lu　延安西路65号
Tel: 6248-1688 x 2340 or x 2341
Hours: 10:00 am - 10:00 pm

## KANETANAKA JAPANESE RESTAURANT　金田中日本料理

(Jintianzhong Riben Liaoli)
57 Maoming Nan Lu　茂名南路57号
Tel: 6258-7882
Hours: 11:00 am - 2:00 pm,
　　　　6:00 pm - 11:00 pm

## KAWAKYU JAPANESE RESTAURANT
河久日本料理

(Hejiu Riben Liaoli)
Shanghai Hotel　上海宾馆
(Shanghai Binguan)
505 Wulumuqi Bei Lu　乌鲁木齐路505号
Tel: 6248-0088
Hours: 11:00 am - 2:00 pm,
　　　　5:00 pm - 10:00 pm

## KISSHO JAPANESE RESTAURANT
吉祥日本料理

(Jixiang Riben Liaoli)
135 Jianguo Xi Lu　建国西路135号
Tel: 6473-1385, 6473-5993
Fax: 6473-6377
Hours: noon - 2:00 pm,
　　　　6:00 pm - midnight
Authentic, superb Japanese cuisine in a simple setting.

## KISSHO SUSHI　吉祥寺日本料理

(Jixiangzhi Riben Liaoli)
11-12 Lane 99, Ronghua Xi Lu
荣华西道99弄11-12号
Golden Lion Flower Circle, Gubei
古北区金狮大厦
Tel: 6219-7609
Fax: 6219-8503
Hours: 11:30 am - 2:00 pm,
　　　　5:30 pm - 10:00 pm

**KISSHO TEPPAN YAKI** 吉祥铁板烧
(Ji Xiang Tie Ban Shao)
5th Fl, 258 Nanjing Xi Lu
南京西路258号5楼
Wan Xiang Department Store
万象帝王百货
Hours: 10:00 am - 10:00 pm

**MATSUWA JAPANESE RESTAURANT**
松和日本料理
(Songhe Riben Liaoli)
3rd Fl, Jinjiang Tower  (Xin Jinjiang)
新锦江3楼
161 Changle Lu   长乐路161号
Tel: 6415-1188 x 80304, 6445-9229
Hours: 11:30 am - 2:30 pm,
         5:00 pm - 11:00 pm
At lunch time find set Sashimi, Teppanyaki and
Tempura courses for RMB90.

**YAMAZATO JAPANESE RESTAURANT**
山里餐厅
(Yinghua Canting)
Garden Hotel   花园饭店
(Huayuan Fandian)
58 Maoming Nan Lu   茂名南路58 号
Tel: 6415-1111
Hours: 7:00 am - 9:30 am,
         11:30 am - 2:30 pm,
         5:30 pm - 10:00 pm

**SHIKI**   世纪餐厅
(Shiji Canting)
Portman Ritz-Carlton   波特曼丽思卡尔顿酒店
(Poteman Lisikaerdun Jiudian)
1376 Nanjing Xi Lu   南京西路1376号
Tel: 6279-8888 x 5898
Hours: 11:30 am - 2:15 pm,
         5:30 pm - 10:15 pm
High-end Japanese dining.

# KOREAN RESTAURANTS

**ARIRANG** ☆ 啊里朗酒家
(Alilang Jiujia)
28 Jiangsu Lu   江苏路28 号
Tel: 6252-7146
Hours: 11:30 am - midnight
Starters are included in your order and consist
of kimchee (hot pickled cabbage), pickled
cucumber, and bean sprouts. Main dishes
consist of a choice of meats cooked over a
central grill, accompanied by savory table
sauces. Lots of garlic is used, so the flavor of
this meal does linger.

**KOREAN BBQ**   韩国馆
(Hanguoguan)
Jinjiang Tower Hotel   新锦江3楼
161 Changle Lu   长乐路161 号
Tel: 6415-1188 x 80306

New Town Club
Hongqiao Development Zone
Tel: 6275-7888 x 251
3rd Fl, 828 Zhangyang Lu   张扬路828号3楼
Tel: 5820-8848
Hours: 11:30 am - 2:00 pm,
         5:30 pm - 10:30 pm

**KOREAN  RESTAURANT**   韩国餐厅
(Hanguo Canting)
Galaxy Hotel   银河宾馆底楼
888 Zhongshan Xi Lu   中山西路888号
Tel: 6275-5888
Hours: 6:00 am - 10:00 am,
         11:00 am - 2:00 pm,
         4:30 pm - 10:00 pm
Lobby level restaurant crisply decorated in pale
wood tones.

# SOUTHEAST ASIAN RESTAURANTS

**THE CAFE** 咖啡厅
(Kafeiting)
1st Fl, Equatorial Hotel
上海国际贵都大酒店1楼
(Shanghai Guoji Guidu Dafandian)
65 Yan'an Xi Lu  延安西路65号
Tel: 6248-1688 x 2337
Open 24 hours and offering a limited selection
of southeast Asian dishes.

**HARRY'S RED APPLE CURRY HOUSE**
红苹果
(Hong Pingguo )
2nd Fl, 129 Yan'an Lu at Wulumuqi Lu,
Overseas Chinese Mansion
延安路129号近乌鲁木齐路 华侨商店2楼
Tel: 6249-1718
Hours: 11:00 am - 4:00 am
Of course, curry is a specialty here but there's
a wide variety of reasonably priced dishes,
including seafood and Indian items.

**YANGTZE CAFE**  扬子咖啡
(Yangzi Kafei)
Yangtze New World Hotel  扬子江大酒店
(Yangzijiang Dajiudian)
2099 Yan'an Xi Lu  延安西路2099号
Tel: 6275-0000
Hours: 11:30 am - 2:30 pm,
       6:00 pm - 10:30 pm
Daily buffets.

# THE NIGHT SCENE

BEER

# BARS

## BANGDE COFFEE, BAR  邦德酒吧
(Bangde Jiuba)
1465 Xinzha Lu  新闸路1465号
Tel: 6247-1757
Hours: 7: 30 pm - 2:00 am
A cozy local pub two blocks north of the Portman.

## BARBYLON FRESH BEER CITY
巴比龙鲜啤城
(Babilong Xianpicheng)
4th Fl, Universal Building
168-172 Yuyuan Lu  愚园路168-172号
Tel: 6249-6511
Hours: 1:00 pm - 1:00 am
A German brew master makes the beer on the premises at this pub, steak restaurant and disco. Russian Cabaret shows on Thursday and Saturday nights.

## BUBBLING WELL BAR-LOUNGE
静安酒廊
(Jingan Jiulang)
2nd Fl, Portman Ritz-Carlton
波特曼丽思卡尔顿酒店2楼
(Poteman Lisikaerdun Jiudian 2 Lou)
1376 Nanjing Xi Lu  南京西路1376号
Tel: 6279-8888 x 5777
Hours: 11:00 am - 3:00 am
1920s decor and quiet atmosphere, perfect for conversation. The atmosphere is elegant and the service good but unobtrusive.

## CAMERA BAR  开麦拉酒家
(Kamaila Jiujia)
359 Xinhua Road  新华路359号
Hours: 2:00 pm - 2:00 am
Tel: 6280-1256
Retro-artsy place close to the Holiday Inn. A pool table is in the front room. The music is quite loud which makes talking a bit difficult.

## CHARLIE'S BAR  查理斯酒吧
(Chalisi Jiuba)
Holiday Inn Crowne Plaza Shanghai
银星假日酒家
388 Panyu Lu  番禺路388号
Tel: 6280-8888
Hours: 11:00 am - 2:00 am
Voted as one of "The Best of Asia" by Time Magazine, with "the friendliest staff in town". Live band plays daily

## CHELSEA BAR  吉尔喜酒吧
(Jierxi Jiuba)
Westin Tai Ping Yang  太平洋大饭店
.5 Zunyi Nan Lu  遵义南路5号
Tel: 6275-8888
Hours: 2:00 pm - 1:00 am
Sophisticated and quiet, which makes it a good place for business discussions. No shorts (even dressy knee-length shorts) allowed.

## CORDON BLEU INTERNATIONAL CENTER  蓝带国际联谊中心
(Landai Guoji Lianyi Zhongxin)
8th Fl, 527 Huaihai Zhong Lu
淮海中路527号8楼
Tel: 5306-9999
Western cuisine, French wines, and KTV rooms (RMB30 - 50 per hour) are available in this bar and cafe. Live music.

## COTTON CLUB  棉花俱乐部
(Mianhua Julebu)
8 Fuxing Xi Lu  复兴西路8号
Tel: 6437-7110
Hours: 8:00 pm - 4:00 am
Reasonable prices on drinks and a nice atmosphere to boot. Some nights there is live music.

## DANNY'S PUB AND CAFE
丹尼斯咖啡厅
(Dannisi Kafeiting)
141 Maoming Nan Lu    茂名南路141号
Hours: 11:00 am - 3:00 am
Tel: 6473-2849
Relaxing bistro decor. A full range of alcoholic beverages and Brazilian coffee are served along with many Western dishes. Reasonable prices.

## DRAGON PUB    巨龙酒廊
(Julong Jiulang)
508 Julu Road    巨鹿路508号
Tel: 6247-7453
Hours: 5:00 pm - 1:30 am Mon. - Fri.
        3:00 pm - 1:30 am Sat. and Sun.

## EDDY'S BAR    名都酒吧
(Mingdu Jiuba)
890 Weihai Lu near Shaanxi Lu
威海路890号 近陕西路
Tel: 6247-7235
Hours: 6:00 pm - 4:00 am

## FEST BREW HOUSE    菲斯特啤酒坊
(Feisite Pijiufang)
11 Hankou Lu    汉口路11号
Tel: 6323-0965
Fax: 6324-8856
Hours: 11:00 am - 1:00 am
This European-style restaurant and bar features Western and Chinese food. Beer is brewed on the spot using standards set by the German Purity Law of 1516.

## FULL HOUSE PUB    德赛咖啡厅
(Desai Kafeiting)
4 Hengshan Lu and 298 Hengshan Lu
衡山路4号和衡山路298号
Tel: 6474-9062
Hours: noon - 2:00 am
Many choices of coffees and teas, as well as alcoholic beverages.

## GROOVE
308 Hengshan Lu
Tel: 6471-8154
Hours: 7:30 pm - 4:00 am Sun. - Thur.
        7:30 pm - 5:00 am Fri. and Sat.
Go for the dancing inside or head outside to the garden. Decor is New Age with nice motif lighting. A nice break from the ordinary.

## HARD ROCK CAFE    硬石咖啡
(Yingshi Kafei)
Shanghai Centre    上海商城
(Shanghai Shangcheng)
1376 Nanjing Xi Lu, 200040
南京西路1376号
Tel: 6279-8133
Fax: 6279-8399
Hours: 11:00 am - 2:00 am (Sun. - Thur.),
        11:00 am - 3:00 am (Fri. -Sat. and
        eves of public holidays)
Adjoining Shanghai Centre at street level on Nanjing Road. Serves some of the best hamburgers in Shanghai. The rest of the menu is authentically American as well.

## HIT HOUSE    黑匣子酒吧
(Heixiazi Jiuba)
2069 Siping Lu, near Guoding Lu
四平路2069号近国定路
Tel: 6548-1001
Hours: 7:00 pm - 2:00 pm
This bar and disco is near Fudan University. The location and the low prices attract the university crowd.

## HYLAND 505    海伦505啤酒吧
(Hailun 505 Pijiuba)
2nd Fl, Hyland Sofitel Hotel    海伦宾馆2 楼
505 Nanjing Dong Lu    南京东路505号
Tel: 6351-5888 x 4281
Hours: 11:00 am - 1:00 am
        (2:00 am on Fri. and Sat.)
A German pub with live bands performing every evening. They brew their own beer and serve German dishes and pizza.

### INTERNET CAFE 英特耐特咖啡
(Yingtenaier Kafei)
3rd Fl, Haodu Plaza  豪都酒楼3楼
400 Jinling Dong Lu (entrance on Guangxi Lu)
金陵东路400号 近广西路
Tel: 6355-7070 x 306

### JUDY'S TOO 杰迪酒吧
(Jiedi Jiuba)
176 Maoming Nan Lu  茂名南路176 号
Tel: 6473-1417
Fax: 6275-0076
Cocktail bar and grill.

### JUICE BAR 热带风情酒吧
(Redai Fengqing Jiuba)
Huating Hotel and Towers  华亭宾馆
1200 Caoxi Bei Lu  漕溪北路1200号
Tel: 6439-1000 x 2880

### JURASSIC PUB 恐龙世界
(Konglong Shijie)
8 Maoming Nan Lu  茂名南路8 号
Tel: 6258-3758
Hours: 2:00 pm - 4:00 am
A very interesting night spot. A dinosaur theme is carried throughout this bar and restaurant, including a two-story Tyrannosaurus Rex skeleton and dinosaur head urinals in the men's room. The first floor offers a bar, cocktail tables and small dance floor to enjoy the live bands that frequent the pub. On the second floor is a popular Teppanyaki restaurant. Table chefs are quite friendly and enjoy talking with their guests. Reservations for dinner are strongly suggested.

### KANSAS CLUB 坎萨斯啤酒屋
(Canshasi Pijiuwu)
35 Anxi Lu (basement)  安西路35号
Tel: 6252-0041
Hours: 7:30 pm - 2:00 am
There is usually live music in this funky bar.

### L.A. CAFE  L.A.咖啡厅
(L.A. Kafeiting)
5th Fl, 188 Huaihai Zhong Lu
淮海中路188 号5 楼
Hours: 5:00 pm - 3:00 am,
         11:00 am - 3:00 am Sun.
Happy Hour: 6:00 pm - 8:30 pm (daily)
Golden Hour:  8:30 pm -3:00 am
Tel: 6358-7097
Monday and Wednesday are Ladies Nights. Half price when you hear the bar bell ring. A large entertainment complex which include the Disco de John Wayne, The Elvis Bar, Take One Karaoke Hall, Hollywood KTV rooms. Jukebox in The Cafe which serves popcorn, pizza and snacks.

### LAFAYETTE BAR
76 Fuxing Xi Lu  复兴西路76号
Tel: 6471-0937
Hours: 2:00 pm - 2:00 am
Scottish motif with Shanghainese waiters in kilts.  More expensive than most pubs, but also a bit nicer.

### LONG BAR 长廊酒吧
(Shanglang Jiuba)
Shanghai Centre, Level 2, 1276 Nanjing Xi Lu  南京西路1276号 上海商城2 楼
Tel: 6279-8888
Hours: noon -3:00 am
In its second incarnation as a 1930s old Shanghai pub, the Long Bar is an institution in Shanghai. Centrally located and convenient, this upscale bar is popular with expats. Live jazz is featured on Tuesday evenings and Sunday afternoons. Drink specials nightly and Wednesday is model night, with a live fashion show.

### MALONE'S AMERICAN CAFE
马龙美式酒楼
(Malong Meishi Jiulou)
257 Tongren Road (just west of the Portman)
铜仁路257号

Tel: 6247-2400
Hours: 11:30 am - midnight Sun.,
        11:30 am - 1:00 am Mon. - Thur.,
        11:30 am - 2:00 am Fri. and Sat.
This "American" cafe is actually Canadian.
Wednesday evenings are movie nights. The
show starts at 8:00 pm.

## MANHATTAN BAR 曼哈顿酒吧

(Manhadun Jiuba)
231 Huashan Lu 华山路231号
Tel: 6747-7787
Hours: 9:00 pm - 6:00 am
Directly across from the Hilton Hotel. This was
the first expat bar in Shanghai. It's been renovated, and now serves quasi-Mexican food.

## MELODY BAR 明都餐厅

(Mingdu Canting)
Yangtze New World Hotel 扬子江大酒店
2099 Yan'an Xi Lu 延安西路2099号
Tel: 6275-0000
Hours: 5:00 pm - 2:00 am

## O'MALLEY'S IRISH PUB 欧玛莉餐厅

(Oumali Canting)
42 Taojiang Lu near Huaihai Lu
桃江路42号近淮海路
Tel: 6437-0667
Fax: 6466-9358
Hours: noon - 2:00 am
Authentic Irish decor, food and the occasional
strolling Irish minstrel make this beer garden/
restaurant a must see. Guinness on tap. Pool
tables on the second floor.

## PAULANER BRAUHAUS 宝莱纳餐厅

(Baolaina Canting)
150 Fenyang Lu near Fuxing Lu
汾阳路150号 近复兴路
Tel: 6474-5700
Hours: 6:00 pm - 2:00 am
A bustling but upscale "big" atmosphere and
hearty food are what you get at this Munich
brewhouse and restaurant that has its own

brew vats making Paulaner beers. Live bands
play nightly.

## PENTHOUSE LOUNGE 采云轩酒吧

(Caiyunyuan Jiuba)
Hilton Hotel 希尔顿饭店
250 Huashan Lu 华山路250号
Tel: 6248-0000
Hours: 8:30 pm - 2:00 am
Elegant atmosphere, magnificent views and
superb live entertainment every night except
Sunday.

## POOLSIDE PUB 湖边咖啡厅

(Hubian Kafeiting)
Galaxy Hotel 银河宾馆
888 Zhongshan Xi Lu 中山西路888号
Tel: 6275-5888
Open 24 hours
Reggae music prevails.

## PUB CRAWLS AND BOOZE CRUISES

Tel: 6279-4336
"China Jim" Nicholson organizes these fun
events. The pub crawls are held twice a year,
around Thanksgiving and in the spring. Everyone meets at a sponsoring bar for an all-you-
can-eat buffet and drinks, then continues on
to other bars. Transportation is provided as
well as free beer on the bus. For the low price
of RMB100, even a lucky draw is included.
The Booze Cruise is held once a year in late
spring. Again, everyone meets at a central
place and takes buses to the boat. On the
boat is all the food one can eat, an open
bar, and live music. The cruise lasts for four
hours and costs RMB200. China Jim also
arranges and caters parties, and runs The
Yellow Submarine restaurants!

## RECREATION BAR 康乐部酒吧

(Kanglubu Jiuba)
3rd Fl, Huating Hotel and Towers
华亭宾馆3 楼
1200 Caoxi Bei Lu 漕溪北路1200 号

Tel: 6439-1000, 6439-6000
Hours: 5:00 pm - 2:00 am

## ROYAL WESTERN FOOD ESTABLISHMENT 皇家西餐厅

(Huangjia Xicanting)
532 Fuxing Zhong Lu 复兴中路532号
Tel: 6318-3117
Hours: 10:00 am - midnight
Walk through the photo gallery on the first floor and ascend to this second floor bar. The best feature of this place is the terrace overlooking Fuxing Lu.

## SHANGHAI WORLDFIELD CONVENTION HOTEL 上海世博国际会议中心

(Shanghai Sibo Guoji Huiyi Zhongxing)
Tel: 6270-3388
Echo KTV and Sparks Entertainment Pub.
虹桥路2106号

## STEP PUB 舞步酒吧

(Wubu Jiuba)
471 Panyu Lu, opposite the Crowne Plaza Shanghai 番禺路471号
Every Saturday and Sunday you will find live music begins at 9:30 pm.
Tel: 6281-6426
Hours: 2:00 pm  4:00 am

## SUPERSTAR 巨星乡村啤酒屋

(Juxing Xiangcun Pijuwu)
Off Xinhua Lu at 155 No. 1 Alley
新华路155号
Tel: 6280-2052
Hours: 10:30 am - 2:00 am
Billiard table, loud music, espresso.

## SKY LOUNGE 空中酒廊

(Kongzhong Jiulang)
Hyland Sofitel Hotel 海仑宾馆
(Hailun Binguan)
505 Nanjing Dong Lu 南京东路505号
Tel: 6351-5888
Hours: 6:00 pm - 1:00 am
Live music nightly and a fantastic view of the Shanghai skyline.

## TIME PASSAGE CAFE 昨天今天明天

(Zuotian Jintian Mingtian)
1100 Huashan Lu 华山路1100号
Tel: 6252-2901
Hours: 11:00 am - midnight
华山路江苏路东面

## TRIBESMAN PUB 部落人酒吧

(Buluoren Jiuba)
2150 Siping Lu 四平路2150号
Tel: 6511-0695
Hours: 7:00 pm - 4:00 am
Artsy and popular with the college crowd.

## ZHOU'S LOBBY BAR 大堂酒吧

(Datang Jiuba)
Portman Ritz-Carlton 波特曼大酒店
(Shanghai Shangcheng)
Lobby Level
1376 Nanjing Xi Lu 南京西路1376号
Tel: 6279-8888
A dignified, sophisticated bar with unobtrusive live Chinese music. A good place to meet business associates.

# NIGHTCLUBS

**CASABLANCA**  凯撒皇宫歌舞厅
(Kaisa Huanggong Gewuting)
30th Fl, Rainbow Hotel
2000 Yan'an Xi Lu
延安西路2000 号 虹桥宾馆30楼
Tel: 6275-3388 x 2826
Hours: 8:30 pm - 3:00 am

**CASABLANCA DISCO AND KARAOKE**
卡桑不来卡
(Kasang Balaika))
Rainbow Hotel   虹桥宾馆
(Hongqiao Binguan)
2000 Yan'an Xi Lu   延安西路2000号
Tel: 6275-3388
Hours: 8:00 pm - 1:00 am

**CASHBOX**  钱柜
(Qiangui)
• 457 Wulumuqi Bei Lu, next to the Shanghai
  Hotel   乌鲁木齐北路457号 希尔顿附近
• 208 Chongqing Nan Lu   重庆南路208号
• 68 Zhejiang Nan Lu   浙江南路68号
Central tel: 6374-1111
Bar, restaurant, and top of the line karaoke.
Credit cards accepted.

**CLUB ABSOLUTE**  新海鲜城大酒店
(Xinhai Xiancheng Dajiudian)
122 Shaanxi Nan Lu   陕西南路122号
Hrs.: 9:30 pm - 2:30 am
Tel: 6279-2111
A great place for dancing.

**CLUB TOP TEN**  上海演歌台
(Shanghai Yangetai)
8th Fl, Portman Ritz-Carlton
波特曼丽思卡尔顿酒店8楼
(Poteman Lisikaerdun Jiudian)
Tel: 6279-8638, 6279-8637
Hours: 8:00 pm - 2:30 am
Floor shows, local singers and models.

**D.D.'S  D.D.咖啡厅**
(D.D. Kafei Ting)
298 Xingfu Lu near Pingwu Lu
幸福路298号 靠近平武路
Tel: 6280-8670
Hours: 6:00 pm - 6:00 am
Popular with the late crowd and conveniently located near the Holiday Inn. Dark underground atmosphere with tables and booths. The DJ is present throughout the evening playing a mix of old and new Western pop and reggae music. Member-ships available. RMB100 cover charge.

**GALAXY**  银河娱乐中心
(Yinhe Yule Zhongxing)
35th Fl, Galaxy Hotel, 888 Zhongshan Xi Lu
中山西路888号 银河宾馆35楼
Tel: 6275-2999
Hours: 8:00 pm - 3:00 am daily
30 KTV rooms and a Piano Lounge, along with dancing to a computer DJ. High tech lighting.

**LAN DAI CLUB**  蓝带娱乐总汇
(Landai Yule Zonghui)
Isetan Department Store building  伊势丹
(Huating Yisidan)
527 Huaihai Zhong Lu  淮海中路 527号
Tel: 5306-9999
Hours: 12:30 pm - 7:00 pm,
        8:00 pm - 3:00 am

**NEW YORK, NEW YORK**
纽约纽约迪斯科
(Niuyue Niuyue Disike)
146 Huqiu Lu (on Suzhou Creek)
虎丘路146 号
Tel: 6321-6097
Hours: 8:00 pm - 2:00 am
        (5:00 am on weekends)

Cover charge: RMB50 includes one drink
The biggest disco in Shanghai. Housed in an old French theater, reminiscent of New York City in the 1920s. The first floor is a disco; the second is a little quieter with lounges, two more bars, a pool table, and KTV rooms. The third floor is a piano lounge.

## NICOLE'S  尼古拉舞厅
(Nigula Wuting)
Huating Hotel and Towers  华亭宾馆
(Huating Binguan)
1200 Caoxi Bei Lu  漕溪北路1200号
Tel: 6439-6000
Hours: 8:00 pm - 2:00 am

## THE TIME  时代歌舞厅
(Shidai Gewuting)
550 Huaihai Zhong Lu (across from Isetan)
淮海中路550号
Tel: 6327-5566 x 6509
Hours: 8:00 pm - 2:00 am
More conservative than most discos. Large dance floor with live D.J.

## TOTAL DISCO  上海通通迪斯科广场
(Shanghai Tongtong Disike Guangchang)
5th Fl, 80 Xingchang Lu  新昌路80号5楼
Tel: 6359-8951
Hours: 7:00 pm - 2:00 am
This is a big place with a relatively quiet bar and lounge next to, but separate from, the dance floor.

## YIN YANG CLUB (Y Y CLUB)
轮回文艺俱乐部
(Lunhui Wenyi Julebu)
125 Nanchang Lu (between Ruijin Lu and Maoming Lu)  南昌路125号
Tel: 6431- 2668
Hours: 9:00 pm - 3:00 am (Mon. - Thurs.),
　　　　9:00 pm - 5:00 am (Fri. and Sat.)
Dance to music provided by DJs. On Mondays, musicians in traditional dress play classical Chinese music and on Thursdays, Foster's Beer sponsors student discounts on beer. Latin night, sponsored by Jose Cuervo, is held on the first Wednesday of each month.

## YUE LONG DISCO  乐龙迪斯科
(Yuelong Disike)
J. C. Mandarin Hotel  锦沧文华大酒店
(Jincang Wenhua Jiudian)
1225 Nanjing Xi Lu  南京西路1225号
Tel: 6279-1888 x 5050
Hours: 8:30 pm - 3:00 am

# SERVICES

Following is a potpourri of establishments offering services. While not all-inclusive, it provides a starting point in the search for service providers.

# BEAUTY SALONS

## BELLE TRESOR
4th Fl, Hilton Hotel　静安希尔顿
250 Huashan Lu　华山路250号
Tel: 6248-0000 x 8774
Hours: 10:00 am - 10:00 pm

## CARITA HAIR AND BEAUTY SALON
锦江佳莉雅美发美容中心
(Jinjiang Jialiya Meifa Meirong Zhongxin)
- West Building, Jinjiang Hotel
  锦江饭店西楼
  59 Maoming Lu　茂名南路59号
  Tel: 6258-2582 x 9281
  Hours: 9:00 am - 10:00 pm
- 4th Fl, JC Mandarin Hotel
  锦沧文华大酒店4楼
  1225 Nanjing Xi Lu　南京西路1225号
  Tel: 6279-1888 x 5404
  Hours: 9:30 am -10:00 pm
- 4th Fl, Equatorial Hotel
  上海国际贵都大饭店4楼
  65 Yan'an Xi Lu　延安西路65号
  Tel: 6248-1688 x 70401
  Hours: 9:30 am - 10:30 pm
- 7th Fl, Hyland Sofitel Hotel　海仑宾馆7楼
  505 Nanjing Dong Lu　南京东路505号
  Tel: 6351-5888 x 4789
  Hours: 9:30 am - 10:00 pm
- 4th Fl, Yangtze New World Hotel
  扬子江大酒店4楼
  2099 Yan'an Xi Lu　延安西路2099号
  Tel: 6275-0000 x 2473,2475,2476
  Hours: 9:00 am - 10:00 pm

## CHARMAINE COIFFURE
露莎莲妮发型美容中心
(Lusha Lianni Faxing Meirong Zhongxin)
1st Fl, Jingming Building　锦明大厦1楼
18 Xianxia Lu, Hongqiao　仙霞路18号
Tel: 6209-6981
Hours: 10:00 am - 9:00 pm

This salon has stylists from France, Hong Kong, and China and uses hair care products from Germany. Artistic nail painting is available.

## CHRIS AND CHRIS BEAUTY SALON
格诗美发美容中心
(Geshi Meifa Meirong Zhongxin)
3rd Fl, Pacific Department Store
太平洋百货3楼
932 Hengshan Lu　衡山路932号
Tel: 6487-8888 x 734
Hours: 10:00 am - 10:30 pm

## HUAN YING 2000　幻影2000美发中心
(Huanying 2000 Meifa Zhongxin)
82 Shaanxi Nan Lu　陕西南路82号
Tel: 6289-1639
Hours: 10:00 am - 10:00 pm

## LASA BEAUTY SALON LASA
LASA 美容美发沙龙
(Lasa Meirong Meifa Shalong)
11-12 Lane 99, Ronghua Xi Lu, Gold Lion Flower Circle, Gubei
虹桥古北新区金狮花苑,荣华西路99弄11-12号
Tel: 6219-7609
Hours: 10:30am - 9:30 pm
All beauty products are imported from France, Japan, and the U.S. Hair products are the "Goldwell" brand from England.

## MODERN CLASSIC BEAUTY SALON
现代经典美容中心
(Xiandai Jingdian Meirong Zhongxin)
#11, Lane 19, Ronghua Xi Lu
荣华西道19弄11号
Golden Lion, Gubei　金狮花苑 古北新区
Tel: 6219-0437
Hours: 9:30 am - 9:30 pm
Classic modern beauty salon.

## PORTMAN BEAUTY SALON
波特曼沙龙
(Boteman Shalong)
7th Fl, Portman Ritz-Carlton
波特曼丽思卡尔顿酒店7楼
1376 Nanjing Xi Lu　南京西路1376号
Tel: 6279-8630
Hours: 10:00 am - 7:30 pm
This salon offers many services in a pleasant atmosphere.

## SALON DE PARIS　巴黎美发美容中心
(Bali Meifa Meirong Zhongxin)
1st Fl, Vanke Plaza　万科广场底层
17 Shuicheng Nan Lu
水城南路17号 (古北新区)
Tel: 6270-2270
Hours: 10:00 am - 10:00 pm
Located in Gubei, art nouveau and Louis XV style furnishings grace this elegant salon. American and European products are used exclusively for full treatment hair styling, facials, body massage, and body wraps.

## SENSE BEAUTY SALON　适仕沙龙
(Shishi Shalong)
878 Julu Lu　巨鹿路878号
Near the Hilton and Equatorial Hotels
Tel: 6247-3443
Fax: 6249-4236
Hours: 10:00 am - 8:00 pm Mon. - Sat.

## WANG LEI HAIR AND FACE　王磊沙龙
(Wang Lei Shalong)
5th Fl, 1038 Nanjing Xi Lu
南京西路1038号
Westgate Mall　梅龙镇广场
(Meilongzhen Guangchang)
Tel: 6218-3096, 6218-3115
Hours: 10:00am - 10:00 pm
From Los Angeles, Wang Lei speaks fluent English and is one of Shanghai's top hair-stylists. All salon staff, some from overseas, are highly skilled. Top-brand imported hair products, color and perms used.

## YELLOW TED HAIR SALON
造形美容院
(Zaoxing Meirongyuan)
- 1st Fl, Building 1　1号楼1楼
  401 Changshou Lu　常熟路401号
  Tel: 6277-8888 x 8166
- 2nd Fl, Sunshine Department Store
  阳光名店街
  700 Caoxi Bei Lu　漕溪北路700号
  Tel: 6438-7420 x 156
  Hours: 10:00 am - 9:30 pm
This salon offers hair styling and coloring, hair repair and conditioning treatments, facials, and beauty and hair care products from Japan.

# HEALTH CLUBS

## D. D.'S PERSONAL CLUB
广林健身中心
(Guanglin Jianshen Zhongxin)
387 Panyu Lu (across from Holiday Inn
Crowne Plaza Shanghai) 番禺路387号近银
星假日酒家
Tel: 6281-5639
Fax: 6281-9590
Hours: 7:00 am - 11:00 pm
A very nice cozy gym with a sauna and a
canteen. Exercise equipment is from the USA.
Aerobic classes and a hair salon are located
next door. Three types of memberships are
offered:
- Regular membership - unlimited use for
  RMB4,800/year.
- Casual membership - use of the club is
  restricted to Monday through Friday from
  7:00 am until 4:30 pm and Saturdays from
  7:00 am to 2:30 pm for an annual fee of
  RMB1,000 plus RMB350 per month.
- Temporary membership - 3 months of un-
  limited use for RMB1,800.
  (Personal trainers are available for
  RMB1,500 for 3 months.)

## GARDEN HOTEL 花园饭店
(Huayuan Fandian)
58 Maoming Nan Lu 茂名南路58号
Tel: 6415-1111
Hours: 7:00 am - 9:30 pm
Facilities include a gym, spa, tennis courts,
and swimming pool. A waiting list is currently
in place. Memberships are RMB10,000 per
year.

## GUBEI GYM CLUB 古北健身俱乐部
(Gubei Jianshen Julebu)
59 Ronghua Xi Dao near Shuicheng Nan Lu
荣华西道59号近水城南路
Tel: 6219-5818
Fax: 6219-2283

Hours: 9:00 am - 2:00 am
Facilities include a swimming pool, sauna,
gym, shooting range, and outdoor tennis
courts. There are also restaurants, karoake,
movie rooms, and shops here.

## HOLIDAY INN CROWNE PLAZA SHANGHAI
上海银星皇冠假日酒店
(Yinxing Huangguan Jiari Jiujian)
400 Panyu Lu 番禺路400号
Tel: 6280-8888
Hours: 6:00 am - 10:30 pm
Facilities include indoor pool, sauna/steam
bath, gym, squash, table tennis, and tennis.
Massages and sports partners are available
at additional cost. There is currently no waiting
list to join this health club. Memberships are
RMB7,000 per year, RMB4,100 for six
months, RMB2,400 on a quarterly basis, and
RMB1,100 for monthly membership.

## HUATING HOTEL AND TOWERS
华亭宾馆
(Huating Binguan)
1200 Caoxi Bei Lu 漕溪北路1200号
Tel: 6439-1000
Facilities include a gym, tennis courts, table
tennis, spa, and swimming pool. Memberships can be purchased for a six month or
one year period. The six-month membership
is RMB5,500 and the year long membership
is RMB8,455.

## HYLAND SOFITEL HOTEL 海仑宾馆
(Hailun Binguan)
505 Nanjing Dong Lu 南京东路505号
Tel: 6351-5888
Hours: 6:00 am - 11:00 pm
The Sofitel offers a gym and spa facility.
Memberships are a monthly RMB550.

## JINJIANG TOWER　新锦江

(Xinjinjiang)
161 Changle Lu　长乐路161号
Tel: 6415-1188
Hours: 8:30 am - 10:30 pm
The Jinjiang health club is equipped with a swimming pool, spa and gym. Memberships run RMB1,200 per month.

## LONGBAI CLUB　龙柏俱乐部

(Longbai Julebu)
2419 Hongqiao Lu　虹桥路2419号
Tel: 6268-8868
Hours: 8:30 am - midnight
Located at the Cypress hotel and offering a wide range of activities, the Longbai club is a nice place to workout or relax. Facilities include swimming pool (indoor and heated), tennis, squash, bowling, billiards, gym, sauna, mahjongg, karaoke, video arcade, and massage. There are three membership plans: individual, family, and firm (corporate). The memberships are US$1,280, US$2,210, and US$4,550 respectively. Members receive a 50% discount on premium services like bowling and massage.

## NEW TOWN CLUB　新虹桥俱乐部

(Xinhongqiao Julebu)
Tel: 6275-7888
35 Loushanguan Road, Hongqiao
娄山关路35号 虹桥
Hours: 8:30 am - 10:00 pm
The New Town Club is open to the public and currently has no membership plans available. The facilities include restaurants, billiards, massage, sauna, karaoke, aerobics, and a beauty salon.

## NOVOTEL HOTEL　园林宾馆

(Yuanlin Binguan)
201 Baise Lu　百色路201号
Tel: 6470-1688
Hours: 8:00 am - 10:00 pm
A swimming pool, spa, gym and tennis courts

are offered at the Novotel under two membership plans; RMB1,280 for three months, or RMB1,800 for six months.

## PHYSICAL LADIES CLUB
舒适堡女子健身美容中心

(Shushibao Nuzi Jianshen Meirong Zhongxin)
- 808 Hongqiao Lu　虹桥路808号
  Tel: 6486-6677
  Hours: 8:00 am - 10:30 pm Mon. - Sat.
  　　　　8:00 am - 9:30 pm Sun.
- 311 Shandong Zhong Lu　山东中路311号
  Tel: 6329-7536
  Hours: 8:00 am - 10:00 pm Mon. - Sat.
  　　　　8:00 am - 9:00 pm Sun.

For women only, offering aerobic classes, body slimming courses, facial treatments, makeup, and massage. There is a gym, sauna, and steam bath. The club on Shandong Lu (behind the Sofitel Hyland Hotel) also has a hair salon. Membership costs RMB1,500 plus a daily usage fee of RMB20. Memberships good at both locations.

## PORTMAN RITZ-CARLTON
波特曼大酒店

(Boteman Dajiudian)
1376 Nanjing Xi Lu　南京西路1376号
Tel: 6279-8888
Gym equipment consists of six treadmills, two step machines, two rowing machines, and four bicycles, all made by Life Fitness. Machines are placed so that one can watch Star TV, CNN and HBO. Weight machines are made by Flex. The health club also offers an indoor-outdoor swimming pool, and tennis, squash, and racquetball courts. In addition, classes are available in aerobics, taijichuan, and children's swimming and ballet for no additional charge. Pre-natal and post-natal exercise classes are planned for the near future. Massage and tanning are available at an additional charge. Expect to be on the waiting list for at least one year. However, tenants of the Portman's apartments are al-

lowed to join immediately. The membership fee is RMB12,000 per annum, RMB7,400 for six months, and RMB4,900 for three months, and a RMB2,000 initiation fee is charged. The guest fee is RMB100.

## RADISSON LANSHENG HOTEL
兰生大酒店

(Lansheng Dajiudian)
1000 Quyang Lu　曲阳路1000号
Tel: 6542-8000
Hours: 8:00 am - 2:00 pm,
　　　　3:00 pm - 11:00 pm
Offering a gym and spa with memberships available at RMB5,800 per year, RMB3,400 for six months, RMB2,000 for three months, and RMB800 for one month.

## RAINBOW HOTEL　虹桥宾馆

(Hongqiao Binguan)
2000 Yan'an Xi Lu　延安西路2000号
Tel: 6275-3388
Hours: 7:00 am - 9:00 pm
Facilities include a gym, spa, and swimming pool. Memberships are RMB7,800 per year, RMB5,200 for six months, RMB2,800 for three months, and RMB980 per month.

## SHANGHAI HILTON HOTEL
静安希尔顿

(Jing'an Xierdun)
250 Huashan Lu　华山路250号
Tel: 6248-0000
Hours: 6:30 am - 11:00 pm
This gym is well-equipped with treadmills, exercise bikes, step machine, and rowing machine made by Life Fitness. The weight room contains equipment by Universal and Flex. Indoor pool and locker room equipped with steamroom, sauna, and massage (extra cost). Membership is limited to 200, and, one can expect to wait four months. Membership is RMB10,000 per annum, and RMB 6,000 for half a year. An RMB2,000 initiation fee is also required. Off-peak memberships, and family and corporate packages are also available. Guest fee is RMB250.

## XIJIAO SPORTS CENTER　西郊体育中心

(Xijiao Tiyu Zhongxin)
1949 Hongqiao Lu　虹桥路1949号
Tel: 6433-6643 x 574
This is a beautiful complex that includes an indoor pool, four outdoor and two indoor tennis courts, squash courts, a bowling alley, billiards, gym, chess/card room, meeting room, beauty salon, restaurant, and video room. Use of the gym is RMB30 per visit. RMB6,000 worth of coupons cost RMB5,000. Tennis and squash extra.

## XIYA SPORTS CLUB
上海西雅健身乐园有限公司

(Shanghai Xiya Jianshen Leyuan Youxian Gongsi)
5th Fl, 163 Songxing Lu　淞兴路163号5楼
Tel: 5662-2540
Fax: 5672-8108
Hours: 11:00 am - 9:00 pm
This is Shanghai's largest sport facility to date. Located in the Baoshan district, Xiya has sauna, swimming, squash, and gym facilities available to its members. Also available is a beauty parlor and facilities for flower and milk baths. There are rooms for rent, a media center, a business center and a tea house.

## YANGTZE NEW WORLD HOTEL
扬子江大饭店

(Yangzijiang Dafandian)
2099 Yan'an Xi Lu　延安西路2099号
Tel: 6275-0000
Hours: 6:30 am - 11:00 pm
The Yangtze offers a gym, spa, and swimming pool. Memberships are RMB6,200 per year, RMB4,600 per half year, RMB3,400 for three months, or RMB2,000 per month.

# SPAS

## CHIVA SOM INTERNATIONAL HEALTH RESORT

73/4 Petchkasem Road
Hua Hin, 771100
Thailand
Tel: (6632) 536-536
Fax: (6632) 511-615
OK, so it isn't in Shanghai, but all expats living here seem to end up in Thailand on vacation. This is an interesting and healthful destination to consider. Chiva Som is Asia's first international health resort and is a twenty-minute flight from Bangkok (or a three-hour taxi ride). Adjacent to the beach, the resort offers pavilions surrounded by lakes and tropical gardens-style rooms. Upon check-in, one receives a consultation that determines the goals one is striving to obtain during the stay. Various forms of exercise, beauty treatments, weight loss programs, or just total relaxation is the regimen. The low calorie menu is satisfying and tasty and may be taken on a terrace overlooking the Gulf of Siam. Accommodation includes three spa meals a day, individual health and beauty consultation, heat treatment of your choice, all fitness classes, and water exercises. Beauty treatments are extra.

# INTERIOR DESIGN

## DECOR UNLIMITED

上海美赞室内艺术装饰有限公司
(Shanghai Meizan Shinei Yishu Zhuangshi Youxian Gongsi)
Room 503, Lane 24, 119 Chengshan Lu
成山路24弄119号503室(浦东新区)
Tel/fax: 5883-1746
Pager: 6253 8880 x 1000
Michelle Mee and her staff have been decorating homes, hotels, and offices in Shanghai for two years. She is willing to visit home or office showing her portfolio. Decor Unlimited can supply draperies, upholstery, window treatments and much more. Ms. Mee speaks English.

## KIS CONSULTING

Tel/fax: 6406-6764
Mobile: 1391620670
Pager: 127-2344816
E-mail: kisinc.@sympatico.ca
Manager: Kate Shung
Kate renovates and outfits office space.

# LANGUAGE

## HUADONG TRANSLATION CENTER

华东翻译中心
(Huadong Fanyi Zhongxin)
418 Guilin Lu    桂林路418号
Haishen Garden    海申花园
Room 503 #39, Lane 125 Songyuan Lu
松园路125弄39号503室
Tel: 6469-1034, 6469-1035
Fax: 6487-9202
Translation from and to English, French, Japanese, and German including essays, books, documents, contracts, regulations, teaching material, etc.

## SPEED TRANSLATION CENTER

上海互通科技公司
(Shanghai Hutong Keji Gongsi)
Shanghai Jiaotong University

上海交通大学
811 Huashan Lu　衡山路811号
Tel/fax: 5681-1540
Pager: 63560220 - 80697
Hours: 9:00 am - 5:00 pm
Technical and commercial English/Chinese translation and interpreting.

## SHANGHAI CENTROID TRANSLATION SERVICE CO.
上海千古翻译服务有限公司
(Shanghai Qiangu Fanyi Fuwu Youxian Gongsi)
Room 302, 706-57 Laohumin Lu
老沪闵路706弄57号302室
Tel/fax: 6477-9770
Mobile phone: 9180-8010
Hours: 8:00 am - 5:30 pm
Manager: Mrs. Run
Translation, interpretation, and tour guidance.

## J.M. AGENCY　杰迈商务谘询公司
(Jiemai Shangwu Zixun Gongsi)
190 Caoxi Lu　漕溪路190号
Room 9006, Hualin Building
华林大楼9006室
Tel: 6486-3162
Fax: 6487-0143
Hours: 9:00 am - 5:30 pm
Manager: Jane Zhang
English/Chinese interpretation and translation, all printing needs, and temporary or full-time personnel trained in all types of office duties.

## ENGLISH FIRST　英利孚语言培训中心
(Yinglifu Yuyan Peixun Zhongxin)
167 Taiyuan Lu　太原路167号
Tel: 6431-6646
Fax: 6415-0076
Hours: 9:00 am - 6:00 pm
Chief representative: Jessica Ryman
Offers English training and assessment for staff in order to solve communication difficulties. Individual, mini-group, and group instruction is available.

# COPY CENTER

## COPY GENERAL　西技图文有限公司
(Xiji Tuwen Youxian Gongsi)
- 1st Fl, 88 Tongren Lu　铜仁路88号1楼
  Tel: 6279-1694, 6279-1563
  Fax: 6279-1563
- 721 Zhangyang Lu　张扬路721号
  Xin Lian Plaza, Pudong　鑫联广场 · 浦东
  Tel: 5835-8223

Fax: 5835 8498
Open 24 hours a day, 7 days a week
Managers: Joy and Patrick Snodgross
Copy General is capable of completing jobs as large as 50,000 copies overnight and can provide plastic spiral, thermal, or hard-cover binding. Courier service is available for pick-up and delivery.

# PRINTING

## SNAP PRINTING
上海时浪印刷有限公司
(Shanghai Shilang Yinshua Youxian Gongsi)
445 Wulumuqi Bei Lu　乌鲁木齐北路445号
Tel: 6248-1248, 6248-2594, 6249-0651
Fax: 6248-7210
Hours: 9:00 am - 6:00 pm
E-mail: snap@public.sta.net.cn
Web page: http://snapprint.co.au
Design, copy, and printing.

## ALPHAGRAPHICS　阿尔法图文
(A'erfa Tuwen)
Suite 455, Shanghai Centre
上海商城东峰4楼455室
1376 Nanjing Xi Lu　南京西路1376号
Tel: 6279-8346

Suite 102, Shartex Plaza　协泰中心102室
88 Zunyi Nan Lu　200335　遵义南路88号
Tel: 6275-8861, 6275-0710 x 20508
Fax: 6275-1626
Design, copy, printing.

## GL STUDIO
上海杰英广告公司
(Shanghai Jieying Guanggao Gongsi)
Room D, 3rd Fl, 248 Tianping Lu
天平路248号3楼D室
Tel: 6464-2614, 6469-5688 x 225
Fax: 6464-2614
Services include computer graphic design, illustration, freehand drawing, photo retouching, professional layout, printing, 3-D design, corporate image design, and computer graphics training.

# CLEANING

## YMCA COLLEGE
上海青年会高级职业培训学院
(Shanghai Qingnianhui Gaoji Zhiye Peixun Xueyuan)
Room 315, 123 Xizang Nan Lu
西藏南路123号315室
Tel: 6326-1040, x 8928 or 6328-3877
Hours: 8:00 am - 5:00 pm
Contact Ms. Zheng Yiming
The Y Advanced Vocational Training College was established by the Shanghai YMCA to train aiyis (maids) in domestic home care. The trainees, aged 35 to 45, are taught cooking, ironing, cleaning, and health care and are selected by their willingness to work, neatness, personality, and educational level.

## C AND C HOME CARE　程成家政
(Chengzheng Jiazheng)
Room 706, Orient International Building (Div. C)　东方国际大厦C座706室
85 Loushanguan Lu　娄山关路85号
Tel: 6278-7728
Fax: 6278-7727
C and C Home Care is jointly established by the Hong Kong Winscore Group and the Shanghai Women's Federation. It specializes in home care service for expatriates living in Shanghai. The company trains women in all aspects of housekeeping, hygiene, nutrition, and English. Each maid is reviewed at three month intervals. Maids are available for RMB15 per hour or on a monthly basis (Mon. - Fri.) for RMB1,800.

# DRY CLEANING

**CHICAGO DRY CLEANERS** 芝加哥乾洗
(Zhijiage Ganxi)
- 41 Hongmei Bei Lu　虹桥北路41号
  Tel: 6262-0924
  Hours: 9:00 am - 9:00 pm

- 195 Tongren Lu (near Shanghai Centre)
  铜仁路195号
  Tel: 6247-7922 x 1
  Customer service: 6492-8120

This company utilizes American dry cleaning methods. Call to arrange pick-up and delivery of your clothing or drop off at store.

# MODELS

**SHANGHAI PIONEER MODEL AND ADVERTISING CENTER**
上海先锋模型广告中心
(Shanghai Xianfeng Moxing Guanggao Zhongxin)
444 Guangzhong Lu　广中路444号

Tel: 5665-7368
Fax: 5665-7368
This company makes models for development projects, machinery, vehicles, and advertisements.

# ENVIRONMENTAL STUDIES

**ERM-ENVIRONOMICS**
巨人内蒙爱普尔药业集团公司
(Juren Neimeng Aipuer Yaoye Jituan Gongsi)
Room C, 21st Fl, 629 Lingling Lu
零陵路629号21楼C座
Tel: 6486-6731
Hours: 9:00 am - 5:00 pm
This company provides environmental services to international clients in Shanghai and the East China region. Services include environmental assessments, site Investigations, pollution reduction, solutions for environmental problems, environmental regulations and licensing requirements, solid and hazardous waste management and disposal, wetland restoration, monitoring air quality, and ground and surface water investigations.

# GUIDES

## HENRY HONG

Tel: 6327-5005
Fax: 5924-1810

Acting as a local guide, Henry will escort individuals or groups around Shanghai for RMB250 or US$35 per day, plus taxi fare. He is experienced and is fluent in English.

# PHOTOGRAPHY

## CHINAPIC　新概念广告摄影室

(Xingannian Guanggao Sheyingshi)
21-A Lezhige, Jade Buddha City
玉佛城乐志阁21A
1076 Jiangning Lu　江宁路1076号
Tel/fax: 6276-3045

Mac McGowan is an American professional photographer who has built a thriving business in Shanghai providing corporate photography for advertisements, annual reports, company image brochures, etc. See the photo of the authors in this book for an example of his work.

## GANG OF ONE PHOTOGRAPHY
王刚锋广告摄影工作室

(Wanggangfeng Guanggang Sheying Gongzuoshi)
3rd Fl, #18 Lane 461, Tianshan Lu
天山路461弄18号3楼
Tel: 6259-9716
Pager: 6215-5775 x 17128

Specializes in high-fashion and book photography.

# RELOCATION COMPANIES

## CROWNE WORLDWIDE　嘉柏有限公司

(Jiabai Youxian Gongsi)
Room 6306, 118 Ruijin Er Lu
瑞金二路118号6306室
Tel: 6472-9470, 6472-0254, 6472-8761
Fax: 6472-0255

## FIRST PACIFIC DAVIES
第一太平戴维斯

(Diyi Taiping Daiweisi)
Suite 9003, Shanghai Novel Building
上海永新大厦9003室
887 Huaihai Zhong Lu
淮海中路887号
Tel: 6474-8908
Fax: 6474-8909

## KOLL RELOCATIONS
科尔房产服务公司

(Keer Fangchan Fuwu Gongsi)
19th Fl, Suite 1913, China Merchants Tower
上海招商局大厦19楼1913室
66 Lujiazui Lu, Pudong　陆家嘴路66号(浦东)
Tel: 5882-2468
Fax: 5882-9860

Koll Relocations is a division of Koll Real Estate Services.

## ORIENT RELOCATION SERVICE
华辉国际工程服务公司

(Huahui Guoji Gongcheng Fuwu Gongsi)
(A division of Sino-Santa Fe)
3rd Fl, Building 8, 137 Xianxia Lu

仙霞路137号8号楼3楼
Tel: 6233-9700
Fax: 6233-9005

## SOURCES RELOCATION SERVICES
渊源远东有限公司
(Yuanyuan Yuandong Youxian Gongsi)
Suite 1-11B, Longbai Apts.　龙柏高级公寓
2461 Hongqiao Lu　虹桥路2461号
Tel: 6268-9850, 6268-9541
Fax: 6268-8004
E-mail: sources@public.sta.net.cn
Web page:
http://www.shanghaisources.com

President: Jennifer Dawson
Vice-president: Douglas Dawson III
*Sources*, a relocation and real estate consultancy, provides relocating personnel with custom-designed orientations to Shanghai and cultural orientation seminars in the United States and China. Sources also provides orientations in Suzhou and Nanjing and is in the process of expanding its services throughout China. Services also include research materials for Human Resource Managers and developers.

# MASSAGE AND ACUPUNCTURE (ZHEN JIU - AN MO)

**DR. WU WEN BING**　吴文斌(医师)
Room 501, No. 8, Lane 2285, Jiaotong Lu
交通路2285弄8号501室
Home tel: 5695 1718
Pager: 6275-7890 x 12060
Dr. Wu is a member of the Shanghai Municipal Acupuncture Association and the Chinese Medical Institute of Restoration of Health. He specializes in massage and acupuncture and makes one-hour house calls. Fee RMB150.

**DR. XU QUANG**　徐强(医师)
11 Xiangshan Lu　香山路11号
Home tel: 6481-3038
Dr. Xu is a doctor at the Shanghai Xiangshan Traditional Chinese Medicine Hospital and is Director of their Massage Division. He is also a member of the Shanghai Qigang Association for Rehabilitation. He charges RMB100 for an hour-long massage at his home or RMB150 for the same massage in your own home. You will need to call for an appointment, keeping in mind that Dr. Xu does not speak English.

# MISCELLANEOUS

Getting around in Shanghai if language-impaired can be a challenge. Stephanie Dawson has an ingenious solution: rings of **laminated address cards** (RMB200) in Chinese and English to show the taxi driver. Never be afraid to venture out again! Contact Stephanie at 6268-6947 or 6268-9541, fax 6268-8004, e-mail: sources@public.sta.net.cn.

# HOTELS

Shanghai no longer wants for satisfactory hotels in every category, which often function as temporary homes for tourists and business travelers alike. Prior to the establishment of good quality privately-run restaurants in Shanghai, resident expats relied solely on five-star joint-venture hotels for Western food and English-speaking service staff, and continue to find the best in Western dining options therein. Also, many of the better hotels now offer high-quality Western-style delis, often with order lists available for faxed orders. These hotel outlets provide an important adjunct to what can be found in supermarkets.

Overall, services and facilities continue to improve in Shanghai's hotels, as foreign management methods are increasingly implemented. And, the number of good hotels in all categories, from budget two-star to luxury five-star, continues to expand at a rapid rate in the local market.

## BAOLONG HOTEL ☆☆☆ 宝隆宾馆

(Baolong Binguan)
70 Yixian Lu    逸先路70号
Tel: 6542-5425
Fax: 5663-2710
250 rooms, Chinese and Western food, gym, business center, karaoke, disco, billiards, and function rooms. Rooms start at US$65, suites start at US$100. Located in the northeastern part of the city.

## BAO SHAN HOTEL ☆☆☆ 宝山宾馆

(Baoshan Binguan)
2 Mudanjian Lu, Baoshan District
宝山区牡丹江路2号
Tel: 5669-8888

## CITY HOTEL ☆☆☆ 城市酒家

(Chengshi Jiujia)
5-7 Shaanxi Nan Lu    陕西南路5-7号
Tel: 6255-1133
Fax: 6255-0211
Centrally located. Facilities include a business center, nightclub, and Cantonese, Sichuan and international restaurants. 257 rooms starting at US$105, with suites starting at US$190.

## CYPRESS HOTEL ☆☆☆ 龙柏饭店

(Longbai Fandian)
2419 Hongqiao Lu    虹桥路2419号
Tel: 6268-8868
Fax: 6242-3739
This hotel has been recently renovated and sits in a beautiful garden environment near the airport. A sports complex is on the grounds and includes a large indoor swimming pool, bowling alleys, billiards, gym, mahjongg rooms, and a sauna/massage room. Double room rates are US$125.

## DONGHU HOTEL ☆☆☆ 东湖宾馆

(Donghu Binguan)
70 Donghu Lu    东湖路70号
Tel: 6415-8158
Fax: 6415-7759
Central location, gym, swimming, chess, billiards, beauty salon, business center, nightclub, function rooms, and Sichuan, Cantonese, and Western restaurants. Rooms start at US$45, suites at US$120. 300 rooms.

## EAST CHINA HOTEL SHANGHAI ☆☆☆
华东大酒店

(Huadong Dajiudian)
111 Tianmu Xi Lu    天目西路111号
Tel: 6317-8000
Fax: 6317-6678
Located next to the Shanghai Railway Station in north Shanghai, this hotel's 327 rooms start at US$77, suites start at US$128. Cantonese, Sichuan, and Shanghainese restaurants. Other facilities include a beauty salon, nightclub, and business center.

## EQUATORIAL HOTEL ☆☆☆☆
上海国际贵都大饭店

(Shanghai Guoji Guidu Dafandian)
65 Yan'an Xi Lu    延安西路65号
Tel: 6248-1688
Fax: 6248-1773
526 deluxe guest rooms (starting at US$120) and suites (from US$300). Restaurants feature an array of French, Japanese, Korean, and Chinese cuisine. Sports and recreational facilities are available for hotel guests and subscribers to the hotel-based Shanghai International Club (which includes a gym, swimming pool, and bowling). A business center, beauty salon, and health services are also available.

## FAREAST EVER BRIGHT CITY HOTEL
☆☆☆
远东不夜城大酒店
(Yuandong Buyecheng Dajiudian)
600 Hengfeng Lu　恒丰路600号
Tel: 6317-8900
Fax: 6317-6989
Located next to the Shanghai Railway Station in northern Shanghai. 132 rooms, Sichuan, Shanghainese and French restaurants, a business center, bowling, gym, medical center, and beauty salon. Rooms start at US$50, suites at US$90.

## FOREIGN LANGUAGE UNIVERSITY GUEST HOTEL ☆☆
国际文化交流中心
(Guoji Wenhua Jiaoliu Zhongxin)
555 Chifeng Lu　赤峰路555号
Tel: 6531-8882
Fax: 6544-8106
This hotel is affiliated with the Shanghai International Studies University and is located in the northeastern part of the city near Luxun Park. Its 160 rooms and suites are equipped with satellite television, central air-conditioning, IDD telephones, and mini bars. Other facilities include a bowling alley, billiards rooms, game room, ballroom, bar, beauty salon, karaoke, and business center. The rate for a standard twin room is US$40. Suites range from US$75 to US$116.

## GALAXY HOTEL ☆☆☆☆ 银河宾馆
(Yinhe Binguan)
888 Zhongshan Xi Lu　中山西路888号
Tel: 6275-5888
Fax: 6275-0039
Adjacent to the western edge of the inner ring road, the Galaxy Hotel is a large international tourist hotel, with 840 guest rooms equipped with closed-circuit color and satellite receiver TVs, automatic program controlled IDD and DDD telephones, stereos, smoke sensors, and automatic sprinklers. The hotel has 15 restaurants serving various Chinese cuisines, Korean cuisine, and European and American dishes and pastries. Facilities include a shopping arcade, gym, sauna bath, beauty salon, multifunction banquet hall, bowling alley, billiard room, karaoke room, discotheque, bar, coffee shop, business center, ticketing office, bank, post office with telecommunication service, and taxi service. Rooms start at US$140 suites start at US$250.

## GARDEN HOTEL ☆☆☆☆☆ 花园饭店
(Huayuan Fandian)
58 Maoming Nan Lu　茂名南路58号
Tel: 6415-1111
Fax: 6415-8866
The 33-story Garden Hotel Shanghai, managed by the Japanese Okura Hotel Group, is surrounded by a seven-acre garden located in the center of the city, within walking distance to major shopping, government and business areas. 500 spacious rooms are tastefully decorated. Rooms start at US$200, while suites begin at US$480.
*Dining:* The Baiyulan, for traditional Chinese cuisine; the Continental Room, offering a variety of European fare; Sakura, for typical Japanese food; Rose Coffee Shop, two bars and the Oasis cocktail lounge.
*Sports:* Indoor pool, gymnasium, sauna, outdoor tennis courts, massage and jacuzzi.
*Additional Features:* Beauty parlor and barbershop, recreation room, eleven banquet rooms (including the original grand ballroom with stained glass ceiling), business center, gift shops, florist, laundry, IDD phones, multilingual staff and satellite TV. 24-hour room service.

## GOLDEN PALACE HOTEL ☆☆☆
金苑宾馆
(Jinyuan Binguan)
215 Huaihai Xi Lu　淮海西路215号
Tel: 6280-6008
Fax: 6280-1022
Rates from US$65 for a Superior room to

US$150 for a Deluxe Suite, subject to a 10% service charge. This hotel is managed by the Huating Hotel and Towers.

## GOOD HOPE HOTEL ☆☆☆
好望角大酒店
(China Science Academic Convention Center)
(Haowangjiao Dajiudian)
500 Zhaojiabang Lu    肇家滨路500号
Tel: 6471-6060
Fax: 6471-0089
Located near Xujiahui, this hotel has 275 rooms beginning at US$48, with suites starting al US $80. Business center, health club, dance hall, billiards, and French, Italian, Cantonese, Sichuan, and Yangzhou restaurant.

## GRAND YOU YOU HOTEL ☆☆☆☆
上海由由大酒店
(Shanghai Youyou Dajiudian)
2111 Pudong Nan Lu    浦东南路2111号
Tel: 5881-0888
Fax: 5881-0511
This new hotel is right at the exit of the Nanpu Bridge on the Pudong side of the river. By highway, it is 30 minutes from Hongqiao Airport. Facilities include a swimming pool and a gym. Rooms start at US$73 plus 10% service charge, and suites start at US$120 plus 10%.

## GROSVENOR HOUSE ☆☆☆☆☆
锦江贵宾楼
(Jinjiang Guibinlou)
59 Maoming Nan Lu    茂名南路59号
Tel: 6258-2582
Fax: 6256-2589
This beautifully restored small hotel/apartment building on the grounds of the Jinjiang Hotel is one of the best kept secrets in Shanghai. The best Shanghai has to offer. No discos or shops in the building (although they are all in the neighborhood), instead, an updated Art Deco ambience is offered.

## HAIGANG HOTEL ☆☆ 海港宾馆
(Haigang Binguan)
89 Taixing Lu    泰兴路89号
Tel: 6255-3553
Fax: 6255-0151

## HENGSHAN HOTEL ☆☆☆ 衡山饭店
(Hengshan Binguan)
534 Hengshan Lu    衡山路534号
Tel: 6437-7050
Fax: 6433-5732
232 rooms starting at US$50, suites from US$165. Located in the Xuhui district, facilities include a business center, bar, karaoke, supermarket, barber shop, sauna, and Sichuan, Shanghainese and French restaurants.

## SHANGHAI HILTON ☆☆☆☆☆
静安希尔顿
(Jing'an Xierdun)
250 Huashan Lu    华山路250号
Tel: 6248-0000
Fax: 6248-3848
To make reservations at a Hilton Hotel anywhere in the world, call Beijing at 1-0-800-8091.
The first five-star hotel in Shanghai, which opened in 1987. Located in the old French Quarter with 775 rooms. The hotel is a 100% foreign-owned joint venture between Hilton International and Cindic Holdings Ltd., a Hong Kong based company. Accommodations include deluxe king and twin bedrooms, as well as Panorama Suites, all with marble bathrooms. Each room is provided with a seating area and executive desk, individually controlled air-conditioning and heating, a refrigerator with mini-bar, and remote control television offering 24-hour satellite programs such as CNN and Star TV. Local radio channels and in-house music are also available. Floors 35-38 are Executive floors featuring luxuriously appointed rooms and suites with extra leisure and bathroom

amenities. Special features include private access to the Executive Lounge with complimentary breakfast, afternoon tea, and pre-dinner cocktails. Additionally, there is an Executive Floor Manager to assist with check-in, airline ticketing, restaurant bookings, etc. The hotel has also introduced a "Wa No Kutsorogi" concept especially designed for its Japanese clientele encompassing two floors of the hotel. A private lounge is provided with Japanese speaking staff. The hotel also provides three non-smoking floors. A 24-hour business center is on the third floor. Function rooms are available, including the Grand Ballroom which can hold 350 seated guests or up to 500 standing guests. The Shanghai Hilton Athletic Club, managed by Clark Hatch International, is open to hotel guests and members only. Its facilities include a fully equipped gym, sauna, steam bath, massage room, whirlpool, indoor swimming pool, sun deck, outdoor tennis court, and two squash courts. Restaurants include Da Vinci's, serving authentic Italian cuisine. Incorporated into Da Vinci's is the Teppan Grill where one may watch Japanese trained local chefs prepare Japanese dishes right at one's own table. On the 39th floor is Sichuan Court, serving Sichuan cuisine and the Penthouse Bar and Lounge featuring international entertainment and a spectacular view. The lower lobby offers Shanghai Express, open 24 hours a day. The Atrium Cafe in the lobby offers a wide variety of buffet and a la carte items. Sui Yuan (Cantonese) on the second floor completes the list. Rooms start at US$235 and suites start at US$350.

## HOLIDAY INN CROWNE PLAZA SHANGHAI ☆☆☆☆
上海银星皇冠假日酒店
(Yinxing Huangquan Jiari Jiudian)
400 Panyu Lu　番禺路400号
Tel: 6280-8888
Fax: 6280-2788

Located close to the consulate district, the Crowne Plaza Shanghai is minutes from the city center and 20 minutes from the airport.

496 guest rooms including 29 suites, each featuring amenities such as color TV with in-house video channel and satellite reception, coffee and tea-making facilities, IDD/DDD phone, individually controlled air conditioning and heating, personal safe, hairdryer and mini-bar/fridge. Six floors comprising the Crowne Plaza Club are designed especially for the business traveler, offering additional comforts and privileges. There is a business center with secretarial services available as well. Leisure facilities include The Health and Fitness Center with private sauna and steam-bath, gym and indoor swimming pool, video games, squash courts, snooker, and table tennis. The Mane Event is the hotel's beauty salon.

*Dining and Entertainment:* Tian Yuan serves tradit-ional Cantonese fare in stylish surroundings. For authentic Sichuan specialties there's Fu Rong Zhen, while Orient Express serves Asian, European and daily theme buffet favorites round the clock. Cheers offers Western cuisine in a relaxing and fun atmosphere. Charlie's pub offers international entertainers. Finally, there's Midnight Star offering Karaoke in private KTV rooms. Rooms start at US$190 and suites begin at US$400. (Some suites include kitchenettes).

## HOLIDAY INN PUDONG SHANGHAI
☆☆☆☆　上海浦东假日酒店
(Shanghai Pudong Jiari Jiudian)
899 Dongfang Lu, Pudong
浦东东方路899号
Tel: 5830-6666
Fax: 5830-5555
E-mail: hipudongsha@poboxes.com
General Manager: Howard T. Bennett
This new hotel opening in March 1998, is located in the center of the Pudong commercial district, and comprises 33 floors containing 320 rooms, including 38 suites, a Presidential

suite, and three floors of Executive Club rooms. All rooms and suites include individual temperature controls, tea and coffee-making facilities, mini-bar, safe, satellite TV reception, and direct fax and internet connections. Shuttle bus service is available for guests to central Shanghai and the airport. You will also find a gym, a swimming pool, sauna and steam rooms, a jacuzzi, aerobics, and massage along with a business center, beauty salon, restaurants, and shops. A Standard Room is US$160, a Business Suite is US$220, an Executive Room runs US$235 and an Executive Suite is US$300.

## HUATING GUEST HOUSE ☆☆☆
华亭贵宾楼

(Huating Guibinlou)
2525 Zhongshan Xi Lu    中山西路2525号
Tel: 6439-1818
Fax: 6439-0322
187 rooms starting at US$85, suites from US$140. Business center, bar, and restaurants. Located in Xuhui District.

## HUA TING HOTEL AND TOWERS
☆☆☆☆☆  华亭宾馆

(Huating Binguan)
1200 Caoxi Bei Lu    漕溪北路1200号
Tel: 6439-1000, 6439-6000
Reservations x 2560
Fax: 6255-0830
This hotel was formerly a Sheraton and was the first hotel in Shanghai to be managed by an international chain. It is located in the southwest part of the city and is housed in an enormous S-shaped building with two exterior glass elevators. There are 1,008 guest rooms and suites. Restaurants include a coffee shop, and French, Italian and Chinese restaurants. Other facilities include a disco, swimming pool, bowling alley, tennis court, health club and gymnasium, billiards, business center, large ballroom and function rooms, and the hotel's own fleet of taxis and a shuttle service

to the airport. Rooms start at US$180 and suites start at US$270.

## HUAXIA HOTEL ☆☆☆  华厦宾馆
(Huaxia Binguan)
38 Caobao Lu    漕宝路38号
Tel: 6436-0100
Fax: 6433-3724
Southwestern location near Xujiahui. Chinese restaurants, beauty salon, business center, and massage. 390 rooms starting at US$40, with suites starting at US$90.

## HUNAN HOTEL ☆☆☆  三湘大厦
(Sanxia Dasha)
1243 Zhongshan Xi Lu    中山西路1243号
Tel: 6275-2468
Fax: 6275-8356
Located in western Shanghai, facilities include business center, health club, beauty salon, nightclub, and Chinese, Western, and Korean restaurants. 130 rooms starting at RMB448, suites from RMB698.

## HYLAND SOFITEL HOTEL ☆☆☆☆
海仑宾馆

(Hailun Binguan)
505 Nanjing Dong Lu, Hailun
南京东路505号
Tel: 6351-5888
Fax: 6351-4088
A hotel with 389 rooms and suites, ranging in price from US$160 - 260 and managed by the French Accor Corporation. Located in the heart of shopping district on Nanjing Lu within walking distance of the Bund. Their restaurants offer Shanghainese, Cantonese, French cuisine, a German micro-brewery and popular venue for Sunday brunch. Other facilities include a business center, beauty salon, health club, deli, and bars. Rooms begin at US$170 and suites begin at US$320.

## JC MANDARIN HOTEL ★★★★☆
锦伦文华大酒店
(Jincang Wenhua Daijiudian)
1225 Nanjing Xi Lu　南京西路1225号
Tel: 6279-1888
Fax: 6279-1822, 6279-1314

Located in the heart of the city, convenient to shops, airline offices, consulates, banks, and entertainment. 480 rooms and 34 suites, each equipped with IDD telephone, satellite television programs, in-house movies and mini-bar. Seven restaurants and bars serve a range of Western and Asian cuisine. Trader's Pub offers live musical entertainment. Fitness center with sauna, steam rooms, massage, fully equipped gymnasium, indoor swimming pool, jacuzzi, tennis and squash courts. Full service business center, large ballroom and banquet facilities, hair and beauty salon, medical clinic, 24-hour room service, airport/hotel shuttle bus service, airport representative. Rooms start at US$210, suites from US$380.

## JIANGSU HOTEL ★★★ 江苏饭店
(Jiangsu Fandian)
888 Wuning Lu　武宁路888号
Tel: 6205-1888
Fax: 6205-2223

In the Changning District. Facilities include mahjongg, karaoke, billiards, beauty salon, disco, and Business Center along with Chinese restaurants. 233 rooms starting at US$50. Suites start at US$154.

## JIANGUO HOTEL SHANGHAI ★★★★
建国饭店
(Jianguo Fandian)
439 Caoxi Bei Lu　漕溪北路439号
Tel: 6439-9299
Fax: 6439-9433

Located in Xujiahui, near the Metro. 475 rooms and suites. A variety of twenty restaurants, bars, lounges and banquet rooms, fully equipped business center, shopping arcade, and health club. Room prices start at US$90 and suites at US$260.

## JING'AN GUESTHOUSE ★★★
静安宾馆
(Jing'an Binguan)
370 Huashan Lu　华山路370号
Tel: 6248-1888
Fax: 6248-2657

Central location. Facilities include a business center, post office, beauty salon, and Sichuan and seafood restaurants. Rooms start at US$135, and suites begin at US$235. 217 rooms.

## JINJIANG HOTEL ★★★★
锦江饭店
(Jinjiang Fandian)
59 Maoming Lu　茂名南路59号
Tel: 6258-2582
Fax: 6472-5588

Twelve years ago this hotel was the premiere facility in Shanghai. Those days are past, but the Jinjiang remains a historical landmark and excellent banquet facility. One building has recently been refurbished and reopened as "Grosvenor House" (see above). 515 rooms starting at US$170 and suites starting at US$240. Chinese restaurants, health club and beauty salon. Twenty-five years ago, the "Shanghai Accord" was signed by Mao and Nixon here.

## JINJIANG PACIFIC HOTEL ★★★
金门大酒店
(Jinmen Dajiujia)
104 Nanjing Xi Lu　南京西路104号
Tel: 6327-6226
Fax: 6372-3634

Located near People's Park, this hotel has a business center and Fujian and Cantonese restaurants. 164 rooms starting at US$50, with suites beginning at US$130.

## JINJIANG TOWER ☆☆☆☆☆ 新锦江
(Xinjinjiang)
161 Changle Lu　长乐路161号
Tel: 6415-1188
Fax: 6415-0048
728 rooms and suites
Restaurants include Blue Heaven Revolving Restaurant, the Bund French Restaurant, Bamboo Garden Restaurant and the Yes Cafe. One block from Jinjiang Hotel. Facilities include a business center, swimming pool, health club, and disco. Rooms start at US $190, suites start at US$350. A state-owned and run hotel.

## JINJIANG Y.M.C.A. HOTEL ☆☆☆
锦江青年会宾馆
(Jinjiang Qingnianhui Binguan)
123 Xizang Nan Lu　西藏南路123号
Tel: 6326-1040
Fax: 6320-1957
Located in the downtown area, this hotel has 154 rooms starting at US$48 and suites starting at US $118. Facilities include business center, karaoke, Chinese and Western restaurants, and health club.

## JINSHA HOTEL ☆☆☆ 金沙江大酒店
(Jinshajiang Dajuidian)
801 Jinshajiang Lu　金沙江路801号
Tel: 6257-8888
Fax: 6257-4149
Sichuan, Shanghainese, and Cantonese restaurants. Other facilities include a business center and a disco. 298 rooms starting at US$50. Suites start at US$90. Located in the northwestern part of the city.

## LANTIAN HOTEL ☆☆☆ 蓝天宾馆
(Lantian Bingguan)
2400 Siping Lu　四平路2400号
Tel: 6511-6666
Fax: 6511-5700
Northwestern location. Cantonese and

Sichuan restaurants, health club, business center, billiards, disco, and travel agency. Rooms begin at US$55 and US$86 for suites.

## LONGHUA HOTEL ☆☆☆ 龙华迎宾馆
(Longhua Yingbinguan)
2787 Longhua Lu　龙华路2787号
Tel: 6457-0570
Fax: 6457-7621
Near Longhua temple and pagoda in the southwestern part of the city, this hotel has 137 rooms starting at US$70 and suites beginning at US$150. Chinese, Western restaurants and vegetarian restaurants. The hotel also features a business center, karaoke, and billliards.

## LONGMEN HOTEL ☆☆☆ 龙门宾馆
(Longmen Binguan)
777 Hengfeng Lu　恒丰路777号
Tel: 6317-0000
Fax: 6317-4099
Adjacent to the train station (the hotel sells railway tickets). Chinese and Western restaurant, business center, billiards, and karaoke. 137 rooms starting at US$70, suites from US $120.

## MAGNOLIA HOTEL ☆☆☆ 白玉兰宾馆
(Baiyulan Binguan)
1251 Siping Lu　四平路1251号
Tel: 6502-6888
Fax: 6502-9499
Northeastern location. Facilities include Sichuan and Cantonese restaurant, health club, and business center. Rooms start at US $70, and US$105 for suites. 231 rooms.

## NANJING HOTEL ☆☆ 南京饭店
(Nanjing Fandian)
200 Shanxi Lu　山西路200号
Tel: 6322-2888
Fax: 6351-6520

## NEW ASIA HOTEL ☆☆☆ 新亚大酒店

(Xinya Dajiudian)
422 Tiantong Lu 天潼路422号
Tel: 6324-2210
Fax: 6393-1262
Located downtown, this 304-room hotel has a business center, beauty salon, and Sichuan, Shanghai, Cantonese, and French restaurants. Rooms start at US$40, suites at US$120.

## NEW GARDEN HOTEL ☆☆☆
新苑宾馆

(Xinyuan Binguan)
1900 Hongqiao Lu 虹桥路1900号
Tel: 6242-6688
Fax: 6242-3256
324-room hotel with Beijing, Sichuan, and Cantonese restaurants and a business center. Rates begin at US$69 for rooms, and US$100 for suites.

## NIKKO HOTEL ☆☆☆☆ 日航龙柏饭店

(Rihang Longbai Fandian)
2451 Hongqiao Lu 虹桥路2451号
Tel: 6268-9111
Fax: 6268-9333
Set amidst a garden not far from Hongqiao Airport, this 11-story hotel has 390 rooms and suites. Japanese, Chinese, and Continental restaurants. Other facilities including a swimming pool, tennis courts, health club, beauty salon, disco, and business center. Rooms start at US$150 and suites at US$220.

## NOVOTEL (YUAN LIN) HOTEL ☆☆☆
园林宾馆

(Yuanlin Binguan)
201 Baise Road 百色路201号
Tel: 6470-1688
Fax: 6470-0008
Situated next to Shanghai's Botanical Garden with 183 guest rooms and forty 140 square meter villas. Facilities include an indoor swimming pool and sun terrace, fitness center with sauna, beauty salon, tennis courts, disco-

karaoke, business center, shopping arcade, snooker room, and meeting and banquet facilities for up to 200 persons. Cantonese and Western restaurants. Rooms start at US$80 and suites from US$110.

## OCEAN HOTEL ☆☆☆ 远洋宾馆

(Yuanyang Binguan)
1171 Dongdaming Lu 东大名路1171号
Tel: 6545-8888
Fax: 6545-8993
The revolving Western restaurant on the 28th floor of this hotel is its most outstanding feature. Located to the north of Suzhou Creek near the Bund, the views are quite spectacular. There are Chinese restaurants as well, and a business center, swimming pool, tennis court, billiards, health club, and game room. Rates start at US$90 for rooms and US$180 for suites.

## OLYMPIC HOTEL ☆☆☆
奥林匹克宾馆

(Shanghai Aolinpike Binguan)
1800 Zhongshan Nan Lu 中山南路1800号
Tel: 6439-1391
Fax: 6439-6295
Located in southwest Shanghai next to both the new and old stadiums. Cantonese, Sichuan, and Western restaurants as well as a business center, bars, health club, squash, beauty salon, billiards, and swimming pool. 200 rooms starting at US$70, suites at US$140.

## PARK HOTEL ☆☆☆ 国际饭店

(Guoji Fandian)
170 Nanjing Xi Lu 南京西路170号
Tel: 6327-5225
Fax: 6327-6958
This historic hotel overlooks People's Park in the heart of downtown. Facilities include a beauty salon, business center, and restaurants featuring French, Beijing, and Cantonese cuisine. 208 rooms starting at US$70 and suites at US$180.

## PEACE HOTEL ☆☆☆☆ 和平饭店

(Heping Fandian)
20 Nanjing Dong Lu 南京东路20号
Tel: 6321-6888
Fax: 6329-0300

Over fifty years old (formerly the legendary Cathay Hotel), the 12-story building has 387 suites and 663 beds and has been renovated in its original Art Deco style. The hotel has several restaurants and excellent banquet facilities including the eighth floor "Dragon and Phoenix" restaurant with an excellent view of the Huangpu River and the Bund. Rooms have been renovated recently and bathrooms are modern and clean. This is also a great venue if you want to host a banquet for Chinese associates. Facilities include a business center, billiards, gym, bars, and karaoke. The bar in the lobby is home to the renowned Shanghai Jazz Band.

## PORTMAN RITZ-CARLTON ☆☆☆☆☆
波特曼大酒店

(Shanghai Shangcheng)
1376 Nanjing Xi Lu 南京西路1376号
Tel: 6279-8888
Fax: 6279-8999 for reservations
Fax: 6279-8800, Business Center

The Portman is a deluxe, international hotel recognized as Shanghai's Best Hotel by the British Chamber of Commerce in Hong Kong, the Best Business Hotel in Shanghai by *Australian Business Magazine*, one of China's 50 Outstanding Joint Venture Hotels by the China Foreign Investment Enterprise Association, and the Best Hotel in Shanghai by *Institutional Investor*. Operated by Ritz-Carlton, with 700 guest rooms and suites. The hotel's Horizon Club comprises 56 rooms and suites on the top three floors and is replete with all amenities for the business and pleasure traveler. Versatile banquet and convention facilities are available. The 510 square meter Grand Ballroom (seating 470) can be divided by sound-proof partitions into three sections

for private parties. Six additional function/banquet rooms are available for smaller gatherings. In addition, the hotel offers satellite TV, room service and business center, a hair salon, and a large health club. Rooms start at US$195.

## QIANHE HOTEL ☆☆☆ 千鹤宾馆

(Qianhe Binguan)
650 Yishan Lu 宜山路650号
Tel: 6470-0000
Fax: 6470-0348

Sichuan and Cantonese restaurants, business center, piano bar, health club, disco and mahjongg rooms. 472 rooms beginning at US $85. Suites are US$170. Western location.

## RADISSON LANSHENG HOTEL ☆☆☆☆
兰生大酒店

(Lansheng Dajiudian)
1000 Quyang Lu 曲阳路1000号
Tel: 6542-8000
Fax: 6544-8400

Located in the northeastern part of the city, Shanghai Lansheng offers elegant guest rooms, conference facilities, restaurants, modern health club, indoor golf, bowling, and business center. 417 rooms beginning at US $135 and suites from US$180.

## RAINBOW HOTEL ☆☆☆☆ 虹桥宾馆

(Hongqiao Binguan)
2000 Yan'an Xi Lu 延安西路2000号
Tel: 6275-3388
Fax: 6275-3736

Located between Hongqiao International Airport and the downtown area. 630 rooms/suites, restaurants, bars, banquet rooms and function halls, as well as service facilities including a business center, shopping arcade, indoor swimming pool, sauna, massage, billiards, gymnasium, karaoke, KTV, and disco. Rooms start at US$150, suites start at US$260.

## REGAL INTERNATIONAL EAST ASIA HOTEL ☆☆☆☆☆ 富豪环球东亚酒店

516 Hengshan Lu  衡山路516号
Tel: 6415-5588
Fax: 6445-8899

This hotel has 300 guest rooms and suites and is located in the Xuhui district. The California Restaurant offers all-day dining. The menu highlights Western fare including American and Italian dishes. The Chinese restaurant, Jade Coral, offers Shanghainese, Pekinese, and Sichuanese choices. The Rivera provides Mediterranean cuisine. The Health Club and Spa is the largest in the city. In addition to extensive exercise facilities, you will find a golf simulator, bowling center, billiards, squash, a 25 meter indoor pool, and a large tennis center. Rooms start at US$200, Regal Club room at US$270, and suites range from US$500 to US$1,400.

## REGAL SHANGHAI EAST ASIA HOTEL ☆☆☆☆ 上海富豪东亚酒店

(Shanghai Fuhao Dongya Jiudian)
666-800 Tianyaoqiao Lu
天钥桥路666-800号
Xu Hui District 200030  徐汇区
Tel. 6426-6888
Fax: 6426-5888

An integrated part of the 80,000 seat multi-functional Shanghai Sports Center, this facility has 350 rooms including 36 suites. Catering to business executives, the hotel offers a business center, meeting and conference facilities, Regal Club Floor and Lounge, seven restaurants and bars, fitness center, beauty salon, and complimentary airport shuttle service. Room rates begin at US$160 and suites begin at US$350. Regal Club rooms begin at US$240.

## RUIJIN GUEST HOUSE ☆☆☆☆ 瑞金宾馆

(Ruijin Binguan)
118 Ruijin Er Lu  瑞金二路118号

Tel: 6472-5222
Fax: 6473-2277

Five older villas in a large garden comprise this 47-room facility. A more traditional choice than the glitzy, new hotels. Restaurants serve Sichuan, Cantonese and Western food. There is also a business center and beauty salon. Prices start at US$65.

## SHANGHAI HOTEL ☆☆☆ 上海宾馆

(Shanghai Binguan)
505 Wulumuqi Bei Lu  乌鲁木齐路505号
Tel: 6248-0088
Fax: 6248-1056

Centrally located, this hotel is run by the Shanghai Tourism Bureau and caters to many tour groups. Facilities include Shanghai, Chaozhou, and Japanese restaurants as well as a business center, karaoke, and bar. 560 rooms starting at US$98, suites from US$198.

## SHANGHAI INTERNATIONAL AIRPORT HOTEL ☆☆☆ 上海国际机场宾馆

(Shanghai Guoji Jichang Binguan)
2550 Hongqiao Lu  虹桥路2550号
Tel: 6268-8866
Fax: 6268-8393

Adjacent to the airport. Rooms start at US $90, suites at US$220. 294 rooms, Chinese, Japanese, and Western restaurants, a bar, business center, a beauty salon, and massage.

## SHANGHAI MANSIONS ☆☆☆ 上海大厦

(Shanghai Dasha)
20 Suzhou Bei Lu  北苏州路20号
Tel: 6324-6260
Fax: 6393-7477, 6306-5147

This historic building is located just north of the Suzhou Creek bridge and overlooks the Bund. Facilities include Cantonese, Western, and seafood restaurants, business center, karaoke, post office, beauty salon, and massage. Rooms start at US$100 and suites at US$125.

# HOLIDAY INN CROWNE PLAZA SHANGHAI

Only minutes away from the city's shopping area and just 20-minutes drive from the airport, the Holiday Inn Crowne Plaza Shanghai is strategically located close to the consulate district and the economic development zones of Shanghai.

## ■ FACILITIES AND SPECIAL FEATURES

The 496 beautifully-appointed guest rooms include 29 suites. Six floors of Crowne Plaza Club are especially for the discerning business traveller and offer additional comforts and privileges. Leisure facilities include exercise machines, sauna and steambath, indoor swimming pool and outdoor tennis court. For the busy executive, there's a business centre equipped with communication facilities and full secretarial services. Conference rooms plus a choice of smaller function rooms are available.

## ■ DINING AND ENTERTAINMENT

Tian Yuan serves traditional Cantonese fare. For authentic Sichuan specialties there's Fu Rong Zhen, while Orient Express serves Asian and European buffet favourites. Akebono welcomes you with authentic Japanese cuisine. Cheers offers western cuisine in a relaxing atmosphere. There's Charlie's, a fun pub with international entertainers. Cafe Journal is where you can relax while enjoying the ambiance of the lobby.

*Reservation Details: Tel: (86-21)6280-8888, Fax: (86-21) 6280-3353, 6280-2788; Domestic Toll Free Reservation Numbers: Tel: 800-820-1988, Fax: 800-820-1688; Web Site: http://www.crowneplaza-shanghai.com, E-mail: hicpsha@uninet.com.cn; 400 Pan Yu Road, Shanghai 200052*

# HOLIDAY INN PUDONG SHANGHAI

Located in the fast developing commercial district of Lujiazui, Holiday Inn Pudong Shanghai is the preferred business location for the executive traveller.

## ■ FACILITIES AND SPECIAL FEATURES

There are 320 well-appointed rooms and suites, including three Executive Club floors and a Penthouse suite. Non-smoking floors are also available.

Holiday Inn Pudong Shanghai offers full support with your seminars through our Conference Network packages, which are tailored to suit your needs. Be it a contract signing event or product launch, our extensive meeting, conference and banquet facilities with a seating capacity of up to 500 guests in our Shanghai Suite are ideal. A further 7 smaller function rooms seating from 6 to 60 guests are also available.

## ■ DINING AND ENTERTAINMENT

When it comes to dining in our restaurants and bars, we have something to suit everyone's taste and mood. Ranging from The Exchange Coffeehouse, Xu Ri Xuan traditional Chinese Restaurant, to the relaxed atmosphere of Oscars Brasserie right down to Flanagan's, the first Irish Pub in Pudong.

*Reservation Details: Tel: (86-21) 5830-6666, Fax: (86-21) 5830-5555, China Toll Free Numbers: For Shanghai & Beijing 10-800-650-8288, other cities in China 108 650 ask for 245-2650; e-mail: hipudongsha@poboxes.com; Website: http://www.hi-pudongsha.com; 899 Dong Fang Road, Pudong, Shanghai 200122 P.R.China*

## SHANGHAI NEW ASIA TOMSON HOTEL ☆☆☆☆☆ 新亚汤臣大酒店

(Xinya Tangcheng Dajiudian)
777 Zhangyang Lu, Pudong　张杨路120号
Tel: 5831-8888
Fax: 5831-7777

The first five-star hotel to open in Pudong, this hotel is located in Lujiazui next to Yaohan New Age Shopping Center. 422 rooms starting at US$160, including 3 executive floors, 78 suites, 2 duplex suites, and a presidential suite. Eleven restaurants, two ballrooms, and ten meeting rooms. Recreational facilities include a health club with gym, indoor/outdoor swimming pool, sauna and steam baths, beauty salon, and an entertainment and shopping center. This hotel is a joint-venture between Shanghai New Asia (Group) Co., Ltd. and Tomson (China) Ltd. and was designed by the American and Shanghai Design Academy.

## SHANGHAI WORLDFIELD CONVENTION HOTEL ☆☆☆☆ 上海世博会议大酒店

(Shanghai Sibuo Huiyi Dajiudian)
2106 Hongqiao Lu　虹桥路2106号
Changning District
Tel: 6270-3388
Fax: 6270-4554

Modern and practical amenities are provided in each of 370 guest rooms. Western, Japanese, and Chinese dining in five restaurants and an array of bars and lounges. These include the Four Seasons Buffet Restaurant, Jing Garden Chinese Restaurant, Ginza Japanese Restaurant, Hong Kong Bistro (snack bar), 24-hour pool-side coffee shop, Lobby Lounge, Sparks Entertainment Pub, Echo KTV Rooms, and Merchant's Bar (recreational pub). This hotel is well equipped for conventions and conferences with a convention space of 3,500 square meters, a Grand Ballroom that can accommodate up to 1,000 persons, fifteen meeting rooms of various sizes, and a 600-seat multipurpose auditorium. These

features are backed by audio-visual equipment and meeting aids including a built-in simultaneous interpretation system, in-house artist production, and a fully equipped secretarial pool. There are also health club and spa facilities, an outdoor swimming pool, a 24-hour Business Center, shuttle buses, and shops. Call extension 67 for more information and/or a tour of the facilities.

## SHANGHAI WUMAO HOTEL ☆☆☆ 上海物贸中心

(Shanghai Wumao Zhongxin)
2550 Zhongshan Bei Lu　中山北路2550号
Tel: 6257-0000
Fax: 6257-7190

219 rooms. Restaurants provide Cantonese, Sichuan, and Yangzhou cuisine. Facilities also include a business center, disco, beauty salon, bar, and billiards. Rooms start at US$55 and US$90 for suites.

## SILK ROAD HOTEL ☆☆☆ 丝绸之路大酒店

(Sichouzhilu Dajiudian)
777 Quyang Lu　曲阳路777号
Tel: 6554-9988
Fax: 6554-8528

Islamic, Cantonese and Western restaurants. 241 rooms, business center, disco, karaoke, health club, beauty salon, and billiards. Rooms start at US$60, and suites at US$120. Located in the northeastern Hongkou district.

## SWAN CINDIC HOTEL ☆☆☆ 信谊宾馆

(Xinyi Binguan)
2211 Sichuan Bei Lu　四川北路2211号
Tel: 5666-5666
Fax: 6324-8002
Sales office tel: 5666-5666 x 2002/2003
Reservation department tel: 5666-5666 x 2104
Business Center tel: 5666-5666 x 2323
Located across from Luxun Park, in Hongkou district. Each of 191 rooms and suites, the

majority of which overlook the park, has central air conditioning, private bath, mini-bar, refrigerator, closed-circuit TV, satellite receiving system, and IDD telephone. Other amenities include eight restaurants, bars, dance hall, beauty salon, shopping arcade, business center, laundry services, and ticket booking services. Rooms begin at US$50, and suites begin at US$100.

### TIAN MA HOTEL ☆☆☆ 天马大酒店

(Tianma Dajiudian)
471 Wuzhong Lu    吴中路471号
Tel: 6401-5888
Fax: 6401-0662
Located in Hongqiao, 5 km from the airport. 199 rooms beginning at US$70 and suites begin at US$170. Facilities include Cantonese, Sichuanese, Chaozhou, and Western restaurants as well as a business center, health club, beauty salon, billiards, and bowling.

### WESTIN TAI PING YANG ☆☆☆☆☆
太平洋大酒店

(Taipingyang Dajiudian)
5 Zunyi Nan Lu    遵义南路5号
Tel: 6275-8888
Fax: 6275-5420
Located in the Hongqiao Development Zone, Shanghai's international trade and commercial district. Accommodations features air conditioning, direct-dial telephone, voice mail message system, remote control color television, mini-bar and alarm clock. Four Executive Floors provide additional amenities. *Dining:* Emerald Garden for Chinese delicacies; Inagiku for Japanese selections; Giovanni's for Italian cuisine; Cafe Bistro for continental and Asian fare; TPY Buffet Restaurant for international buffet selections. *Sports:* Outdoor swimming pool, tennis court, gymnasium, sauna, Japanese style hot-tubs, massage and billiards room. *Additional Features:* Meeting and convention facilities for

up to 1,200, business center, shopping arcade, beauty and barbershop, same-day laundry and dry cleaning, 24-hour room service. 578 rooms starting at US$195, with suites starting at US$350.

### WINDSOR EVERGREEN HOTEL ☆☆☆
金岛温莎大酒店

(Jindao Wensha Dajiudian)
189 Baise Lu    百色路189号
Tel: 6470-0888
Fax: 6470-4832
Located near Longhua temple and pagoda in the southern part of the city. 175 rooms with Cantonese and Western restaurants, karaoke, and a business center. Room prices start at US$80, suite prices at US$150.

### WUGONG HOTEL ☆☆ 吴宫饭店

(Wugong Fandian)
431 Fuzhou Lu    福州路431号
Tel: 6326-0303
Fax: 6328-2820
Located at the corner of Fuzhou Lu and Fujian Lu near the Bund, this nine-story hotel houses 190 rooms including 21 suites. Rooms are equipped with central air conditioning, pay television, and Star TV. The hotel has many restaurants including the Golden Dragon Palace, which serves dishes that were once served to emperors. A business center and beauty salon are also located on the premises. Room rates range from RMB385 to RMB462.

### XIJIAO GUEST HOUSE ☆☆☆☆☆
西郊宾馆

(Xijiao Binguan)
1921 Hongqiao Lu    虹桥路1921号
Tel: 6219-8800 or 6433-6643
Fax: 6433-6641
Located in Hongqiao in a garden setting. 150 rooms starting at US$110, suite prices at US$210. Facilities include a sophisticated health club which includes bowling, and indoor swimming pool, gym, billiards, and tennis.

*Bicycles are still the major mode of transportation in Shanghai.*
*Sony televisions on the back of a bicycle rickshaw.*

## XING GUO GUEST HOUSE ☆☆☆☆
兴国宾馆
(Xingguo Binguan)
72 Xingguo Lu  兴国路72号
Tel: 6212-9998, 62129070
Fax: 6251-2145

Set in spacious gardens in central Shanghai.
28 old Western-style villas. Rooms in the
various buildings start at US$75 and suites
at US$180. Facilities include Chinese
restaurants, a business center, travel service,
and post office.

## YANAN HOTEL ☆☆☆ 延安饭店
(Yan'an Fandian)
1111 Yan'an Zhong Lu  延安中路1111号
Tel: 6248-1111
Fax: 6247-7149

Well situated in central Shanghai. 418 guest
rooms and suites, 5 meeting rooms, and 14
restaurants, serving Sichuan, Fujian, Yangzhou
Cantonese and Western cuisine. Guest rooms
have IDD and satellite television. Beauty salon,
shops, a business center, gym, medical clinic,
a billiard room, and laundry service. Rooms
begin at US$60, while suites start at US
$120.

## YANGTZE HOTEL ☆☆ 扬子饭店
(Yangzi Fandian)
740 Hankou Lu  汉口路740号
Tel: 6351-7880, 6322-5375
Fax: 6320-6974

This hotel near the Bund classifies itself as a
"business hotel" in that it has excellent facilities
for meetings and has computers, fax machines,
and access to the Internet in its rooms. It is
also equipped with a beauty salon, sauna,
gym, and shops as well as several restaurants.

## YANGTZE NEW WORLD HOTEL
☆☆☆☆  扬子江大酒店
(Yangzijiang Dajiudian)
2099 Yan'an Xi Lu  延安西路2099号
Tel: 6275-0000
Fax: 6275-0750

Midway between the airport and city center.
553 guest rooms and suites centrally air-
conditioned with individual controls. All rooms
are appointed with a business desk, ensuite
bathroom, remote control color TV, in-house
movies, mini-bar, IDD telephone and 24-hour
room service. A wide range of accommodation is available from deluxe and standard
rooms to duplex suites and executive floors.
There are 9 restaurants and lounges. Other
facilities include a ballroom and function
rooms, swimming pool, health club, sauna,
gymnasium, shopping arcade, valet shop,
medical clinic, chauffeured limousine, and a
free shuttle bus to/from airport and downtown.
Rooms start at US$200 and US$350 for
suites.

## ZHAO AN HOTEL ☆☆☆ 兆安酒店
(Zhao'an Jiudian)
195 Hengtong Lu  恒通路195 号
Tel: 6317-2221
Fax: 6317 0338

This new hotel has 270 rooms, including
superior and deluxe rooms, one-bedroom
suites, and duplex suites. The suites contain
kitchenettes. The duplex suites are designed
to allow you to use the living area as an office
while maintaining a private bedroom. Room
service is available. The 24 hour Cafe Pavilion
offers Western, Chinese, and Asian cuisine.
Chinese restaurant, business center, swimming
pool, and gym. Rates range from US$88 to
US$200.

## CONSULATES

All consulates request that their citizens register with them upon establishing residence in Shanghai or nearby counties. This enables consulates to contact individuals in case of public or private emergency and provide them with useful information on various aspects of life in Shanghai.

**AUSTRALIA** 澳大利亚领事馆
(Aodaliya Lingshiguan)
17 Fuxing Xi Lu 复兴西路17号
Tel: 6433-4604
Fax: 6437-6669

**AUSTRALIA TRADE OFFICE**
澳大利亚领事馆商务处
(Aodaliya Lingshiguan Shangwuchu)
2nd Fl, North Building, Peace Hotel
20 Nanjing Dong Lu
南京东路20号 和平饭店北楼2楼
Tel: 6321-1333
Fax: 6321 1222

**AUSTRIA** 澳地利领事馆
(Aodili Lingshiguan)
3rd Fl, Suite A, Qihua Tower 启华大厦3楼
1375 Huaihai Zhong Lu 淮海中路1375号
Tel: 6474-0268
Fax: 6471-1554

**BELGIUM** 比利时领事馆
(Bilishi Lingshiguan)
127 Wuyi Lu 武夷路127号
Tel: 6437-6579
Fax: 6437-7041

**BRAZIL** 巴西领事馆
(Baxi Lingshiguan)
Qihua Tower, 10B 启华大厦10楼
1375 Huai Hai Zhong Lu 淮海中路1375号
Tel: 6437-0110
Fax: 6437-0160

**CANADA** 加拿大领事馆
(Jianada Lingshiguan)
Suite 604, West Tower
American Int'l. Center
Shanghai Centre 上海商城西峰604室
1376 Nanjing Xi Lu 南京西路1376号
Tel: 6279-8400
Fax: 6279-8401

**CHILE** 智利领事馆
(Zhili Lingshiguan)
Equatorial Hotel, Suite 305A
贵都国际大酒店305
65 Yan'an Xi Lu 延安西路65号
Tel: 6249-8000, 6249-4933
Fax: 6249-8333

**CUBA** 古巴领事馆
(Guba Lingshiguan)
Room 501, New Town Mansion,
Hongqiao area, 200335
虹桥开发区新虹桥大厦501室
55 Loushanguan Lu 娄山关路55号
Tel: 6275-3078
Fax: 6275-3147

**CZECH REPUBLIC** 捷克领事馆
(Jicke Lingshiguan)
12th Fl, Qihua Tower 启华大厦12楼
1375 Huaihai Zhong Lu 淮海中路1375号
Tel: 6471-2420
Fax: 6474-1159

**DENMARK** 丹麦领事馆
(Danmai Lingshiguan)
International Trade Center, Suite 701
国贸中心701室
2200 Yan'an Xi Lu 延安西路2200号
Tel: 6209-0500
Fax: 6209-0504

**FINLAND** 芬兰领事馆
(Fenlan Lingshiguan)
Qihua Tower, 7A 启华大厦7楼
1375 Huaihai Zhong Lu 淮海中路1375 号
Tel: 6474-0068
Fax: 6474-3485

**FRANCE** 法国领事馆
(Faguo Lingshiguan)
21st Fl, Qihua Tower 启华大厦21楼
1375 Huaihai Zhong Lu 淮海中路1375号
Tel: 6437-7414
Fax: 6433-9437

Commercial Section
Tel: 6351-9400, 6351-9405, 6351-9406

## GERMANY 德国领事馆
(Deguo Lingshiguan)
181 Yongfu Lu 永福路181号
Tel: 6433-6951
Fax: 6471-4448

## HONG KONG TRADE DEVELOPMENT COUNCIL 香港贸易发展局
(Xianggang Maoyi Fazhangu)
East Ocean Center 东海商业中心
588 Yan'an Dong Lu 延安东路588 号
Tel: 6352-8488
Fax: 6352-3454

## INDIA 印度领事馆
(Yindu Lingshiguan)
1008 Shanghai International Trade Center
国贸中心1008室
2200 Yan'an Xi Lu 延安西路2200号
Tel: 6275-8885
Fax: 6275-8881

## IRAN 伊朗领事馆
(Yilang Lingshiguan)
296 Xinhua Lu 新华路296号
Tel: 6281-4666
Fax: 6281-0502

## ISRAEL 以色列领事馆
(Yiselie Lingshiguan)
Suite 703, New Town Mansion
新虹桥大厦703室
55 Loushanguan Lu, Hongqiao
娄山关路55号
Tel: 6209-8008
Fax: 6209-8010

## ITALY 意大利领事馆
(Yidali Lingshiguan)
11th Fl, Qihua Tower 启华大厦11楼
1375 Huaihai Zhong Lu 淮海中路1375号

Tel: 6471-6980
Fax: 6471-6977

## JAPAN 日本领事馆
(Riben Lingshiguan)
1517 Huaihai Lu 淮海路1517号
Tel: 6433-6639
Fax: 6433-1088

## KOREA (NORTH) 朝鲜领事馆
(Chaoxian Lingshiguan)
4th Fl, Shanghai Int'l. Trade Center
国贸中心4楼
2200 Yan'an Xi Lu 延安西路2200号
Tel: 6219-6417
Fax: 6219-6918

## MEXICO 墨西哥领事馆
(Moxige Lingshiguan)
20th Fl, Qihua Tower 启华大厦20楼
1375 Huaihai Zhong Lu 淮海中路1375号
Tel: 6437-9585
Fax: 6437-2397

## NETHERLANDS 荷兰领事馆
(Helan Lingshiguan)
4th Fl, East Tower, Sun Plaza
88 Xianxia Lu 仙霞路88号太阳广场4楼
Tel: 6209-9076
Fax: 6209-9079

## NEW ZEALAND 新西兰领事馆
(Xinxilan Lingshiguan)
15th Fl, Qihua Tower 启华大厦15楼
1375 Huaihai Lu 淮海路1375号
Tel: 6433-2230
Fax: 6433-3533

## NORWAY 挪威领事馆
(Nuowei Lingshiguan)
8th Fl, Qihua Tower 启华大厦8楼
1375 Huaihai Zhong Lu 淮海中路1375号
Tel: 6431-4725
Fax: 6431-7169

## POLAND 波兰领事馆
(Bolan Lingshiguan)
618 Jiangguo Xi Lu   建国西路618 号
Tel: 6433-9288
Fax: 6433-0417

## RUSSIA  俄罗斯领事馆
(Eluosi Lingshiguan)
20 Huangpu Lu   黄浦路20号
Tel: 6324-2682
Fax: 6306-0699

## SINGAPORE   新加坡领事馆
(Xinjiapo Lingshiguan)
400 Wulumuqi Lu   乌鲁木齐路400号
Tel: 6437-0776
Fax: 6433-4150

## SWEDEN   瑞典领事馆
(Ruidian Lingshiguan)
6th Fl, Qihua Tower   启华大厦6楼
1375 Huaihai Zhong Lu   淮海中路1375号
Tel: 6474-1311
Fax: 6471-6343

## SWITZERLAND   瑞士领事馆
(Ruishi Lingshiguan)
3rd Fl, Sun Plaza, 88 Xianxia Lu, Hongqiao
西霞路88号 太阳广场3楼
Tel: 6270-0519
Fax: 6270-0522

## UK  英国领事馆
(Yinguo Lingshiguan)
Suite 301, Shanghai Centre  上海商城301室
1376 Nanjing Xi Lu   南京西路1376 号
Tel: 6279-7650
Fax: 6279-7651

## UNITED STATES OF AMERICA
美国领事馆
(Meiguo Lingshiguan)
1469 Huaihai Zhong Lu   淮海中路1469号
Tel: 6433-6888
24-hour Emergency: 6433-3936
Fax: 6433-4122

The Commercial Section of the consulate (美国领事馆商务处) is located at Shanghai Centre, Suite 631, 1376 Nanjing Xi Lu. 上海商城631室 南京西路1376号
(Meiguo Lingshiguan Shangyechu)
Tel: 6279-7630
Fax: 6279-7639
The United States Agricultural Trade Office (美国领事馆农务处) also has a separate location in Suite 331, Shanghai Centre. 上海商城331室 南京西路1376号
(Meiguo Lingshiguan Nongmaochu)
Tel: 6279-8622
Fax: 6279-8336
The American Consulate's Citizens Services Office at tel. 6433-6880 has information as to what services the consulate provides. Register here once you have established residence in Shanghai. To vote by absentee ballot, contact Citizens Services and request a Federal Post Card Application (FPCA). This form is used when requesting registration and/ or an absentee ballot from local election offices. The Voting Assistance Guide is also available through Citizens Services, wherein you can check the section regarding home state rules and regulations. Some states allow you to fax the application and the completed ballot. If your state does not allow this, mail the FPCA to the local election office. You will receive an absentee ballot to fill out and return to the US by election day. DHL in Shanghai will mail ballots to the States at no charge. (In some states, late absentee ballots may still be counted in the event of a close or contested election.) American citizens may vote in the state of last residence immediately prior to departing the US even if many years have elapsed and the voter maintains no residence in the state and the intent to return to that state may not be certain. For further information, contact the Voting Information Center's 24-hour recorded service for information on current and upcoming elections at tel: 1-703-693-6500.

**FOREIGN BANKS**

## ABN AMRO BANK
荷兰银行上海分行
(Helan Yinhang Shanghai Fenhang)
20 Zhongshan Dong Yi Lu 中山东一路20号
Tel: 6329-9303
Fax: 6329-5199
Hours: 9:00 am - noon, 2:00 pm - 6:00 pm

## AMERICAN EXPRESS
美国运通国际股份有限公司
(Meiguo Yuntong Guoji Gufen Youxian Gongsi)
Level 2, West Wing, Shanghai Centre
上海商城西峰2楼
Tel: 6279-8082
Fax: 6279-7183
Hours: 9:00 am - 5:00 pm

## ASAHI BANK 旭日银行上海分行
Room 1403, International Trade Center
国贸中心1403室
2200 Yan'an Xi Lu 延安西路2200号
Tel: 6275-8111
Fax: 6270-2701
Hours: 8:30 am - 5:30 pm

## AUSTRALIA AND NEW ZEALAND BANK
澳大利亚与新西兰银行
(Aodaliya Xinxilan Yinhang)
10th Fl, 128 Nanjing Xi Lu
南京西路128号10楼
Tel: 6350-9599
Fax: 6350-9590
Hours: 8:30 am - 5:30 pm

## BANCA COMMERCIALE ITALIANA
意大利商业银行
(Yidali Shangye Yinhang)
10th Fl, China Merchants Tower, Room 1
招商局大厦
66 Liujiazui Lu 陆家嘴路66号
Tel: 5879-9930
Fax: 5879-9945
Hours: 9:00 am - 4:00 pm

## BANCA DI ROMA 罗马银行上海分行
Room 603, Zhonhui Building 中汇大厦603室
16 Henan Nan Lu 河南南路16号
Tel: 6355-8008, 6355-9010
Fax: 6355-9003
Hours: 9:00 am - 6:00 pm

## BANCA NAZIONALE DEL LAVORO
意大利国民劳动银行
(Yidali Guomin Laodong Yinhang)
Unit 505, Equatorial Hotel
国际贵都大饭店505室
65 Yan'an Xi Lu 延安西路65号
Tel: 6249-0462
Fax: 6249-0338
Hours: 9:00 am - noon, 2:00 pm - 6:00 pm

## BANCO SANTANDER
西班牙国际银行
(Xibanya Guoji Yinhang)
Room 803, Equatorial Hotel
国际贵都大饭店803室
65 Yan'an Xi Lu 延安西路65号
Tel: 6249-1677
Fax: 6249-4945
Hours: 9:00 am - noon, 1:00 pm - 5:30 pm

## BANGKOK BANK 盘谷银行上海分行
7 Zhongshan Dong Yi Lu 中山东一路7号
Tel: 6323-3788
Fax: 6323-5400
Hours: 9:00 am - 4:30 pm

## BANK OF AMERICA 美国美洲银行
(Meiguo Meizhou Yinhang)
18th Fl, Shanghai Security Exchange Building,
South Tower 上海政券大厦
528 Pudong Nan Lu 浦东南路528号
Tel: 6881-8686
Fax: 6881-8816
Hours: 9:00 am - 5:00 pm

## BANK OF EAST ASIA LTD.　东亚银行

(Dongya Yinhang)

- 299 Sichuan Zhong Lu　四川中路299号
  Tel: 6329-7338
  Fax: 6329-1813
  Hours: 9:00 am - noon,
  　　　　1:00 pm - 5:00 pm
- 1st and 2nd Fl, Huadu Mansion
  华都大厦1-2室
  838 Zhangyan Lu　张扬路838号
  Tel: 5820-8583
  Fax: 5820-1169
  Hours: 9:00 am - noon,
  　　　　1:00 pm - 5:00 pm

## BANK OF TOKYO MITSBISHI LTD.
东京三菱银行

(Dongjing Sanling Yinhang)
Room 1207, Ruijin Bldg　瑞金大厦1207室
205 Maoming Nan Lu　茂名南路 205号
Tel: 6472-3166
Fax: 6472-7540
Hours: 9:00 am - 4:30 pm
20th Fl, Senmao International Building
森茂国际大厦20楼
101 Yincheng Dong Lu　银城东路101号
Tel: 6841-1515
Fax: 6841-1843
Hours: 9:00 am - 4:30 pm

## BANQUE INDOSUEZ SHANGHAI
东方汇理银行

(Dongfang Huili Yinhang)
17th Fl, Marine Tower　船舶大厦17楼
1 Pudong Dadao　浦东大道1号
Tel: 5879-5559
Fax: 5879-4303
Hours: 9:00 am - 6:00 pm

## BANQUE  NATIONAL DE PARIS
巴黎国民银行

(Bali Guomin Yinhang)
Room 102-105, Garden Hotel
花园饭店102室 - 105室
58 Maoming Nan Lu　茂名南路58号

Tel: 6472-8762
Fax: 6472-8748
Hours: 9:00 am - 6:00 pm

## BANQUE PARIBAS　巴黎巴银行

31st Fl, China Merchants Tower
招商局大厦31楼
66 Lujiazui Lu, Pudong　浦东陆家嘴路66号
Tel: 5879-7725
Hours: 9:00 am - 6:00 pm

## BARCLAYS BANK　巴克莱证券有限公司上海办事处

(Bakelan Zhengquan Youxian Gongsi
Shanghai Banshichu)
651 Shanghai Centre　上海商城651室
1376 Nanjing Xi Lu　南京西路1376号
Tel: 6279-8279
Fax: 6279-8239
Hours: 9:00 am - 5:00 pm

## CHASE MANHATTAN BANK
美国大通银行上海分行

(Meiguo Datong Yinhang Shanghai Fenhang)
700A Shanghai Centre　上海商城700A座
1376 Nanjing Xi Lu　南京西路1376号
Tel: 6279-7288
Fax: 6279-8101
Hours:  9:00 am - 5.30 pm

## CITIBANK　花旗银行

(Huaqi Yinhang)
1st and 2nd Fl, Marine Tower
船舶大厦1-2楼
1 Pudong Dadao　浦东大道1号
Tel: 5879-1200
Fax: 5879-1132
Hours: 9:00 am - 6:00 pm

## CITIC INDUSTRIAL BANK
中信实业银行上海分行

(Zhongxing Shiye Yinhang Shanghai Fenhang)
61 Nanjing Dong Lu　南京东路61号
Tel: 6350-6350
Fax: 6350-6156
Hours: 9:00 am - 4:30 pm

One of the historic banks on the bund near the intersection with Nanjing Lu. These banks prospered before WW II and are being bought by international banks and reopened as such.

**COMMERZBANK**　德国商业银行
(Deguo Shangye Yinhang)
701 Central Place　中汇大厦701室
16 Henan Nan Lu　河南南路16号
Tel: 6374-7680
Fax: 6374-7681
Hours: 9:00 am - noon, 1:30 pm - 5:00 pm

**CREDIT LYONNAIS**
法国里昂信贷银行上海银行
(Faguo Li'ang Xindai Yinhang Shanghai Fenhang)
36th Fl, China Merchants Tower
上海招商局大厦36楼
66 Lujiazui Lu　陆家嘴路66号
Tel: 5887-0770
Fax: 5887-7037
Hours: 9:00 am - 4:30 pm

**CREDIT SUISSE**　瑞士信贷银行
(Ruishi Xindai Yinhang)
17th Fl, Shanghai Security Exchange Building
上海政券大厦
528 Pudong Nan Lu　浦东南路528号
Tel: 6881-8418
Fax: 6881-8417
Hours: 8:30 am - 5:30 pm

**DAI-ICHI KANGYO BANK**
株式会社第一劝业银行
(Zhushe Huishe Diyi Quanye Yinhang)
- 1107 Ruijin Bldg.　瑞金大厦1107室
  205 Maoming Nan Lu　茂名南路205号
  Tel: 6472-3651
  Fax: 6472-7679
  Hours: 9:00 am - 4:30 pm
- 25th Fl, Senmao International Building
  森茂国际大厦25楼
  101 Yincheng Dong Lu　银城东路101号
  Tel: 6841-0001
  Fax: 6841-0002
  Hours: 9:00 am - 4:30 pm

**DAIWA BANK**　大和银行上海分行
Room 2790, International Trade Center
国贸中心2790室
2200 Yan'an Xi Lu　延安西路2200号
Tel: 6275-5198
Fax: 6275-5229
Hours: 8:30 am - 5:30 pm

**DEUTSCHE BANK**　德意志银行
2 Guangming Mansion　光明大厦2室
2501 Jinling Dong Lu　金陵东路2501号
Tel: 6323-9884
Fax: 6323-9858
Hours: 9:00 am - 6:00 pm

**DEVELOPMENT BANK OF SINGAPORE**
新加坡发展银行上海分行
28th Fl, China Merchants Tower
上海招商局大厦28楼
66 Lujiazui Lu　陆家嘴路66号
Tel: 5876-7698
Fax: 5876-7839
Hours: 9:00 am - 4:30 pm

**DRESDNER BANK**　德累斯登银行
(Deleisideng Yinhang)
2nd Fl, Yangtze New World Hotel
扬子江大酒店2楼
2099 Yan An Xi Lu　延安西路2099号
Tel: 6275-5904
Fax: 6219-1433
Hours: 9:00 am - 5:00 pm

**FIRST SINO BANK**　华一银行
Basement Level, Shanghai International Building　新上海国际大厦底层
360 Pudong Nan Lu　浦东南路360号
Tel: 5888-1234
Fax: 5840-8080
Hours: 9:00 am - 5:00 pm

## FUJI BANK LTD
株式会社富士銀行上海分社
(Zhushi Huishe Fushi Yinhang Shanghai Fenshe)
7th Fl, Senmao International Building
森茂国际大厦7楼
101 Yincheng Dong Lu　银城东路101号
Tel: 6841-1000
Fax: 6841-2000
Hours: 9:00 am - 4:00 pm

## GEN BANK (BELGIUM)
比利时通用银行
(Bilishi Tongyong Yinhang)
Unit 601, Equatorial Hotel
国际贵都大酒店601室
65 Yan'an Xi Lu　延安西路65号
Tel: 6248-6600
Fax: 6248-9966
Hours: 9:00 am - 5:30 pm

## HANG SENG BANK
恒生银行上海代表处
(Hengsheng Yinhang Shanghai Daibiaochu)
12th Fl, Marine Tower
中国船舶大厦
1 Pudong Dadao　浦东大道1号
Tel: 5882-1338
Fax: 5882-9600
Hours: 9:00 am - 5:00 pm

## HANIL BANK　韩一银行
(Hanyi Yinhang)
Room 2302, Shanghai Int'l. Trade Center
上海国际贸易中心2302室
2200 Yan'an Xi Lu　延安西路2200号
Tel: 6219-0606
Fax: 6219-5543
Hours: 9:00 am - 4:30 pm

## HONGKONG AND SHANGHAI BANK
香港上海汇丰银行
(Xianggang Shanghai Huifeng Yinhang)
• Room 504, West Wing, Shanghai Centre
上海商城西峰504室

1376 Nanjing Xi Lu　南京西路1376号
Tel: 6279-8582
Fax: 6279-8586
Hours: 9:00 am - noon,
　　　　1:00 pm - 4:30 pm
• Room 102, Marine Tower　中国船舶大厦
1 Pudong Dadao　浦东大道1号
Tel: 5876-1111
Fax: 5879-2238
Hours: 9:00 am - noon,
　　　　1:00 pm - 4:30 pm

## INDUSTRIAL BANK OF JAPAN
日本兴业银行上海分行
(Riben Xinye Yinhang Shanghai Fenhang)
• Room 401, Marine Tower　中国船舶大厦
1 Pudong Dadao　浦东大道1号
Tel: 5879-0611
Fax: 5879-0600
Hours: 8:30 am - 5:20 pm
• Room 1601, Shanghai International Trade Center, 2200 Yan'an Xi Lu
延安西路2200号国际贸易中心1601室
Tel: 6275-1111
Fax: 6275-1769
Hours: 8:30 am - 5:20 pm

## INTERNATIONAL BANK OF PARIS AND SHANGHAI　上海巴黎国际银行
(Shanghai Bali Guoji Yinhang)
13rd Fl, Shanghai Security Exchange Building
上海政券大厦
528 Pudong Nan Lu　浦东南路528号
Tel: 5840-5500
Fax: 5888-9232
Hours: 9:00 am - 5:30 pm

## ING BANK　荷兰商业银行
(Helan Shangye Yinhang)
2nd Fl, Central Place　中汇大厦2楼
16 Henan Nan Lu　河南南路16号
Tel: 6355-6006
Fax: 6355-6001
Hours: 9:00 am - 5:00 pm

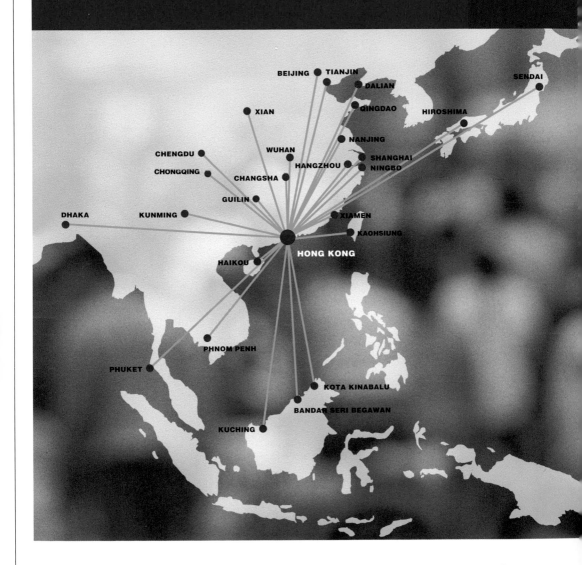

# What's the best way to get from Hong Kong to 26 Asian destinations? Fly Dragonair.

DRAGONAIR

## JAPAN NO. 16 BANK
日本十六银行上海代表处
(Riben Shiliu Yinhang Shanghai Daibiaochu)
Room 1007, Ruijin Bldg.  瑞金大厦1207室
205 Maoming Nan Lu  茂名南路205号
Tel: 6473-1616
Fax: 6472-8881
Hours: 9:00 am - 5:30 pm

## LONG-TERM CREDIT BANK OF JAPAN
日本长期信用银行
Suite 550, Shanghai Centre  上海商城550室
1376 Nanjing Xi Lu  南京西路1376号
Tel: 6279-8855
Fax: 6279-8856
Hours: 8:30 am - 5:30 pm

## MEES PLERSON N.V.
荷兰万贝银行上海分行
(Helan Wanbei Yinhang Shanghai Fenhang)
809 Central Place  中汇大厦809室
16 Henan Nan Lu  河南南路16号
Tel: 6311-2789
Fax: 6311-2444
Hours: 9:00 am - 5:30 pm

## MITSUBISHI BANK LTD  东京三菱银行
(Dongjing Sanling Yinhang)
1207 Ruijin Bldg.  瑞金大厦1207室
205 Maoming Nan Lu  茂名南路205号
Tel: 6472-3166
Fax: 6472-7540
Hours: 9:00 am - 5:30 pm

## NATIONAL WESTMINSTER BANK
英国国民西敏银行上海代表处
(Yingguo Guomin Ximin Yinhang Shanghai Daibiaochu)
708 Shanghai Centre (West)
上海商城西峰708室
1376 Nanjing Xi Lu  南京西路1376号
Tel: 6279-8820
Fax: 6279-8491
Hours: 9:00 am - 5:30 pm

## NOMURA SECURITIES CO LTD.
野村证券上海代表处
(Yecun Zhengquan Shanghai Daibiaochu)
601 Garden Hotel  花园饭店601室
58 Maoming Nan Lu  茂名南路58号
Tel: 6415-1200
Fax: 6415-1317
Hours: 8:30 am - 5:00 pm

## OVERSEAS-CHINESE BANKING CORP.
华侨银行上海分行
(Huaqiao Yinhang Shanghai Fenhang)
- 23rd Fl, Tomson Commercial Building
  汤臣金融大厦23楼
  710 Dongfang Lu, Pudong
  浦东 东方路710号
  Tel: 5820-0200
  Fax: 5830-1925
  Hours: 9:00 am - 5:00 pm
- 120 Jiujiang Lu  九江路120号
  Tel: 6323-3888
  Fax: 6329-0888
  Hours: 9:00 am - 5:00 pm

## PO SANG BANK  宝生银行上海分行
668 Beijing Dong Lu  北京东路668号
Tel: 6361-8888
Fax: 6361-8338
Hours: 9:00 am - 5:00 pm

## ROYAL BANK OF CANADA
加拿大皇家银行
(Jianada Huangjia Yinhang)
12th Fl, Shanghai Security Exchange Building
Room 1205  上海政券大厦1205室
528 Pudong Nan Lu  浦东南路528号
Tel: 6881-5001
Fax: 6881-5232
Hours: 8:30 am - 11:15 am,
       1:00 pm - 5:00 pm

## SAKURA BANK LTD.
株式会社樱花银行上海分行
(Zhushi Huishe Yinghua Yinhang Shanghai Fenhang)
4th Fl, Senmao International Building
森茂国际大厦4楼
101 Yincheng Dong Lu     银城东路101号
Tel: 6841-3111
Fax: 6841-4113
Hours: 8:30 am - 5:30 pm

## SANWA BANK LTD
三和银行上海分行
(Sanhe Yinhang Shanghai Fenhang)
- Room 1408, Orient International Plaza
  东方国际大厦1408室
  85 Loushanguan Lu     娄山关路85号
  Tel: 6295-5858
  Fax: 6295-0085
- 16th Fl, Marine Tower
  中国船舶大厦16楼
  1 Pudong Dadao     浦东大道1号
  Tel: 5879-3818
  Fax: 5879-3816
  Hours: 8:30 am - 5:30 pm

## SOCIETE GENERALE
法国兴业高城证券
(Faguo Xingye Guochen Zhengchuan)
342 Shanghai Centre, East Wing
上海商城东峰
1376 Nanjing Xi Lu     南京西路1376号
Tel: 6279-8471
Fax: 6279-7091
Hours: 9:00 am - 5:30 pm

## STANDARD CHARTERED BANK
标准渣打银行上海分行
(Biaozhun Zhada Yinhang Shanghai Fenhang)
- 35th Fl, China Merchants Tower
  上海招商局大厦35楼
  66 Lujiazui Lu     陆家嘴路66号
  Tel: 5887-1230
  Fax: 5876-7308
  Hours: 9:00 am - 4:00 pm

## SUMITOMO BANK LTD
住友银行上海分行
(Zhuyou Yinhang Shanghai Fenhang)
30th Fl, Senmao International Building
森茂国际大厦30楼
101 Yincheng Dong Lu     银城东路101号
Tel: 6841-5000
Fax: 6841-5111
Hours: 8:30 am - 5:30 pm

## TM INTERNATIONAL BANK
泰华国际银行
1st Fl, Yonghua Building     永华大厦1楼
138 Pudong Dadao, Pudong
浦东大道138号
Tel: 5888-6688
Fax: 5888-6609
Hours: 9:00 am - 4:30 pm

## TOKAI BANK LTD     东海银行
(Donghai Yinhang)
18th Fl, Pudong Nextage Business Center
浦东新世纪商厦18楼
1111 Pudong Nan Lu     浦东南路1111号
Tel: 5830-6570
Fax: 5830 6450
Hours: 8:45 am - 5:45 pm

## TOYO TRUST AND BANKING CO
东洋信托银行上海办事处
(Dongyang Xintuo Yinhang Shanghai Banshichu)
Room 1901, Ruijin Bldg.     瑞金大厦1901室
205 Maoming Nan Lu     茂名南路205号
Tel: 6472-1394
Fax: 6472-9554
Hours: 9:00 am - noon, 1:00 pm - 5:00 pm

# TELECOMMUNICATIONS

### Emergency Telephone Numbers

| | |
|---|---|
| Ambulance | 120 or 6324- 4010 |
| Fire Department | 119 or 6321- 3535 |
| Police | 2321- 5380 |
| Public Security for foreigners | 110 or 6321- 5380 |

# INTERNATIONAL DIALING

## To call Shanghai from abroad, dial 86 21 + local number

*Note:*

*On November 25, 1995, Shanghai added an additional digit to its seven digit telephone numbers. To "old" numbers that begin with 2, 3, 4, or 5 add a 6 at the beginning. If the old number begins with 6, 7, 8, or 9, add a 5 in front. For mobile phones that begin with 9, add 1 after the initial 9. Shanghai is the fourth city in the world to go to an eight digit telephone system. The others are Paris, Tokyo, and Hong Kong. The new system expanded the number of lines available from eight million to eighty million. If every urban family in China has a telephone (the goal of the Ministry of Posts and Tele-communications by the year 2000), 105 million lines will be required for this alone. Shanghai switched from six to seven digit telephone numbers as recently as November 1989.*

*There are few telephone books, as we know them, in Shanghai. One is left to compile one's own. Although there are no Western-style English-language "white pages" residential telephone directories in Shanghai, there are at least two English-language yellow pages directories of commercial and industrial listings. The STDC puts out the Shanghai Yellow Pages, and the CTDC publishes the China Telephone Directory, both sold at most hotel bookstores. One way to acquire a partial expat residential listing is through the Shanghai Expatriates Association (see "Clubs and Organizations chapter). The SEA publishes a yearly listing of all its members (about 1500 in 1997) which is distributed to members only.*

## Telephone Installation

Most apartments and offices will already have phone lines installed. However, if a new or additional line is needed, apply at one of the Shanghai Post and Telecommunications offices listed below. For a business line, bring identification, business license and/or a letter of introduction. If you are applying for a residential line, bring identification in the form of your Residence or Temporary Residence Certificate and your housing lease or deed. Once you are notified that your line is available, return to the same office with the documents described above and the notice that you have received stating that the line is available. You will also need a receipt for your telephone purchase. At this time, costs are RMB3,500 for a personal line and RMB4,500 for a business line. It will take another month for the line to be installed.

Presently, extended telephone services offered in Shanghai in addition to basic line installation are:

| | | |
|---|---|---|
| Call waiting | Out-going call barring | Do not disturb |
| Call transfer | Security code calling | Abbreviated dialing |
| Conference calling | Wake-up calls | Hot-line service |

Apply for these services either at the time of line installation or thereafter. There is an application fee of RMB10 and a monthly fee of RMB2 for individuals and RMB6 for businesses.

Any telephone line that is to be used with a fax machine must be registered. One must obtain an application and apply at the Shanghai Post and Telecommunications office at either 260 Suzhou Bei Lu (北苏州路260号) or 700 Gubei Lu (古北路700号). Return the completed application form to the same office along with RMB100 and the MPT Network Entry License and SPT Examination and Approval Certificate (you will be given these when you purchase the fax machine), and a copy of your monthly phone bill or your line installation receipt, which you must "chop" or sign.

## SHANGHAI POST AND TELECOMMUNI-CATIONS (SPT) OFFICES

| | |
|---|---|
| 915 Caoxi Bei Lu | 6468-7002 |
| 700 Gubei Lu | 6275-0812 |
| 232 Jiangxi Zhong Lu | 6323-1490 |
| 717 Pudong Nan Lu | 5884-1616 |
| 260 Suzhou Lu | 6324-6544 |
| 313 Xinchuan Lu | 5898-1776 |

## SERVICES

| | |
|---|---|
| International Operator | 6258-3322 |
| Domestic Operator | 5666-7321 |
| Telephone Information | 114 |
| Long distance, domestic | 113 |
| Long distance domestic inquiries | 116 |
| Long distance, service inquiries | 5696-2820 |
| Telephone repair | 112 |
| Time | 117 |
| Weather | 121 |
| Airport Information | 6268-8899 |
| Taxi | 6258-0000 |
| Railway | 6317-9090 |
| Boat schedules | 6326-1261 |
| Tourist Information | 6439-0630 |
| CITS | 6321-7200 |
| Water supply | 6321-5577 |
| Electric supply | 6321-7272 |
| Gas supply | 6322-2333 |
| Public security | 6321-5380 |

## TELEPHONE CITY CODES FOR CHINA

For domestic calls, dial 0 + city code

| | |
|---|---|
| Anqing | 556 |
| Anshan | 412 |
| Anyang | 372 |
| Baoji | 917 |
| Beijing | 10 |
| Bongbu | 552 |
| Benxi | 414 |
| Chang'an | 918 |
| Changchun | 431 |
| Changsha | 731 |
| Changzhou | 519 |
| Chengdu | 28 |
| Chongqing | 023 |
| Dalian | 411 |
| Fusun | 413 |
| Fuzhou | 591 |
| Guangzhou | 20 |
| Guiyang | 851 |
| Hangzhou | 571 |
| Haerbin | 451 |
| Hefei | 551 |
| Huzhou | 572 |
| Jiaxing | 573 |
| Jilin | 432 |
| Jinan | 531 |
| Jinzhou | 416 |
| Kaifeng | 378 |
| Kunming | 871 |
| Lanzhou | 931 |
| Luoyang | 379 |
| Nanchang | 791 |
| Nanjing | 25 |
| Nanning | 771 |
| Nanyang | 377 |
| Ningbo | 574 |
| Qingdao | 532 |

| | |
|---|---|
| Quanzhou | 595 |
| Shaoxing | 575 |
| Shenyang | 24 |
| Shijiazhuang | 311 |
| Suzhou | 512 |
| Taiyuan | 351 |
| Tianjing | 22 |
| Wuhan | 27 |
| Wuhu | 553 |
| Wuxi | 510 |
| Xiamen | 592 |
| Xian | 29 |
| Xining | 971 |
| Xinjiang | 373 |
| Xinxiang | 373 |
| Xuchang | 374 |
| Xuzhou | 516 |
| Yan'an | 911 |
| Yangzhou | 514 |
| Yanji | 433 |
| Yinchuan | 951 |
| Zhangzhou | 596 |
| Zhengjiang | 511 |
| Zhengzhou | 371 |

## INTERNATIONAL COUNTRY CODES

Dail 00 + country code + telephone number

| | |
|---|---|
| **Australia** | **61** |
| Adelaide | 8 |
| Brisbane | 7 |
| Canberra | 62 |
| Darwin | 89 |
| Hobart | 02 |
| Melbourne | 39 |
| Perth | 9 |
| Sydney | 2 |
| **Austria** | **43** |
| Graz | 316 |
| Innsbruck | 512 |
| Linz | 90 |
| Salzburg | 662 |
| Vienna | 1 |
| **Belgium** | **32** |
| Antwerp | 3 |
| Brussels | 2 |
| Ghent | 9 |
| Liege | 4 |
| **Brazil** | **55** |
| **Canada** | **1** |
| Calgary | 403 |
| Edmonton | 403 |
| Montreal | 514 |
| Ottawa | 613 |
| Quebec | 418 |
| Toronto | 416 |
| Vancouver | 604 |
| **Denmark** | **45** |
| **Egypt** | **20** |
| **Finland** | **358** |
| **France** | **33** |
| Marseille | 491 |
| Monte Carlo | 93 |
| Nice | 493 |
| Paris | 1 |
| **Germany** | **49** |
| Bonn | 228 |
| Bremen | 421 |
| Cologne | 221 |
| Dusseldorf | 211 |
| Frankfurt | 69 |
| Hamburg | 40 |
| Munich | 89 |
| West Berlin | 30 |
| **Greece** | **30** |
| **Guam** | **671** |
| **Hong Kong** | **852** |
| **Hungary** | **36** |
| **India** | **91** |
| New Delhi | 11 |
| **Ireland** | **353** |
| Dublin | 1 |
| **Italy** | **39** |
| Florence | 55 |
| Genoa | 10 |
| Milan | 2 |
| Naples | 81 |
| Rome | 6 |
| Venice | 41 |

| | | | | |
|---|---|---|---|---|
| **Japan** | **81** | Birmingham | 121 |
| Hiroshima | 82 | Bristol | 117 |
| Kobe | 78 | Cardiff | 1222 |
| Kyoto | 75 | Edinburgh | 131 |
| Nagasaki | 958 | Glasgow | 141 |
| Osaka | 6 | Leeds | 113 |
| Sapporo | 11 | Liverpool | 151 |
| Tokyo | 3 | London | 171/181 |
| Yokohama | 45 | Manchester | 161 |
| **Korea** | **82** | Southampton | 1703 |
| **Kuwait** | **965** | **United States** | **1** |
| **Macau** | **853** | Atlanta | 404 |
| **Malaysia** | **60** | Boston | 978 |
| **Mexico** | **52** | Chicago | 312 |
| **Netherlands** | **31** | Cincinnati | 513 |
| Amsterdam | 20 | Cleveland | 216 |
| Rotterdam | 10 | Dallas | 214 |
| Hague | 70 | Denver | 303 |
| **New Zealand** | **64** | Detroit | 313 |
| Wellington | 4 | Hawaii | 808 |
| **Norway** | **47** | Houston | 713 |
| **Pakistan** | **92** | Jacksonville | 904 |
| Islamabad | 51 | Kansas City | 816/913 |
| **Philippines** | **63** | Los Angeles | 213/310 |
| Manila | 2 | Memphis | 901 |
| **Russia** | **7** | Miami | 305 |
| **Singapore** | **65** | Minneapolis | 612 |
| **Spain** | **34** | New Orleans | 504 |
| Barcelona | 3 | New York City | 212 |
| Madrid | 1 | Philadelphia | 215 |
| **Sweden** | **46** | Salt Lake City | 801 |
| Goteborg | 31 | San Francisco | 415/650 |
| Stockholm | 8 | Seattle | 206 |
| **Switzerland** | **41** | Washington DC | 202 |
| Berne | 31 | | |
| Geneva | 22 | | |
| Lausanne | 21 | | |
| Lucerne | 41 | | |
| Zurich | 1 | | |
| **Thailand** | **66** | | |
| Bangkok | 2 | | |
| **United Kingdom** | **44** | | |
| Aberdeen | 1224 | | |
| Belfast | 1232 | | |

## PHONERENT

Tel: 6327-4974

E-mail: phonemt@public.bta.net.cn

Rent mobile phones through this company even for only one day. Their phones have coverage throughout the major cities in China and you can make international calls. Offices are in Shanghai and Beijing with a drop-off service in Hong Kong. Major credit cards are accepted.

## SPRINT EXPRESS

From China, dial 10813 for a Sprint operator. Bill to your Sprint FONCARD, your USA local calling card, or call collect.

## GLOBAL ONE

Tel: 6279-8538

Fax: 6279-8561

Money saving telephone system with fiber optic network.

## TELEPHONE CARD

This card can be purchased at any Post Office and can be used to make local and long distance calls in special telephone booths. With each use the card will be returned with the proper amount deducted from its value to pay for your call. Cards values of RMB100, 50, 30, and 20 are available.

## KALLBACK

Useful for those who call overseas on a regular basis. Kallback's rate to call from China to the United States is currently US$1.30 per minute, billed in 6 second increments with a 30 second minimum. There is no charge for incomplete calls. Compared to the local IDD provider in China, the savings are significant. Sign up with Kallback and provide billing information (credit card). After your application has been processed, you will receive a personal trigger number. To make a call, simply dial your trigger number, wait for one ring, and hang up. Kallback's computer will call back with a line (dialtone). Dial the intended number, anywhere in the world. Your call is billed to your credit card, and you receive a monthly statement from Kallback. Kallback also offers other services such as Faxaway, an e-mail-to-fax service. For as little as US$0.10, a fax can be sent to the U.S. from anywhere in the world. To sign up or get more information you can call or fax the following numbers, or you can visit Kallback's website.

Tel: 1-206-284-8600

Fax: 1-206-270-0009

Website: http://www.kallback.com

## NEWWORLD

Suite 114, 1402 Teaneck Road,

Teaneck, New Jersey 07666 USA

Tel: 1-201-488-0131

Fax: 1-201-488-0675

E-mail: newsweek@newworldtele.com

Web-page: www.newworldtele.com

24-hour muiti-lingual operators

This company provides services similar to Kallback and saves money on international calls originating outside of the USA.

## NET2PHONE

Website: http://www.net2phone.com

Net2Phone is a new technology which makes it possible to place domestic and international calls from a personal sound-equipped computer to any telephone in the world. Because the signal is carried over the Internet until it reaches IDT's US-based phone switches, rates are not dependent upon the country of origin. In effect, all calls originate in the United States. This means that users pay as little as 10 cents a minute for calls to the United States from anywhere in the world. You may call any telephone in the US for these low rates **including** all 800 numbers. Although you can call any country from Shanghai using

Net2Phone, the distinct advantage it offers is when making calls to the US.

## INTERNET ACCESS

Accessing the Internet in Shanghai is not as difficult as one might think. At this time, access is obtained by signing up with either ChinaNet, Eastern Web Services, or CompuServe. ChinaNet is a country wide general purpose public data network that covers all provincial capital cities and is managed by the Ministry of Posts and Telecommunications (MPT). ChinaNet does provide Internet applications such as FTP (file transfer protocol), Archie, Golpher and Telnet. To register for ChinaNet service, you or someone on your behalf must go to Room 406 in the Long Distance Telephone building at 333 Wusheng lu. While you can register as either a corporate or individual user, it is more convenient to register as an individual. To apply, you must provide the following information: your name, billing address, passport number, proposed e-mail address (your e-mail address should be between 4 and 8 digits or letters), modem type and desired payment plan. If you are a foreign citizen applying as an individual, a Chinese citizen must sign your application to guarantee that you will pay your bill.

Eastern Web Services provides Internet access and e-mail accounts through Uninet. In addition to this service, Eastern Web Services can also assist in creating custom web sites (business or personal) and graphics as well as end to end Internet and Intranet solutions. To sign up, or get more information on web services, call 6437-7050 x 9061, or fax 6437-7050 x 9063

CompuServe now has local access here in Shanghai. If you already have an account with CompuServe, simply change your access phone number in Session Settings to 6251-8008 and select SCITOR as your default network. Be prepared for a busy signal when you dial. Supposedly, the SCITOR network is the same network used by the airlines to communicate via computer. It is usually much easier to connect in the evening. To contact CompuServe in Hong Kong, call (852) 2304-1332 in Hong Kong and call 1-614-529-1340 in the USA.

# SHANGHAI INTERNET USER'S GROUP

The Shanghai Internet User's Group was organized by Breaux Walker of CBV Communications' and is intended to provide the city's users with a means of exchanging information about the Internet and computer related topics. (See the Shopping chapter's Electronics section on pages 70 to 72). The group sends out notices of meetings by fax. To participate, call CBV Communications at 6248-0066.

## A word to the wise on using the Internet in China...

It is illegal in China to view pornographic materials or any other materials considered to be illicit or immoral via the Internet. It is believed that the authorities can monitor usage via software installed on local servers. Certain sites are simply unavailable, and the browser will indicate that it is unable to open the site. The CNN.com site, though not pornographic or illicit, is one example of this type of governmental restriction on Internet usage within China.

## Some useful links

| | |
|---|---|
| http://www.shanghaisources.com | *Relocation and Real Estate services in Shanghai* |
| http://www.shanghai-ed.com | *The definitive on-line guide to Shanghai* |
| http://www.sit.online.sh.cn/shangbop.htm | *The Shanghai Museum* |
| http://www.china-collection.com/consulat.htm | *Foreign Consulates in Shanghai* |

☛ Please note that these addresses tend to change every so often. A good place to start surfing in China, is via Sources' links page at http://www.shanghaisources.com.

Every effort is made to keep it all up to date. There are over 100 links related directly to Shanghai and China in general.

# COMPUTER CONSULTING AND SALES COMPANIES

## BELLSOUTH

Suite 437, Shanghai Centre
(Shanghai Shangcheng)
1376 Nanjing Xi Lu    南京西路1376号
Tel: 6279-8900 (Stella Wu)

BellSouth offers classes in English or Mandarin to those who wish to enhance their computer skills on IBM compatibles or Macintosh. Professional instructors teach basic and intermediate level courses for the most popular softwares. Adult classes are usually 2-3 hour sessions. Children's classes (minimum age 5) are half-hour sessions, 2 days a week for 4 weeks. BellSouth's computer services include network integration services, computer hardware installation, maintenance, software upgrades, virus checks, and Internet installation. Other services include office packages for a "virtual" office with a business address, phone and fax number, or for offices with desks that are either 10 square meters or 14 square meters. BellSouth also provides a graphic arts studio for brochures, name cards, flyers, advertisements, design.

## TRAYTON SYSTEMS

上海特雷通系统公司
(Shanghai Teleitong Xitong Gongsi)
Suite 5-E2, Tsengchow World Trade Building
增泽世贸5楼E2室
1590 Yan'an Xi Lu    延安西路1590号
Tel: 6280-6598 x 2528
Hours: 9:00 am - 5:30 pm
Computer troubleshooting.

## DRAGONSON COMPUTER SERVICE

上海龙强科贸有限公司
(Shanghai Longqiang Kemao Youxian Gongsi)
Room 604, #10 Lane, 99 Caobao Lu
漕宝路99弄10号604室
Tel/fax: 6470-1233
Mobile: 1391742699
Pager:    127-8262138
E-mail: dragon@public.sta.net.cn
Service, training, and consulting.

# COMPUTER SALES

see *Shopping*

# RADIO

The English radio channel is at 105.7 FM. It airs eight hours a day from 9:00 am to 5:00 pm. Along with music and news, there is book reading.

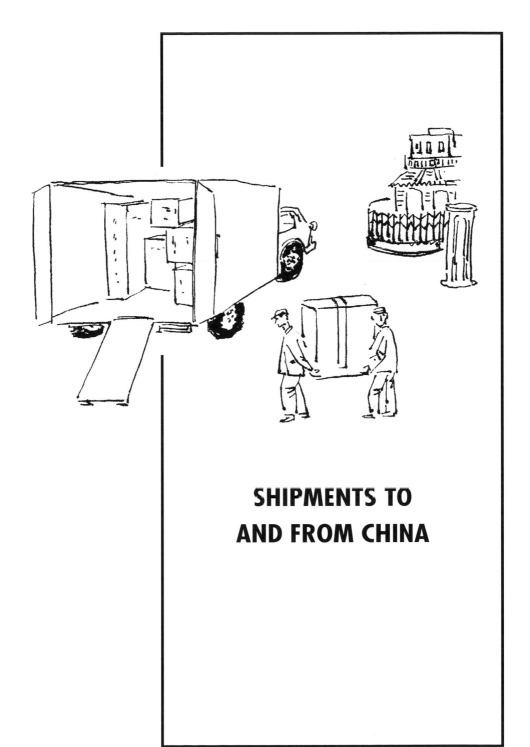

# SHIPMENTS TO
# AND FROM CHINA

Most personal and household items can be found in Shanghai these days, though prices are high and selection is still rather limited. It is most frustrating to comb the stores here, in need of a particular item, only to come up empty-handed or overcharged. Therefore, expats relocating to Shanghai naturally feel compelled to bring many things with them from home, even though shipping costs are often high.

Good quality outergarments, such as jackets, sweaters, gloves and scarves can easily be purchased here, but well-fitting undergarments and larger-sized shoes can be a problem. Formal wear should also be brought from home, as expat life in Shanghai often involves many formal evening events.

Obviously, with respect to household items, it helps to be able to see one's residence prior to moving here, so that precise needs can be assessed. Some homes have no lighting fixtures or appliances, while some are fully furnished right down to the bed linens. However, even fully-furnished homes do not come with dishes and glassware, pots and pans, or silverware, which need to be purchased locally or shipped over.

*Note: In light of the above, it may be worthwhile to check out the discount prices offered on overseas appliances at:*

### APPLIANCES OVERSEAS

*Suite 407, 276 Fifth Avenue (at 30th St.)*
*New York, NY 10001-4509 USA*
*Tel: 001-212-545-8001*
*Fax: 001-212-545-8005*
*Every 220v appliance imaginable is available through this outlet, along with multi-system TVs, VCRs, and stereo systems. They also carry all types of transformers. Shipping, usually through one's designated mover, is one of their services.*

*Corporate employees need to inquire about specific company guidelines for shipping personal belongings from home, as provisions naturally vary from company to company.*

*There is extensive bureaucratic boondoggle in clearing shipments through customs in Shanghai. Larger multinationals experienced in moving families abroad have sufficient experience and manpower to handle this in-house. However, those without company support, or who are in the vanguard of a company's move to Shanghai should enlist the aid of a shipping company to help navigate the maze of paperwork and procedures. The relocation experts at Sources can provide a broad overview of the process, but situations may arise which require expert help.*

*One must show evidence of official residence in China before goods can be released from customs. The first step in this process is to acquire a "Z" visa by applying at a Chinese Embassy or through consultants in the travel or shipping businesses. Once in China with a "Z" visa, one must present certain documents to the Public Security Bureau (PSB) which they will retain for three to five days. These documents are:*
*• one's passport bearing the "Z" visa; and*
*• a Medical Examination Certificate from:*

### SHANGHAI HEALTH AND QUARANTINE VERIFICATION OFFICE  上海卫生检疫局

(Shanghai Weisheng Jianyiju)
701 Hami Lu   哈密路701号
Tel: 6268-6171
Fax: 6268-6286
Hours: 8:30 am - 11:00 am,
         1:00 pm - 3:00 pm
The requirements for this certificate seem to change case by case, but basically they include an examination of all family members, blood work, and AIDS and

Hepatitis test. Many feel squeamish about having this exam done in China, preferring to have the physical and the lab work done in their own countries and presenting certified documents to the quarantine service. This used to be acceptable practice, but is no longer allowed. The process is not intimidating and new disposable needles are used. The Human Resources department of one's employer can help with this issue. Independent individuals should visit Hami Road with a translator on the initial trip to Shanghai to assess methods that are used.

If you work for a representative office of a foreign company, you will need to present the "Representative Card" issued to your business by the government. New representative offices may have to wait up to three months for this card to be issued. Goods will be sitting in customs accruing storage charges until this card is issued. Therefore, it is recommended by the experts to have any shipments held at the point of origin until this card is in hand. After receipt of this card, there is an additional two weeks before one receives a residency card. One also must submit a form for Residency Registration for Personnel of Foreign Offices and a letter from one's representative office confirming employment by them. Heads of representative offices can present a letter authorizing employment from the Chinese host organization.

"Green Cards" are issued within one to two weeks, making one an official Chinese resident! Now, an application for import of personal effects can be submitted to the customs bureau. When this application is approved, there is a time-frame of six months to bring in personal goods, which need to be listed on the application. Only one application may be made, but items may be brought in more than once, until the six month window has expired. For example, one may send a shipment from the US, and also bring items listed from a trip to Hong Kong. Therefore, the initial list should list anything and everything that one wants to bring into China during a six month period. It isn't necessary to import everything on the list, so feel free to make it extensive. One may not, however, bring in an unreasonable quantity of one thing, especially electronic equipment. The application is for personal goods only but putting one desk-top office computer on your list will not present a problem. Buying one with dual voltage in one's home country may save a lot of money.

As for the question of duty on goods shipped to China, at one time foreigners were allowed one duty-free shipment of personal goods. As of January 1, 1995, this changed and the new guidelines are blurry. It is difficult to estimate what duty a shipment will incur. Contact a shipping company that has experience in clearing goods from customs in Shanghai for help. They can answer such questions as "Will the higher price I pay for a computer in Shanghai be offset by the shipping price and the duty payment required?"

Once the application for personal affects has been approved, one must then make a list for a particular shipment and apply for what is called a "Customs Sealed Letter". This list will be presented with the original customs list, one's residence permit, and passport. One copy is for the applicant to keep, another is for the customs office, and the third copy will be sealed in an envelope and be given to the applicant to use during customs clearance. This envelope is to be opened **only** by the customs officials clearing your shipment.

Once one's personal items enter the door, it'll feel like a giant step has been taken toward creating a real home in Shanghai.

## ALLIED PICKFORDS

联合百福有限公司上海办事处

(Lianhe Baifu Youxian Gongsi Shanghai Banshichu)

808 Hongqiao Lu 虹桥路808号

A 8501B Jiahua Business Center

加华商务中心A栋8501B室

Tel: 6486-0833

Fax: 6486-0831

Hours: 8:30 am - 5:00 pm

- International Household Relocation
- Settling In Services
- Handyman/Maid Services
- Local Household Removals
- Office and Warehouse Relocation
- Short and Long Term Storage

## ASIA-PACIFIC WORLDWIDE MOVERS

上海亚太包装运输服务有限公司

(Shanghai Yatai Baozhuang Fuwu Youxian Gongsi)

PO Box 1724

Richardson, Texas 75080 USA

225 Chongqing Nan Lu, Block 5, Room 403

重庆南路225号5座403室

Shanghai

Tel: 6374-0408

Fax: 6320-2736

Hours: 9:00 am - 5:00 pm

Asia-Pacific specializes in door-to-door worldwide service, household goods packing and removals, office removals, museum inspections, China and destination customs clearance, car import and export service, packing supplies, and cargo freight forwarding.

## CROWN WORLDWIDE 嘉柏有限公司

(Jiabai Youxian Gongsi)

6306 Room, 118 Ruijin Er Lu

瑞金二路118号6306室

Tel: 6472-9470, 6472-0254, 6472-8761

Fax: 6472-0255

Hours: 8:30 am - 5:30 pm

Crown has extensive experience dealing with western companies and is generous with advice to expatriates needing assistance with the bureaucracy involved in shipping items to Shanghai.

## GLOBAL SILVERHAWK 北京环球货流保税有限公司上海办事处

101-102, 780 Lane, 67 Hongzhong Lu

虹中路780弄67号101-102室

Tel: 6405-4120

Fax: 6401-8631

E-mail: glbhawk@public.sta.net.cn

## INTERCONEX 美国康利运通公司

(Meiguo Kangli Yuntong Gongsi)

New Garden Hotel, Room 2128 新苑宾馆

1900 Hongqiao Lu 虹桥路1900号

Tel: 6242-6810 or 6242-6688 x 2116

Fax: 6242-6810

Hours: 8:30 am - 5:00 pm

- International household and commercial moving
- International trade shows and exhibits
- International packing specialists
- Door-to-door service
- World-wide agency network
- One control - one responsibility
- Free international estimates and counseling

## ORIENT PACIFIC INTERNATIONAL MOVERS

美国东方太平洋包装服务有限公司

Room 208, Education Hotel

教育活动中心宾馆208室

3 Fenyang Lu 汾阳路3号

Tel: 6466-6163/0500 x 208

Fax: 6466-5152

E-mail: sopisc@npc.haplink.com.cn

## SINO SANTA FE INTERNATIONAL

华辉国际工程服务公司

(Huahui Guoji Gongcheng Fuwu Gongsi)

3rd Fl, #8, Lane 137, Xianxia Lu

仙霞路137弄8号3楼

Tel: 6233-9700

Fax: 6233-9005

Hours: 9:00 am - noon, 1:00 pm - 5:30 pm

- Pre-move consultations
- International removals
- Local removals
- Door-to-door service
- Custom-made crating
- Antique inspection
- Fully licensed customs staff

## TCI WORLDWIDE MOVERS

泛美国际运输有限公司

(Fanmei Guoji Yunshu Youxian Gongsi)

2-D Taitech Business Center

科美商务大厦2-D室

1245-2 Zhongshan Xi Lu

中山西路1245—2号

Tel: 6278-7204

Fax: 6278-7207

E-mail: tcis@public.sta.net.cn

TCI Worldwide Movers is an International moving company with over 25 years experience in moving families around the world. Based in Hong Kong, TCI operates seven offices throughout China. TCI services international moves through a network of affiliated offices around the world, and domestically through its own offices within China. Door-to-door service is provided for local moves. Warehouse storage is specially designed for household goods and personal effects, with a humidity-controlled section for delicate items.

## VIRGOWILL

威高利有限公司上海办事处

(Weigaoli Youxian Gongsi Shanghai Banshichu)

Room 102 , Marseille Garden

马赛花园102室

#2 Lane 79, Ronghua Dong Dao, Gu Bei

荣华东道79弄2号 (古北新区)

Tel: 6278-7070, 6278-7070

Fax: 6278-6060

Mobile: 1391751157

Hours: 9:00 am - 5:30 pm

Manager: Kevin Drisko

- Local moves in Shanghai and to other cities in China
- Packing and transportation of household effects with door-to-door or door-to-port service
- Scheduling of cultural relic appraisal
- Special antiques packing and crating
- Long/short term storage facilities

# PET CARE

Pet ownership is on the rise in Shanghai, as owning them has become a status symbol for the "nouveau riche". However pet care is only just beginning to emerge. Following are some newer pet-related care and retail facilities. Officially, it is against Shanghai municipal regulations for dogs to be on the streets between 6:00 am and 9:00 pm. In Beijing, dogs over 33 centimeters tall are not allowed at all within city limits.

# VETERINARIANS

## PENG DENG ANIMAL CLINIC
鹏峰兽医院
(Pengfeng Shouyiyuan)
Dr. Geoffrey Chen    陈鹏峰兽医师
Shanghai  Pet Market    上海宠物市场
Rooms 10-12, 18 Caodong San Lu
漕东三路18号10-12座
Tel:  6482-6886
Fax: 6244-3599
Pager: 127-2300711
Hours: 9:00 am - 5:00 pm

## SHU JIA MO    舒家模
Director and Professor
Shanghai Animal Hospital
Lane 2200, Xietu Lu    斜土路2200弄

Tel:  6404-6132, 64331790 x 28,
      6443-8957
Tel:  6317-4386 (home)
Hours: 8:30 am - 5:00 pm
Mr. Shu speaks English quite well and will treat your pet either at the hospital or via private home consultation.

## YANG QI QING    杨其清
Shenlong Animal Clinic
161 Zhizhong Lu    自忠路161号
Tel: 6385-5905
Pager: 128 x 131897
Hours: 9:00 am - 8:00 pm
Dr. Yang speaks some English and will make house-calls.

# PET SUPPLIES

## BIRD AND FLOWER MARKET
江阴路花鸟市场
(Jiangyin Luhua Niaoshichang)
Jiangyin Lu (near Huangpi Bei Lu)
江阴路靠近黄彼北路
Pick a nice sunny day to walk through this open alley bird and flower market. Ornate cages, crickets, fish, turtles, rabbits, (and believe it or not) squirrels and adorable Pekinese puppies are for sale. Pet supplies are available, as well as flowers and plants.

## SHANGHAI NAUGHTY FAMILY PETS CO. 上海顽皮家族宠物有限公司
(Shanghai Wanpi Jiazu Chongwu Youxian Gongsi)
2293 Hongqiao Lu    虹桥路2293号
Tel:  6268-9507
Fax: 6268-9507
Hours: 9:30 am - 5:30 pm
Look for a blue and white building that looks like a miniature castle. One can buy pets and

pet supplies in the front shop. In the back, there is a veterinarian's office, with a new Taiwanese vet.

## SHANGHAI PET MARKET (ALSO CALLED DOG TOWN)    上海宠物市场
(Shanghai Chongwu Shichang)
18 Caodong San Lu (off Caoxi Bei Lu)
漕东三路18号近漕溪北路
Tel: 6482-6885
This is south of and across the street from the Huating Hotel and Towers near Caoxi Park. Dogs, cats, birds, fish, and monkeys are for sale, as well as imported pet care products and food. There is also a veterinary clinic and access to imported vaccines for your pet.

*Note: Pet food is also available at most grocery stores.*

# BRINGING PETS TO SHANGHAI

Chinese rules in this area aren't very clear cut. What applies in one case doesn't always apply in another. The following information pertains to pets coming from the United States. Readers from other parts of the world may already have a good idea as to how to initiate the pet transport process.

The first step is to contact the air carrier that will bring the pet to Shanghai. All airlines have guidelines available regarding their policies. They should also be able to provide regulations pertaining to the destination. The cage used for the pet during transport must stand up straight, be fairly easy to move and have ventilation on all sides. Cages may be purchased from the airline or a pet store. (Airlines will not provide a free cage for one-time use.)

Next, contact your veterinarian and ask for the required USDA paperwork. If your vet does not have these papers, contact the USDA directly. The vet will need to administer all required innoculations three months prior to departure. If your pet has had regular, documented care and shots with no lapses, acquire this documentation from the vet so that innoculations can be done closer to departure. The vet must fill out all the USDA-required forms, but you must send them to the USDA yourself.

The USDA will then approve or disqualify your pet for overseas travel.

Upon arrival in Shanghai, take your pet directly to the Quarantine Bureau in the airport terminal, keeping the animal in the cage. From this point, things may be a bit touch-and-go. A one-month quarantine is mandatory under Chinese law, but can be accomplished either in the airport facility or at your home in Shanghai. Obviously, the latter is preferable, so put on your bargaining hat. Try not to show any impatience or irritability. Be as polite as possible, present all paperwork and try to negotiate for at-home quarantine, which is more than likely to be granted. Have on hand a minimum of RMB2,000 in cash (the US$ equivalent, about $240, is also acceptable) for documentation procedures. Papers will be issued allowing your pet to enter the PRC. Remember to also obtain exit papers for the pet. These should be issued along with the entry papers. With at-home quarantine, officials will definitely visit your home within 30 days to give your pet a cursory examination.

Smaller pets have a greater chance of being accepted into the PRC. Regulations bar entry of very large dogs, but like most things in China, this is negotiable.

# PROFESSIONAL PET TRANSPORT AGENCIES

Many expatriates choose to have their animals shipped by professional pet transport agencies because the documentation involved can be so complex. An individual who acts alone cannot count on the airlines to check documentation. If you decide to transport your pet without professional assistance, research the current regulations carefully and follow them to the letter. Then, sit back and try to relax as one diplomat did who purchased a seat for his German Shepherd. Detailed advice is available from the following companies in the US who provide relocation and moving services for pets. Call them with more specific questions.

## COSMOPOLITAN CANINE CARRIERS
5 Brook Street
PO Box 3271
Darien, CT 06820, USA
Tel: 1-800-243-9105 or 1-203-655-7295
Fax: 1-203-656-2527
Canine Carriers is a pet transportation agency, independent of IPATA (Independent Pet Animal Transportation Association). This company works directly with over 300 boarding kennels and veterinarians (all of which it has inspected), throughout the United States and abroad. Canine Carriers uses only the select few quarantine facilities that meet their standards. Unlike IPATA, Canine Carriers transports only dogs and cats. (It will include a rabbit in a dog or cat shipment). It will not however, transport birds, snakes, rodents, horses, or exotics. Like IPATA, Canine Carriers provides all documentation needed to ship an animal, including health certificates. This company can provide service for travelers from anywhere in the USA and is licensed by the Interstate Commerce Commission.

## AIR ANIMAL "THE PET MOVERS"
Toll-Free number for USA and Canada (1-800-635-3448)

## AMERICAN PET MOTELS, INC.
Toll-Free number for USA (1-800-728-7387)

## WORLD WIDE PET TRANSPORT
Toll-Free number for USA (1-800-545-PETS)

Most pet transportation companies can provide the following services or a tailored package:
- Health certificate(s)
- Veterinary certificate(s)
- Airline-approved flight kennels (all sizes)
- Boarding
- Flight arrangements
- Transportation from kennel to airport

## A LIST OF IPATA MEMBERS (all in the US):

### AIR ANIMAL, INC.
Tampa, FL 33607
1-813-879-3210 or
1-800-635-3448

### AIR PET TRANSPORT
River Forest, IL 60305
1-708-366-7080

**AMERICAN PET MOTELS, INC.**
Prairie View, IL 60069
1-708-634-9447

**ANIMAL CARE CENTER**
Houston, TX
1-713-774-7688

**ANIMAL MOTEL**
Butler, WI 53007-0228
1-414-781-5200

**ANIMAL PORT HOUSTON**
Houston, TX 77205
1-800-235-8744

**ANIMAL TRAVEL AGENCY**
Grayslake, IL 60030
1-708-362-3567

**ANIMAL TRAVEL AGENCY**
Deer Park, NY 11729
1-516-667-8924

**A PET TRANSFER**
Santa Ana, CA 92707
1-714-660-9390

**ATWOOD'S PET TRANSPORT**
Seattle, WA 98168
1-206-241-0880

**BELIEBEN KENNEL SERVICES**
Houston, TX 77064
1-713-466-1378

**BRETON'S SCHOOL FOR DOGS**
Danville, CA 94506
1-415-736-6231

**CANINE COUNTRY CLUB**
Phoenix, AZ 85034
1-602-244-8171

**COLLEYVILLE KENNEL**
Colleyville, TX 76034
1-817-498-6410

**DAY HILL KENNELS**
Windsor, CT 06095
1-203-688-2370

**THE FUNNY FARM**
Carlisle, PA 17013
1-717-249-5512

**GOLRUSK PET CARE CENTER**
Green Bay, WI 54311
1-414-468-7956

**HORKY'S PAWS INN, INC.**
Charlotte, NC 28208
1-704-399-1609

**JET-A-PET**
Westport, CT
1-203-227-3276

**KENILRIDGE KENNEL**
N. Ridgeville, OH 44039
1-216-327-8281

**KENNELWOOD VILLAGE, INC.**
St. Louis, MO 63114
1-314-429-2100

**KEYSTONE KENNELS, INC.**
Bethany, CT 06525
1-203-393-3126

**KONTINENTAL KENNELS**
Clinton, MD 20735
1-301-297-9244

**KRISDAN KENNELS**
Orlando, FL 32810
1-407-293-4645

**MIKE AND MAFF TRANSPORT**
Syracuse, NY 13224
1-315-445-9758

**MITCHVILLE K-9 KENNELS**
T-92 Seletar West
Farm Way 1
Singapore 790000
65-481-0084

**PARKWAY KENNELS**
Coraopolis, PA 15108
1-412-262-2727

**PEGASUS PET SHIPPING**
Arvada, CO 80001
1-303-431-4951

**PET EXPRESS**
San Francisco, CA 94107
1-415-821-7111

**PET EXPRESS, INC.**
Hanover Park, IL 60403
1-708-289-3900

**PET SET-COZY PET INN**
Gardena, CA 90249
1-213-644-2938

**PET TRAVEL AGENCY**
Schenectady, NY 12306
1-518-355-1749

**PROFESSIONAL PET SERVICES**
Palm Desert, CA 92260
1-619-345-8668

**ROXDANE KENNELS**
Warren, NJ 07059
1-908-755-0227

**STARWOOD KENNELS**
Oxford, MA 01540
1-508-987-0077

**THE KENNEL CLUB OF SOUTHERN CALIFORNIA**
Los Angeles, CA 90045
1-213-338-9166

**TRANSPET: AUSTRALIA**
Australia, N.S.W, 2171
61-2-606-6655

**VALLEY PET SERVICE**
Towson, MD 21204
1-301-821-1065

**WOODLAWN KENNEL, INC.**
Alexandria, VA 22309
1-703-360-6161

**WORLD WIDE PET SHIPPING**
South El Monte, CA 91733
1-818-448-6143

**WORLD WIDE PET TRANSPORT**
College Point, NY 11356
(718)539-5543/5547
1-800-545-PETS

# TRAVELING WITH PETS

Pets should be as comfortable and prepared as possible for the journey. The following suggestions will help make this transition easier.

- If the pet is traveling with you, make airline reservations early. Pets will normally travel in the cargo area of the plane. Call the airline a week before departure to remind them that you will be taking a pet.

- A travel identification tag is essential. In addition to a permanent identification collar and rabies tag your dog or cat should have a special tag with enough information on it to ensure the animal's return in the event it gets lost. A luggage-type tag should also be made out that includes your pet's name, your name, your destination address and telephone number, and an alternative contact person and telephone number, perhaps a business connection.

- There are stringent regulations regarding the size and type of container in which your pet must travel. Pet transportation companies and some airlines have kennel containers available for purchase in various sizes. Make certain that the container is large enough for your pet to stand, lie down, and turn around comfortably. Mark the container "LIVE ANIMAL" and indicate which side is up with an arrow.

- Print your name and destination address clearly on the container. Write your pet's name on the container so that the attendant can call it by name. Also, indicate any temperament problems or special needs.

- Provide containers for food and water along with feeding instructions. Dry food is best.

- Help your pet adjust to the travel container before the trip. Equip the kennel with a comfortable, absorbent pad and a safe, favorite toy. For the trip, it's a good idea to put an article of your worn clothing inside the kennel. Your scent will be comforting to the animal.

- Feed your pet about six hours before departure. Unless the weather is very hot, or your pet is very young, do not give it any water within two hours of the flight.

- Make sure your pet has been sufficiently exercised before the trip. Exercise helps to alleviate anxieties and will allow your pet to sleep.

- Tranquilizer drugs can decrease respiratory function and breathing difficulties may occur. Check with your veterinarian before dispensing tranquilizers.

# THE TALE OF THE PAINTED DOG
Jennifer Dawson
President, Sources Far East Ltd.

Last year, my son and business partner, Doug, and I were shopping for office equipment on Nanjing Lu. We barely noticed a man, who was leaning against a building with a small bag in his arms, but for a tiny face poking from the top of the bag. It was an animal of an unrecognizable variety, with a face resembling a dog's or cat's, but with coloring more like a tiger. The fur on the fuzzy face was black with a perfect copper-colored mask. The black body was striped with matching copper stripes. The animal was so small that it could be held in the palm of one's hand.

We were captivated, however neither of us needed or wanted a dog. Doug already had a dog in Shanghai and I was too busy to take on the added responsibility. We started to walk away. We made it about twenty feet before we stopped and looked at each other. After about two minutes of trying to talk each other out of making a rash, emotional decision, we turned and walked back to the man. Of course, we ended up with the dog. And, of course the dog decided to do his business on my coat on the way home. We were still smitten however, and decided that his name had to be Tigger.

Now, we faced another problem. We knew Doug's five-year-old son would really enjoying having Tigger around, but we weren't so sure Doug's wife, Stephanie, would be so happy with this turn of events. As it turned out, she was just as charmed by Tigger as we were, and gave us only token grief. Everyone who saw the dog was incredulous of its coloring and Tigger soon became a minor celebrity in the neighborhood.

We continued to ponder how a dog could possibly look like this, and felt certain that he was dyed, though we couldn't imagine anyone being able to do a dye job of this sort, especially around the eyes. We decided that if it was indeed dye, the person who did it was a genius and should be working in a Fifth Avenue salon.

Eventually, rumors began to circulate of other dogs similar to Tigger being sold on the streets in Shanghai. Some were similarly striped and others bore perfectly round copper spots. Although Tigger held his stripes for about two months, we were sure that they were artificial. Then, lo and behold, we started to notice a gradual change. The dog was slowly becoming blacker, and a bald spot developed on his head due to chemical irritation, though this was only temporary, fortunately.

So we now have a full-grown dog that is totally black. We always said that even if Tigger lost his stripes he would still be cute (and he is), but that people who encountered him would wonder about his name.

This tale points up the fact that Chinese ingenuity never ceases to amaze. I've lived here for quite some time and it still throws me sometimes. And, I always seem to learn the hard way.

# RELIGIOUS ACTIVITIES

Formal churches that provide services in English are few and far between here, but there are a few. To make up for this lack, there are many Bible Study groups for foreigners in Shanghai that are usually special interest groups within larger social organizations such as the Shanghai Expatiates Association. If you're looking for a study group to suit your needs, ask around among the expatriate population.

The Chinese government does not mind that expatriate religious groups exist, but a problem definitely arises if expatriates include local Chinese in their informal groups. Proselytizing is not permitted. Local Chinese are free to worship at Chinese-organized churches of their choice, but private expatriate religious groups that include locals may be forced to disband, and organizers may be expelled from China.

# PROTESTANT

These services are frequently attended by expatriates:

## SHANGHAI COMMUNITY CHURCH
国际礼拜堂
(Guoji Libaitang)
Protestant, non-denominational.
53 Hengshan Lu  衡山路53号
Tel: 6437-6576
Services: 7:30 am, 10:00 am and 7:00 pm
        Sundays.

English translation is sometimes available. This is a lovely, quaint church located in Xuhui district in the former French Concession. Special lofts for foreigners and translation machines exist, but the machines are used only for certain services. The church is always overflowing with Chinese devotees.

## Others

### BEI QIAO CHURCH  北桥耶稣堂
(Beiqiao Yeisutang)
Beiqiao Town  北桥镇
Tel: 6490-1374
Services: Fri. 8:00 am - 10:30 am,
        Sun. 8:00 am - 10:30 am and
        12:30 pm - 2:30 pm

### HUAI'EN CHURCH  怀恩堂
(Huai'en Tang)
375 Shaanxi Bei Lu  陕西北路375号
Tel: 6253-9394
Services are held on:
        Wed. 7:30 am - 8:00 am,
        Thur. 1:30 pm - 3:30 pm,
        Sat. 8:30 am - 10:00 am and
        Sun. 8:30 am - 10:00 am and
        6:30 pm - 8:00 pm

### HU DONG CHURCH  沪东教堂
(Hudong Jiaotang)
350 Guohe Lu  国和路350号
Tel: 6533-5963
Services: Sat. 6:30 am - 8:00 am;
        Sun. 6:30 am - 8:00 am,
        9:00 am - 10:30 am, and
        6:30 pm - 8:00 pm

### HUXI CHURCH  沪西基督教礼拜堂
(Huxi Jidujiao Libaitang)
1465 Changning Lu  长宁路1465号
Tel: 6259-7389
Services: Sun. 7:30 am - 8:30 am and
        9:30 am - 10:30 am

### KUNSHAN CHURCH  基督教景灵堂
(Jidujiao Jinglingtang)
135 Kunshan Lu  昆山路135号
Tel: 6324-3021
Services: Sun. 7:30 am and 9:30 am

### MU'EN (BAPTISED WITH MERCY) CHURCH  沫恩堂
(Mo'en Tang)
316 Xizang Zhong Lu  西藏中路316号
Tel: 6322-5069
Services: Wed., Thu., and Fri. 7:00 pm - 8:30 pm; Sat 1:30 pm - 3:30 pm; Sun 7:30 am - 9:00 am, 9:30 am - 11:30 am, 2:00 pm and 7:00 pm
Xizang Zhong Lu (between Jiujiang Lu and Hankou Lu)
Used as a school until 1979, this was a former Methodist Church. In 1988, some 1,500 Protestants packed this church for the consecration of two bishops, the first to be installed in China in over 30 years.

**XIN EN CHURCH** 新恩堂
(Xin'entang)
25 Wulumuqi Bei Lu 乌鲁木齐北路25号
Tel: 6258-0451
Services: Sun. 7:30 am - 8:30 am and
9:30 am - 10:30 am

**ZHABEI CHURCH** 基督教闸北堂
(Jidujiao Zhabeitang)
340 Baotong Lu 宝通路340号
Tel: 5662-9409
Services: Sun. 7:30am and 9:30am

**ZHU SHENG CHURCH** 诸圣堂
(Zhusheng Tang)
425 Fuxing Zhong Lu 复兴中路425号
Tel: 6385-0906
Services: Sat. 7:00 am - 8:00 am;
Sun. 7:00 am - 8:00 am,
9:30 am - 10:30 am and
7:00 pm - 8:00 pm

# CATHOLIC

These churches are frequently attended by expatriates:

## CHRIST THE KING CATHOLIC CHURCH
天主教上海教区君王堂
(Tianzhujiao Shanghai Jiaoqu Junwangtang)
361 Julu Lu at Maoming Lu 巨鹿路361号
(First floor of white high-rise building)
Tel: 6217-4608
Services: Sat. 5:00 pm (Fnglish),
Sun. 8:30 am (Chinese),
Sun. 10:30 am (English)
Both masses are in English. The congregation is primarily expatriate and the program and presentation is very similar to church abroad.

## ST. IGNATIUS CATHEDRAL
徐家汇天主教堂
(Xujiahui Tianzhujiaotang)
158 Puxi Lu, Xujiahui Qu
蒲西路158号 徐家汇
Tel: 6469-0930
Services: Sunday 5:30 am, 6:00 am,
7:00 am and 8:00 am
Several masses are offered on religious holidays such as Christmas and Easter. As the church has only 2,500 seats, thousands of people stand in the courtyard listening to the services over loudspeakers. Times of services during these holidays vary from year to year. The church was founded by the Jesuits in 1848 and during the Taiping Rebellion (in the mid-19th century) it served as headquarters for the rebel forces. It has also served as a missionary seminary, orphanage, library, and publishing house. It was closed during the cultural revolution, but reopened in 1979. Masses in this cathedral are in Chinese.

## DA GONG SUO CATHOLIC CHURCH
大公所天主教堂

(Dagongsuo Tianzhi Jiaotang)
Congming County　崇明县港沿镇
Tel: 5946-1272
Services: Mon. - Sat. 6:15 am - 7:15 am,
　　　　 Sun. 2 services at 6:00 am and
　　　　 8:30 am

## FU JIA ROSE CHURCH
付家玫瑰圣母堂

(Fujia Meigui Shengmutang)
1115 Pudong Dadao (near Taixing Plaza)
浦东大道1115号近泰星广场
Tel: 5885-3172
Services: Mon. - Sat. 7:00 am - 8:00 am;
　　　　 Sun. 6:30 am - 7:30 am and
　　　　 8:00 am - 9:00 am

## NANSHI DISTRICT CATHOLIC CHURCH
南市区董家渡天主堂

(Nanshiqu Dongjiadu Tianzhutang)
185 Dongjiadu Lu　董家渡路185号
Tel: 6377-5665
Services: 6:30 am - 8:00 am, daily

## QI CHANG QIAN CATHOLIC CHURCH
其昌浅天主教堂

(Qichangqian Tianzhujiaotang)
666 Pudond Dadao, Education House
浦东大道666号
Tel: 5876-9532
Services: Sat. 5:00 pm - 6:30 pm

## YANGPU DISTRICT CATHOLIC CHURCH
天主教和平之后堂

(Tianzhujiao Hepingzhihuotang)
692 Huimin Lu　惠民路692号
Tel: 6546-0067
Services: Weekdays 6:45 am;
　　　　 Sat. and Sun. 7:00 am

## ZHABEI CATHOLIC CHURCH
闸北天主教堂

(Zhabei Tianzhujiaotang)
289 Yuyingtang Lu　育婴堂路289号
Tel: 5662-4172
Services: Mon. - Sat. 6:15 am - 7:00 am
　　　　 Sun. 7:00 am - 8:00 am

## ZHANGYAN BAI JIA CATHOLIC CHURCH　百家天主教堂

(Baijia Tianzhujiaotang)
Jinshan County　金山县张堰
Tel: 5721-3372
Services: Sat. and Sun 7:00 am

## ZHU JIA JIAO CATHOLIC CHURCH
朱家角天主教堂

(Zhujiajiao Tianzhujiaotang)
Qingpu County　青浦县朱家角
Tel: 5924-0877
Services: Sat. 3:00 pm; Sun. 7:00 am

# WOMEN'S BIBLE STUDY GROUPS

Meetings are held every Wednesday at 10:00 am at the Portman Ritz-Carlton. For information about this group call either Louise Lipman at 6358-9267 or Pat Wilson at 6279-8499 or fax at 6279-8339. There is also a group in Gubei that meets on Thursdays at 9:30 am. Please contact Kelly Thompson at 6270-3437 or Ann Kedl at 6280-2906.

# JEWISH

There is an active group in Shanghai that celebrates Jewish holidays and holds services. Contact Seth Kaplan 6482-7230 or the Israeli Consulate General at 6209-8008 以色列领事馆 (Yiselie Lingshiguan)

Suite 703, New Town Mansion
新虹桥大厦703室
55 Loushanguan Lu, Hongqiao
娄山关路55号
Tel: 6209-8008
Fax: 6209-8010

# ISLAMIC

**HU XI MOSQUE**  沪西清真寺
(Huxi Qingzhensi)
3 Changde Lu, Lane 1328
常德路1328弄3号
Tel: 6277-5966
Hours: 6:00 am - 10:00 pm

**XIAO TAO YUAN MOSQUE**
小桃园天灵寺
(Xiaotaoyuan Tianlingsi)
52 Xiaotaoyuan Jie   小桃园路52号
Tel : 6377-5442
Hours: 8:00 am - 4:00 pm
Built in 1925. Services are at the traditional times of day for Moslems.

# BUDDHIST AND TAOIST

**BAIYUN TAOIST TEMPLE**  白云观
(Baiyun Guan)
100 Lane,  8 Xilinhou Lu   西林后路100弄8号
Tel: 6377-2800
Hours: 8:00 am - 4:00 pm

**GUANG FU TEMPLE**  广福寺
(Guangfu Si)
Congming County   崇明县
Tel: 5944-1939
Hours: 7:30 am - 11:00 am

**JADE BUDDHA TEMPLE**  玉佛寺
(Yufusi)
170 Anyuan Lu   安远路170号
Tel: 6266-3668
Hours: 8:00 am - noon, 1:30 pm - 5:00 pm

**JING'AN TEMPLE**  静安古寺
1700 Nanjing Xi Lu   南京西路1700号
Tel: 5648-6366, 6248-6366

**LONG HUA TEMPLE**  龙华寺
(Longhuasi)
2853 Longhua Lu   龙华路2853号
Tel: 6456-6085
Hours: 7:00 am - 4:30 pm

**LONG WANG MIAO TAOIST TEMPLE**
龙王庙道观
(Longwangmiao Daoguan)
Gong Lu   龚路
Tel: 5856-2332
Hours: 7:00 am - 4:00 pm

## SHANGHAI BUDDHISM INDUSTRIAL ORGANIZATION 上海佛教之实业社

(Shanghai Fujiao Shiyeshe)
418-A Changde Lu    常德路418号A座
Tel: 6247-5098
Fax: 6247-5098
Hours: 8:30 am - 4:30 pm

## SHANGHAI TAOIST ASSOCIATION 上海市道教协会

(Shanghaishi Daojiao Xiehui)
Lane 100, 8 Xilinhou Lu    西林后路100弄8号
Tel: 6377-5402

## SHESHAN XIAN LING TEMPLE 西林寺

(Xilnsi)
Songjiang County    松江县
Tel: 5781-3454
Hours: 5:00 am - 4:00 pm

## XIA HAI TEMPLE 下海庙

(Xiahaimiao)
73 Kunming Lu    昆明路 73号
Tel: 6541-0761
Hours: 6:00 am - 4:00 pm

# NUNNERIES

## CHEN XIANG GE NUNNERY 沉香阁

(Chenxiangge)
29 Chenxiangge Lu    沉香阁路29号
Tel: 6320-3431
Hours: 7:00 am - 7:00 pm

## CI XIU NUNNERY 慈修庵

(Cixiu'an)
15 Qinling Jie    溱岭街15号
Tel: 6328-8550, 6328-2892
Hours: 6:00 am - 4:00 pm

## CONVENT IN SHANGHAI SUB-REGION OF CATHOLICISM 修女院

(Xiunuyuan)
201 Caoxi Bei Lu    漕溪北路201号
Tel: 6438-2695

*Chen Xiang Ge Nunnery and Ci Xiu Nunnery are both open to visitors to worship during the hours shown.*

# TRAVEL AND
# TRANSPORTATION

For airport and flight information
at Hongqiao Airport
call 6268-8918 or 6253-7664.

# TRAVEL AGENCIES

## AMERICAN EXPRESS TRAVEL RELATED SERVICES 美国运通国际股份有限公司

(Meiguo Yuntong Guoji Gufen Youxian Gongsi)

Level 2, West Wing, Shanghai Centre

上海商城西峰2楼

Tel: 6279-8082

AMEX bills paid here will be credited on the same day. They can also book travel packages.

## EVROKONTAKT

永祥实业顾问上海有限公司

(Yongxiang Shiye Guwen Shanghai Youxian Gongsi)

Room T, 9th Fl

Tseng Chow Commercial Mansion

增泽世贸大楼9楼T座

1590 Yan'an Xi Lu    延安西路1590号

Tel: 6280-9579, 6280-6598

Fax: 6280-9579

This German travel agency is European-managed and all staff are fluent in English. Evrokontakt is part of a world wide network of travel agents and has connections with professional tour organizations, airlines, and hotels all over the world.

## GREAT WEST CORP.

大希角贸易有限公司

(Daxijiao Maoyi Youxian Gongsi)

Suite 330, Shanghai Centre  上海商城330室

1376 Nanjing Xi Lu    南京西路1376号

Tel: 6279-8219, 6279-8489

Fax: 6279-8488

Airline tickets, tours, and hotel bookings. This company also provides customized secretarial services and company registration.

## HARVEST TRAVEL SERVICES LTD.

夏怡旅游咨询公司

(Xiayi Luyou Zixun Gongsi)

16-A6 Harvest Bldg.

585 Longhua Xi Lu    龙华西路585号

Tel/fax: 6469-1860

Reservation representative: Anita Wang

Harvest Travel Services offers international ticketing and hotel bookings, package tours for individual and groups, incentive tours to North America and southeast Asia, and cruise bookings. Harvest Travel has been in operation for about twenty years and maintains offices in Hong Kong, Honolulu, Los Angeles, London, Vancouver, and Toronto.

## SEA WORLD TRAVEL AGENCY

海上世界航空售票处

(Haishang Shijie Hangkong Shoupiaochu)

169 Jianguo Zhong Lu    建国中路169号

Tel: 6431-1600, 6471-9170

Fax: 6431-3475, 6471-9170

24-hour automatic service: 6460-0047

Authorized agent for Lufthansa.

## SHANGHAI JEBSEN AIR SERVICE CO. LTD.  捷成航空

(Jiecheng Hangkong)

Central Place  中汇大厦

16 Henan Lu    河南南路16号

Tel: 6355-4001, 6355-4002, 6355-4003

Fax: 6355-3010

Hours: 9:00 am - 6:00 pm Mon. - Fri
　　　 9:00 am - 1:00 pm Sat.,Sun., holidays

Contact: Miss Ranny Ip

Full-service travel agency. They accept American Express, Visa, Diner's Club, Mastercard, and JCB credit cards. Sino/Hong Kong joint venture.

**INTERNATIONAL TRAVEL SERVICE**
中国国际旅行社外航售票处
(Zhongguo Guoji Luxingshe Waihang
Shoupiaochu)
Jiahua Business Center  加华商务中心
Room 8116A, 808 Hongqiao Lu
虹桥路808号8116A
Tel: 6486-0681, 6486-0682, 6486-4519

Fax: 6486-4520
E-mail: irs@gate.ininet.co.cn
This agency can handle all international and
domestic business and pleasure travel. Dis-
counted domestic hotel packages are also
available.

# AIR TRAVEL

## Airline Offices

### AIR CHINA  中国航空公司
(Zhongguo Hangkong Gongsi)
600 Huashan Lu  华山路600号
Tel: 6327-2676
Fax: 6327-2762
Hours: 8:30 am - 6:00 pm
Flights to and from Anchorage, Frankfurt,
Fukuoka, Hiroshima, Kuala Lumpur,
Melbourne, Nagoya, New York, Osaka,
Paris, San Francisco, Sydney, Tokyo, and
Vancouver.

### AIR FRANCE  法国航空公司
(Faguo Hangkong Gongsi)
Room 1301, 128 Nanjing Xi Lu
南京西路128号1301室
Tel: 6360-6688
Fax: 6360-6655
Two direct Shanghai-Paris flights per week,
on Tuesdays and Sundays. Flights from Beijing
to Paris on Tuesday, Friday, Saturday, and
Sunday. Hong Kong to Paris daily and
Bangkok to Paris daily.

### AIR NEW ZEALAND  新西兰航空公司
(Xinxilan Hangkong Gongsi)
Round-trips to Sydney and Auckland on
Sundays.

### ALL NIPPON AIR (ANA)  全日空
(Quanrikong)
Level 2, East Wing, Shanghai Centre
上海商城西峰2楼
1376 Nanjing Xi Lu  南京西路1376号
Tel: 6279-7000
Flights to and from Osaka and Tokyo.

### ANSETT AUSTRALIA AIRLINES
澳洲安捷航空公司
(Aozhou Anjie Hangkong Gongsi)
918 Huaihai Zhong Lu  淮海中路918号
Tel: 6415-5210
Fax: 6415-5209
This airline offers two direct flights per week
on Thursdays and Sundays from Shanghai to
Sydney.

### ASIANIA  韩亚航空公司
(Hanya Hangkong Gongsi)
2000 Yan'an Xi Lu  延安西路2000号
Tel: 6219-4000
Daily round-trips to Seoul.

### AUSTRIAN AIRLINES  奥地利航空公司
(Aodili Hangkong Gongsi)
303 Equatorial Hotel
上海国际贵都大饭店303室
65 Yan'an Xi Lu  延安西路65号
Tel: 6249-1202
Fax: 6249-1205
Two weekly flights to Vienna.

## CANADIAN AIRLINES INTERNATIONAL

加拿大航空公司

(Jianada Hangkong Gongsi)

City Ticket Office

Jinjiang Tower, 6th Fl　新锦江6楼

161 Changle Lu　长乐路161号

Tel: 6415-3091

Fax: 6415-3096

Suite 104, Lufthansa Center, Beijing

北京燕莎中心104室

Tel: 6463-7901, 6463-7902,
　　　6463-7903, 6463-7904, 6463-7905

Fax: 6463-7906

Non-stop service from Shanghai and Beijing to Vancouver twice a week on Tuesdays and Saturdays.

## CHINA EASTERN AIRLINES

中国东方航空公司

(Zhongguo Dongfang Hangkong Gongsi)

Main office: 200 Yan'an Xi Lu

延安西路200号

Domestic information: 6247-5953

International information: 6247-2255

For groups of nine or more,
contact 6247-1152

Fax: 6247-6761

Open 24 hours daily

- 330 Dongchang Lu　东昌路330号
  Tel: 5887-1111
  Fax: 5887-3797, 5831-6039
  Hours: 8:30 am - 6:00 pm
- 370 Huashan Lu　华山路370号
  Tel: 6248-1888 x 2100
  Hours: 8:00 am - 5:30 pm
- 2099 Yan'an Xi Lu　延安西路2099号
  Tel: 6275-0000 x 57
  Fax: 6275-6813
  Hours: 8:00 am - 8:00 pm
- 860\3 Nanjing Xi Lu　南京西路860弄3号
  Tel: 6255-1925
  Fax: 6271-4956
  Hours: 8:00 am - 8:00 pm

Flights to Bangkok, Brussels, Chicago, Fukuoka, Hong Kong, Los Angeles, Madrid, Munich, Nagasaki, Osaka, Seattle, Seoul, Singapore, Sydney, and Tokyo.

## CHINA NORTHERN AIRLINES

中国北方航空公司

(Zhongguo Beifang Hangkong Gongsi)

1394 Yan'an Xi Lu　延安西路1394号

Tel: 6280-0800

Fax: 6280-3604

Hours: 8:30 am - 4:30 pm

## CHINA SOUTHWESTERN AIRLINES

中国西南航空公司

(Zhongguo Xinan Hangkong Gongsi)

150 Maoming Nan Lu　茂名南路150号

Tel: 6433-3355

Fax: 6471-1676

Hours: 8:30 am - 11:30 am,
　　　　1:30 pm - 4:30 pm

## DRAGONAIR　港龙航空公司

(Ganglong Hangkong Gongsi)

Room 202, West Tower, Shanghai Centre

上海商城西峰202室

1376 Nanjing Xi Lu　南京西路1376号

Tel: 6279-8099

Fax: 6279-7189

Office hours: 9:00 am - 5:00 pm daily,
　　　　　　　including Sundays

*Baggage allowance:* 20 kg. for economy class, 40 kg. for first class

*Carry on:* One bag, not larger than 22x13x9 inches, and weighing no more than 5 kg.

*Reconfirmation:* Required 72 hours before departure

*Payment:* Credit cards and cash are acceptable.

*Check-in:* Counters open 2 hours before departure and close 30 minutes before departure.

## FINNAIR

SCITE Tower, Room 204,

22 Jianguomen Waidajie

Beijing 100004

Tel: 6512-7181
Fax: 6512-7182

## JAPAN AIRLINES (JAL)  日本航空公司
(Riben Hangkong Gongsi)
Room 201, Ruijin Building  瑞金大厦201室
205 Maoming Nan Lu  茂名南路205号
Tel: 6472-3000, 6258-8588
Fax: 6472-9071
Daily round-trips to Tokyo and Osaka

## KOREAN AIRLINES  大韩航空公司
(Dahan Hangkong Gongsi)
Room 104, Hotel Equatorial
国际贵都大酒店104室
65 Yan'an Xi Lu  延安西路65号
Tel: 6275-6000
Fax: 6275-2777

## LUFTHANSA  德国汉莎航空公司
(Deguo Hansha Hangkong Gongsi)
Hilton Hotel  静安希尔顿
250 Huashan Lu  华山路250号
Tel: 6248-1100
Fax: 6248-1133
Round-trips to Frankfurt

## MALAYSIA AIRLINES
马来西亚航空公司
(Malaixiya Hangkong Gongsi)
Suite 209, Level 2 East Wing,  东峰209室
Shanghai Centre  上海商城
1376 Nanjing Xi Lu  南京西路1376号
Tel: 6279-8607
Fax: 6279-8657
Non-stop flights to Kuala Lumpur every Tuesday
and Saturday.

## NORTHWEST AIRLINES  西南航空公司
(Xinan Hangkong Gongsi)
- Level 2, East Wing, Shanghai Centre
  上海商城东峰2楼
  1376 Nanjing Xi Lu  南京西路1376号
  Tel: 6279-8088
  Fax: 6279-8007

- Beijing  北京
  Tel: 010-6505-3505
  Fax: 010-6505-1855
- Tokyo  日本
  Tel: 81-03-3533-6000

## QANTAS AIRLINES  澳大利亚航空公司
(Aodaliya Hangkong Gongsi)
203A Shanghai Centre  上海商城203A室
1376 Nanjing Xi Lu  南京西路1376号
Tel: 6279-8660
Fax: 6279-8650
Four direct flights weekly to and from Sydney.

## RUSSIAN INTERNATIONAL AIRLINES
俄罗斯国际航空公司
(Eluosi Guoji Hangkong Gongsi)
70 Donghu Lu  东湖路70号
Donghu Hotel, New Wing  东湖宾馆新楼
Tel: 6415-8158 x 77403, 6415-6700

## SAS  斯堪的纳维亚航空公司
(Sikandinaweiya Hangkong Gongsi)
- JinJiang Hotel
  锦江饭店 外国航空公司服务部
  59 Maoming Nan Lu  茂名南路59号
  Tel: 6472-3131
- Scandinavian Airlines
  CVIK Tower
  22 Jianguomenwai Dajie
  建国门大街22号
  Beijing
  Tel: 010-512-0575/76
Four weekly non-stop flights from Beijing to
Copenhagen on Monday, Tuesday, Thursday,
and Sunday.

## SHANGHAI AIRLINES
上海航空公司
(Shanghai Hangkong Gongsi)
- 555 Yan'an Zhong Lu  延安中路555号
  8:00 am - 9:00 pm, everyday
  Tel: 6255-0550
  Fax: 6255-0251
- 385 Maiyuan Lu  梅园路385号

8:00 am - 6:00 pm, every day
Tel: 6317-8178

- 534 Hengshan Lu　衡山路534号
  Hengshan Hotel　衡山宾馆
  8:30 am - 3:30 pm Mon. - Fri.
  8:30 pm - noon Sat.
  Tel: 6437-7050 x 734
- 422 Tiantong Lu　天通路422号
  New Asia Hotel　新亚大酒店
  8:30 am- 4:30 pm Mon. - Fri.
  8:30 am - noon Sat.
  Tel: 6324-0549
- 111 Jiangwan Lu　江湾路111号
  Swan Cindic Hotel　天鹅信谊宾馆
  8:30 am - 11:00 am
  noon - 4:30 pm Mon. - Fri.
  8:30 am - 11:00 am Sat.
  Tel: 6325-5255 x 2105
- 650 Yishan Lu　宜山路650号
  Qianhe Hotel　千鹤宾馆
  8:00 am - 7:30 pm, every day
  Tel: 6470-1733
  Fax: 6470-0348
- 35 Xizang Nan Lu　西藏南路35号
  9:00 am - 5:00 pm, every day
  Tel: 6328-8292
- 1465 Pudong Nan Lu　浦东南路1465号
  Tel: 5831-9090
  Fax: 5830-0471
  8:30 am - 5:00 pm
- 777 Hengfeng Lu　恒丰路777号
  Longmen (Dragon Door) Hotel　龙门宾馆
  Tel: 6317-0000 x 2722
- 131-133 Lanxi Lu　兰溪路131-133号
  Tel: 6254-3086
  8:30 am - 6:00 pm
- 200 Renmin Dadao　人民大道200号
  Tel: 6311-9946
  9:00 am - 5:00 pm
- 1912 Yan'an Xi Lu　延安西路1912号
  Tel: 6219-3090
  Fax: 6219-3090
  8:00 am - 6:00 pm
- 7 Xilingzhai Lu　西凌宅路7号
  Tel: 6312-1829

Fax: 6312-1829
8:00 am - 6:00 pm

## SINGAPORE AIRLINES
新加坡航空公司
(Xinjiapo Hangkong Gongsi)
Level 2, East Wing, Shanghai Centre
上海商城东峰2楼
1376 Nanjing Xi Lu　南京西路1376号
Tel: 6279-8000, 6255-8703
Fax: 6279-8027, 6279-8028
Daily flights to and from Singapore

## SWISSAIR　瑞士航空公司
(Ruishi Hangkong Gongsi)
Room 203 Level 2, West Wing, Shanghai
Centre　上海商城西峰2楼
Tel: 6279-7381, 6279-7383
Fax: 6279-7384
Three times weekly between Shanghai and
Switzerland and three times a week to and
from Zurich via Beijing

## THAI AIRWAYS INTERNATIONAL
泰国航空公司
(Taiguo Hangkong Gongsi)
Room 201 Level 2, West Wing, Shanghai
Centre　上海商城西峰2楼
1376 Nanjing Xi Lu　南京西路1376号
Tel: 6279-7175, 6248-7766
Fax: 6248-8144
To Bangkok and back three times a week

## UNITED AIRLINES　联合航空公司
(Lianhe Hangkong Gongsi)
Level 2, West Wing, Shanghai Centre
上海商城西峰2楼
1376 Nanjing Xi Lu　南京西路1376号
Tel: 6279-8010
Tel: 6279-8009 for reservations
Tel: 6268-8818 for incoming flight informa-
tion
Fax: 6279-8853
Beijing tel: 10 463-1111
Daily flights to and from Tokyo.

## Private Charters

**VIP CHARTER SERVICE** 贵宾包机服务
(Guibin Baoji Fuwu)
China Hainan Airlines   中国海南航空公司
(Zhongguo Hainan Hanghong Gongsi)
- Haikou head office
  Tel: 0898-670-4399
  Fax: (0898) 671-2974
- Beijing base
  Tel: (010) 6506-8300, 6506-8282
  Fax: (010) 6506-8221

- Hong Kong Agency
  Tel: (852) 2723-3981
  Fax: (852) 2723-3931
  Mobile phone: (0898) 908-7245,
  1391035180
  Pager: (010) 65258861 x 3841
  E-mail: vcs@public.hk.hq.cn
Web site: http://www.hpis.com/partners.htm
Based at Beijing Capital International Airport,
this company's Learjets can take off from any
city at any time for business travel or emergency evacuation.

# GROUND TRANSPORTATION

Cars owned or leased by one's employer are the chief mode of transportation for foreigners in Shanghai. Most joint ventures and representative offices provide their managers with a car and driver. Each company forms its own policy as to the availability of the vehicle to spouse and family.

Transportation by taxi is quite reasonably priced and all Shanghai taxis are metered. Ordering a taxi by telephone costs an additional RMB4. Fares start at RMB10.60 for the small vehicles, and Santanas start at RMB14.40. The meter runs more slowly if the car is not moving, therefore, most drivers are hesitant to wait if you prefer to keep the car to go on to another destination. In this case, make it clear to the driver that you are willing to pay an additional fee, over and above the metered fee. One should judge this amount by the amount of "down time" your driver has endured. Tipping is not required, but it is expected that you will round-off the fare and not expect the driver to return small change. If you are traveling from Shanghai proper (Puxi) to Pudong there is no additional charge. However, the return trip from Pudong to Puxi requires an additional fee of RMB15. If you are traveling one-way from Puxi to Pudong, your driver will ask for the RMB15 he requires to return. This is standard practice.

If you have not mastered saying your destination in Chinese, you will have difficulty. You have three options in this case:

- Carry cards with you that have your destination written in both Chinese, pinyin, and English. (These can be purchased from Stephanie Dawson at 6268-6947 or 6268-9541 or by fax at 6268-8004 or e-mail at sources@public.sta.net.cn.)

- Ask a nearby hotel doorman to assist you. Most of them are familiar with the English names of places foreigners frequent.
- Order your taxi through the reception desk at the major residential complexes or hotels.

# TAXI COMPANIES

| Dazhong Taxi | 大众出租 | 6258-1688 |
|---|---|---|
| Friendship Taxi | 友谊出租 | 6258-4584 |
| Zhendong Taxi | 振东出租 | 5887-1890 |
| Baolong Taxi | 宝隆出租 | 5610-7400 |
| Nonggong Shang Taxi | 农工商出租 | 6214-5588 |
| Jing'an Taxi | 静安出租 | 6258-4000 |
| Tourism Taxi | 旅汽出租 | 6464-8888 |
| Waimao Taxi | 外贸出租 | 6321-0493 |
| Zhenhua Taxi | 振华出租 | 6275-8800 |
| Qiangsheng Taxi | 强出生租 | 6258-0000 |

One also has the option of renting a vehicle for the entire day. Although presently there are no foreign rental car companies operating in Shanghai, it is rumored that Hertz is looking into opening an operation here soon. Don't imagine renting a Hertz car and heading out for the day by yourself however. These cars will be provided with a chauffeur.

## Leasing of passenger vehicles

**FRIENDSHIP CAR LEASING COMPANY**
上海友谊汽车服务公司
(Shanghai Youyi Qiche Fuwu Gongsi)
54 Wuzhong Lu 吴中路54号

Tel: 6270-1671, 6256-2158, 6256-2153
This company has the most extensive list of cars for lease:

| Model | Daily Rental | Monthly Rental | Half Year Rental | Yearly Rental |
|---|---|---|---|---|
| Santana | 320/120 km | 9,000 | 51,000 | 97,200 |
| Santana 2000 | 450/120 km | 13,500 | 72,000 | 132,000 |
| Audi 100cc | 480/120 km | 12,000 | 69,000 | 132,000 |
| Audi 100U | 580/120 km | 17,500 | 96,000 | 180,000 |
| Nissan VIP | 936/100 km | 18,000 | 108,000 | 216,000 |
| Chevrolet 7 seat | 800/100 km | 19,600 | 108,000 | 205,200 |
| Chrysler Van | 1,100/100 km | 20,000 | 108,000 | 180,000 |
| Chrysler Car | 1,100/100 km | 30,000 | 150,000 | 264,000 |
| Mercedes-Benz | 3,000/100 km | negotiable | negotiable | negotiable |
| Cadillac | 2,800/100 km | negotiable | negotiable | negotiable |

*All figures in RMB*

The above prices are without a driver. The Mercedes-Benz and the Cadillac require drivers from the leasing company. Drivers are an additional charge of RMB2,000 per month or RMB100 per day. The rental pay-ment must be made in advance along with a deposit of RMB15,000. If a foreigner wants to lease a vehicle in his/her own name, he/she has to provide a guarantor (preferably a company, or a local Chinese resident with an established reputation).

## SHANGHAI FRIENDSHIP TAXI SERVICE COMPANY 上海友谊汽车公司

(Shanghai Youyi Qiche Gongsi)
Room 202, 847 Yan'an Zhong Lu
延安中路847号202室
Tel: 6279-1279 x 220 or 227 (Ms. Zhang Meiping) 张美萍小姐
This company has recently imported 100 Ford Tempos that rent for RMB468 per day or RMB12,000 per month.

## AN JI CAR LEASING COMPANY 安吉汽车租赁公司

(Anji Qiche Zulin Gongai)
1387 Changning Lu 长宁路1387号
Tel:6229-1119 (Headquarters)
The An Ji Car Leasing Company also has a satellite office located at the International Terminal of the Hongqiao International Airport. The telephone number there is 6268-7788 x 6723. Foreigners can rent a car by showing a passport, driving license, and major credit card. They will also provide a temporary driving license (at a fee of RMB50) if you already possess an International driving license. The temporary license is to be returned upon termination of the Lease Agreement. The only car available is the Volkswagon Santana, and the deposit is RMB5,000.

## Passenger Vehicle Sales

Policies

Wholly owned foreign enterprises (WFOEs), joint ventures, and foreign representative Offices all have the right to buy a number of vehicles for foreign employees (foreign employee vehicles will have a blue license plate which allows them into town every other day). Additionally, high level managers, chief representatives, and officials of an Embassy or Consulate can buy vehicles in their own names (these officials will be issued a black license plate which allows entry to the downtown area on any day). Individuals who wish to buy a private car and are not affiliated with a company with a vehicle quota must buy a car license for RMB150,000. When applying for a license plate, foreigners shall produce the following documents:

- Business license
- Passport
- Certificate of residence
- Invoice of purchase of vehicle
- Commodity inspection paper (for imported vehicles only)

Fees

In addition to the price of the vehicle, the purchasing party must pay other taxes and fees, the majority of which follow:

- Car purchasing fee (10% of purchase price)
- Insurance fee (depending on type of insurance desired. Minimum of RMB1,500.00)
- Commodity inspection fee (in cases involving imported vehicles, RMB2000.)
- Other government administration fees (a number of small fees that amount to approximately RMB 2,000.00)

## Passenger vehicle sales companies

### SHANGHAI UNION AUTO TRADE MARKET　上海联合汽车交易市场
(Shanghai Lianhe Qiche Jiaoyi Shichang)
130 Gansu Lu　甘肃路130号
Tel: 6325-9197
Fax: 6306-0868

### SHANGHAI AUTOMOBILE AND PARTS COMMERCIAL CENTER
上海汽车汽配商厦
(Shanghai Qiche Qipei Shangsha)
No. 350 Weihai Lu　威海路350号
Tel: 6267-4536, 6267-3472
This company deals with all kinds of vehicles.

### SHANGHAI HEPING AUTOMOBILE TOWN　上海和平汽车城
2418 Hunan Lu, Pudong　浦东沪南路2418号
Tel:5843-9532

Following is a list of vehicle prices for general reference:

| Model | Price |
| --- | --- |
| Toyota Crown 3.0 | RMB470.000 |
| Audi 2.6 V6 | RMB430,000 |
| Mercedes-Benz S320 | RMB920,000 |
| Volkswagen Santana 2000 | RMB198,000 |
| Volkswagen Santana | RMB140,000 |
| Chevy Van (15 seat) | RMB415,000 |
| Chevy Van (7 seat) | RMB390,000 |
| Omica Opel | RMB370,000 |
| Nissan Bluebird | RMB320,000 |
| Lexus | RMB700,000 |
| Honda Accord | RMB425,000 |
| Toyota Costa (26 seat) | RMB660,000 |
| BMW 525 | RMB620,000 |
| Ford Tempo | RMB226,000 |
| Dodge Ram Van | RMB380,000 |

# TRAINS AND SUBWAYS

### SHANGHAI TRAIN STATION
上海火车站
(Shanghai Huochezhan)
303 Moling Lu　秣陵路303号
Tel: 6317-9090

The Shanghai Railway Bureau is in the process of replacing slower trains with express trains. There are now three express trains to Nanjing daily. With the addition of 50 new cars, by April 1, 1998 the Shanghai - Nanjing and Hangzhou area will have six pairs of express trains daily, plus the addition of express trains on the Shanghai - Beijing route, shortening the trip from 17 1/2 hours to 14 hours. The bureau also runs a special train from Shanghai to Kowloon making the 1,983 kilometer trip in 28 hours. Identify the fastest trains by the "K" (which stands for *kuai* meaning "quick" in Chinese) in the identification number. Tourist trains are labeled with a "Y" (*you* in Chinese meaning "tourist") while Express Trains are identified by a "Z".

### SHANGHAI SUBWAY COMPANY
上海市地铁总公司
(Shanghai Shi Ditie Zonggongsi)
12 Hengshan Lu　衡山路12号
Tel:6318-9188

Shanghai has one subway line in place, running north and south. The second line running east to west is now under construction. The second line, which is scheduled to open January 1, 2000, will be 13.6 kilometers long and run from the Jing'an central area to Longdong Lu near the new Pudong International Airport. The subway is clean, efficient, and safe. The first line runs from Shanghai Railroad Station (Shanghai Huochezhan) in the north to its terminus, Jinjiang Park (Jinjiang Leyuanzhan) in the south. Intermediate stops

from north to south are:

|  |  |  |
|---|---|---|
| Shanghai Train Station | Shanghai Huochezhan | 上海火车站 |
| Hanzhong Road Station | Hanzhong Lu Zhan | 汉中路站 |
| Xinzha Road Station | Xinzha Lu Zhan | 新闸路站 |
| People's Square Station | Renmin Guangchang Zhan | 人民广场站 |
| Huangpi South Road Station | Huangpi Nan Lu Zhan | 黄坡南路站 |
| Shaanxi South Road Station | Shaanxi Nan Lu Zhan | 陕西南路站 |
| Changshu Road Station | Changshu Lu Zhan | 常熟路站 |
| Hengshan Road Station | Hengshan Lu Zhan | 衡山路站 |
| Xujiahui Station | Xujiahui Zhan | 徐家汇站 |
| Shanghai Stadium | Shanghai Tiyuguan Zhan | 上海体育馆站 |
| Caobao Road Station | Caobao Lu Zhan | 漕宝路站 |
| Xinhua Road Station | Xinhua Lu Zhan | 新华路站 |
| Jin Jiang Amusement Park | Jinjiang Leyuan Zhan | 锦江乐园站 |
| Xin Zhuang Area Station | Xinzhuang Zhan | 辛庄站 |

# BUS TRANSPORTATION

## ZHENHUA EXPRESSWAY PASSENGER CO. 振华旅行社

(Zhenhua Luxingshe)
58 Laochongqing Zhong Lu
老重庆中路58号
Tel: 6358-8089

Fax: 6358-9193
Hours: 8:30 am - 5:30 pm
A Deluxe Coach "Setra" will take you between Shanghai and Nanjing in comfort. The trip takes 3 1/2 hours and costs RMB86.

## City Bus Routes

This is a last resort for getting around Shanghai. Riding the local buses is only for the most intrepid among us. They are overcrowded and breakdown frequently. Although Shanghai is very safe, pick-pocketing is a common occurrence on buses. The good news is that there are 1,000 new air-conditioned 72-seat Volvo buses in Shanghai, and new "911" double-cleckers.

* Please note that route numbers and destinations were correct at time of going to press.

| | From | To | |
|---|---|---|---|
| 6 | Liyang Lu - Tumen Lu | | 溧阳路 - 图门路 |
| 8 | Yangshupu Lu - Wujiaochang | | 杨树浦路 - 五角场 |
| 11 | Zhonghua Lu via Renmin Lu | | 中华路人民路环行 |
| 13 | Tilanqiao - Caojia Du | | 提蓝桥 - 曹家渡 |
| 14 | Dongxin Lu - Dahushan Lu | | 东新路 - 打虎山路 |
| 15 | Shanghai Stadium - Tianmu Dong Lu | | 上海体育馆 - 天目东路 |
| 16 | Huanghe Lu - Dongxin Lu | | 黄河路 - 东新路 |
| 17 | Ruijin Nan Lu - Tongbei Lu | | 瑞金南路 - 通北路 |
| 18 | Xinzhaozhou Lu - Luxun Park | | 新肇周路 - 鲁迅路 |
| 19 | Tilanqiao - Aomen Lu | | 提蓝桥 - 澳门路 |

| 20 | Jiujiang Lu, Waitan - Zhongshan Park | 九江路外滩 - 中山公园 |
| 21 | Jing'ansi - Luxun Park | 静安寺 - 鲁迅公园 |
| 22 | Minhang Lu - Jungong Lu | 闵行路 - 军工路 |
| 23 | Gaoxiong Lu - Xinkang Lu | 高雄路 - 忻康路 |
| 24 | Laoximen - Yichang Lu | 老西门 - 宜昌路 |
| 25 | Dongyuhang Lu - Jungong Lu | 东余杭路 - 军工路 |
| 28 | Tilanqiao - Zhong Yuan Lu | 体蓝桥 - 中原路 |
| 37 | Jing'ansi - Qiqiha'er Lu | 静安寺 - 齐齐哈尔路 |
| 40 | Tongren Lu - Lishan Lu | 铜仁路 - 骊山路 |
| 41 | Tianmu Dong Lu - Shuangfeng Lu | 天目东路 - 双峰路 |
| 42 | Guangdong Lu, Waitan - Yude Lu | 广东路外滩 - 裕德路 |
| 43 | Nanpu Bridge - Shanghai Teacher's University | 南浦大桥 - 上海师大 |
| 44 | Longhua Town - Yangliuqing Lu | 龙华镇 - 杨柳青路 |
| 45 | Jiangbian Dock - Caojia Du | 江边码头 - 漕家渡 |
| 46 | People's Square - Pengpu Xincun | 人民广场 - 彭浦新村 |
| 47 | Huimin Lu - Lishan Lu | 惠民路 - 骊山路 |
| 48 | Lianyun Lu - Siqi Gongsi | 连云路 - 四汽公司 |
| 49 | Hankou Lu - Dong'an Lu | 汉口路 - 东安路 |
| 50 | Xujiahui - Zhujiahang | 徐家汇 - 朱家行 |
| 51 | Baochang Lu - Wusong Dock | 宝昌路 - 吴淞码头 |
| 52 | Baotong Lu - Wusong Gas Factory | 宝通路 - 吴淞煤气厂 |
| 54 | Jiangning Lu - Huining Lu | 江宁路 - 徽宁路 |
| 55 | Shiliupu - Wujiaochang | 十六铺 - 五角场 |
| 56 | Xujiahui - Changqiao Xincun | 徐家汇 - 长桥新村 |
| 57 | Jing'ansi - Shanghai Zoo | 静安寺 - 上海动物园 |
| 58 | Qufu Xi Lu - Qilianshan Lu | 曲阜西路 - 祈连山路 |
| 59 | Liping Lu - Wujiaochang | 黎平路 - 五角场 |
| 60 | Dinghui Lu - Jingyu Dong Lu | 定海路 - 靖于东路 |
| 61 | Tiantong Lu - Gongnong Xincun | 天潼路 - 工农新路 |
| 62 | Meiliyuan - Luyangqiao | 美丽园 - 绿杨桥 |
| 63 | Beihaining Lu - Putuo Hospital | 北海宁路 - 普陀医院 |
| 64 | Yangjiadu - Shanghai Train Station | 杨定渡 - 上海火车站 |
| 65 | Nanpu Bridge - Gonghexin Lu | 南浦大桥 - 共和新路 |
| 66 | Jiangbian Dock - Minyan Lu | 江边码头 - 民晏路 |
| 67 | Zhongshan Park - Zhenbei Lu | 中山公园 - 真北路 |
| 68 | Cangping Lu - Pingli Lu | 晶平路 - 平利路 |
| 69 | Gongxing Lu - Loushanguan Lu | 公兴路 - 娄山关路 |
| 70 | Luxun Park - Yangshupu Lu | 鲁迅公园 - 杨树浦路 |
| 71 | Yan'an Xi Lu - Shuicheng Lu | 延安西路 - 水城路 |
| 72 | Chalin Bei Lu - Tianshanzhi Lu | 茶林北路 - 天山支路 |
| 73 | Longhua Town - Zhongshan Park | 龙华镇 - 中山公园 |
| 74 | Maotai Lu - Zhudi Town | 茅台路 - 诸翟镇 |
| 75 | Wujiaochang - Zhayin Lu | 五角场 - 闸殷路 |
| 76 | Changhua Lu - Xuhong Bei Lu | 昌化路 - 徐虹北路 |
| 77 | Fuxing Lu - Yingkou Lu | 复兴路 - 营口路 |

| 78 | Gongxing Lu - Xixiang Lu | 公兴路 - 西乡路 |
|---|---|---|
| 79 | Pingliang Lu - Wanrong Lu | 平凉路 - 万荣路 |
| 80 | Yangshupu Lu - Busin Lu | 杨树浦路 - 埠新路 |
| 81 | Lujiazui - Gaoqiao Town | 陆家嘴 - 高桥镇 |
| 82 | Lujiazui - Zhoujiadu | 陆家嘴 - 周家渡 |
| 83 | South Dock - Xiying Lu | 南码头 - 西营路 |
| 84 | Zhoujiadu - Lingshao Xincun | 周家渡 - 凌兆新村 |
| 85 | Dongchang Lu - Boxing Lu | 东昌路 - 博兴路 |
| 86 | Dongchang Lu - Yaohua Lu | 东昌路 - 耀华路 |
| 87 | Longhua Lu - Qibao Town | 龙华路 - 七宝镇 |
| 88 | Zhongshan Park - Honggu Lu | 中山公园 - 虹古路 |
| 89 | Nanpu Bridge - Tianlin Xincun | 南浦大桥 - 田林新村 |
| 90 | Kongjiang Lu - Shuichan Lu | 控江路 - 水产路 |
| 91 | Beixinjing - Xinzhuang Town | 北新泾 - 辛庄镇 |
| 92 | Shanghai Stadium - Shanghai Agronomy University | 上海体育馆 - 上海农学院 |
| 93 | Changle Lu - Nongyuancun | 长乐路 - 农苑村 |
| 94 | Xiangyang Bei Lu - Luding Lu | 向阳北路 - 芦定路 |
| 95 | Shanghai Train Station - Tiehejin Lu | 上海火车站 - 铁合金路 |
| Zx95 | Shanghai Train Station - Sitang Xincun | 上海火车站 - 泗塘新村 |
| 96 | Xizang Nan Lu - Zhongshan Park | 西藏南路 - 中山公园 |
| 97 | Luxun Park - Jingwan Town | 鲁迅公园 - 江湾镇 |
| 98 | Yanchang Lu - Yunzao Nan Lu | 延长路 - 蕴藻南路 |
| 99 | Wujiaochang - Wuchuan Lu | 五角场 - 武川路 |
| 100 | Kunshan Lu - Quyang Lu | 昆山路 - 曲阳路 |
| 101 | Hongxing Lu - Shuichan Lu | 鸿兴路 - 水产路 |
| 102 | Guoding Lu - Nenjiang Lu | 国定路 - 嫩江路 |
| 103 | Haimen Lu - Songhuajiang Lu | 国定路 - 松花江路 |
| 104 | Shanghai Train Station - Longhuazhen | 上海火车站 - 龙华镇 |
| 105 | Changhua Lu - Caoyangba Cun | 昌化路 - 曹杨八村 |
| 106 | Shanghai Train Station - Shanghai West Station | 上海火车站 - 上海西站 |
| 107 | Ganquan Xincun - Liangcheng Xincun | 甘泉新村 - 凉城新村 |
| 108 | Songshan Lu - Pingxingguan Lu | 嵩山路 - 平型关路 |
| 109 | Shanghai Train Station - Nanpu Bridge | 上海火车站 - 南浦大桥 |
| 110 | Pengpu Xincun - Dachang Town | 澎浦新村 - 大场镇 |
| 111 | Shanghai Stadium - Changqiao Xincun | 上海体育馆 - 长桥新村 |
| 112 | People's Square - Guanlong Xincun | 人民广场 - 管弄新村 |
| 113 | Shanghai Train Station - West Bus Station | 上海火车站 - 西区汽车站 |
| 114 | Shanghai Train Station - Tiehe Jinchang | 上海火车站 - 铁合金厂 |
| 115 | Shanghai Train Station - Shuangyang Lu | 上海火车站 - 双阳路 |
| 116 | Quyang Xincun - Qibao Town | 曲阳新村 - 七宝镇 |
| 117 | Shanghai Train Station - Taopu Xincun | 上海火车站 - 桃浦新村 |
| 118 | Pengpu Xincun - Antu Lu | 澎浦新村 - 安图路 |
| 119 | Taidong Lu - Lancun Lu | 泰东路 - 兰村路 |
| 123 | Yunguang Xincun People's Square | 远光新村—人民广场 |
| 120 | Honggu Lu - Pingtang Lu | 虹古路 - 平塘路 |

| | | |
|---|---|---|
| 121 | People's Square - Yunguang Xincun | 人民广场 - 远光新村 |
| 124 | Liping Lu - Zhongyuan Lu | 黎平路 - 中原路 |
| 125 | Guohe Lu - Songbin Xi Lu | 国和路 - 松滨西路 |
| 126 | Xinkai He - Wukang Lu | 新开河 - 武康路 |
| 127 | Yan'an Dong Lu Waitan - Shuicheng Lu | 延安东路外滩 - 水城路 |
| 128 | Nanyang Middle School - Hutai Xincun | 南洋中学 - 沪太新村 |
| 129 | Jiaotong Lu - Shanghai West Station | 交通路 - 上海西站 |
| 130 | Yiangjiadu - Jiepu Lu | 杨家渡 - 歇浦路 |
| 132 | Yongxing Lu - Anda Lu | 永兴路 - 安达路 |
| 133 | Wujiaochang - Liangcheng Xincun | 五角场 - 凉城新村 |
| 135 | Huaihai Dong Lu - Liping Lu | 淮海东路 - 黎平路 |
| 139 | Wujiaochang - Luxun Park | 五角场 - 鲁迅公园 |
| Tunnel 1 | Dapuqiao - Changli Xiaqu | 打浦桥 - 昌里小区 |
| Tunnel 2 | Fenglin Lu - Hongshan Lu | 枫林路 - 洪山路 |
| Tunnel 3 | Shanghai Train Station - Rushan Xincun | 上海火车站 - 乳山新村 |
| Tunnel 4 | Lianyun Lu - Weifang Xincun | 连云路 - 维坊新村 |
| Tunnel 5 | Tanshui Lu - Nanquan Xincun | 谈水路 - 南泉新村 |
| Tunnel 6 | People's Square - Jinqia Xincun | 人民广场 - 金桥新村 |
| Tunnel 7 | Chaling Lu - Dezhou Xincun | 茶陵路 - 德州新村 |
| Tunnel 8 | Longhua Dong Lu - Meiyuan Xincun | 龙华东路 - 梅园新村 |
| Bridge 1 | Chongqing Nan Lu - Linyi Xincun | 重庆南路 - 临沂新村 |
| Bridge 2 | Huining Lu - Donggang Lu | 徽宁路 - 东方路 |
| Bridge 3 | Luoshan Xincun - Wujiaochang | 罗山新村 - 五角场 |
| Bridge 4 | Lanyang Lu - Zhoujiazui Lu | 兰阳路 - 周家嘴路 |
| 502 | Shanghai Train Station - Gaojingzhen Zhengfu | 上海火车站 - 高境镇政府 |
| 506 | Shanghai Train Station - Guiqing Lu | 上海火车站 - 桂青路 |
| 507 | Shanghai Train Station - Gongnong Xincun | 上海火车站 - 工农新村 |
| 508 | Shanghai Train Station - Baoshanzhen | 上海火车站 - 宝山镇 |
| 512 | Guotai Lu - Ganquan Xincun | 国泰路 - 甘泉新村 |
| 510 | Huimin Lu - Hutai Lu Bus Station | 惠民路 - 沪泰路长途站 |
| 511 | Nanpu Bridge - West Bus Station | 南浦大桥 - 西区汽车站 |
| 526 | Xinkaihe - Yishan Bei Lu | 新开河 - 宜山北路 |
| 571 | Hengda Lu - Hudong Xincun | 恒大路 - 沪东新村 |
| 572 | Shanghai Stadium - Sanling Cheng | 上海体育馆 - 三林城 |
| 573 | Liangji Lu - Shanghai Train Station | 良基路 - 上海火车站 |
| 574 | People's Square - Xiying Lu | 人民广场 - 西营路 |
| 575 | Duhang - Huaihai Dong Lu | 杜行 - 淮海东路 |
| 591 | Waigaoqiao - Longmai Xincun | 外高桥 - 龙梅新村 |
| 592 | Waigaoqiao - Shanghai Train Station | 外高桥 - 上海火车站 |
| 593 | Waigaoqiao - Shanghai Stadium | 外高桥 - 上海体育馆 |
| 820 | Changqiao Xincun - Dapu Bridge | 长桥新村 - 打浦桥 |
| 821 | Jinjiang Amusement Park - Huashan Lu | 锦江乐园 - 华山路 |
| 822 | Caohejing - Changle Lu | 漕河泾 - 长乐路 |
| 901 | Changning Train Station - Tilanqiao | 长宁火车站 - 提蓝桥 |
| 902 | Shanghai Train Station - Yangjia Du | 上海火车站 - 扬家渡 |

| 903 | Shanghai Train Station - Shanghai Stadium | 上海火车站 - 上海体育馆 |
|------|-------------------------------------------|----------------------|
| 904 | Shanghai Train Station - Nanpu Bridge | 上海火车站 - 南浦大桥 |
| 905 | Changning Train Station - Tilanqiao | 长宁火车站 - 提蓝桥 |
| 906 | Shanghai Train Station - Dongfang Lu | 上海火车站 - 东方路 |
| 911 | Laoximen - Shanghai Zoo | 老西门 - 上海动物园 |
| 912 | Shanghai Train Station - Pengpu Xincun | 上海火车站 - 澎浦新村 |
| 302 | Shanghai Train Station - Baojiao Gongsi | 上海火车站 - 宝交公司 |
| 303 | Shiliupu - Tianlin Xincun | 十六浦 - 田林新村 |
| 304 | Huancheng Waixian - Yichang Lu | 环城外线 - 宜昌路 |
| 305 | Shanghai Train Station - Nanpu Bridge | 上海火车站 - 南浦大桥 |
| 306 | Shanghai Train Station - Jiangbian Dock | 上海火车站 - 江边码头 |
| 307 | Shiliupu - Wujiaochang | 十六铺 - 五角场 |
| 308 | Shanghai Train Station - Songhuajiang Lu | 上海火车站 - 松花江路 |
| 309 | Gongxing Lu - Tianshan Lu | 公兴路 - 天山路 |
| 310 | Shanghai Train Station - Yangshupu Lu | 上海火车站 - 杨树浦路 |
| 311 | Shiliupu - Beixinjing | 十六铺 - 北新泾 |
| 312 | People's Square. - Shanggang #1 Iron And Steel Factory | 人民广场 - 上钢一厂 |
| 313 | Dongchang Lu - Gaoxiong Lu | 东昌路 - 高雄路 |
| 314 | Lujiazhui - Zhoujia Du | 陆家嘴 - 周家渡 |
| 315 | Shanghai Train Station - Shanghai Stadium | 上海火车站 - 上海体育馆 |
| 316 | Shiliupu - Gongjiao Tianshan Lu | 十六铺 - 公交天山路 |
| 317 | Shiliupu - Jungong Lu | 十六铺 - 军公路 |
| 318 | Xinzhaozho Lu - Luxun Park | 新肇周路 - 鲁迅公园 |
| 319 | Shanghai West Bus Station - Tilanqiao | 上海西站 - 提蓝桥 |
| 320 | Yan'an Lu Waitan - Tianshan Lu | 延安路外滩 - 天山路 |
| 321 | Tongren Lu - Hutai Xincun | 铜仁路 - 沪太新村 |
| 322 | Shanghai Train Station - Baoshan Town | 上海火车站 - 宝山镇 |
| 323 | Tongten Lu - Taopu Xincun | 铜仁路 - 桃浦新村 |
| 324 | Shanghai Train Station - Yangjia Du | 上海火车站 - 扬家渡 |
| 325 | Pingliang Lu - Zhayin Lu | 平凉路 - 闸殷路 |
| 326 | Fenglin Lu - Changqiao Xincun | 枫林路 - 长桥新村 |
| 327 | Jiangbian Dock - Caojia Du | 江边码头 - 曹家渡 |
| 328 | Shanghai Train Station - Shanghai Zoo | 上海火车站 - 上海动物园 |
| 329 | Shanghai Train Station - Gongnong Xincun | 上海火车站 - 公农新村 |
| 330 | Zhongshan Park - Qiqiha'er Lu | 中山公园 - 齐齐哈尔路 |
| 331 | Taidong Lu - Nanquan Lu | 泰东路 - 南泉路 |
| Tunnel 24 hr service | Shanghai Train Station - Weifang Xincun | 上海火车站 - 维坊新村 |
| Tunnel 24 hr service | Fenglin Lu - Hongshan Lu | 枫林路 - 洪山路 |

# MANNERS, CUSTOMS, AND TRADITIONS

East is East and West is West and never the twain shall meet? The old adage doesn't necessarily have to be one's experience in China if a little effort is made towards understanding the Chinese way of thinking and behaving.

Chinese and Western traditions are vastly divergent and it is often hard for foreigners to decipher and accept such a different code of behavior. Things which by Chinese standards are not offensive offend foreign sensibilities, and vice versa. Time is the best teacher, though even after many years in China, one still has much to learn. This writer has learned the hard way – through embarrassing mistakes, which are part of one's initiation, a rite of passage so to speak, that cannot be avoided. These mistakes point up the fact that the more one learns about the Chinese mentality, the more one realizes how much more there is to learn. When trying to understand Chinese behavior, it helps to visualize an inverted triangle whose base extends towards infinity.

The Chinese readily excuse and forgive foreign naivete on the grounds that the nuances of their ancient and superior culture are complicated and difficult for fumbling foreigners to understand. Of course, it helps to have a close Chinese friend who can truthfully explain the convoluted path to behavior that is proper in Chinese eyes.

Perhaps a small head start in cultural orientation can be gained by some of this writer's examples. One of the most important things to remember, particularly in mainland China, is to be extremely judicious in requesting help or anything that can be even remotely construed as a favor. Make sure the request is important enough that it warrants the other person's time and energy. A Chinese friend or associate will move mountains to accommodate you, drawing upon their personal relationships and thereby incurring relationship debts of their own in the process. The concept of *guanxi*, (meaning relationships, ties or connections) is and always has been central to the entire social and business fabric of China. The entire structure of contemporary society is based on one's network of friends, relatives and associates. The quality of these networks is assessed by the power one has at hand as a result of the network. In recent years, particularly during the 1950s, 60s and 70s, money had little relevance, as the average citizen had little or none. Therefore, power became the valued commodity, in the sense of power as a way to get something done, whether large or small in significance. Trading of favors throughout the *guanxi* network is still how most life issues are dealt with. An individual's relationships are his/her most valued possession, with years of careful nurturing having been invested in development of this guanxi.

The delicate balance of give and take is crucial within these relationships. Relationships which are not attentively nurtured will be lost. The Chinese feel most comfortable, and in fact strive to have the scales tipped in their direction, with others owing them for favors received. This feeling of security equates to the Western feeling of having a large bank account that cushions one against the foibles of life.

This writer first arrived in Shanghai in 1988 to look for housing and get the lay of the land. The generosity of the Chinese people deputed to assist me was overwhelming, and still is. However, one comes to realize that the term "generosity" should not be applied. In Western culture, generosity is something that is given freely, above and beyond basic standards, with nothing expected in return. In China, generosity is essential to quality of life. Without giving of themselves, the Chinese have no means of asking for reciprocity from others, and are stymied in achieving their own goals. This is not to say that the generosity and warmth one is given here is artificial. Rather, it is simply considered essential as opposed to optional. Friendship or any relationship in China carries with it an obligation that is not akin to the foreign way of thinking. Life in China becomes a little easier when one accepts this fact and swims with the current, rather than fighting it. One is usually led, kicking and struggling, to this realization through unfortunate experiences, or witnessing of them.

One such experience stands out in this writer's mind. Years ago, I was asked by an American friend to help her find an *ahyi* (housekeeper). I casually asked a Chinese friend if he knew of anyone. Two weeks later, the Chinese friend called and said that he had someone for the job. By then, however, the American friend had found someone, and thanked me anyway. Much to my surprise and confusion, the Chinese friend was quite distressed over this news. Because we were good friends, he did not simply swallow his anger, as is usually the case. Instead of leaving me ignorant of the bind I had put him in, he explained, after some prodding, that in order to give me "face" with my American friend, he had been combing through his relationships to find someone. This had required many meetings, and he had assured the best candidate that the position was a sure thing. He explained that he would seriously lose face in reneging on the deal, not just with the individual involved, but also with the friends and family who had been involved in the process. In order to prevent my Chinese friend's loss of face, I was obligated to find the ahyi another position, in the meantime meeting with her several times to explain the delays. To my tremendous relief, I was finally able to match her with another employer, with whom she was quite happy. The Chinese friend and I received abundant praise from the *ahyi* and her family as a result. The obvious lesson here is to ask for something only if you are certain you can follow through, as a Chinese person will never forget to see to a favor that is requested of him. And, the Chinese are usually not inclined to frank discussion of matters that the other party causes to go awry. Instead, they will remain silent, harboring a festering anger which colors the rest of your dealings with that person and anyone else involved in the helping process.

Frankly, foreigners can very easily be undermined by Chinese associates. Foreigners tend to be very isolated and out of the Chinese loop in their positions here, and must rely on Chinese associates and friends for many things, both personally and business-wise. Value their assistance by giving it due respect, taking care to nurture the relationship. What is happening beneath the surface, and something always is, can affect one's success or failure here to a much greater extent than most foreigners are aware.

# NAMES

In China, the surname precedes the given name. Instead of calling a Chinese individual by their surname only, one should add a more polite "Xiansheng" (Mr.) or "Xiaojie" (Miss) after the surname. If this proves intimidating, even the English "Mister" or "Miss" in front of the surname is an improvement. A less formal alternative would be to precede the surname with "Xiao" (meaning small) or "Lao" (meaning old) as in "Xiao Zhang", and one must consider the person's age and position. If he is considerably older and/or has a position of power, it's best to stick with Mr. or Xiansheng.

A younger driver would best be addressed as "Xiao Zhang". For an older male friend or employee, "Lao Zhang" would be preferable. Expats tend to feel that calling someone "Small" or "Old" is insulting. In China, however, no such stigma is attached to addressing a person as such. The terms convey endearment and friendship.

A person's work title can also be used following the surname as a form of address. A Chinese language teacher could be called "Zhang Laoshi", *laoshi* meaning teacher, or even "Laoshi" alone.

Chinese women do not assume their husband's family name upon marriage. Therefore, it would be incorrect for you to call Zhang Ding's wife "Mrs. Zhang". She should be addressed by her own name, for example, Xie Xiaojie (Miss Xie). If her name is unknown to you, use "Zhang Tai Tai" (meaning that she is the wife of Mr. Zhang).

A Chinese person is seldom called his given name alone, unless it is "doubled", as in "Ding Ding".

# DINING WITH CHINESE

When in Shanghai on business, one will undoubtedly be entertained by Chinese business associates. Eating, not necessarily for sustenance but for pleasure, is a primary source of enjoyment for the Shanghainese. And if it's at company expense, so much the better.

Banquet and formal dinners usually revolve around business. The more regard for you that your host has, the more extensive and exotic the dishes will be. The honor of being served exotic dishes is usually lost on foreigners, who are prone to be put off by deep-fried scorpions, sea slug, and fish lips. However, one is not really required to eat everything on one's plate. Accept what your host puts on your plate, but don't eat it if it doesn't appeal or you'll be served more of the same. Dirty dishes are changed frequently, so eventually uneaten remains will disappear into the kitchen. One needn't pretend to love every Chinese dish, as the Chinese have no qualms about adamantly and enthusiastically denouncing Western food.

The guest of honor is seated on the host's (who will be facing the door) right. Spouses will generally be seated to the left of the host. The host will begin the meal by serving the guest(s) of honor, then everyone may begin. After the first course, he or she will propose a toast which you should return after the next course is served. Others take their turns at toasts throughout the meal. It's great sport for the Chinese to see foreigners get tipsy, but drinking is not mandatory. If you don't want to partake, establish this right at the beginning. You can always say you are taking antibiotics and cannot drink, but don't expect to get away with this time after time.

Many Chinese serve themselves from common dishes with used chopsticks. Sometimes, serving spoons or serving chopsticks are provided. That failing, turn used chopsticks upside down, and serve with the clean ends. Pointing chopsticks at anyone is considered insulting. Also, don't stick chopsticks into a bowl of rice, as this signifies death.

And don't worry about making a certain amount of noise when eating noodles, as no sound at all is considered gauche by the Chinese.

No one lingers after the meal at a banquet. After dessert, the host will propose another closing toast and everyone begins to leave.

When reciprocating, it's easiest to book the banquet through one of the hotels. Their food and beverage department has set menus to choose from in different price ranges, making thing fairly simple. Just remember the guidelines for seating and opening and closing the banquet.

When ordering food for a more casual meal with Chinese guests, remember that the minimum number of dishes to show proper respect is seven. These would include a soup, vegetable, some type of fowl, a meat dish, and a fish dish. The other two dishes could be rice or noodles, dim sum, fruit, or appetizers.

Chinese don't ever split the bill or "go Dutch". One individual, usually the inviting party, will pay for the entire meal. Nor does anyone order a dish for themself exclusively.

# PUBLIC HOLIDAYS,
# COMMEMORATION DAYS, AND FESTIVALS

Chinese New Year, also called Spring Festival, is the most important holiday of the year in China. Its date varies year to year, but falls between late January and early February. There is a fixed cycle of twelve animals that signify each year. See the table below to determine which animal signifies your year of birth. Each animal sign carries with it different qualities, much like our Western horoscope. When a Chinese asks you what animal represents you in the Chinese zodiac, your age can easily be determined by your answer (unless you look twelve years younger or older than your actual age).

According to legend, just before departing this earth, Lord Buddha summoned all the creatures of the world to his side. Only twelve creatures made the effort to attend this farewell and so, in recognition of their fidelity, Buddha named a year after each one of them in accordance with the order that they reached his side. Therefore, the years are named in the sequence below.

## Year of the.....

| Rat | 1900 | 1912 | 1924 | 1936 | 1948 | 1960 | 1972 | 1984 | 1996 |
|---|---|---|---|---|---|---|---|---|---|
| Ox | 1901 | 1913 | 1925 | 1937 | 1949 | 1961 | 1973 | 1985 | 1997 |
| Tiger | 1902 | 1914 | 1926 | 1938 | 1950 | 1962 | 1974 | 1986 | 1998 |
| Rabbit | 1903 | 1915 | 1927 | 1939 | 1951 | 1963 | 1975 | 1987 | 1999 |
| Dragon | 1904 | 1916 | 1928 | 1940 | 1952 | 1964 | 1976 | 1988 | 2000 |
| Snake | 1905 | 1917 | 1929 | 1941 | 1953 | 1965 | 1977 | 1989 | 2001 |
| Horse | 1906 | 1918 | 1930 | 1942 | 1954 | 1966 | 1978 | 1990 | 2002 |
| Sheep | 1907 | 1919 | 1931 | 1943 | 1955 | 1967 | 1979 | 1991 | 2003 |
| Monkey | 1908 | 1920 | 1932 | 1944 | 1956 | 1968 | 1980 | 1992 | 2004 |
| Rooster | 1909 | 1921 | 1933 | 1945 | 1957 | 1969 | 1981 | 1993 | 2005 |
| Dog | 1910 | 1922 | 1934 | 1946 | 1958 | 1970 | 1982 | 1994 | 2006 |
| Pig | 1911 | 1923 | 1935 | 1947 | 1959 | 1971 | 1983 | 1995 | 2007 |

### Rat
Persistent, charming, but mercurial, who can resist partying with you at every occasion? You symbolize wealth and prosperity but beware of acquiring it from others' Achilles Heels. Ox, Dragon, or Monkey are your safest allies, but stay clear of Rabbit, Horse, and Sheep.

### Ox
Quiet and patient, you are the strong, silent type. Beware that your stubborn streak doesn't come to the fore! You symbolize longevity and family values. Give your affection to those born in the years of the Snake, Rooster, or Rat, and tread warily in the presence of those of the Horse, Sheep, or Dog.

### Tiger
A rebel with a hot-headed cause, you are the pushy type that gets his own way, or else. Your tendency to find fault can be irksome but you inspire loyalty and are true in return. Your ideal match is the Dragon. Those born under the sign of the Snake or Monkey will make unsuitable companions.

### Rabbit

Yours is the voice of reason that often soothes quarrels. Therefore, a career in local government or public relations would suit you. Wealth and success are like an aura around your sign. You favor people who were born under the sign of the Ram, Dog, or Pig. Those who ruffle your genial nature are the Dragon or Rooster.

### Dragon

Hail! Yours is the symbol of majesty! You exude vitality and health and your natural leadership makes it easy for others to fall in with your decisions. Form your alliances with those born under the signs of the Tiger, Rat, Monkey, or Rooster. Keep an arm's length from anyone linked to Rabbit, Dog, or even your own sign, the Dragon.

### Snake

Your heart rules your head more than you like to admit and you are an exasperating opponent in any debate that goes against you. With someone born under the Ox or Rooster beside you, a formidable duo would be born; those born under the Tiger, Monkey, or Pig are your life-long stumbling blocks.

### Horse

Symbol of masculinity, helpfulness, and strength, you are a thoroughly good type all around. As a result, others often use you for their own purposes or take advantage of your easy-going ways. Go with those born under the signs of the Tiger, Ram, or Dog. Guard against the Rat, the Ox, and your fellow Horses.

### Sheep

Mild-mannered and likable, you are a peacemaker. You are moral and positively austere in your integrity. The priesthood beckons! You are very creative, which bodes well for links with those born under the Rabbit, Horse, or Pig. Try to keep your cool around those born under the Rat or Ox.

### Monkey

You are intelligent if a little hot tempered and a definite actor at heart whose bohemian nature cries out for a career on the stage. You are best teamed with anyone who is a Rat or Dragon. Problems lie ahead for any relationship involving the Tiger, Serpent, or Pig.

### Rooster

You are the one with stamina, a stayer who sees a project through to the end. You are fond of applause and it often shows in your behavior, so beware playing to the gallery. Marriage does not usually appeal to you but when Cupid strikes, it would be best if it were with the Ox, Dragon, or Snake. Your fellow Rooster is not a wise ally, nor is the Rabbit or the Dog.

### Dog

You are protective and would make a good administrator or wise High Court Judge. In marriage, you tend to be henpecked, so at least make wedded bliss a little easier by seeking out those who came into this world under the signs of the Rabbit or Horse. Steer away from the Ox, Dragon, or the Ram.

### Pig

You symbolize leisure and gracious living, as well as good fortune. You are never happier than when calculating the odds on some gamble or turning your fingers over the abacus. Happy marriage awaits with one born under the Tiger, Rabbit, or Ram. Beware of your own sign and the Snake or Monkey.

Chinese New Year lasts for five days, beginning with New Year's Day. The first three days are official holidays, but one week's vacation is the norm for Chinese staff. It is next to impossible to conduct business during this week and most expatriates leave China for a holiday during this week as well. This leaves most businesses, including foreign companies, completely shut down. Hotels and most restaurants operate during this period, but with reduced staff.

So what to do? Enjoy the fun! Most of the better hotels will provide entertainment on

New Year's morning in the form of Dragon or Lion dances and also provide special meals in their restaurants. A strong cup of coffee is welcome after the barrage of fireworks exploding the evening before. Even though the government is trying to control the use of fireworks by local citizens during the holiday, they are set off during the entire week, as they are the main theme of the celebration.

Chinese families prepare for the holidays by sprucing up their homes and themselves in preparation for the many visits to and from relatives and friends. The intent is for all relationships to be renewed and to erase any bad feeling or debt left from the previous year. Families stage special dinners on New Year's Eve and/or New Year's Day with special dishes. A red envelope (*hong bao*) of money is given to small children and employees are rewarded in the same manner for their work during the past year. The standard greeting is "Gongxifacai" which is a wish for wealth and prosperity, or "Xinnianhao" which simply means "Happy New Year".

## LANTERN FESTIVAL  元宵节
(Yuanxiaojie)
This falls on the 14th, 15th, and16th days of the 1st lunar month. Public and private parks are festooned with lanterns and Yuanziao dumplings, made with glutinous rice, are eaten.

## INTERNATIONAL WORKING WOMEN'S DAY  三八国际妇女节
(Sanba Guoji Funujie)
March 8th  3月8日
Women are given at least one-half day off from work. They are recognised by the government and their individual enterprises for contributions made to the economy during the past year.

## QINGMING FESTIVAL  清明节
(Qingmingjie)
Qingming means "pure brightness" and is the annual day for showing respect to deceased relatives. Temples provide memorial services requested by family members. The old tradition of sweeping graves has little relevance in contemporary China due to the fact that cremation is required for everyone below head of state caliber. This holiday is usually celebrated around April 4th or 5th.

## DRAGON BOAT FESTIVAL  端午节
(Duanwujie)
Held on the 5th day of the 5th lunar month and celebrated by eating *zongzi* (a pyramid-shaped dumpling made of glutinous rice wrapped in reed leaves), and by burning insect-repellent incense.

## INTERNATIONAL LABOR DAY
五一国际劳动节
(Wuyi Guoji Laodongjie)
May 1st  5月1日

## YOUTH DAY  青年节
(Qingnianjie)
May 4th  5月4日

## INTERNATIONAL CHILDREN'S DAY
国际儿童节
(Guoji Ertongjie)
Celebrated on June 1st 6月1日. Children are allowed a day off and are treated to special events.

## ANNIVERSARY OF CHINA'S COMMUNIST PARTY  中国共产党诞生纪念日
(Zhongguo Gongchandang Dansheng Jinianri)
July 1st  7月1日

## ADMINISTRATIVE REGION ESTABLISHMENT DAY (HK)
香港特别行政区成立纪念日
July 1st    7月1日
Acknowledging the handover of Hong Kong to China.
This holiday commemorates the establishment of the Communist Party in 1921. Until 1997 people continued to work on this day, but now that the celebration of the Hong Kong Handover shares the same day, workers are given the day off.

## ANNIVERSARY OF THE FOUNDING OF THE PEOPLE'S LIBERATION ARMY
中国人民解放军诞生纪念日
(Zhongguo Renmin Jiefangjun Dansheng Jinianri)
August 1st    8月1日

## MID-AUTUMN FESTIVAL    中秋节
(Zhongqiujie)
Commonly called the "Moon Festival", this holiday is held when the moon is at its fullest phase of the year, around the 15th day of the 8th lunar month. One spends the evening admiring the beauty of the moon and eating moon cakes, which are frequently given as gifts during this period.

## DOUBLE NINTH FESTIVAL    重阳节
(Chongyangjie)
Also called Chongyang Festival, held on the 9th day of the 9th lunar month. 9月初九 Ascending heights and eating Chongyang cakes (sweet cakes made of rice flour) is the traditional way to celebrate.

## NATIONAL DAY    国庆节
(Guoqingjie)
October 1st    10月1日
The entire nation enjoys two days off to commemorate the founding of the People's Republic of China.

## CHRISTMAS    圣诞节
(Shengdanjie)
December 25th    12月25日
Celebrated in China's Christian churches.

# CHINESE FABLES

*Fable 1*
## THE PEASANT AND THE SNAKE

One winter day a kindly peasant who was walking in the woods found a snake buried in the snow. The snake was cold and not moving. The peasant felt sorry for the snake and decided to put the snake inside his shirt so it could be warm. When the snake came out of its dormant state due to this warmth, it dealt a deadly bite to the peasant.

*Moral: Beware of doling out inappropriate kindness.*

*Fable 2*
## THE OLD MAN AND HIS HORSE

When neighbors came to offer consolation to an old man whose horse had disappeared, they were surprised and puzzled to find him undisturbed and saying that it may have been a good thing in the long run. Eventually, the horse returned, accompanied by a younger, faster horse. Again, the neighbors were surprised that he was not overjoyed and was actually worried that something bad may come of his purported good luck. As it turned out, the old man's son went for a ride on the fast horse and was thrown off, resulting in a broken leg.

*Moral: Sometimes blessings come in disguise.*

*Fable 3*
## THE SPEAR AND THE SHIELD

There was a man who made and sold weapons for a living. He bragged that his spears were so sharp that they could pierce anything. He also claimed that his shields were so strong that nothing could pierce them. Onlookers began to laugh at him and one asked if it was possible to pierce his shields with his spears. Of course, the man selling the weapons was made to look foolish when he could provide no answer.

*Moral: Don't make arguments that are unjustifiable*

*Fable 4*
## THE HORSE JUDGE

A horse that could formerly run 1,000 *li* a day was ravaged by old age. In spite of this, his owner forced him to haul a cart full of salt up a mountainside. Becoming exhausted quickly and bathed in sweat, the horse finally stopped, unable to continue his ascent. A carriage passing by carried a renowned judge of horses. This judge could immediately see that this exhausted animal had once been a magnificent steed and was overcome with pity at the horse's condition. He alighted from his carriage with tears in his eyes and covered the once fine animal with his own robe. The horse was filled with joy at the judge's acknowledgement of his former worth and snuggled his head in the judge's arm.

*Moral: Don't take others at face value.*

*Fable 5*
## PLAYING A LUTE FOR A COW

A cow was grazing in a nearby field as a musician was playing his lute. Having an audience, the musician decided to play his most exquisite piece for the animal's pleasure. Noticing that the cow completely ignored the music, the musician tried playing a tune that imitated the buzzing of mosquitoes and the cry of a calf. This caught the cow's attention and interest and the cow, thereafter, listened intently.

*Moral: Don't cast pearls before swine.*

# LIVING IN **SHANGHAI**

JENNIFER DAWSON & DOUGLAS DAWSON III

# LIVING IN SHANGHAI

has been specially written for you and for people who want
to know more about living in Shanghai.

# LIVING IN SHANGHAI

is the first guide of its kind giving you an in-depth, informative and practical source to help
you find what you are looking for quickly and easily.

**Pacific Century Publishers** is pleased to be able to specially
customize this guide as a corporate gift for your valuable
clients and associates or as a special gift for staff relocating
to Shanghai.

We can help you with gold stamping, tailor-made covers
and inserts at a reasonable cost.

Simply fill out this form and return it to:
**Pacific Century Publishers**
Tel: (852) 2376-2085
Fax: (852) 2376-2137
E-mail: airman@gateway.net.hk

## ENQUIRY DETAILS

Name: _____     Date: _____

Company Name: _____     Title: _____

Nature of business: _____

Address: _____

_____

Tel: _____     Fax: _____

E-mail: _____